P9-CEQ-235

TO PEKING AND BEYOND—
A REPORT ON
THE NEW ASIA

Previous books by Harrison E. Salisbury

The Many Americas Shall Be One

The War Between Russia and China

The 900 Days: The Siege of Leningrad

Orbit of China

Russia

Behind the Lines—Hanoi

The Northern Palmyra Affair

A New Russia?

Moscow Journal—The End of Stalin

To Moscow and Beyond

The Shook-Up Generation

American in Russia

Russia on the Way

The Soviet Union—The Fifty Years

The Eloquence of Protest: Voices of the Seventies

The Soviet Union (commentary by Harrison E. Salisbury)

TO PEKING— AND BEYOND

A Report on The New Asia

By
Harrison E. Salisbury

Quadrangle/The New York Times Book Co.

 For information, address: Quadrangle Books, Inc., 330 Madison Avenue, New York, New York 10017. Manufactured in the United States of America. Published simultaneously in Canada by Fitzhenry & Whiteside, Ltd., Toronto.

I.S.B.N. No.: 0–8129–0333–1

Library of Congress Catalog Card Number: 72–90467

Book design by Clinton J. Cowels
Jacket design by Diane and Leo Dillon

For Ed Snow and the Old China Hands

CONTENTS

CONTENTS

TO PEKING AND BEYOND— A REPORT ON THE NEW ASIA

1

The Sleeping Giant

The night lay on Peking like velvet, and the moon was silver. It was so quiet I heard the crunch of a bicycle tire on a dry leaf a block away and, under the shadow of the plane trees, silence flowed in an invisible stream. I have never felt a city so silent, and yet, behind the endless walls, within the narrow courtyards, the dark *hutungs,* a million people slept—or rather, not one million, but seven—in a stillness so profound I could almost hear the soft inspiration and exhalation of their breaths—men lying beside their wives on the broad *kangs;* infants nursing their mothers' breasts; children with flushed faces and open mouths, twitching in dreams, as they still ran at play; old men with wispy whiskers, awakening a dozen times to remember other days; statesmen stretched motionless, their brains sleepless with the problems of the world; students, limbs swollen with exhaustion, backs stiff, hands raw, from a day of digging in the fields; old women whose bound feet ached through their slumbers; athletes, relaxed and dreamless; diplomats, perplexed and puzzled and (I had no doubt), here and there a man or woman tight in the throes of a nightmare, gripped by Freudian guilt; criminals—but no whores and no robbers; soldiers and politicians; the whole of a great city—sleeping.

It was my first night in Peking. The hour was a little after 1 A.M., and I was moving through streets infinite in their emptiness, from a hotel whose name I hardly knew, to the Foreign Office whose location I could only vaguely guess, in a taxi whose driver knew no word of my language and of whose tongue I was equally ignorant. Not one automobile broke the muffled stillness. We came to a broad avenue—it led, I believed, to Tien-an Men, the Imperial Palace and the Forbidden City. For a moment we halted as red light changed to green, but whether this was automatic, or by the hand of a hidden traffic officer, I could not judge. The car hesitated a moment then sped across the vast avenue and plunged into a narrow street where the curving branches of the plane trees made a canopy overhead. And again we were lost in a world of shadows. Ahead I saw a bicycle, and then another, two solitary cyclists and myself. No one else in Peking was awake.

A little more than 12 hours earlier, the Ilyushin-18 from Canton had let down smoothly through the cloud cover and leveled off over a world of ochre—ochre land, ochre villages, ochre houses, a horizon of soft ochre dust. Earth brown. As we dropped lower, I stared out the window at China. China was brown, brown as earth, villages everywhere on the vast plain, their walls geometric quadrants of baked clay, brown and ochre against the overcast sky; the houses of baked clay, their roofs earthen and ochre; rectangle within rectangle, village walls, courtyard walls, walls around each house, walls around each building, courtyards within courtyards—like the Chinese chest of drawers on my childhood desk, concealing one box within another and another within that, until you could not believe the final cube was solid, impermeable.

This was China. The villages spaced across the plain, each village within sight of three more villages, and village succeeding village, until the last was lost against the landscape. And everywhere the color of earth. The color of China.

At first I saw no green, then the wing lifted slightly and I caught a quick reflection of silver strips among the straight squares of the fields, and a thin gleam of green—rice and water, wheat and water, millet and water. The irrigated fields of north China and an arrow-straight canal. The Grand Canal. It had to be. The Grand Canal from Canton to Peking. Marco Polo saw it. Now, for a quick minute, the Ilyushin followed the canal and then left it behind, as we came down straight, no circling, on an approach to Peking over open country, the rice paddies plain and visible now, the wheat plantings geometric and meticulous, the villages coming up under the wing, the ochre of the earth redder and richer, the walls about the courtyard plots, the small earthen enclosures (pigsties), the narrow paths across the paddy fields, the highway suddenly straight and tree-lined, the landscape greener and greener with each hundred feet of descent. And then we slipped down on the Peking runway, still and quiet, taxiing past two or three TU-104's, and pulled up before the airport building. It looked familiar. I had seen it in all the Nixon television.

5
The Sleeping Giant

It had been a long, long journey to Peking, so long that I could hardly say when it began. Did it start in the mystic days before World War I, when, my hand in my mother's, we went to my favorite spot, the Chinaman's shop on Western Avenue, a block or two from our old house—a cavern, dim and mysterious and filled with the scent of ginger and lichees and candied lilacs and dried ginseng with rat's tails (I firmly believed) hanging, tied one-to-one in the window, and sallow-faced men endlessly playing cards under a dim electric bulb in the rear? That was China to a six-year-old—mysterious, romantic, inviting, frightening.

Had it begun at the university, when I studied Chinese history and "diplomatic relations" and dreamed of shipping on a freighter to the China coast and working as a reporter on the Shanghai *Morning Post*?

Or in World War II, when I set off from Moscow to make the long and perilous trip, down the Volga steppes, across the Elburz Mountains, into Persia, thence to India and then "over the hump" into China and Chungking—a trip aborted by sudden orders to return to New York?

Or did my journey stem from more recent times, from the hundred telegrams, letters and cables to Mao Tse-tung and Chou En-lai, the first one hand-delivered by myself to the Chinese Embassy in Moscow during Mao's negotiations with Stalin from December, 1949, to February, 1950?

I could not really say.

All I knew on this cool May day was that I had been on the way to Peking for so long that when I stepped out of the plane at the airport and looked up at Chairman Mao's picture, it seemed that I had seen it all before. I picked up my typewriter and briefcase and walked up the steps into the air terminal. No big thrill.

But now, 12 hours later, moving through the dark Peking streets, it came to me that I *was* in China. In the heart of China. In the Forbidden City itself. Peking. Moving through shadowy streets, not one of whose names I could recite if my life depended upon it, driving with a man who knew neither my name nor my nationality, who could take one sudden turn from this dim street into a dimmer *hutung* and I would vanish from the face of the earth, no one, Chinese or American, ever being the wiser. I could not help smiling. This was China. And it was a China I had not dreamed of.

I was not, after all, merely driving through the Peking night on some romantic adventure. I had not flown 6,000 miles simply for the sake of letting my pulse beat faster. I had not dedicated the last dozen years of my life to journeying again and again into the Asian heartland, crisscrossing Siberia, penetrating the very core of Central Asia (Soviet and non-Soviet), traveling for months around the whole perimeter of China, visiting every country in Asia (and many of them again and again); I had not painstakingly interviewed every visitor I could find who had been into China in the last decade; sought out Chinese diplomats and newsmen in a dozen countries (enduring rebuff after rebuff in the days when no Chinese would even speak with an American); I had not devoted years to studying the tangled skein of Soviet-Chinese relations; plunged behind the lines into North Vietnam; assiduously cultivated the prickly North Koreans; turned myself into a Mongologist—I had not devoted a quarter of my adult life to the Chinese vortex and the problems that swirled around it simply from vagrant curiosity.

There was serious, deadly purpose behind all this. China and the Asian heartland—I had long since come to believe—held the key to the future of the world; to the fate of America; to the critical question of war and peace; to the nuclear issue that humanity confronts: survival. And on this ancient Chinese soil, it well might be that the dreams of mankind were being given living shape.

It is always difficult to single out a specific circumstance that can later be seen to determine a life's course. So it is with my conviction about China, my dedication to the unearthing of the real nature of China, of her relationship to her neighbors and to the world; of our relationship to her. I could say, in all truthfulness, that my interest was strongly engaged nearly 25 years ago, in the period of Mao Tse-tung's long visit to Moscow in 1949–50. Those were the silent years of Stalin, years when I was a correspondent in Russia, struggling against impossible odds to penetrate the enigma of the great dictator's design and strategy. No one there in those times could fail to sense curious and inexplicable signs in the Soviet-Chinese negotiations. Perhaps it was not entirely strange that Mao himself came to Moscow only two and a half months after proclaiming his Chinese Revolution on October 1, 1949. But surely it was unusual that he stayed in Moscow for two months or more. Never before had any Communist chief of state spent so long a time in Moscow (nor ever again would this happen). Surely it was unusual that after a few days of ceremonial visits, Mao's name dropped out of *Pravda*, and he himself fell so completely from sight that I addressed an inquiry to the Soviet Foreign Office as to whether he was still in Moscow, and, failing an answer, went out to the Chinese Embassy myself in hopes of securing some clue to his whereabouts.

And it seemed strange that, more than six weeks after Mao came to Moscow, Chou En-lai was suddenly summoned, as well, and then more weeks passed before, finally, on St. Valentine's Day, 1950, as odd a communiqué as ever formalized a diplomatic dialogue was made public in Moscow—a treaty of friendship, mutual aid and assistance, predicated not upon the obvious common enemy—the United States—but upon Japan and "any powers associated with Japan." It was a treaty which, with the passage of two decades, looked stranger and stranger—a treaty which, for the most part, preserved Russia's special status in Manchuria and north China; which preserved the Soviet bases in Dairen and Port Arthur; which maintained the Soviet foothold on the Manchurian railroads; which established joint Soviet-Chinese companies for the exploitation of natural resources in Sinkiang—that westernmost Chinese province that Russia, by one stratagem or another, had been trying to annex for three quarters of a century; and which provided the munificent sum in aid loans (not grants) to China of $300 million to be allotted over five years—that is, some $60 million a year, all to be repaid at three percent interest.

What did it mean? Was it a treaty that actually bound China and Russia in eternal friendship? Did it forge an alliance of 200 million Russian Communists and 800 million Chinese Communists, an axis of titans that confronted the world with a Red monolith extending from the Bering Strait to the Elbe? That surely was the reading placed upon it by John Foster Dulles. That certainly was the verdict of the cold warriors.

Of course, they had long since concluded that China and Russia were one, that Mao was a mere pawn of Stalin, and that, as Dean Acheson proclaimed in the famous State Department White Paper of July 30, 1949:

"The heart of China is in Communist hands. The Communist leaders have foresworn their Chinese heritage and have publicly announced *their subservience to a foreign power, Russia* [my italics] which during the last 50 years, under Czars and Communists alike, has been most assiduous in its efforts to extend its control to the Far East . . . The Communist regime serves not their [Chinese] interests but those of Soviet Russia . . . We continue to believe that however tragic may be the immediate future of China and however ruthlessly a major portion of this great people may be exploited by a party *in the interest of foreign imperialism* [my italics] ultimately the profound civilization and the democratic individualism of China will reassert themselves and she will throw off the foreign yoke."

Or, as Senator Joseph McCarthy was saying by March 30, 1950: "It was not Chinese democracy under Mao that conquered China as Acheson, Lattimore and Jessup contended. *Soviet Russia conquered China* [my italics], and an important ally of this conqueror was the small left-wing element in our Department of State."

Or, as Dean Rusk was to put it about a year later, on May 18, 1951: "We do not recognize the authorities in Peiping for what they pretend to be. *The Peiping regime may be a colonial Russian government*—a Slavic *Manchukuo* [my italics] on a larger scale. It is not the Government of China. It does not pass the first test. It is not Chinese."

Or, as Captain Joseph Alsop, then aid to General Chennault, put it so simply and plainly much earlier (in February, 1945): "We are childish to assume that the Chinese Communists are anything but *an appendage of the Soviet Union*" [my italics].

Thus, they (and most other Americans as well) saw the alliance as a mere ratification of the Russification of China. To them there was no China. There was merely a Red Empire; Headquarters, the Kremlin; Ruler, Stalin.

It never seemed so simple to me. It did not seem so during those faceless days in Moscow when security was so tight that, in theory, a correspondent might be sent to a labor camp if he even telephoned the Moscow weather bureau to ask if it was going to rain. Nor did it seem so as the years ran by in Russia, some even grimmer, and then, finally, lightening a bit with the death of Stalin on March 5, 1953. But we never knew. I never had any evidence to prove a case one way or the other.

To be sure, I wondered. I wondered particularly one sultry night in the summer of 1954. Chou En-lai was being entertained in Moscow by the Russian Politburo at Spiridonovka House, on his way back through Russia, having signed the Geneva agreements, which brought the fighting in Indochina to a halt. When I came upon him he was circling the table of his Russian hosts—Malenkov, Molotov, Bulganin, Khrushchev, Mikoyan, Kaganovich and the others—offering toasts to each. But he was speaking in English—a language none of them understood (although, of course, it was perfectly comprehensible to the correspondents and diplomats present—the English, the Swedish, the

Indian and other ambassadors). I thought it was very strange, and apparently the Russians did, too, for when Chou approached Anastas Mikoyan and offered a toast in English, Mikoyan said through an interpreter, "Why don't you speak in Russian, Chou—you know our language perfectly well."

Chou rejoined saucily: "Look here, Mikoyan, it's time you learned to speak Chinese. After all, I have learned to speak Russian."

Chou's remarks had to be interpreted into Russian for Mikoyan who sulkily grumbled: "Chinese is a difficult language to learn."

"No harder than Russian," Chou snapped back. "Come down to our embassy in the morning. We'll be glad to teach you Chinese."

Kaganovich then intervened with a rude remark in Russian, but Chou, continuing to speak in English, said: "There's no excuse for you people."

Was this just hijinks? Was it simply Chou's ebullience over the success (as it seemed then) of Geneva—the first international diplomatic meeting he had participated in? Perhaps, but it did not seem so to me and as the years have gone by it has seemed less and less like mere horseplay. I suspected (but could not prove in 1954) that Chou's remarks reflected a deep bitterness in Sino-Soviet relations—the existence of which no western statesmen, least of all Mr. Dulles, then in his glory, would have been prepared to admit. In fact, even to suggest such a thing at that time was to invite ridicule and contempt.

It was years before the suspicions touched off in my mind that summer night won confirmation. Not, in fact, until five years later, when I found myself, surprisingly but not by accident, in Ulan Bator, capital of Outer Mongolia, the guest of Premier Tsedenbal at a great official reception on the occasion of Nadam, the traditional Mongol holiday, July 11. As I entered the ballroom, I saw a strange spectacle. On one side of the room stood the Russian guests, on the other the Chinese. Between the two groups, rushing back and forth with determined hospitality, were the Mongol hosts, doing their best to make it appear that the party was gay and joyous. But, alas, the evidence was inescapable. One half of the party was not speaking to the other half. The Russians and the Chinese were drawn up in aloof ranks of icy hostility.

I had to make a quick choice—which side of the room would I stand on? I knew from past experience that the Chinese would not shake hands with me, let alone speak. I quickly strode to the Russian side where the Soviet diplomats and military men greeted me with great joviality. Before the evening was over, I found myself confronting a massive Soviet officer who insisted on my drinking *Brüderschaft* to Soviet-American friendship. Then, putting one great paw around my shoulder, he leaned over confidentially and said: "Now, honestly, don't you feel more at home on *our* side? We must stand together against *them*." And lest there be any mistake, he waved grandly toward the Chinese standing polite but silent on the other side of the room.

On that evening, all doubt fled my mind as to the true and inner nature of the relationship between these two great Communist empires. Whatever they might have been in the past, they were now naked, acknowledged, deadly enemies. And if this were true—as I now was convinced—there was no single fact in world politics more important. No longer did we live in a bipolar world. We lived in a triangular world, with all the infinite complications that might bring.

To be sure, the full implications of this did not leap into my mind that evening in Ulan Bator. But I did have the wit to realize that I had got on to what must be the most awesome development in world politics since the rise of Hitler. And, as I suppose is inevitable, I found very quickly that not only was it extraordinarily difficult to get anyone to listen to my story (although it was, of course, published in *The New York Times*) but so far as the officials who concerned themselves with such matters—the White House, the State Department, Defense, the CIA and the rest—my words and my evidence and my conclusions were treated as a rather poor joke. Everyone *knew* that the Sino-Soviet alliance was the Gibraltar of the Communist world. Everyone *knew* that Communism was a monolithic doctrine. No one was really interested in the social notes from Ulan Bator. They did not fit Washington's preconception.

All this changed with time—quite rapidly, too; within a year or so the first open polemics between Moscow and Peking began. But if this brought the rift between Soviet Russia and Communist China into the open, it by no means clarified its meaning for us as Americans, or for the Russians, for the Chinese, for their Asian neighbors or for the world.

Nor were those implications by any means clear even now, on this night in May, 1972, some two months after President Nixon's visit to Peking and on the eve of his trip to Moscow. China had moved. The United States had moved. The Soviets had moved. But where did this leave the pieces on the chessboard of the world? What *really* was the nature of China and what *really* were her intentions?

This night, as I drove through Peking's darkened streets, 1 million Soviet troops stood on the alert on China's northern frontiers: in deep concrete ravelins along the Amur and the Ussuri, in mobile missile bases south of the Gobi in Mongolia, at strategic air stations east of Baikal, in armored concentrations near Khalkin-gal, in rocket silos positioned in the mountains of Mongolia, in hardened installations in eastern Kazakhstan. "They are not there for a simple excursion," a Chinese had told me only a few hours earlier. And I had already seen in that hasty cab ride through the Peking streets the carelessly strewn pre-stressed concrete arches, the house-high stacks of bricks and the long steel girders that were stockpiled for one of the most massive construction projects of our day—the Peking anti-nuclear, air raid-shelter system.

The evidence of a continent in precarious balance was everywhere. The Sino-Soviet frontier was not the only trouble spot. The dust had hardly settled from the India-Pakistan war, and the agonies of Bangladesh were vivid in my mind.

Southward, in the Indochinese archipelago, the horror of war, lately easing, was now rising to a new crescendo, as President Nixon multiplied the B-52 strikes, razed the bomb-shattered towns and cities of North Vietnam yet once again, and blockaded Haiphong and the Vietnam coast. The world trembled on the brink of disaster. The errand that had sent me off through the darkness of this Peking night was a formal Chinese protest against the President's acts. Minutes later, I was standing in the bright lights of the Foreign Office, receiving a copy of the Chinese declaration, then hurrying back once again through the empty streets to the Tsin Chiao Hotel, climbing the staircase to my fifth-floor room (no elevators running at this hour), calling a sleepy Chinese telephone operator, giving the number of *The New York Times*, and, a half hour later, miraculously dictating to New York China's warning that President Nixon was guilty of a "grave new step," and pledging China's support to North Vietnam so long as the war went on.

At 2:30 A.M., I put down the telephone and sat for a few moments in silence. I had turned off the light and, from the window, I could see far out over the low walls and courtyards of the Peking expanse. My hotel was a biggish building, one of several put up in the heyday of

Soviet-Chinese collaboration to house some of the thousands of Russian technicians and engineers who were sent to help China industrialize, and whose sudden withdrawal in August, 1960, marked the real opening of the Moscow-Peking cold war. The building towered over the Peking houses at the back of the old legation quarter.

Looking out over the city bathed in the gentle silver of the moon, I thought again of the millions of sleeping people, and I thought, too, of the millions throughout the country—the greatest population of any nation, greater than any the world had ever seen, a force that was epic in its totality, tidal in its sweep, a force of which I knew so little. Nothing was older on the earth, no human society was older than the Chinese nation. It had endured 5,000 years before the first white colonists had settled in the United States. It had been an advancing civilization when the red men were first penetrating North America (having probably come from within a thousand miles of the spot where I now sat). China had been China when the Roman legions fought blue-clay spattered Picts in the wilderness we now know as pastoral England. What presumption on my part to think that, within a few moments of time, I might begin to understand the deep and complex forces from which the fabric of Chinese policy and the structure of a New Chinese society were being constructed.

And yet it seemed to me that there could be no more vital task than to apprehend in some measure the density, the velocity, the viscosity, the sheer magnitude of the Chinese spirit. For it took little wit to see that, before my very eyes, within my own lifetime, the whole fulcrum of the earth had shifted from the west toward China.

I was born into a world that revolved around the four poles—London, Paris, Berlin and Moscow. Nothing else mattered. Washington was a provincial outpost. India a colony. Japan an upstart. China a debauchee tottering toward final ruin. Africa did not exist.

But after World War I this all had changed, although few statesmen realized it. Lord Grey of Fallodon was more right than he knew when he said in August, 1914: "The lamps are going out all over Europe. We shall not see them lit again in our lifetime." They were going out not just for his time. But for our era. Perhaps they did not light immediately in Asia, but when Russia plunged out of the old imperial system and Japan became the equal of any European power, the world's weight shifted to the east.

How could we have been so naïve, I thought, as to suppose that World War II was about Europe? Of course the Europeans thought that. But *our* war had begun in Asia, and not by accident. It was the cataclysmic movement of the Asian continent, the inexorable rise of Japan that smashed the old system and dragged us into belligerency. And Asia was still in motion. Japan had failed to create an Asian empire, but with her failure, China had risen, and Japan started on her climb toward the world's greatest GNP. Even tonight, as I sat in the window of the Tsin Chiao Hotel, the Asian continent still shuddered. We were wearily fighting our third war of the quarter century —in Asia. Japan, Korea, Vietnam—all Asian wars. Still, we had not really learned the lesson. Or had we? Had Nixon's trip to China marked the beginning of our greater wisdom?

Where, indeed, did greater wisdom begin with China? What manner of state was this ancient nation to which I had finally come? It had undergone not just one revolution, not merely a Communist military success that had crushed the corrupt legions of Chiang Kai-shek. At this moment it was only just emerging from something far more profound—the Great Proletarian Cultural Revolution, an event that the world had perceived as some kind of bewildering anarchistic madness—the Russians called it a precursor of Asian Hitlerism, and labeled Mao a new Genghis Khan. Was that what it was all about? Or did I now stand in the presence of a New Man, a new being born out of chaos, and endowed with moral qualities such as had never been seen before? And if this were so, what did it portend for the world?

There were no end to the questions that night as I looked out over the unlit city, the silent, sleeping city. Could we live in amity with this new-born man and his society of equals? Or was he bent on setting the world ablaze—carrying the red torch of revolution, first through the backways of Asia, into the jungles of the subcontinent, through the desert heartland which Sir Halford Mackinder insisted was the fulcrum that controlled the world, into the uneasy structure of the Middle East, deep into Africa and into restless Latin America? Would India stand or fall in some coming Chinese whirlwind?

There were questions, but only guessed-at answers. I had come to China to see whether the pieces of the puzzle might be fitted together. I was not optimistic about getting final solutions. I distrusted them deeply. The world was far too complicated for simplistic absolutes of the kind that once rolled from the lips of John Foster Dulles. I knew a great deal about China from the outside. I had stood at her frontier in the Himalayas. In Indochina. In Siberia. In Outer Mongolia. Now

I was going to see not only China, but the last of the Communist states I had not yet visited—North Korea, the true hermit kingdom of the modern world. Soon my wife Charlotte would join me. We would have a rendezvous in Peking. Then we would tour China. Possibly I would go again to North Vietnam and Outer Mongolia. If answers were to be found by persistent investigation, some should be forthcoming. At least few persons in the world would have made a more comprehensive exploration of Red Asia.

Finally, I turned away from the window. Did my ears deceive me, or did I hear in the distance a faintly rhythmic beat? I listened more closely and smiled. It was not, as my imagination for a moment had suggested, the heartbeat of a great nation. It was the comfortable distant chuff of a switch engine shuttling through a marshaling yard. Somewhere in the great city, someone else was awake in the stillness of the night. But for the rest, the city slept, a giant drowsing peacefully, but a giant that would soon awaken.

2

Journey to Another Century

I caught my first glimpse of China through the slit of an observation post atop the barbed-wire-nested guardhouse at Lo Wu station, terminus of the 27-mile railroad that runs from Kowloon through the Leased Territories to the Chinese frontier. I looked through the slit, focusing my binoculars as directed by the chief of the Hong Kong defense battalion, and saw through the lens the grim visage of People's Liberation Army soldiers on guard on *their* side of the Lo Wu Bridge, the Shumchun side, behind *their* barbed wire. The year was 1966, and China was tense with the exploding Cultural Revolution. No one in Hong Kong understood what was going on (and, as later became evident, not so many on the China side understood either) but to all, it was apparent that this was a critical moment in the turbulent history of the People's Republic. I was permitted only a minute or two in the observation post—lest, as the British said, the Chinese detect that "something was going on." I stayed just long enough to fix in my mind the stern and hostile look of the PLA men, with their sloppy uniforms and Tommy guns at the ready. I did not want to tangle with them. I caught one other image when I shifted my focus a few points to the east. There, across the Shumchun River, I saw cattle grazing in the green meadows on the China side and a few peasants tending them. The peasants and the cattle looked exactly like the peasantry and the cattle on the British side of the river.

I had two other snapshots of China from afar. One was from Macao, the 400-year-old Portuguese trading center. Here I stood on a dismal creek bank, where refugees, ragged and dirty, huddled in tin and wood shacks or cinderblock huts, while outside, the children with pus and sores on their faces begged for alms. Many had not long before fled from Communist China. Across the creek, on the Chinese side, stood a small blockhouse, neat, well-tended, and three PLA soldiers at their post, looking across a checkerboard paddy field to the rubble and refuse of Macao, standing unblinking, as a gentle wind wafted smoke from the burning garbage heaps over to the China side.

My third glimpse came from a Russian TU-104, tossed like a chip by a thunderstorm over the Ussuri River. The Soviet pilot, rather than detour over the Chinese frontier and escape the jagged lightning that exploded over, under and around the plane, doggedly flew straight into the very eye of a 5,000-foot thunder cap, more fearful of Chinese anti-aircraft batteries than of lightning shafts. From the pitching plane, I saw the Chinese shores of the Ussuri, the very shores where, two months earlier, the Russians and the Chinese fought a deadly rocket battle which left casualties admitted to number 200 or 300, and which rumor persistently placed at much more.

Three images of China, each menacing and dangerous; each stern, chilling, forbidding. Approach China with caution—this was the message. And there was, too, an implicit contrast in discipline, the ragged individualism of the marginal western world on one side, and the strict law and order and neat landscape of China on the other.

I thought I had a good idea of what China would be like, partly formed from these furtive glimpses, and partly from remembered fragments of a hundred crossings of Communist frontiers. I have been across them all in the last quarter century—the sullen Russian frontier, so monotonous in its eternal suspicions that somewhere, somehow, you have concealed in your luggage, possibly between your shirts or in a hollow heel, a potent Capitalist leaflet, which might, in a twinkling, topple the Communist Paradise. At least that is what the green-capped Customs men *seem* to be searching for, as they painstakingly turn over each sheet of paper, glancing in frowning suspiciousness at copies of *Portnoy's Complaint* or *Playboy* magazine. I have stood by as a broad-beamed Mongol Customs lady delved into every nook and cranny of my bags, hunting determinedly for film which she seemed convinced might betray the secrets of the Gobi to Pentagon war planners. I have been awakened by Czech frontier police, insistent on searching my compartment in the Orient Express, and have spent half a day while Polish and Russian guards and police sorted through the luggage of the East Berlin-Brest Litovsk-Moscow Express. I mean I have been through the mill in the Communist countries. I know what to expect. I am braced for unpleasantness when I hand over my passport to the unsmiling border guard, with his bayonet or Tommy gun.

Which is by way of saying that when I walked across the bridge at Lo Wu, typewriter in one hand, briefcase in the other, camera around my neck, I was prepared for a grim encounter. I was not expecting the shy grin that appeared on the faces of the two PLA men with their back-slung Tommy guns at the China side of the bridge, and it unnerved me so much that I whipped out my camera and took a picture. Nothing happened. No remonstrance from the soldiers, just another tired smile that told me I was only one of a thousand who had done the same thing. A moment later I was turning over my passport to a border official who said "Welcome to China," and I had hardly put my bags on the Customs bench before a gentle little Chinese Customs lady quietly said: "The Customs examination is completed."

First impressions are important. My first impression of China stood in stark contrast to my expectation of China, and to my experience with Communist countries in general and the Soviet Union in particular.

But, I thought, of course, the Chinese may simply be putting their best foot forward. This may not *really* be their style at all. Think again of the Cultural Revolution. The terror and the rioting. The attacks on the foreigners. Remember the faces of the PLA men through the observation slit at Lo Wu. Don't leap to hasty conclusions. I thought of this as I wandered down the corridor of the long Shumchun reception building and into a cheerful dining room. A hundred foreigners were going into China that day and a hundred were going out—students, delegations. Inevitably, I ran into a friend.

The waitresses were clean, neat, friendly. They did not seem to think that it was an indignity that I had interrupted their leisure by sitting down at a table—as Russian waitresses usually seemed to do. They brought the food with a smile. And it was good food. Hot. Chinese. Clean. Eggdrop soup, chicken and green peppers, breaded oysters, pungent pork meatballs and orange pop. The tablecloth was clean. The chopsticks clean. I felt myself relaxing. Why, I suddenly thought, it's pleasant to be in this country!

I didn't know why, but I felt at home. And it was a feeling that never left me. Not even in the depths of the countryside; not even on that curious midnight ride through Peking. Not in Yenan. Not in the great cities—Shanghai, Wuhan or Canton. Wherever I went, China felt like China. There is no other way of putting it. It was Chinese, recognizably Chinese. It was strange, but not hostile; it was different, but not alien. And nowhere did I feel that I was intruding or that I was seen as an intruder or an enemy. It was a country of dignity and respect and the people seemed to respect both themselves and their visitors.

I had come expecting to find tensions, to find harsh lines of worry curving the lips of officials, to see worn and sullen looks. But as I stood on the balcony of the reception building at Shumchun and looked across the hot courtyard to the street, no one even glanced my way. It was obvious that this was simply an ordinary village street in an ordinary Chinese village, yet it was right at the Leased Territories line, the frontier. A hundred yards away lay Capitalism, the outside world, the enemy. Where was the vigilance, the surveillance, the electrified barbed wire, the watchtowers, the trained police dogs?

It was difficult to believe that I was plunging into a nation on guard, a nation pregnant with xenophobia and fear. What was the scene? Ordinary Chinese coming and going, coming to the station to wait for the train to Canton, strolling down the street to buy in the shops. Three Chinese ladies, one young, rather pretty, very buxom, in a kind of *café-au-lait* jump suit and blue plastic boots, just off a train, with enormous bundles and great cord-bound boxes on carrying poles, haggling with a pedicab driver, striking a bargain, hoisting box after box into the pedicab and then hoisting themselves (one carried a babe in arms) into the remaining space, seating themselves imperiously. And, a moment later, incredibly, the pedicab driver mounting his bicycle and somehow causing the wheels to turn and the great assemblage majestically to roll off in the hot sunshine.

An ambulance slowly halted outside the station. Two young medical attendants with white smocks and nose masks opened the back and helped out an elderly man, probably a patient going to Canton for treatment. He stepped down carefully, then walked over to the station steps and relaxed, fanning himself in the shade, before gathering his strength to board the train. It was a quiet scene and I stared in utter fascination. As long as I looked it did not change. Presently, a man from the travel service came along. The train for Canton was about to leave. Let's go.

First impressions . . . I leaned back against the lace antimacassar, neatly pinned to the blue upholstery of the train seat. It was a clean train, decorated in blue and gray, lace curtains at the window, many excited Japanese tourists taking pictures of each other, and at one end, a rather poor painting of the famous new bridge across the Yangtze at Nanking.

I turned my eyes to the window and watched China . . . emerald-green countryside, the emerald of rice paddies (I thought of the Emerald City in the land of Oz), terraces in the red earth climbing every hillside; gray water buffalo in the ponds and paddies, knee-high corn, women in conical straw hats transplanting the rice; new orchards on the hillsides, new pine stands, and in some places people setting out the trees; fields of cabbage, beans, peas, squash, melon and cucumbers; walled gray-brick villages, each with a two- or three-story tower. Grain elevators? Or watchtowers?

I lost track of time as field succeeded endless field, then looked at my watch with a start. We had traveled for an hour and a half through the countryside and I had yet to see a car or a truck or a tractor or any kind of farm machinery more complex than a shovel. I had not even seen a road, only narrow paths wandering through the fields, curving around the paddies, linking village to village. The countryside lay quiet, verdant, planted to the last inch; the villages seeming to grow out of the very fields, the people moving slowly across the horizon at their traditional tasks, backs bent as they set out the rice, backs bent as they set out the new young trees, backs bent as they pulled their barrows along the narrow paths.

As I watched a man trundle his barrow through the field, I realized that I had done more than simply walk across the plank boards of the little bridge over Shumchun River, passing from one country into another. I had walked across an invisible line that took me from one century to another. On the Lo Wu side I was in the 20th century, the 20th century of industrialism, of tin cans, of paper wrappings, of gasoline engines, of urgent motors, of blazing billboards, of crashing sounds—the world of waste and garbage and litter and junk, the land of machines and hurry and hustle.

Now from the window of a 19th-century railroad car I looked out at the 17th century. There was nothing in this cavalcade of villages, this checkerboard of rice paddies, this world of men and women and animals and simple tools, hand made, hand wielded, that would startle the eye of a traveler to China in 1672 or even 1572. The people wore the same conical hats, the same simple blue trousers and formless jackets that march across those willow pattern dishes of grandmother's day that introduced most of us to the land of China.

The rice grew in the same way, its green as brilliant as ever. The water buffalo had not changed. The meticulous orchards and precise terraces had been transferred from some ancient scroll.

There were no archers on the village walls but, perhaps, they still stood guard within the watchtowers. I knew the great iron-bound gates in the village walls still clanged shut at sundown. This was not a journey into nostalgia. It was a genuine journey backward in time, a backward leap of centuries into a coherent and compatible way of life in which the land and the people, their animals, their rice and their millet lived and grew in harmony, all things falling into the place that nature and nature's bondsman, man, had intended them to fall.

Well, perhaps, I exaggerate a little. It is true that I saw striding across the countryside, heedless of fields, heedless of villages, the conventional stilts of an electric line, starting somewhere behind and extending as far as my eye could see. But there was only this single standing line. It is true that the train's presence, moving easily across the fields, quiet, no sound from its whistle, smooth on the well-ballasted rails, was a 19th-century anachronism. But there were no other signs my eye could detect that I had not suddenly and improbably been propelled backward into a century that was coterminous with the one in which one of my ancestors set out in a small sailing vessel from Bristol, hoping, in a matter of months, to make landfall somewhere in the New World, a hope fulfilled, providentially, in Rhode Island in 1640.

The implications of this discovery I did not attempt immediately to fathom, but they were obviously profound. I had come on a journey to the Future. But I was first plunging deep into the Past.

Could it be that the path to the Future led backward in time to the 17th century, rather than forward across the industrial battlements of the 19th century? Could it possibly be that the Industrial Revolution in grimy Birmingham and Manchester, that cataclysmic event that Marx saw, analyzed and then employed as the launch-point for his vision of a new society and a new man, arising out of the factory-created proletariat, could it be that this outward thrust of humanity, idealized in the west, carried to almost mythological perfection in computerized America—could this be in reality a cul-de-sac with no opening to the future, a cul-de-sac that China with its ancient roots so firmly imbedded in the soil had already discovered led only to disaster?

Or was this Chinese landscape the simple product of austerity? Perhaps the Chinese, lacking machinery, lacking modern tools and instruments of production, had simply settled for an interim solution—to put their traditional agriculture into order, to practice the art of farming as it had always been practiced, without introducing the machine age, imposing only on the simple landscape certain basic new patterns—better organization of labor; lifting the yoke of landlord oppression and debt; an end to starvation, undernourishment and epidemic disease; and, for the soil itself, better seed, better fertilizer, herbicides and pesticides.

For any judgment on this, a train window was hardly sufficient. It would require first-hand knowledge, visits to the communes, talks with the peasants, a close-up look at what well might prove to be a blend of China's oldest folkways with some of the new weapons in the 20th century's armory of technology.

This question remained for later resolution. But there was another—equally pressing. Was China, in fact, the land of "blue ants" as so many writers had insisted, a nation of 800 million human robots, dressed in blue denim, emotionless, faceless, automatonistic creations bent to the inscrutable will of unseen masters pushing buttons in the depths of some secret retreat in the inner recesses of the Forbidden City?

That was a concept toward which I myself had been drawn more than ten years earlier, when I had my first glimpse of Chinese workers in Outer Mongolia. There were then in Mongolia some 40,000 Chinese—sent there as a contribution to mutual aid. I saw them everywhere—in Ulan Bator, building apartment houses; outside the city, throwing bridges across the Tola River, installing water conservancy systems in the dry steppes, building roads, doing the thousand-and-one tasks that an underdeveloped country urgently needs to have done. As they went about their work, they fitted perfectly the "blue-ant" tag. They wore identical dark blue trousers and dark blue tunics (both men and women, although most of the workers were men); blue caps of identical cut. They rode bicycles in almost military formation (no one else in Mongolia rode bicycles). At 6 A.M., I saw them on the stony banks of the Tola River doing their calisthenics—hundreds of them, bending, twisting, jumping, turning, like a mechanistic ballet. I saw them march in the Nadam parade, a blue clockwork brigade, their clothes baggy but their pace machine-like amid the turbulent outpouring of Mongols, arms swinging and legs uplifted with almost Prussian rhythm. Blue ants. It was easy to believe their minds and thoughts were as disciplined as their arms and legs.

22
TO PEKING—AND BEYOND

It was but one short step from the concept of "blue ants" to the concept of the Chinese colossus—the titanic China, 800 million strong; the world's greatest mass of humanity, trained, obedient, ritualistically ready to do the bidding of their mythic leaders. It was, of course, out of this construct that the Russians had fashioned their terrifying image of China as the new Mongol horde. The question was simple: Were the Chinese, in fact, "blue ants" or was this just one more of the pejorative epithets that foreigners had applied to China over the years? Was it, in fact, merely a color shift from "yellow peril" to "blue ant"? Were these concepts, in fact, merely two sides of a common coin?

Here the evidence was swift and persuasive. It took no time to see that the Chinese did not *look* like blue ants. True, they dressed more or less uniformly, but the uniformity of dress did not stifle diversity in personality and temperament. After my first glimpse of the waitresses in the restaurant at Shumchun, I could no longer believe in the "blue ants." These girls—pretty, jolly, not the slightest sign of stress or self-consciousness—kept up a constant stream of jokes and chatter as they waited on the foreigners. There was nothing rude or inattentive about that. It was simply the mark of warm and easy relations among themselves. They went about their tasks not like automatons, not like soldiers obeying orders, but like simple youngsters, enjoying their work and enjoying each other. I could not think of these pretty girls as "blue ants."

But in Canton, and then in Peking, in one Chinese city after the other, I saw how the concept had taken shape. Many Chinese do dress in baggy cottons or synthetics, and the predominant color is blue. But it is not one standard shade of blue (as had been the case with the labor battalions in Mongolia). The blues ranged from horizon to midnight. Some were fresh and some were faded. Some were new and some were shabby. And the color monotony was broken by the blouses of the girls and women. Though simple, they embraced a range of colors and combinations. If they were not yet what we would call bright, they were not monotonous or uniform. And the children were a delight. Their clothes came in every shade and style, the gayer the better; and it quickly transpired that a quiet effort was being made by the government and, I suppose, the party, to persuade both men and women to express greater individuality in clothing. A visit to any department store confirmed it. Dress goods counters were a riot of colors and patterns—patterns being bought, and obviously not entirely for children.

But the "blue-ant" image didn't apply simply to uniformity of dress. It was intended to describe uniformity of conduct, uniformity of thought, uniformity of habit, perfect obedience, submissiveness to orders, subordination of personality to some higher scheme. If this concept were valid, the New Man (and New Woman) of China would emerge as a kind of stamped-out product of the modern ideological factory—labor cadres, cannon fodder, disciplined soldiers in civilian dress.

One warm night in Peking I was riding from the Chien Men Hotel toward the Central Telegraph Office on the Tien-an Men. It was sweltering, and all of Peking seemed to be on the street. As we approached the broad boulevard where the new Peking subway is being built, I saw two youngsters, nine or ten years old, on a pedestal in the center of the intersection where the traffic officer normally stood. The officer had gone off duty and the two youngsters stood in his place, wildly flinging their arms about, directing traffic to their hearts' content. The performance upset no one. There were no hasty calls for the police; only chuckles from passing truck drivers. I tried to visualize a similar scene on Gorky Street in Moscow, but my imagination broke down. In the first place, the traffic officers *never* go off duty in Moscow, not even at 4 A.M. In the second place, not the boldest street urchin would dare offer what would be understood in Russia as a challenge to constituted authority. In Peking it was seen for what it was—a small boy's innocent joke.

That same evening a bit further down the street, my way was almost barred. Some youngsters had opened a street hydrant in the time honored fashion of the old Lower East Side of New York. The water was gushing halfway across the street, and a hundred joyous boys and girls were splattering themselves. Once again there was no call for higher authority. No cops came and turned the hydrant off. No youngsters were scolded. No one was arrested. On my way back from the telegraph office I stopped three times under street arcs to see what had caused a crowd to collect. In one case it was two young men seriously pondering a chessboard. In the other two, it was games of cards. I don't know what the game was but I don't think it was Old Maid—unless in China they play Old Maid for money. One day at the Ming tombs in the lovely western hills of Peking, we walked through a shady park where sightseers were having their lunch and a quiet drink. At three tables I saw card games in progress—nothing furtive about any of them. Just people enjoying themselves.

I don't want to make a big point out of a few games of fan-tan. But I don't want to dismiss the card-playing either. China is just emerging from the Great Proletarian Cultural Revolution, the turbulent and traumatic upheaval which, it is said, has transformed her society. And I am prepared to believe that this is so. But I think it is also apparent that the Great Proletarian Cultural Revolution has not created a generation of "blue ants." As always, Chinese society is a diversified whole. Perhaps it has more discipline than in the past. Perhaps not. China has always been a disciplined and cultured nation, and if it seemed to old China hands that it was not, it is likely that it was the disturbing influence of western materialism and amorality that corrupted the personality of the Chinese who were in contact with it, and who thus became, in essence, its victims.

There are certain main lines of contemporary Chinese character. There is even, as we shall see, important evidence that something like a New Man (and New Woman) has been created, at least, in part, in China. But the image of the "blue ant"—this is a caricature that never had more than a vague authenticity.

To be sure, China is a homogeneous nation. Her population is more than 90 percent Han, that is, ethnic Chinese. Less than ten percent of China's residents have other ethnic origins—Mongol, Kazakh, Uighur, Manchu (if that can be still distinguished) and many small fragments of ethnic groups like the Hakka and the Wei people. Both of these are probably basically Han, maybe even the building blocks from which the Han people arose. This does not mean that the Han stock is pure. Far from it. Again and again, outside races have swept into China and conquered her. But each of them has been numerically small compared to the Han mass and each has been culturally inferior to the Hans. As a result, the Huns, the Mongols, the Manchus, and all the others who fought their way to the Dragon Throne became, after one or two hundred years, indistinguishable from the Hans, the world's oldest and strongest people.

When the integral nature of China is perceived (and Americans, coming from the most diverse of populations, find it extremely difficult to adjust to the idea of a nation made up of the same people, possessing the same racial stock and the same culture, with infinitesimal variations north and south, east and west) then the small core of truth that is encrusted by the "blue ant" fallacy becomes plain.

For instance, in the days of the Empire, the common people, the ordinary people, the peasantry, were forbidden to dress in the gay and luxurious silks and satins and velvets and cloths of gold that were the mark of the Empire and the ruling class. It was not, thus, necessary for any Communist regime to insist by edict, indoctrination or egalitarian principle that all people dress more or less alike. The fact was that the people in China had *always* dressed alike as far as the memory of history goes, and that is close to 5,000 years. No Chinese looking out on the hurrying throngs in the shopping streets just off the Tien-an Men sees anything new or strange about the fact that everyone dresses very much the same. His eyes would be offended if people appeared suddenly in the galaxy of colors, shapes and sizes that characterize the crowds thronging into Rockefeller Center of a summer day.

The same is true of Peking itself. To many visitors, Peking streets seem gray and drab, lined as they are by endless blocks and squares of Peking courtyard houses, all one story tall, all with nothing distinguishing on the outside, all enclosed within gray or tan walls that give no hint of what is inside, most of them with access through narrow streets or *hutungs*, blind alleys between encroaching, barren walls. And no other building more than one story high, except a few put up by foreigners before 1949 and, here and there, a hotel or a ministry built by the present government. (I am not counting the big new quarters of four-, six- and eight-story apartment houses that have been built in the city's outskirts under the new regime, largely to house the hundreds of thousands of new residents, many of them workers in new suburban industries.)

The façade of Peking, its inward-looking drabness, grayness, monotony (which quickly turns out to have its own attractiveness) is not, as the thoughtless visitor may think, a product of the stern puritanism of the new regime, but rather the cultural heritage of the great Empire, which remorselessly refused to the very end to permit anyone to build in Peking any structure that would in any way, by height or design, detract from that most dramatic of all creations, the Imperial City, the Forbidden City itself, with its infinity of towers and courtyards, its rich décor, its marvelous walls of imperial red-purple or purple-red, its battlements, and that wonder of the past, the Peking wall and its towers, a thing of soaring imagination that loomed out of the great northern plain like a dream from the red chamber, one of the unique sights of man, now vanished and forever gone (the greatest cultural loss of the Revolution), only a few of its remarkable towers —Bell Tower, Drum Tower, the Chien Men, the Northern Gate, the Western Gate—still standing as footnotes to the past, small reminders of a glory that never again will be seen, the very stones that formed the wall dispersed, and hidden deep in the bowels of Peking, to provide the foundations and walls of the great underground shelter system.

Here, then, is a lesson I quickly learned in this new society: The first and most important step toward its understanding is to know not only what is real and what is apparent, what is genuine and what is sloganeering (either domestic or external) but, more important, to know what *is* China, the eternal China, the China that has existed for 5,000 years, and what it is that has been changed, augmented, diminished, or modified by one of the great transformations of our time.

Only when I began to be able to distinguish old from new, real from false, would it be possible to make valid judgments about the nature of this new civilization.

3

"People Were Killed"

The professor was a worn, gray man with the quiet manner of one who has experienced more than he would like to remember. He wore a neat, tan suit of some light material, probably a synthetic, well-cut and not baggy in the knees or floppy at the cuffs like those of many of his colleagues. When he spoke he was quite firm, although his voice was soft. "You must understand," he said, "that it was a real *revolution*. People fought one another. People were killed."

We were talking of the Cultural Revolution. Everywhere in China I asked about the Cultural Revolution, because it seemed to me the most important thing to understand—the most important and the most difficult. I am sure that there is much that I still do not understand, but I have learned enough to know no one can begin to comprehend China today, no one can begin to draw conclusions about the nature of the country, the quality of the people, the inner meaning of Chinese policy, the psychology of her leaders or her attitude toward the world and toward the United States, without grasping the essentials of the Cultural Revolution. If there is in China a New Man, if China is creating the pattern of the world's future, the secret, I think, must lie in the Cultural Revolution.

I first heard the words "Cultural Revolution" in Hong Kong in 1966. I had just come out to Asia, and I found the specialists of Hong Kong puzzling over what was happening within China. The commonest and easiest explanation, the one most often heard, was that a "power struggle" had broken out among the Chinese leaders. But precisely who was fighting whom was not clear, and each specialist had his own interpretations.

Power struggles in Communist countries were nothing new to me. I had been through that several times in the Soviet Union. They were complex affairs, I knew, and looking from the outside, one was as apt as not to get the line up wrong. As for predicting the outcome—it was only a little less risky than playing roulette.

But there were those who felt that what was happening in China was no ordinary power struggle, and my instinct supported that view. So did one of the few Chinese with whom I had direct contact. To his mind, something entirely different was happening. He called the Cultural Revolution a deliberate "tempering" experience for China's youth, launched with full understanding of its consequences, because Chairman Mao feared that soon China would be confronted by war with the United States. It was necessary to steel and harden China's youth for the terrible experience that lay ahead. The young people of China, he said, had grown up not knowing the hardships and perils of the revolutionary generation, the generation of Yenan. They had not fought in the Civil War; they had not gone on the Long March; they had not been tested in battle against the Japanese and Chiang Kai-shek. They were becoming effete and soft, thinking of themselves, living a life of comparative ease and luxury. It was necessary to "blood" them, to instill in them a knowledge of hardship and danger and sacrifice, so that they could stand up to the threats that lay just ahead.

This interpretation, heavy with doomsday psychology, and rooted in President Johnson's escalation of the Vietnam War, then in full progress, carried a good deal of conviction. Moreover, it matched the rhetoric that was coming out of China, even though I thought it a massive over-reaction to the American effort in Vietnam. But my Chinese friend insisted: What could the American purpose in Vietnam be if not to establish a *place d'armes* for attacking China? If Vietnam had no other strategic purpose, and if Johnson was now escalating the war—sending his bombers closer and closer to China—was not the situation parallel to the Korean War, which had inevitably brought China into conflict with the U.S.A.? I did not accept this thesis but, on the other hand, I did not think it unrealistic for the Chinese to interpret Vietnam in these terms.

There were other interpretations of the Cultural Revolution. Later on that year, I talked with my Russian friends and found them saying that China had fallen into complete anarchy. They talked seriously about the possibility that Mao Tse-tung had simply gone mad. They compared him with Hitler. The Red Guard movement, they insisted, was simply the invocation in Asian terms of the Nazi youth movement. They cited reports that young Red Guard detachments had sacked the houses of persons accused of kowtowing to foreigners, of the burning of "foreign" books (and Chinese classics) in the streets of Peking, just as the Nazis burned books on the streets of Berlin in the 1930's. They mentioned the indignities heaped upon famous writers like Kuo Mo-jo (who at one point proclaimed publicly that "all I have written should strictly speaking be burned. It has no value."). There were rumors that the Red Guards had even broken into the Shanghai apartment of Madame Soong Ching-ling, widow of Dr. Sun Yat-sen and the Vice-Chairman of the People's Republic, and reproached her for her "foreign" way of life. Then, too, there had been physical attacks on Soviet diplomats; their cars had been surrounded and the occupants dragged out and pummeled on the street; the assault and sacking of the British Embassy; the beating up of the British chargé d'affaires, the house arrest of the Reuter correspondent and warnings to foreigners not to appear in public in Peking because of the danger of physical attack. Foreigners in cities like Tientsin and Harbin had been assaulted by Red Guards, apparently in the belief that they were Russians. A deep strain of chauvinism and xenophobia seemed to have surfaced.

Rumor followed rumor. There were disorders in Chinese cities. The universities had shut down. Millions of young people were wandering about the country, confronting officials, haranguing, arguing. There were reports of armed clashes, of disruption of industry, of disruption of the very process of government. The trouble spilled out across the border. There were riots in Hong Kong and Macao.

I met a European Communist, an old friend of mine and an old friend of China. He had actually been to Peking and he could hardly bear to talk about it. His Chinese friends would not see him—even party friends whom he had known before 1949. He had been told to stay in his hotel room (he was actually just in transit through China) and not to venture onto the streets. When he went to the Foreign Office to get his exit visa, no one would speak to him except in Chinese, which he did not understand. He was rudely given a form to fill out —all written in Chinese. As he sat at a desk, bewildered and wondering what to do, one of his oldest Chinese friends chanced to pass through the waiting room. She silently befriended him, filled out the form in Chinese, and then vanished, without a word, a finger to her lips.

Now, of course, it was over. Or so I thought. Officials were back in their offices (although many, I believed, had vanished); the Red Guards were dispersed to the countryside; things were moving along more or less normally, it seemed. But what *had* happened and *why* did it happen and what was the legacy of the Cultural Revolution to China and to the world?

One of my first discoveries was that the Cultural Revolution was not over, at least not in the words and attitude of the Chinese. When I asked to visit some more remote and exotic regions—Tibet, Sinkiang, Inner Mongolia—I was quickly told that this was not possible because "the Cultural Revolution is still in progress in those areas." And the same explanation was offered to proposals to visit out-of-the-way cities like Chungking and Kunming. There, too, the Cultural Revolution was said still to be in progress.

Exactly what this meant I was never able to determine precisely, but it seemed to be a way of saying that the Peking authorities had not yet completely restored their authority in such outlying regions, and that the turbulence, disorder and struggle that had characterized the Cultural Revolution still prevailed there, at least to such an extent that Peking was not yet ready to permit visits by an American correspondent. I knew, however, that this did not necessarily mean acute trouble, because a few foreigners had been permitted into those regions. John S. Service, the old China hand of the State Department who had been persecuted for his accurate and prescient reports from China during World War II, was permitted to visit Chungking (where he was born) and found no evidence of trouble; and the Canadian Ambassador, Ralph Collins, born in Kunming, was permitted to visit his birthplace and saw nothing untoward there. There had also been a visit or two by foreigners to Sinkiang and possibly Inner Mongolia (but none, so far as I could ascertain, to Tibet).

But the use of the phrase "the Cultural Revolution is still in progress" indicated that the Revolution was regarded in Peking as a continuous process and not one that had come to an arbitrary or predetermined end.

This was reflected, too, in many other comments that seemed to indicate that while the Cultural Revolution had passed its peak, it was by no means a dead letter—rather, it was being treated as a more or less permanent factor in Chinese life—a factor, incidentally, that many individuals regarded as of transcendental importance. But to get to the root of the feeling was by no means simple. I quickly found that it was much easier to discover what had happened in physical terms than to grasp its metaphysical essence.

My first effort to come to grips with the Cultural Revolution arose in discussion with the students and faculty of Tsinghua University. Tsinghua, the Chinese MIT, is located on a 500-acre campus northwest of Peking, a lovely spot, with trees, park-like avenues and a sprawling jumble of buildings. It was founded in 1911 by Americans, with funds from the indemnity China was compelled to pay foreign countries in compensation for damage done and lives lost in the Boxer Rebellion. The U.S. remitted its share of the indemnity to China, and the funds were used for the establishment of the university. It was supposed to be an institution for training China's new leaders and it carried this out, quickly becoming a hotbed of intellectual activity and playing a leading role in China's revolutionary movements, from the time of its inception in 1911—the very year that Dr. Sun Yat-sen's independence movement toppled the old Manchu Dynasty.

In a sense, Tsinghua had been the birthplace, too, of the Cultural Revolution, or at least of the Red Guards. It was at Tsinghua that students in the secondary school of the university had first called themselves Red Guards. They were repressed by the authorities, but six of them wrote to Mao Tse-tung and he came to their rescue with a letter dated August 1, 1966: "I hereby give you my enthusiastic support." And so the Red Guard movement took off. Thus, when we drove out of Peking on a warm June day, past the factory district that encroaches on the city's northwest corner, into the countryside where already the fierce hot winds from the Mongolian plain were beginning to yellow the wheat and burn the grain, we were driving in a sense right into the heart of the Cultural Revolution, its germinal center. Or at any rate one of them.

But there was little of this atmosphere as we sat down to talk in a big airy room on the second floor of the administration building with two or three professors, several members of the Revolutionary Committee that now administered the university (every institution in China, even kindergarten, is now administered by a "Revolutionary Committee") and two or three students. One student, a sparkling black-eyed girl, with her hair in pigtails and wearing a pretty blue and pink plaid, silk blouse, gave her name as Tsao Yu-chien and said she was 24 years old and had been a member of the Red Guards at the university during the Cultural Revolution. She was one of the very few Red Guard students still at the university, and she it was who began talking about the Cultural Revolution, quickly to be joined by almost all those present. It was, I learned, one of the rare occasions on which the participants at Tsinghua had talked in detail about the conflict and the fighting. There had been earlier discussions at Tsinghua with foreigners but rarely was the question of physical violence mentioned.* As time went on and I engaged in similar discussions at other universities in other cities, I found that they, too, were talking for the first time to foreigners about these remarkable events.

Tsinghua began to be caught up in the revolutionary struggle in May of 1966 and on May 29 the secondary-school students set up an organization which they called the Red Guards. Sentiment moved very rapidly and soon the whole university was ablaze with talk, debate, demonstrations and argument. To Americans familiar with "The Movement" at Columbia in 1968, or at Berkeley in 1966, or on any of the campuses where the great wave of turbulence erupted in 1968, 1969 and 1970, the story had a familiar ring.

By June the students and faculty were ranged in violent disagreement over the educational system, methods of study, the rights of students, the content of courses, the attitudes of professors, the whole aim and objective of education. This was a subject with which Chairman Mao had been concerned for several years. He had sought repeatedly to get a national debate going, to win changes in the direction of China's educational system, without success. Now, suddenly, the system was racked by an explosion which, beginning as at Columbia and Berkeley with academic questions, quickly swept into the basic issues of the political and social direction that the People's Republic should take.

There were then in Tsinghua about 12,000 students and 2,600 faculty and staff, all living in dormitories or houses within the 500-acre campus. By June there were few who had not involved themselves in

---

* Compare, for instance, the account of Maria Antoinetta Macciocchi, *Daily Life in Revolutionary China* (Monthly Review Press, New York, 1972). However, a remarkable and detailed inquiry into the Tsinghua events has been made by William Hinton who interviewed a large number of participants at Tsinghua and in Peking during the summer of 1971. This account has been published under the title *Hundred Day War: The Cultural Revolution at Tsinghua University* (Monthly Review Press, New York, 1972). This is the finest account of any aspect of the Cultural Revolution yet to appear.

the struggle. Classes and formal activity at the university had ground to a halt.

At this point there appeared on campus a "work team" of about 500 senior party members, headed by Wang Kuang-mei, the wife of Liu Shao-chi, President of the People's Republic, and the man who, as it was soon to develop, was Chairman Mao's principal ideological opponent.

"But, of course, that wasn't clear to us then," said Professor Chien Wei-chang, one of China's leading specialists in thermodynamics and the H-bomb, and a one-time Caltech student. Professor Chien played a leading role in Tsinghua's Cultural Revolution, first as a target of students who branded him "old stubborn," and later as one of the faculty members who helped set the university up along new lines.

The "work team" set about to restore order by insisting that classes resume. When objections were raised, some 150 leading student and faculty members were ousted on charges that they were "anti-party elements." When this did not halt the agitation, the work team branded another 800 faculty and students "anti-revolutionaries" and confined them to quarters. But even this did not quiet the university. Agitation rose more strongly, and finally the Liu Shao-chi work team had to be withdrawn, and the Red Guards, victorious, took over the university. Thus, by autumn, there was full victory of the Cultural Revolution at the university, but no classes, no teaching, no curriculum. Everyone was talking and agitating, and (with the personal encouragement of Chairman Mao) many young people had left to travel about the country—all transportation was free. They could go where they liked and when they liked. In theory, they were "studying local conditions" and taking word of the Cultural Revolution to every nook and cranny of the land. They still were paid their student stipends even though no classes were held; and local authorities fed and housed them on demand.

At the university, the Red Guards were busy "cleansing" the thought of the university and of its professors. (This was when Professor Chien was labeled as "old stubborn.") Professors and students were subjected to a re-education process, which often meant that they had to stand up before enormous disorderly congregations of students who hurled insults and reprimands at them while they "confessed their sins." If the Red Guards did not find the confession credible, it was made over and over. Sometimes the more stubborn cases (or those thought to be so) were paraded through the campus with dunce caps on their heads and mocking signs saying "jackass" or "stupid" around their necks.

This process was not unique at Tsinghua. The same thing was going on at every university and every educational institution in the country. And not only in educational institutions. It was happening in factories, government offices, stores, theaters, hospitals, city councils, communes—every kind of institution that existed in China.

But the course of the Revolution by no means ran smoothly. As 1967 advanced, there was serious trouble at Tsinghua and many other places. At Tsinghua, the Red Guards had split into two factions, each of which regarded itself as the true defender of the faith, the only protector of Mao Tse-tung's thought. One was known as "The Regiment," the other as "The Fours." The whole group originally called itself the "Tsinghua University Chingkangshan Regiment." Each regarded the other as traitorous renegades. The factions were in touch with Red Guards at other universities—particularly with those at nearby Peking University—but gradually they became more and more isolated as the struggle began to be of a quasi-military character and students began to barricade themselves in university buildings.

"Our group [The Regiment] set up its headquarters in this building," Tsao Yu-chien said, her eyes sparkling even more than usual. "The other group [The Fours] was in the science building."

The science building was just down the university street from the ten-story administration building where we were sitting—plainly visible from the windows. The group in the science building had an advantage over the administration-building group, because in the laboratories it was possible to make bombs, grenades and rockets. There was also a machine shop, and here the Red Guards managed to construct a makeshift tank by fastening steel plates to the sides of a tractor.

On the other hand, the Red Guard group in the administration building had the advantage of superior elevation; they could fire right down on the science building from the higher floors of the building.

How did things come to such a pass? Professor Chien insisted that it was not entirely the fault of the protagonists. "Class enemies," he said, passed back and forth between the factions, stirring up hatred and convincing each side that the other was the foe of the Cultural Revolution. As time went on, a siege mentality took over. Each group began to think that it was an outpost surrounded by the most treacherous enemies of Chairman Mao. They threw up higher and higher barricades and prepared for a battle to the end. Sentries were mounted around-the-clock, every possible access was closed and guards watched with fieldglasses from rooftops to spy out any movement of the enemy. There were frequent exchanges of fire.

"Most of the students had gone home," Tsao Yu-chien said, "before the worst fighting in the spring of 1968."

But she stayed on, helping to prepare meals for her comrades and to participate in the "artistic department" of the Red Guards.

The faculty members who continued to live on the campus tried to mediate between the groups; to no avail. Representatives of the PLA came into the campus and tried to cool things down. It did not help. Both sides engaged in periodic skirmishing and there were occasional exchanges of fire, but it was not until April 23, 1968, that the most serious battles began.

Each side attempted to take the other's position by direct assault. Fire bombs burned out the science building. Then the factions started to tunnel underground, each hoping to plant a bomb under the other's headquarters and blow it up. At this point, Tsao Yu-chien finally slipped away from the campus and made her way to her home in a nearby village. Only the most fanatic students remained, but these numbered several hundred.

Many of the dormitories on the campus were badly damaged by gunfire or burned out. One student was killed just outside the administration building by a rooftop sniper. Still the battling went on. It continued for three months. On July 22, 1968, some 30,000 workers[1] from Peking were mobilized and marched into the university grounds, surrounding the besieged factions and calling upon them to halt their battle. By that time, ten students had been killed. The workers were not armed. Their task was to bring the conflict to an end by persuasion. But one Red Guard faction, The Regiment, did not believe that the workers were genuine supporters of Chairman Mao. These students were convinced it was a trick. Arming themselves with grenades and machine guns, they fought their way through the throng of workers, killing five of them in the battle, and fled into the countryside, hoping to make contact with "true Mao Tse-tung supporters."[2]

[1] Some estimates of the size of the workers' group are as high as 100,000.

[2] William Hinton reports 731 persons were wounded in the fighting and 143 taken prisoner. Chou En-lai used the figures five killed and 751 wounded in speaking to the Association of Concerned Asian Scholars in 1971.

It was not until days later, when they had wandered for miles from village to village, that they finally realized that they had been living in a world of chimera and delusion. The countryside was not against Mao, the city was not against Mao, the workers were not against Mao. They were, in fact, victims of their own paranoia.

Most of the Red Guards, Professor Chien said, finally came back to the university, and there were subjected to an "intensive struggle" to reform their thought and correct their errors. Once that was achieved, they were graduated and sent out to make their way in the world. But not all met that fate. Those who were particularly recalcitrant were made objects of public meetings. And some who were adjudged to be "evil elements," guilty of deliberately stirring up trouble and sabotaging the Cultural Revolution, were placed under close supervision and put to work on "university farms" maintained in the deep countryside. No one was convicted of murder, the faculty said, because it was felt that these were special circumstances and the young people had been misled.

That was the end of the physical struggle at Tsinghua. But it was far from the end of the story. All faculty and administration members, without exception, were sent to the countryside to so-called "May Seventh" schools founded by Chairman Mao for the purpose of "remolding" thought. Most of them spent two years living a peasant life, digging in the fields, planting rice, driving the night-soil carts, studying Marxism-Leninism and *The Thought of Chairman Mao*. Some—but not any great number—were still in the countryside but almost all were back at the university and most were at their old jobs. Not all, however. Shih Kuo-hong, for instance, a Harvard student from 1945 to 1948 and a sociology professor before the Cultural Revolution, was now the university librarian. Sociology, as an academic subject, had been abolished. The university itself was still moving only in low gear. It was closed for four years and received its first class of 2,800 students only in September, 1970, and its second class of 2,000 in May, 1972. It would be several years before its enrollment approached pre-Cultural Revolution levels. Its basic character had been considerably altered. At Chairman Mao's insistence, no students were admitted who had not completed at least three years' work in the fields or factories or served three years in the armed forces after finishing secondary school. They were meticulously screened for political reliability and, once they were at the university, there was intensive emphasis on vocational training. The university had installed its own machine shops and small factories. Students spent one third of their time on practical tasks and in work in the fields, whither they were sent during the critical labor periods at planting and harvesting time. The faculty, having completed its tours in the May Seventh schools, would now spend a month or so working with the peasants every year.

This was the story of the Cultural Revolution as it was told to me at Tsinghua.* It seemed to provide a reasonably complete microcosm of the *physical* aspects of the Revolution, and it provided some clue to institutional changes that had occurred. But it did not tell me *why* the Revolution had occurred, what it was intended to accomplish, what, actually, it had done to the character and psychology of the country and how it had changed human beings.

I raised the question again at Wuhan University and got somewhat the same answer. I knew that Wuhan had been the scene of pitched battles during the Cultural Revolution (probably the most savage fighting of the Revolution occurred there) and in the very first classroom we visited, I noticed broken window panes. I could not help asking whether here, too, there had been violent physical combat and I was told that there had been—but not quite so violent as that at Tsinghua. Here, too, the students had barricaded themselves in classroom buildings. There had been much rifle fire. The windows had, indeed, been shattered during the battles of the Cultural Revolution. But no one had been killed on the campus, although certainly some had been wounded in exchanges of rifle fire and pitched battles with bricks, stones, sticks and fists. The worst fighting had occurred late in 1967, but fortunately, most of the firing had been intended to frighten rather than to kill.

But if the casualty list had been lighter at Wuhan University, it seemed to me that the impact of the Revolution had, perhaps, been more profound. As at Tsinghua, enrollment at Wuhan was only a fraction of its former total—2,200 compared with 5,000. The university had set up what it called two branches out in the countryside, one at Hsiang-yan and the other at Shayang. But they sounded to me more like labor camps. At one, the curriculum seemed to be largely

* To get a feeling of the utter madness of this struggle, particularly in its later phases, and of the remarkable role of Kuai Ta-fu, leader of The Regiment, the reader is directed to William Hinton's *Hundred Day War*. Kuai's conduct was still under investigation in 1972 to determine his relationship to the so-called "May 16th" group and possibly to Lin Piao.

forestry work (timbering?) and at the other, manual farm labor. Both student and faculty were working in these branches. There had been, I learned, a sharp split within the Wuhan faculty even before the Cultural Revolution. Chairman Mao visited the university on September 12, 1958, and laid down a comprehensive program of part-time study and part-time work, designed to integrate academic life with the life of peasants and workers. But, said Tung Nao-lin, the small, energetic woman who headed the university's Revolution-in-Education Committee, the Chairman's guidance was blocked by ideological opponents in the university, "capitalist roaders," as she called them. The capitalist roaders, she explained, were persons who carried out a "revisionist line," that is, persons who sided with President Liu Shao-chi and who, in general, were inclined toward the Soviet approach to education. I asked who these persons were, specifically, and it turned out that they were the university rector and the whole administrative leadership of Wuhan University. Not very surprisingly, there had been some changes in the university administration. More surprisingly, however, all of the faculty was said to be back on the job, having gone through two to three years of rehabilitation through physical labor in the countryside.

I could not help wondering what had happened to human relations during such violence—violence, as it was becoming more and more clear, being one of the salient features of the Cultural Revolution. I raised the question when talking with a faculty-student group at Hunan Science and Engineering University at Changsha. Hunan has always been one of China's top engineering schools and before the Cultural Revolution it had an enrollment of 5,000. In June of 1972, the enrollment was 1,079 and the expectation was that it would not reach normal figures for another three or four years, even though the curriculum had been revised so that students now graduate in three rather than four years.

There had been, the faculty conceded, a certain amount of disorder and violence at Hunan University during the Cultural Revolution but, they hastened to assure me, not as much as there was in some places. True, the students had split into two factions by the end of 1966; it was also true that in 1967 they barricaded themselves in buildings and fought, sometimes with their fists, and also with home-made weapons. "What kind of home-made weapons?" I asked. Cannon, they replied. Cannon made from seamless tubes, which they had converted in the university's excellently equipped machine shops.

Was anyone wounded in this fighting? Yes, came the answer, some were. And was anyone killed? Yes, some were killed. How many? Wang Wi-chun, assistant group leader of the Revolution-in-Education Committee, a competent-looking man in a blue shirt, lifted his hand, extending his five fingers. He clenched his fist, extended the fingers again. He clenched the fist a third time, then held up four more fingers. "Fourteen were killed?" I asked in wonderment. "That's right," he said, "fourteen," "But no one was killed on the campus," Chen Tsai-kang, Vice-Rector of the University hastily added. "They were killed in fighting at Changsha and other places nearby."

I had a sudden thought.

"Were any faculty members hurt in the fighting?" I asked. Eyes met eyes around the room. "Yes," someone said. "Were any faculty killed?" I pressed. "Yes," Wang admitted sadly, "three were killed." "But," interjected Chen, "not on the campus. They were killed outside." The three, it developed, all members of the electrical engineering faculty, had been in Changsha and were returning to the city when they were caught in a crossfire and killed.

What, I wondered, had happened to the students? They returned to the university in March of 1968, the faculty said. They were sent back to their classrooms briefly and then directed out to the countryside and to the factories. There were some isolated cases of students who were punished for committing crimes, including murder. These were sent to labor camps under close custody. But the faculty? What about the faculty? Almost everyone in the faculty had engaged in the Revolution, had taken positions, had argued, had fought as hard as the students. What had happened to them? They, too, I was told, had all gone to the countryside. Now they were all back, and, it was insisted, "relatively speaking," were on good terms with each other. It seemed impossible to define "relatively speaking" with any precision. Having regard for Chinese tact, it seemed to me that this probably meant wounds were far from healed.

This, then, was the pattern. I talked to factory directors and got much the same story. The director of the big Wuhan Iron & Steel Company, the Bethlehem Steel of China (No. 2 to the great Anshan works in Northeast China) said that his plant had been closed for brief periods during the Cultural Revolution, especially when what he called "extreme leftist and anarchistic elements" came to the fore. But, later on, these elements were criticized and repudiated. He lost some production and one blast furnace was forced to halt operations, but by the time it was over, the spirit of the workers had been stimulated, and production boomed. In his plant, he insisted, the fighting was confined to fists; no guns were used.

Fu Dan University at Shanghai rounded out my picture of the physical side of the Cultural Revolution. Here, too, enrollment was only a fraction of what it had been before the Cultural Revolution, 1,790 compared to 6,500. Here, too, the Cultural Revolution was marked by the fiercest kind of struggle, but a struggle punctuated by considerably less physical violence than at the other universities. It opened with adherents of the educational line of Liu Shao-chi in command and ended when members of the Shanghai working class, factory workers from all over the city, entered the university and took over a leading role in its administration. Here, too, the students had split into two factions. But, despite heated debate, there was never a physical struggle, no barricades, no arms. The strongest weapons were loudspeakers, blaring denunciations and curses, from one side to the other. The most dramatic event at the university came when one Red Guard faction kidnapped Hsu Ching-hsien, Vice-Chairman of the Shanghai Revolutionary Committee, and held him prisoner for a week in a university dormitory. Government troops entered the university grounds and compelled the Red Guards to hand over their captive.

These stories, I realized, actually told me nothing so far as principles were concerned. These were stories of violence, of conflict, of a clash of student and faculty forces. The violence apparently had been set in motion when Chairman Mao encouraged the students to take the field against constituted authority. But why? What was Chairman Mao's objective, and what did the students accomplish? How was China changed by the Cultural Revolution? Did it redistribute power? Did it change attitudes and policy?

I knew that battle lines had been drawn over issues that aroused men and women to fight and die. "People were killed," as the professor said. It *had* been a revolution. But I was still to learn the nature of the revolution and what its legacy to China and the world might be. Only on the very eve of my departure did I begin to get an inkling of what it was all about.

4

Where It All Began

It was my next-to-last evening in China. Charlotte and I were sitting in a cream and gold suite of the Park Hotel in Shanghai. Before 1949, the Park was a luxury residence hotel, a 20-story skyscraper, sleek, suave, rich. Now, nearly 25 years into China's revolution, the Park had not lost its character. We were whisked up to the eighth floor in a silent, carpeted elevator, with an upholstered chair for anyone who was tired. Dinner had been served in high style. If it was not the finest meal we had enjoyed in China, that was because we had so many remarkable dinners that only an epicure could choose the best among them. The linen was white and gleaming; the waiters silent, quick and efficient; the dishes one surprise after the other—the climax a vegetable platter surmounted by two pheasants carved from winter melons—and the menu itself a glorious thing, each dish listed in beautiful calligraphy on a sheet of crimson and gold paper. It is hard to believe dinner at the Park had been more luxurious before 1949. When we finally finished, we rose and went to the next room to relax over a bowl of fruit (oranges cut in frescoed shapes of baskets), Cuban cigars and excellent brandy.

Finally our host, a dark-haired, good-looking, thirtyish man with a quick grin, a quicker wit and a direct and authoritative way of speaking that told you that he knew what he was talking about and had the authority to express himself, squared his shoulders and, smiling quizzically, said in a quiet voice: "I can tell you something about the Cultural Revolution in Shanghai. I only participated in it here. I wasn't in other parts of China. But it is true that it all began here."

I had spoken in Peking about my confusion over the Cultural Revolution. Now I was to get my answer.

The speaker was Chu Yung-chia, member of the Standing Committee of the Shanghai Revolutionary Committee—a title that conveys little until you learn that the Standing Committee is, in essence, the Politburo of Shanghai and that Chu is a leading member of this inner circle, one of the most important members of the Shanghai group. Then you begin to understand that he spoke with such quiet authority because as a member of the Shanghai group he is one of the most powerful (if little known) men in China.

Dinner begins early in China. Dinner with Chu began at 6:30. It was after midnight, a good bit after midnight, before we left, and all that time Chu had been talking to me about the Cultural Revolution. He could, he said, have talked until morning. It was a long, complex story, but by the time he finished I understood a good deal of what the Cultural Revolution had been about and I thought I knew where it was going.

Chu began by talking about the nature of Chinese society under the Revolution. In simplest terms, he said, there were two possibilities after 1949. One was to consolidate the Revolution under the dictatorship of the proletariat and state ownership of the means of production. The other was to start back on the road toward capitalism. The Cultural Revolution he pictured as a continuation of the struggle between these two lines—in a sense, an inevitable result of that struggle, a struggle to continue the Revolution and to prevent a turning back toward "bourgeois restoration," such as he believed had occurred in the Soviet Union.

In more specific terms, I found, the Hong Kong analysts in 1966 had been, in a sense, right. The Cultural Revolution *was* a struggle for power, a struggle between Mao Tse-tung and the chief of state, Liu Shao-chi, but not simply a struggle based on personalities. It was a struggle over policy, and it had been going on for a long time before the Cultural Revolution occurred.

Chu took a deep breath and began to trace for me the tortured history of the dispute between the two men. Sometimes, he said, Liu Shao-chi adopted right-wing tactics to oppose Mao, sometimes ultra-leftist positions. But regardless of the policy that Liu proclaimed at any given moment, he was actually seeking to move the country toward a less revolutionary position and away from the line consistently advocated by Mao Tse-tung.

The dispute between the two men could be traced back at least to 1958 and the Great Leap Forward and, more specifically, to 1959 and the following years, when China was encountering very critical difficulties. These were the years when China suffered several great catastrophes—drought, floods, crop failure, very serious breakdowns in agriculture and also in industry. These, too, were the years when the Soviet Union reneged on its obligations—pulled out all its experts and refused to fulfill contracts for delivery of machinery and essential parts. In these times, Liu Shao-chi, swinging hard to the right, wanted to reverse policy in agriculture and go back to reliance on private farming. In the international sphere, he favored reconciliation with the Soviet Union. Under the sway of Liu Shao-chi's policies, Chu said, the enemies of the revolutionary regime—the former Capitalists, the rich peasants, the former landlords—began to see hope for better days.

In the beginning, the dispute was contained within the organs of the party. But Liu Shao-chi was in Peking. He was running the government and giving the orders. Mao argued with him but to no avail. The quarrel became sharper in 1962, particularly at the tenth plenary meeting of the Eighth Party Congress.

Why did Liu Shao-chi act like this? Chu answered his own question: It had something to do with his personal history. Liu, like Mao, was a product of Hunan. But three times, it was known now, Liu had betrayed the party. Once back in the Hunan days, again later in the critical times in Wuhan in 1927, and, finally, when he was fighting against Chiang Kai-shek in the Northeast.

I could not help interrupting: How could this be? Here is a man who was associated all his life with the Communist movement. He had been close to Mao Tse-tung since the earliest days. He had risen through the ranks to the supreme position in the People's Republic. He was chief of state. How could such a man be a betrayer of the party, and how could such betrayals only now come to light?

Chu smiled. That was, he said, a perfectly reasonable question. The treachery of Liu Shao-chi had not been known. It had not even been suspected. It was only during the Cultural Revolution that it all came out. Until that time it had been supposed that the quarrel between Mao and Liu was simply one of politics, policy and, perhaps, principles. But now Liu's old inner history had been uncovered and, against the background of that conduct, it was easy to understand why Liu had adopted a regressive position.

During the early days of the Japanese war, Chu said, Liu Shao-chi now was known to have issued orders to 60 Communist Party members to confess that they belonged to the party. He gave them permission to sign declarations saying that they renounced the party and would support Chiang Kai-shek. That had happened when Liu Shao-chi was in Nationalist territory. It had never been known until Red Guard detachments dug into the old files in the libraries and turned up the evidence.

But, wait a minute, I interjected. This doesn't seem reasonable to me. Certainly the party has its security controls. Certainly all this would have come to light long ago. How can it be that the discovery is made only now, 30 years after the event?

Chu was not shaken. He was absolutely confident of his facts. Liu had used a false name—Hu Fo. Liu and all of the 60 men who had gone over to Chiang Kai-shek had had a common motivation for saving their necks. They had protected each other and, as Liu rose in the party and government, he advanced his own men, members of this group of 60.

Even if someone had come forward with this evidence, Chu said, even if an ordinary person had suspected Liu Shao-chi, he would not have dared raise such a question. If he had it would have gotten nowhere. These people were in high office. They protected each other.

Thus, Chu went on, the Cultural Revolution was, in reality, not unlike the struggle between the Communists and Chiang Kai-shek's Kuomintang. The difference was that in the battle against Chiang you knew at once who was a member of the Kuomintang. The enemy wore uniforms and insignia. But in this battle there were no insignia. It was a battle within the party. You could not readily distinguish whether a person was a good person or a bad person. The task was to weed out the bad person.

"It is not easy to fight such a war," he said seriously. "How do you carry out such a war? Mainly by mobilizing the masses against what we call the 'black liners.' Our task was to seize back into our hands those positions of power that had been usurped by them. This is a very difficult struggle."

I said nothing but I felt most skeptical. The belated revelations of treachery gave me a sense of *déjà vu*. So often, in Communist Party struggles, I had heard the same kind of charge. There leapt to my mind Stalin's ridiculous (but deadly serious) allegations against Voroshilov and Molotov—that they had long been agents of British intelligence—charges that would have cost both their lives had not Stalin fortuitously died before he could stage a trial. I remembered the charge by Trotsky that Stalin had once been an informer for the

Czarist *okhrana* (a charge which, psychologically at least, seemed to have little sounder base) and I remembered those other nightmarish fantasies—Stalin's claim that the Kremlin doctors had conspired with British and American intelligence and Zionist organizations to take the lives of high Soviet military and political figures, and then, that ironic touch of the post-Stalin epic, the indictment brought by his colleagues against Lavrenti P. Beria, Stalin's police administrator, that Beria had, in fact, been an agent of British intelligence since his early manhood.

But if I was skeptical of the treason charge, at least I was beginning to see more clearly the nature of the personalities and politics that underlay the Cultural Revolution.

This, then, said Chu, was the background of the Revolution. But the movement did not actually get started until November, 1965, and then it began in a most curious way.

A man called Wu Han, the Vice-Mayor of Peking, had written a play. It was about a famous minister in the Ching Dynasty, an honest public servant, who was dismissed from office by a tyrannical emperor. The play was called *Hai Jui Dismissed from Office*. Not exactly the material out of which a government crisis was likely to be created. But China is different. The play was no mere exercise in historiography. In 1959, Defense Minister Peng Teh-huai had been dismissed from office at the insistence of Chairman Mao. Thus, by historical analogy, the Ching Dynasty play was in reality an attack on Chairman Mao, a comparison of the arbitrary dismissal of Hai Jui by a capricious emperor with the Chairman's action. It was not exactly a subtle slap.

I could not help asking how such an attack on Mao could have been permitted.

"The answer is simple," said Chu. "Wu Han was a henchman of Peng Chen, the First Secretary of the Peking Party Committee, the Mayor of Peking and one of the most important of Liu's 60 traitors."

The Party Committee in Peking was controlled by Peng Chen. No orders of Chairman Mao were accepted in Peking. When Mao read the play he tried to get someone in Peking to take up the cudgels in his behalf. No one was willing to do so.

"That's why Chairman Mao had to come to Shanghai," said Chu. The fact was that Mao had been spending more and more time in Shanghai as his influence waned in Peking and in the central party and government apparatus. His wife, Chiang Ching, had roots in

Shanghai. It was her home base; she was very active there in cultural circles. When Mao found that he could get no one in the national capital to write in his behalf, he turned to Shanghai and to Yao Wen-yuan, a very well known journalist who had written for many years for the Shanghai *Liberation Daily*, the *Jie Fang*, and for the leading cultural paper of Shanghai, *Wen Wei Pao*. Yao was an ideological critic who was not at that time associated with any newspaper or government office and who had written before in support of Mao's cause.

Yao wrote an attack on *Hai Jui Dismissed from Office*, and it was published on November 10, 1965, in *Wen Wei Pao*.

"Chairman Mao thought, of course, that the Peking papers would republish the article," said Chu. "But to his surprise they ignored it."

Mao then persuaded the Shanghai *Liberation Daily* to publish the article. Still Peking paid no attention, and Mao decided to print the article as a small pamphlet in order to give it national distribution. Advertisements for the pamphlet appeared in the Shanghai papers.

"We called Peking and asked: 'How many copies do you want?' " Chu said. "They said they didn't want any."

However, by this time, Premier Chou En-lai had become aware of what was going on (whether through another telephone call from Shanghai or by other means Chu did not make clear). Chou intervened, and the article was finally published in the *Liberation Army Daily* in Peking on November 29, 1965, and then in the *People's Daily* on November 30.

What Chairman Mao had hoped to stimulate, of course, was discussion of the political aspects of the article. However, through the influence of Mayor Peng Chen of Peking, the *People's Daily* instructed readers to limit their criticism to the play's literary qualities and not to discuss its politics.

The discussion initiated by Peng Chen would deal with such questions as: Are there any good officials in China's past? What can we learn from the conduct of these officials? How should we evaluate historical personages?

"But our aim," said Chu, "was to get a political discussion going. We wanted to discuss such questions as: What is the political aim of the play?"

Mayor Peng Chen, Chu admitted, was a powerful opponent. He was a secretary of the Central Committee. He was in Peking. He commanded a very strong position, and he was not going to be moved easily. Determined to keep the political discussion in his own hands, he issued an outline for its conduct and, in effect, tried to set the guidelines for the Cultural Revolution. His slogans were: "Do away with scholastic tyrants!" and "Everybody is equal before the truth!" These theses were circulated all over the country. But Chairman Mao was not going to let go. He summoned a special meeting of the Central Committee on May 16 to expose Mayor Peng, and at his direction a circular of the Central Committee was sent out, criticizing Mayor Peng's guidelines and warning the party that they must always be on the alert against "Khrushchev-like people who are nestling beside us."

"The Cultural Revolution officially began on May 16, 1966," Chu said. "Very soon Mayor Peng Chen was exposed. Big Character posters (wall posters hand-lettered in very large ink-drawn Chinese ideographs called *ta tze pao*) went up at Peking University and other universities exposing the Peking Party Committee which Peng headed. The Party Committee was reorganized and Peng Chen was dismissed. The students and the masses wanted to make an investigation and study of the Peking Committee."

Now, said Chu, Liu Shao-chi moved into action. This was when he sent "work teams" into the universities to suppress the mass movements. The team that went into Peking University (like the one that went to Tsinghua) labeled the revolutionary students counter-revolutionary. They sought to suppress the Big Character posters the students had put up all over the campus.

Chairman Mao intervened again. The Peking students had written a Big Character poster attacking Lu Ting, Rector of Peking University. It had been suppressed by the Liu Shao-chi work team. Mao interceded and at his direction it was published on June 1, 1966, in the *People's Daily* and its text was broadcast throughout the country.

The pace of the Cultural Revolution began to move faster. On August 5, the 11th plenary session of the Eighth Party Congress was summoned in Peking and there Chairman Mao wrote his own Big Character poster, which he called "Bombard the Headquarters." It did not mention Liu Shao-chi by name but it was apparent that it was he whom Mao regarded as the main enemy.*

* Mao's text read: " 'Bombard the Headquarters—My Big Character Poster.' China's first Marxist-Leninist Big Character poster (the Peking University poster of June 1) and commentator's article on it in the *People's Daily* are indeed superbly written! Comrades, please read them again. But in the last 50 days or so some leading comrades from the central down to the local levels have acted in a diametrically opposite way. Adopting the reactionary stand of

Then, on August 18, Chairman Mao appeared on Tien-an Men Square himself. He, too, wore a red armband. It carried the single Chinese character *ping*, which means "soldier." He received the Red Guards and wished them well. From that moment forward, the Red Guards swarmed over the country. Six times Chairman Mao received them in Tien-an Men Square, and before it was over more than 13 million had come to Peking. Never in the history of China (or perhaps any country) had so many youngsters taken to the road. The only youth movement that compared with it was the Children's Crusades of the Middle Ages. It seemed, sometimes, that everyone in China under the age of 20 and over the age of eight was on the road.

Yet, despite all this activity, Chu said, many people did not know what was going on.

"The ordinary party members," he said, "didn't know what had happened at the 11th plenary session. It wasn't reported in the newspapers. We in Shanghai didn't know anything about Chairman Mao's Big Character poster. And the reason for this was that the Shanghai party leaders were afraid of the masses and afraid of exposure by Big Character posters. They were hostile to Chairman Mao's movement. If it had not been for the Red Guards, the country would never have known what was happening."

One morning, Chu recalled, as he was going to work, he saw plastered up on the wall Chairman Mao's Big Character poster proclaiming: "Bombard the Headquarters."

---

the bourgeoisie, they have enforced a bourgeois dictatorship and struck down the surging movement of the great Cultural Revolution of the proletariat. They have stood facts on their head and juggled black and white, encircled and suppressed revolutionaries, stifled opinions differing from their own, imposed a white terror, and felt very pleased with themselves. They have puffed up the arrogance of the bourgeoisie and deflated the morale of the proletariat. How poisonous! Viewed in connection with the right deviation in 1962 and the wrong tendency of 1964 which was 'left' in form but 'right' in essence, shouldn't this make one wide awake?" (*Peking Review* No. 33, August 11, 1967). It is characteristic of the difficulties encountered in western reporting on the Cultural Revolution that no mention of Chairman Mao's Big Character poster appeared in *The New York Times* during 1967; there was no mention of Mao's order that the Peking University Big Character poster of June 1 be published; nor was the text of this poster published; nor was there any mention of Chairman Mao's approving letter to the Tsinghua Red Guards. The first mention of *Hai Jui Dismissed from Office* and Wu Han came in a dispatch from Hong Kong by Seymour Topping on May 6, 1966. On August 12 the Central Committee approved a 16-point decision on the Cultural Revolution, spelling out clearly the target of the Revolution: "Those in power who take the Capitalist road."

"I rushed straight to the old Shanghai Party Committee headquarters," he said, "and asked: 'Have you heard anything about this poster by Chairman Mao?' No, they said, they hadn't heard anything about it. They were so afraid of Liu Shao-chi they didn't even want to mention the Chairman's poster. But with the Red Guards coming forward everywhere, it broke down the old atmosphere."

Chu said that only a small percentage of party members were bad and traitorous people who didn't want the Cultural Revolution to succeed. But this bad percentage was not unimportant—it included, in Shanghai, Mayor Tsao Ti-chin and Party Secretary Chen Pei-hsien. They were very much afraid of the people becoming aroused and were also afraid of the Red Guards, Chu said. So they organized their own Red Guards to protect themselves from the Red Guards who came to Shanghai from other cities. And now things became very complicated—so complicated that many people in Shanghai were confused as to what was going on.

The Mayor and Party Secretary did not stop with organizing their own Red Guards. They did another thing. They incited the workers to come out against the students by telling them that the students had gone into the streets to oppose the Communist Party. "Go out and give those students a good lesson," they told the workers, according to Chu. The students fought back. They went to the factories and told the workers about the Cultural Revolution and Chairman Mao's views. But they got little attention. Not until late in the fall did some factory workers begin to join the Cultural Revolution in Shanghai. Finally on November 9, 1966, the workers of about a dozen factories formed their own headquarters which they called the "Workers' Revolutionary Rebel Headquarters." They held a big rally at Shanghai's Cultural Square and demanded that Mayor Tsao come out and answer their criticism. When Tsao refused, they marched to the railroad station and seized a train, determined to go to Peking and present their case to Chairman Mao. Since many of them were railroad workers, they had no trouble getting a train and starting off. But they had gone no farther than Anting station when Party Secretary Chen had them halted. That made the workers even angrier. They said that if they couldn't get to Peking, no one else would, and they stopped all train traffic between Shanghai and Peking.

"That was the famous Anting incident," Chu said.

Concerned by the situation in Shanghai, Chairman Mao sent Chang Chun-chiao, now Chairman of the Shanghai Revolutionary

Committee and a member of the Politburo in Peking, to Shanghai. Chang had been one of Mao's closest allies from the beginning of the Cultural Revolution and, despite being a Shanghai Party Secretary, had actually been spending all of his time in Peking.

Chang had been the person to whom Mao first turned when he found himself unable to mount an attack on *Hai Jui Dismissed from Office*. While Chang was still in Peking, Mayor Tsao and Party Secretary Chen stormed at him: "You've never had a taste of what a mass movement is like. Now that you are coming here you will get a taste." They thought that Chang would come to Shanghai and suppress the movement. Instead Chang went to Anting to listen to the workers. He told them that they were right and proffered his support. "Return to Shanghai, and organize, and solve the problems there," he said. They came back and gathered again in Shanghai's Cultural Square. Chang appeared before them and said: "We recognize you officially as the Revolutionary Rebels. You can go ahead and carry out your revolutionary activities."

Enraged at Chang, Mayor Tsao and Secretary Chen sent inquiries to the Central Committee asking what powers had been given to Chang. Contending he had betrayed party principles, they persuaded hecklers to surround him night and day, questioning him without cease, so that he could neither work nor sleep. Finally he went back to Peking.

Hardly had Chang departed when the Mayor and Party Secretary organized their own revolutionary group, the Red Defense Detachment, making the *Liberation Daily* their organ. The Workers' Revolutionary Rebel Headquarters then set up their own newspaper, the *Red Guard Combat Bulletin*, but the Mayor and Secretary suppressed it. Whereupon the Revolutionary Rebels occupied the *Liberation Daily* plant, declaring: "If you don't let us publish our paper we won't let you publish your paper."

Mayor Tsao organized several hundred thousand people to demand that the *Liberation Daily* be published. He expanded the Red Defense Detachment to 800,000 members, far outnumbering the tens of thousands who supported the Revolutionary Rebels. The *Liberation Daily* was surrounded, hundreds of thousands of people outside, thousands inside.

"That," said Chu, "was the so-called '*Liberation Daily* incident.' "

News of the huge demonstration reached Peking, the Party Central Committee and Premier Chou En-lai. Once again the Premier intervened, criticizing Tsao and Chen and ordering that for every copy of the *Liberation Daily* that was circulated, there must be circulated a copy of the *Revolutionary Bulletin.*

"So Tsao and Chen were defeated and didn't have much prestige," Chu commented. But they fought on. They ordered the Red Defense Detachment suppressed and, as a result, the Red Defense Detachment attacked the Mayor, sending several thousand members to the Kang Ping Road headquarters of the old party committee, and demanded that they be recognized as a revolutionary organization. Realizing that Mayor Tsao and Secretary Chen had reached the end of the road, the Revolutionary Rebels sent several thousand workers to seize party headquarters. This so angered the Red Defense Detachment that they determined to go to Peking and protest. They started off, some by train and some by truck. The Revolutionary Rebels, however, headed them off at Kunshan station, compelling them, after some argument, to return to Shanghai.

"That," said Chu, "was the third incident—the 'Kang Ping Road incident.' " It occurred on December 27–28, 1966. By this time, Shanghai was paralyzed. Many workers had simply left their jobs. The port was affected. So were the factories. Railroads and docks suffered most. Ships lay unattended in the harbor. Train service had virtually halted. Some workers, on December 27 and 28, wanted to cut off all electric power in Shanghai. Others threatened to stop the water supply. Industry ground to a halt. Foreign ships were not being unloaded. The Red Defense Detachment, Chu said, wanted to bring everything to a stop in order to show the Central Committee that the Cultural Revolution could not be carried any further.

At this point, the Revolutionary Rebel Headquarters drafted an open letter to the workers, calling for a halt to disorders and resumption of work in the city lest anarchy result in the defeat of the Cultural Revolution. Every revolutionary worker was asked to remain at his post. By dint of this appeal, the city was saved from complete collapse.

Actually, Chu said, a factual revolution had occurred in Shanghai. Power had flowed into the hands of the Revolutionary Rebel Headquarters and no one was paying heed either to the Mayor and the Party Secretary or to the Red Defense Detachment.

"This is what we call the 'Seizure of Power,' " Chu explained. It was formalized when Mao sent Chang into Shanghai on January 4 to help the Rebel Revolutionaries take over. First, they formally adopted the newspaper *Wen Wei Pao* as their official organ on the evening of January 4. Then, on January 9, the unified Rebel organization issued a call to the people of Shanghai to resume work and defeat the "reactionary economists," as they called those who were trying to bring about a total work stoppage. On January 11, the seizure of power was ratified by a cable of congratulations from Peking, signed by all the party and government organs, and on January 12 a rally of a million people in Shanghai celebrated the revolutionary success.

"The Rebel Revolutionaries," Chu said, "then had a discussion about forming their own power organs and what to call them. There were a number of suggestions, but it was decided to call it the 'Shanghai People's Commune.' " After the formal inauguration of the Shanghai People's Commune on February 5, 1967, Chairman Mao asked Chang and Yao Wen-yuan (author of the original *Hai Jui* criticism) to come to Peking. He expressed himself as very pleased with events in Shanghai, except for one thing. The name "Shanghai People's Commune" worried him. If that name was used, what, he asked, will we call our country? It will make things very complicated. It might affect diplomatic relations. If Shanghai insisted on using the name People's Commune—all right, it could go ahead. But, perhaps, it would be better to call the new organ the Revolutionary Committee. So Chang and Yao went back to Shanghai and the comrades there agreed to accept Chairman Mao's suggestion.

"All these events," said Chu, "are what we call the 'January Storm.' "

We had now been talking for hours. I was tired but fascinated. Chu seemed as fresh as when he started. But Yao Wei, our interpreter, and the other members of the group were weary.

"Let's go on a bit longer," I said. "This is the first time I have ever understood how all these events fitted together."

Chu agreed. "I can talk all night if you can."

Chu turned back to the outcome of the struggle in Shanghai. Why had Mayor Tsao and Party Secretary Chen fared so badly? The fact was they had both done bad things in the past. When Tsao was very young, he had had relations with the enemy. He had been captured when leading a scouting expedition and had worked for the enemy for a while. He was afraid the masses would find out. Chen had a bad record too. He had close relations with Liu Shao-chi during the New Fourth Army period, and in early 1934 had betrayed the party, telling all he knew about it to the enemy. So it was not surprising that these two men took the wrong line. But the more they tried to repress the people, the more the people stood up against them.

And that, said Chu, is why Chairman Mao intended that the Cultural Revolution be a revolution from the bottom up—because the masses in due course would expose every element in power. Those bad elements, he repeated, were nothing more nor less than the Kuomintang (Chiang's Nationalists) without labeling themselves Kuomintang.

I did not challenge this assertion about Tsao and Chen, but in my mind I put it alongside his claim of prior treachery on the part of Liu Shao-chi. What is it, I wondered, that compels Communists always to label their enemy a total enemy, totally black, evil from the very beginning? There could be no grays, no shades of evil. Only total evil —the doctrine of original sin dialecticized.

"So far," I said, "no one seems to have been killed in Shanghai."

"That's right," Chu agreed. "No one had been killed up to now."

"And," I added, "unlike those in other cities, the students there don't seem to have played a very important role."

"True," he agreed, "up to now, the students had not played a very important role. They played an instigating role, but the workers took the main part. All the Revolutionary Committee members were workers. Wang Hung-wen, Vice-Chairman of the Revolutionary Council of Shanghai, was the commander-in-chief of the Rebel Headquarters. He was a worker of the 17th Textile Mill, and there were some other good people from the past. For instance, Ma Tien-shui, Vice-Mayor before the Cultural Revolution, is Vice Chairman of the Revolutionary Committee now."

After the January Storm, Chu continued, there were many twists and turns. Every organization formed its own Revolutionary Committee. Often there were two factions in the factories and this produced incidents and conflicts. In August, 1967, the situation grew tense, particularly in the eastern district of Shanghai around the Shanghai Diesel Engineering Factory, a very big plant with 7,500 workers. There were two factions here—the "East is Red" faction, and the United Headquarters faction. There were some bad elements in the United Headquarters faction. They had links to other conservative and reactionary groups in the city. They suppressed the "East is Red" group and ran things with an iron hand. Any worker who disagreed was beaten or tortured. A worker named Hsieh Sun-hsi of the East is Red faction was killed by the United Headquarters and all members of the East is Red faction were driven from the factory. Then the United Headquarters group went on a rampage. They overturned cars and burned them and blocked streets. They equipped themselves with homemade weapons and attacked other factories. Production was disrupted.

The Revolutionary Committee decided the situation must be brought under control. It organized a mass demonstration at the Diesel Factory and more than 100,000 workers turned out on August 4, 1967, demanding that the East is Red group be permitted to go back to work. They sought to reason with the United Headquarters faction, but the UH attacked them with homemade grenades and bottles of sulphuric acid. The Revolutionary Committee men then fought their way into the factory and occupied it, shop by shop. A number of persons were wounded but only one was killed. The ringleaders of the United Headquarters were captured.

That was the biggest battle in Shanghai. From then on, the Revolutionary Committee gradually took over the city, weeding out "bad elements" and "purifying class ranks." Persons who were willing to accept the new order were permitted to go on working. But bad elements were arrested.

"How many 'bad elements' were there?" I asked. "A few thousand?"

"More than that," Chu said.

"Ten thousand?"

"No, not 10,000, but more than a few thousand. We arrested only those who were engaged in counter-revolutionary activities—those who were poisoning or killing people. The others weren't arrested. So long as they confessed their former crimes in the old society they were given work like anyone else."

Chu insisted that the great majority of party members behaved well. He put the number of "bad elements" at one or two percent. Three or four leaders of the United Headquarters, he said, were still in jail.

Well, I said, what happened once the Revolutionary Committee was in power—what changed?

There was, he said, mass revolutionary criticism of Liu Shao-chi and his methods in every field. Thus, people got to know the right line and the erroneous line. And the masses were mobilized to reform outmoded and irrational regulations that restricted and repressed their work. This led to liberation of production forces and an increase in output. Administration was simplified at all levels, red tape was cut and party workers went into the workshops to work with their hands. This brought about better feeling as well as better production. And, of course, all the cadres and government people went to May Seventh schools for a year or two and came back mentally and physically stimulated.

There was one more thing I wanted to know. What about ultra-leftists? Liu Shao-chi had been a rightist. He and his followers were defeated. Had there not been ultra-leftists, too?

Chu looked at me as though he was dealing with a rather tiresome child. To be sure there were ultra-leftists. Especially after the January Storm they had appeared. For instance, there was one Red Guard organization in Shanghai that played a positive role in the early days but then went wrong. It was one of the 38 organizations that participated in the January seizure of power but then these Red Guards developed their own ideas. They organized peasants, workers, soldiers and students to go to the different organizations and take away their seals, their symbols of office and power, by force. They wound up with a whole bagful of seals. This same group—very isolated, but centered at Fu Dan University—was strongly opposed to Chang. It was they who kidnapped Hsu Ching-hsien, the Vice-Chairman of the Revolutionary Committee, and held him for a week. Their idea was to force him to tell some things that would discredit Chang. But troops went in and freed Hsu.

"They stirred up a lot of trouble," Chu said. "People came out and demonstrated against the Revolutionary Committee. Actually this was sabotage of the Revolution."

Well, I said, that was ultra-leftism on a lower plane. What about on a higher plane?

Chu gave me an odd glance. But, of course, there was ultra-leftism higher up. Some people questioned everything that was done. Some people on a higher level were backing these lower-echelon ultra-left organizations. There were bad people higher up, too—members of the Central Cultural Revolution Group in Peking, persons like Wang Li, Kuan Feng and Chi Pen-yu.

"And," said Chu with a significant look, "why were these people there? Why were they in the Central Revolutionary Group? They had to have support from the top. Those people exposed themselves later on."

We went on talking a little while longer. He spoke of some of the tendencies of ultra-leftism—not to treat the enemy in accordance with the policy of the party (that is, with respect) and not to treat cadres that way. Sometimes, there was nothing in the record of the ultra-leftists, and it took a long time to understand what they were about. Some of them did not treat intellectuals in accordance with the policy of the party. And, sometimes, they doubted and suspected people unduly; all of these, he said, were ultra-leftist tendencies.

After all, he said, the class struggle was bound to be reflected in the party. The representatives of the bourgeoisie adopted either a rightist or an ultra-leftist position. That was true of Liu Shao-chi and his like. . . .

We left it there. I thanked him—for the dinner and for the meticulous account of the Cultural Revolution, as seen from Shanghai, as seen from the inside, as seen by one of those who made it. Then we descended in the purring elevator and went out to the gleaming, long, Shanghai-model car, just off the assembly line, that awaited us. It was the only car in sight, and the great clock in the old Shanghai Customs House was just striking one. We drove back to another luxury hotel, the Palace, not quite as chic as the Park but almost so. Shanghai streets at 1 A.M. were not as deserted as those of Peking. Here and there, people were still strolling; here and there a bicycle moved; here and there a couple sat on a bench or doorstep, quietly talking. There were more lights and I could clearly see the great buildings on the Bund, their magnificent façades a little dreary and run down.

Physically, it was much the same city it had been at the heyday of pre-revolutionary China, but it was like an empty monument to that past—gone were the prostitutes, the seven-year-old pimps and the six-year-old "little sisters"; gone were the coolies, dying on the street of starvation or cholera; gone were the Sissoons, the Hardoons, the Kadories (their palace now a children's museum); gone the josshouses, the gamblers, the thieves; gone the filth and the millionaires, the White Russian whores and the Sikh police; gone the signs in the parks—"Dogs and Chinese not allowed"; gone the British, gone the Americans, gone the Japanese, gone the Germans. Tonight we drove through a Chinese metropolis—no glitter, no glamor, no slums, no horror. This was New China inhabiting the house of the old.

I thought as we drove up to the Palace Hotel and a sleepy young woman in blouse and trousers fumblingly unlocked the gate and let us in, that I now understood a great deal about the Cultural Revolution—perhaps more than Chu Yung-chia intended me to, although I might be mistaken in that. I might still have some points out of perspective, but one thing I knew positively from his last words: I knew the name he had not spoken, I knew the name of the "ultra-leftist" who, in his position "from the top," had given support to the other ultra-leftists. There was only one man this could be: Defense Minister Lin Piao. It was many months since Lin Piao's mysterious disappearance in autumn, 1971. Not one word had yet been said publicly within China about him. But there could be no doubt from the description. I matched this conversation with others and concluded that the time was fast approaching when Lin Piao would be named publicly and his crimes placed on record (as, indeed, they were only three weeks later). He was, it appeared from the official story, the arch-traitor on the left, the symmetrical twin of Liu Shao-chi on the right, and with this, the Cultural Revolution might be said to have reached its artistic completion.

But what of its effects? Had it changed man? Had it created a new China? Armed with Chu's chart of these extraordinary events, I thought that I could begin to rough out some general answers.

5

The More *Luan* The Better

There is an old Chinese proverb that says: "Those who labor with their minds are the rulers; those who labor with their hands are the ruled."

Long before I left China, this saying had been engraved in my mind, because it was reported so often as conveying one of the absolutes—possibly the most important absolute—of what the Cultural Revolution was about. The Revolution was designed not to eliminate the distinction between physical and mental work, one of the familiar *leitmotifs* of Marxism. That was manifestly impossible in the present state of Chinese industrial and technological development. Instead, it was intended to change profoundly the psychology of the Chinese people, here and now, so that whether they labored with their minds or their hands, they would feel neither superiority nor inferiority.

This concept was considerably more difficult to grasp than some of the basic goals of the Cultural Revolution as outlined to me by Chu Yung-chia in Shanghai. It was obvious from what he said that Chairman Mao had been deeply dissatisfied with the political direction of his country. He felt that it was veering far from the revolutionary simplicity of Yenan; that it had begun to cater to the deeply ingrained bourgeois, acquisitive instincts of the Chinese; and that, internationally, it was seeking to make peace with the hated Russians. In terms of his own person, his influence had been overriden by men who sought to relegate him to the sidelines. The Cultural Revolution put him back on top. It defeated, once and forever, Liu Shao-chi and his supporters. Now they had all been blackened as renegades and traitors. They were finished. Nor had the Revolution halted there. It had gone on and destroyed its Robespierre, Defense Minister Lin Piao, once marked as Mao's successor. Now Lin Piao and his group of generals and party chiefs were gone. Only the Chairman remained—the Chairman and Premier Chou En-lai, upon whom so much depended.

But this was politics and personalities, not philosophy and metaphysics. Was it true, as so many believed, that the Cultural Revolution had changed China's soul? Had it created a New Chinese Man and Woman? Was this the reason why China, in James Reston's phrase, had become a "sink of morality"? Or, as John King Fairbank said, the reason why the Chinese man now stood on his own feet?

In 1919 Lincoln Steffens had gone to the new-born Soviet Union and, returning, proclaimed to Bernard Baruch: "I have been over into the Future—and it works." Could it possibly be that China was the Future of our generation?

This was a question that stood in my mind before I arrived in China, but I could hope to answer it only by talking to individual men and women. It called for subjective judgments. If a man felt he was new-born, then, I supposed, at least in a sense, he was new-born. And so, wherever I went in China, I asked those whom I met what had happened to them in the Cultural Revolution. How had it changed their lives? What difference had it made in their world? I must admit that I embarked on this inquiry with great temerity. I could talk to only a few score or a few hundred of China's hundreds of millions and I had certain doubts. To be sure, Steffens and many others had gone to Russia, and in the enthusiasm of the '20's, had thought that a new man, Soviet man, a man of ingrained morality, free of the defects and distortions inspired by greed and hatred, hypocrisy and oppression, was being created. And even I was prepared to believe that in those days newer and better human beings were being forged in Russia. But, alas, what had happened to those brave hopes 40 or 50 years later? Where, today, in materialist, careerist, alienated Russia did one find those splendid new men and women? I did not like to be cynical and I hoped that I might find the New Man and the New Woman in China, but I set out on my quest determined to keep my feet firmly planted on the ground.

It proved to be a task both fascinating and frustrating. Not all the answers I got were satisfactory. That is, I did not always feel that I was being told the truth. And, sometimes, I felt that those with whom I was speaking were not certain what they felt. And sometimes, I thought, they were somewhat too certain.

The answer that impressed me most was one that emerged from a talk with a Chinese in his late 30's, a remarkably intelligent man in the lower bureaucracy, a man who was well educated and who had seen a great deal of the Cultural Revolution.

"First of all," he said, "you can't imagine how exciting it all was. Every morning, you came to your office. You could hardly wait to get there to see what was new, to see what the new posters said."

He used to ride his bicycle to work through the Peking streets, and all the way, he would look at the walls to see the posters put up during the night by the Red Guards. Then, at his office, he would hurry through the halls. There would be new posters about individuals in his organization. They were put up by workers in the office, some belonging to one faction, some to another. And there would be posters about other political leaders in Peking, and the leaders of the national government and the party itself. The posters would argue with each other, back and forth, often quoting from secret documents and files. Walking up and down the corridors and halls would be the workers, also arguing and talking. There were meetings from early morning until late at night. Sometimes all night long. The head of the office was denounced. (All persons holding responsible positions all over China were denounced.) Then the persons who denounced the chief were themselves criticized. There were angry quarrels. Sides shifted.

"You never knew when you yourself might be attacked," he said. "Often you and your comrades would make up a Big Character poster attacking someone in the morning, and in the afternoon another poster would denounce that of the morning. It was a continuous fever. Everyone was swept up in it. There were meetings in the Tien-an Men. Something was happening all the time."

His young son became a Red Guard and traveled around the country with the hundreds of thousands of other Red Guards. "He would be gone for weeks or even months," he said. "There was no stopping him. All the youngsters went."

Only those who lived through this experience could really understand the emotional exaltation, the engagement, the deep searchings of conscience that went on. The most violent disagreements sprang up. This man worked for an organization that had contacts with foreign countries. Some extreme radicals demanded that all contacts with foreigners be halted, except those with foreign revolutionaries friendly to the Chinese Revolution. This would have put the organization out of existence but, as a matter of fact, it was not functioning anyway, because no one had time for work—everyone was too busy agitating.

This went on for a year or more, reaching an early peak in summer, 1966, and continuing with lessening momentum through most of 1967 and into 1968. By this time, most of the old leadership had been driven out. Revolutionary Committees in which the army played a major role began to be set up and people were starting to go to the newly formed May Seventh schools—schools established on the basis of a directive of Chairman Mao of May 7, 1966. These had, as their basic task, to teach others to learn from the people. Officials, party members, bureaucrats, members of the party apparatus were sent to live, to work with their hands, to "cleanse their thought," to get back to Marxist and Maoist fundamentals. Everyone went. My friend went. So did most of his organization. They stayed for about two years in the countryside, living under rugged conditions. (Rural life in China can best be compared to rural life in the United States in about 1820.) They built their own huts with crude brick or baked mud walls. They broke ground, planted crops, irrigated the land. They worked to exhaustion and suffered freezing cold in winter and the blazing-oven heat of China's summer.

"It was a wonderful experience," the official said. "It was the great experience of my life."

And that was true. I knew it had to be true from the emotion in his voice, from the reverence with which he spoke. He had always been a city dweller, he said. He had lived comfortably, rather bookishly. For the first time, he learned what it meant to have every muscle in his body aching, to rise at four in the morning and sink exhausted on his pallet at ten in the evening.

"Now I know what life in China means," he said. He felt that the experience had rid him of selfishness, of his natural tendency to put himself first, to think of his life in individual terms, to put his career and personal well-being first. Now he lived—and he said it quite simply—for others. He was not envious of his fellow workers. He was happy when he could help them and he understood how much he owed his country—a debt he would never be able to pay.

He told me all this without any sense of trying to convince me of something. He was simply putting into words the feelings that were in his heart.

I have talked to many foreigners who have been in China since the Cultural Revolution, and I know that my friend's emotional response is not unusual. Indeed, I met many variations of it in talks with other Chinese.

But there was another kind of response, too. Perhaps my talk with Professor Sung Chiang-ching, a professor of botany at Wuhan University, is a good example. Professor Sung, at 64, is something of an extrovert. He enjoys talking and he doesn't mind admitting that he has been—and still is—attached to the theories of Professor Trofim Lysenko, the notorious Stalinist agronomist who caused such havoc in Soviet genetic science. In fact, he and his department were once a citadel of Lysenkoism, and he still thinks there is a good deal in Lysenko's theories. But that was not the principal thrust of his conversation. He wanted me to know what the Cultural Revolution had done for him. He had not been attracted to the Cultural Revolution at all. It was disorderly and interfered with his routine, and, he thought, had nothing to do with him. He was criticized, but he didn't think the criticism was valid. He was not conscious of any divorce between himself and the basic life of the country. He felt he knew the countryside, because he was in the habit of spending a great deal of time there, collecting botanical samples with his students.

The professor, a gray man with a grayish-blue suit, gray hair and a rather prominent wen on his cheek, gave the impression that he had not yielded much ground in his discussions with the Red Guards.

But when he, with most of the other faculty, finally went to the countryside, he began to realize that he had been, indeed, divorced from life. He knew a lot about plant systems but nothing about peasant life and farming. The peasants began to bring him problems. They would say: "We have a botanist—let's ask him." But, alas, he didn't know the answers because what he had spent his life doing, actually, was hunting for new species of plants—not growing old ones.

"I'll give you an example," he said. "It was very educational for me. We were planting seed potatoes—sweet potatoes. Someone said: 'How do you plant them—with the eye perpendicular or leaning over?' I said: 'Any way you want—they will still grow.' But they said: 'Which is the best way?' I just didn't think it made any difference. But, later on, a poor peasant showed me how he planted potatoes standing up—and the production was much better. I could give you lots of examples like this in the remolding of the ideology of an intellectual."

He was, he said, born into the old society of China and brought up in feudalistic and bourgeois conditions, and, quite naturally, his thinking tended to be bourgeois. He had often been abroad, had studied in Edinburgh, and that had strengthened these tendencies. Yet he had always thought of himself as contributing to the construction of his motherland. But now he realized that his chief motivation was personal pride. He was always on the lookout for new plant species, hoping to write new scientific theses and enhance his personal reputation.

"But," he said, "in the countryside, I lived in close contact with the workers and the peasants and came to understand that they had very lofty ideals. They work very hard the year around. What for? To contribute to the building of the motherland."

He said, at his age, he was not able to do a lot of manual labor, but he had been able to learn very valuable lessons in patriotism from poor peasants. He had learned that nothing was more important than a selfless contribution to his country. No longer did he look down on those who worked in the fields.

"I'm more than 60 years old," he said. "But I consider that my remolding is only beginning. I am determined to continue my remolding, filled with revolutionary vigor."

How was I to evaluate Professor Sung's remarks? I couldn't look into his heart and see how much sincerity was there. My feeling was that the professor thought of himself as honest, but I did not take him to be a very profound man. His affection for the notorious Lysenko teachings did not testify to his intellectual vigor, and yet he did seem to have a certain humility, which probably had not been present before the Cultural Revolution. In talking with him I felt a bit as I once did when talking with a businessman who had gone through a Billy Graham revival. The businessman had emerged filled, as he said, with the spirit of the Lord. And I could not doubt that this was an accurate description. Both the Billy Graham convert and Professor Sung had gone through a powerful emotional experience. Its depth, however, was something I could not help questioning.

The problem of moral transformation was put into a broader context by Hsu Yu-lin, leader of the administration of Fu Dan University at Shanghai. In his view, before the Cultural Revolution not only were any relations between intellectuals, workers and peasants sorely lacking, but there was no such thing as democratic relations between students and teachers. Now, he said, the intellectuals were integrated with workers and peasants, and students and teachers were learning from each other and teaching each other.

In old China, he said, the scholar was at the top of the pyramid. Everyone bowed low before him. He was a pillar of the Empire, its chief support, and was taken as the model that everyone should imitate and emulate. Naturally, these intellectuals had little to do with the lowly workers. That was the root of the proverb about the difference between mental and manual labor. It was a tradition more than a thousand years old. Naturally, it had not been changed a great deal by the Revolution of 1949. The divisions in Chinese society persisted. The scholars and intellectuals held themselves aloof from those who worked with their hands. They did not understand peasants, and saw no reason for understanding them. There was no bond between them, and in this way Chinese society, even after the Revolution, remained dangerously fragmented. But now, as a result of the Cultural Revolution, that had been changed. People had actually been changed inside themselves.

Now, everyone had a common aim in life—to serve the people. All Chinese considered themselves ordinary laboring people, whether they worked in the paddies or in the physical-engineering laboratories of the university. The differences were only superficial, and the intellectual did not hold himself superior to the factory worker nor did the factory worker denigrate those who did not work with their hands because even that distinction had been partially eliminated. Not only had all the party workers and intellectuals spent two or three years digging in the fields, sharing the physical hardships of the country, but they now worked in plants, alongside the industrial workers. Everyone's hands were dirty. Manual work had actually been brought into the ivory tower—each university and school had its own factory, where teachers and students spent a part of their time, and every intellectual spent a month or more of every year in the countryside, in physical chores.

All of this, Hsu Yu-lin emphasized, had been achieved through the turbulent struggle of the Cultural Revolution and through its sequel, the May Seventh schools.

What was a May Seventh school? There were, I learned, several hundred of these institutions in China, including more than 40 in Peking alone. There had been a good deal of consolidation but, basically, there were local schools for the party workers of Changsha, for example, and those of other cities; and special schools for institutions like the Ministry of Foreign Affairs, the Ministry of Foreign Trade and all the principal departments of government. There were schools for the universities and for the cadres—the Central Committee, the Secretariat and municipal and provincial government workers and officials. They varied a good deal, I gathered, in the conditions of life and work and, particularly, as between the schools as they were originally set up and as they exist today. The difference was both physical and psychological.

The institutions stemmed from a general directive of Chairman Mao's, which said that the army should be the model in educating the country, and which called on everyone to engage in industrial, agricultural and military activities.

"Conditions permitting," the Chairman said, "workers in the commercial sector, employees of administrative services, party cadres and members of the state administration should do the same.

"Going back to manual work at the base is an excellent opportunity for leaders in the highest positions to relearn everything. Except for the old, the sick and the infirm, everyone should follow this road. Those who are designated to remain in leadership positions must also, when the time comes, go as a group to do manual work at the base."

During the anarchistic period of the Cultural Revolution, nothing was done toward fulfilling the Chairman's directive. That began only in 1968 when, by the decree of October 4, 1968, the establishment of the "schools" was ordered.

In theory, the students volunteered for training. But, as was now admitted, it did not work that way in the early days. There was a tendency to use the schools for punishment, to send to them the officials and workers who had proved "recalcitrant," or were thought to be, in "cleansing their thought." There was, in a word, a strongly punitive element in the schools; not as much as in the labor camps of Siberia, but the schools might easily have developed in that direction since, of course, the original rationale for the labor camps of Russia was not unlike that of the May Seventh schools—to "re-educate" individuals through wholesome "corrective labor." The aim in the early Soviet period was to purify the citizenry by subjecting them to the moral benefits of fresh air, healthy, hearty work with their hands, and substantial doses of Communist moral platitudes.

That was not far from the May Seventh rationale. The first "enrollees" were sent out in the fall of 1968 to make their way in a grim world. I visited the May Seventh school of the eastern district of Peking, for example, located about 50 kilometers out of Peking. It had been founded on November 7, 1968. Some 1,000 students—all drawn from the party and the administrative structure of the eastern district of Peking, were set down on a raw and wind-swept field, without houses, shelter, kitchens or workshops—beyond what they could build for themselves. They lived in tents (Peking is bitterly cold in winter, with the temperature often dropping to 20 below zero, and the wind whipping dust in from the Gobi) and a few were accommodated by peasants in a nearby village. Their first task was to put up huts to live in. None had ever built a house. These were city workers, used to warm offices, desks and fountain pens. It was not easy, and the houses (of which they are very proud today) are filled with irregularities—bricks laid unevenly, windows askew, roofs that don't jibe. But they were glad to have them. The housing was far from complete by the time spring came in 1969, and then they had to plow and make ready the 2,000-*mu* (a *mu* is about 1/6 of an acre) fields that were to provide them with food and sustenance—again not an easy task for city hands, most of which had never held a spade.

"You must understand that the people had never built houses or tilled fields before," said Li Chang-chun, Vice-Chairman of the Revolutionary Committee that runs the school. Li had been there from the beginning. He was a trade union leader with the Eastern Peking district before he was assigned to the school. The majority felt that their position had completely changed. They had been leaders in offices, issuing orders and giving instructions. Now they had to learn from peasants and workers who told them what to do. The teachers who came there had taught others for many years. Now they themselves were being taught.

"Many of these people had thought they were doing quite well," Li said. "But when they came here, they realized their shortcomings. It was very good for the intellectuals who had never been to the country. Some of them had the bad habit of looking down on peasants."

Some 60 to 70 percent had neither factory nor farm experience. Even if they had come originally from the country, they had not lived there for years. They were sent to work with production teams in the local communes in order to learn how to cultivate the earth and plant the crops.

No one knew when they first arrived how long they would be there. It might be one year, it might be five, it might be ten. (Actually, most stayed about two years.) The fact was, although Li did not mention it, that Peking had been the stronghold of Liu Shao-chi and Mayor Peng Chen and the first "class" of May Seventh students was made up of strong supporters of the opposition line. A few of these officials were still in the camp—the man in charge of pig production, for instance. He was named Chen Yi-ju, and he had once worked in the administration of the East Peking Party Committee. He had known nothing about pigs when he arrived, but now he was in charge of a 160-pig farm and, as he said, had become "quite skilled" at his task. In his neat city suit, however, he still looked a good deal more the bureaucrat than the swineherd.

I asked Shao Sung-ling, who had been in charge of the school's political work since it was founded, what he personally had gained from the experience. He said that he had learned the truth of Chairman Mao's teaching—that the masses were the makers of history.

"Take my experience," he said. "When I was working in the office (he had formerly been in the party's industrial department) I gave orders—do this, don't do that. Without close control, no one would know whether my work was being done well or not.

"Now, here, the cadres are all equal. No one gives orders to anyone else. The teacher and the students are equal. The lecturers are criticized, and the students criticize themselves."

Li Chen, another veteran party worker, said that for the first time in 23 years he had had a chance to seriously study Marxism-Leninism and Chairman Mao's thought.

"Now I know how to become a successor of the Revolution," he said. "I've learned how to carry out the educational line put forward by Chairman Mao for the cadres. I have come to understand much more deeply why the line of Liu Shao-chi is wrong. He always advocated that the cadres be divorced from labor and reality. I worked with the people before the Cultural Revolution, but now I realize that we haven't served the people heart-and-soul as pointed out by the Chairman. We are bound to be bureaucrats if we are divorced from the masses and from productive labor."

By this time, most students in the camp had little in common with the first wave. They were spending only six months there. They were, so far as I could ascertain, genuine volunteers. In fact, I had the impression that it was a status symbol of considerable weight to get sent to the camp. The students were medium-level bureaucrats and civil servants, and many were teachers from the middle schools, particularly history and political science instructors. Most of the teachers were women, and they had left their families, including children, in the city, while they spent six months in the country. They usually went back to Peking to visit their families every week, or every other week. They lived in barracks, which they kept spotlessly clean, ate their meals in a big communal dining room and worked on the farm in teams. The food—like the food all over China—was exquisite, and the living quarters—if Spartan—were comfortable.

Ku Ching-he, 32, a history teacher, with a husband and four-year-old boy in Peking, was typical of these students. She was cheerful and serious. Her husband was a librarian in Peking and he had attended a similar school in Hupei, run by the Ministry of Culture. Now he was back in Peking, having spent the year 1970 at the school.

Students rose at six and did ten minutes of setting-up exercises before dressing and going to breakfast. Ku Ching-he felt that her world outlook had been changed by her studies, that she was more realistic in her thinking and closer to the peasants and workers.

I had no doubt that she felt she had been bettered by her experience. Most of the students gave that impression. Certainly, they did not seem oppressed, nor were they under any constraint. They were healthy and vigorous and seemed to be enjoying themselves.

After we were served a meal that included at least a dozen succulent dishes, the students put on an amateur entertainment—songs and dances. The titles provided an idea of the school's style: "We All Have Embarked on the Road Pointed out by the May Seventh Directive" (a group chorus); "Chairman Mao Has Sent Us Revolutionary Seed" (young woman's solo); "The May Seventh Fighters Are Busy Transplanting Rice" (dance by men and women); "Drying the Grain Reserve" (dance by men and women); "Happy is He Who Drives the Night-soil Cart" (tenor solo); "Song of the Pig Breeders" (girls' dance and song); "It's Good to Be Tempered" (chorus); "Song of the May Seventh Fighters" (ensemble).

That was it. That was the May Seventh school. They were just at that time studying Engels' "Anti-Dühring." Before this, they had studied Lenin's *State and Revolution, The Communist Manifesto* and Mao's five philosophical works. The curriculum was not completely standardized. They were experimenting with it, just as they were experimenting with the duration of the stay at the school. Perhaps there would be changes later on, but one thing seemed to be certain. From now on, the schools would be a permanent feature of Chinese life. Party and state workers would attend them regularly, taking turns with their jobs. After an initial course of six months or a year, there would be annual refresher courses of at least a month's duration. Every effort would be made to see that the link between the bureaucrat, the intellectual, the scholar, the white-collar worker and the blue-collar worker would not be severed.

Alongside this, there would be a massive effort to keep the educational system from producing a generation of lily-white youngsters, of youngsters divorced from the reality of labor in the city or in the country; but that, the education of youth, was a different story, a story all in itself.

So far as adult China was concerned, there seemed to be three elements in the creation of the new man and the new woman. First, there was the Revolution itself, its liberating force, its idealism, its transformation of the subservient, slave-like Chinese peasants and workers into self-sufficient men and women. The workers "stood up." The peasants "stood up." That was the phrase that was used, and it was used almost in a physical sense, to describe the poverty-stricken, disease-ridden, debt-burdened, debased Chinese men and women, their backs literally bent by the burdens of life, who now, with the liberating force of the Revolution, literally stood up.

Second, there was the exhilaration, the sheer anarchistic stir of the Cultural Revolution, what Chairman Mao called the *luan*, which is the Chinese word for confusion. As the Red Guards of Peking expressed it in June, 1966:

"We want to wield the massive cudgel (of Mao's thought) to express our spirit, invoke our magic influence and turn the whole world upside down, smash things into chaos, into smithereens, smash things *luan-luan-ti*, and the more *luan* the better."

Or as Chairman Mao put it: "As I see it, shocking people has its good points. For many years I thought about how to administer a shock, and finally conceived the shock of the Cultural Revolution."

The shock and the *luan* did shake China, especially the Chinese intelligentsia, the Chinese bureaucrats, the Chinese white-collar class. It did break the pattern of Chinese life, of life as it was evolving under the Communist rule. There was no doubt that the shock was real. One had only to talk to the Chinese people. It was something they had experienced themselves. They were not always articulate about it. Often they said: "Well, we don't entirely understand it ourselves." Or they would say: "There is much about the Cultural Revolution that is not yet clear." But it did administer a social shock to the whole body politic, in addition to the specific shock of breaking up organizations and removing not only many leaders at the top but the top veneer of leaders right across the country.

This created an atmosphere that changed men and women, just as, on a lesser scale, the traumatic events at Columbia, say, changed all of those who participated in them.

But the process did not end there. Having shocked the white-collar class by the violence, turbulence and raw drama of the Cultural Revolution, most of the leading participants were plunged into something that I can only describe as a combination of a YMCA Camp and a Catholic retreat—with no offense intended to either. The Chinese were lifted up out of their urban milieu, transported deep into the countryside, set to doing physical tasks of great hardship under primitive conditions and exposed to an evangelical campaign to reorder their thinking, to instill in them patriotic love of country, dedication to the common good, to the philosophy of the golden rule (all China today lives, almost literally, by the Confucian precept of "Do Unto Others as Thou wouldst be Done to Thyself") and adoration of the personality of Chairman Mao.

It was more than a little reminiscent of Chautauqua and the old Methodist camp-meeting grounds—the combination of pure air, pure living and pure thought, a notoriously exhilarating mixture, particularly for urban dwellers. There was no reason to suppose that it would not have an impact upon the Chinese, psychologically and physiologically, just as it would upon Americans.

This, it seemed to me, constituted the ingredients of the Cultural Revolution—the ingredients out of which the new Chinese national psychology had been formed. And I believe that it *is* a national psychology, one that has deeply affected the Chinese white-collar class and the intelligentsia (although I would enter major reservations about the artistic milieu).

But what of the peasantry and what of the workers—what of these paradigms that the white-collar class had been set to emulate? Were they, too, deeply transformed, deeply imbued with this new spirit of China? Were they, too, China's New Men and Women?

That was a question to which the spiritual transformation of the intellectuals by the Cultural Revolution and the revivalist spirit of the May Seventh camps could provide no answer. Workers and peasants were not sent to May Seventh camps. Peasants had little or no part in the Cultural Revolution—that is, in the violent and traumatic sense in which it was carried through in the cities. As for the workers, they were deeply engaged in certain areas. But in others, they seemed to have been hardly touched.

Before I was prepared to accept any generalization about China's new man and new woman, I would have to look much closer at the countryside and at the great industrial works in the city. For, important as they were, the intelligentsia and the cadres were not China.

6

The Countryside

The Peking train pulled into Anyang about 6 A.M., but as our sleeping car, plain but comfortable, glided to a slow stop, I saw that the city had long been awake and that the streets were already alive with movement—heavy trucks weaving through the throng, their horns going constantly.

Anyang is a city the size of Indianapolis, 600 kilometers south of Peking, and we came to it as a take-off point for a venture deep into the Honan countryside. After a quick breakfast, we set out from the city on a highway that was narrow, but paved for a few miles, and heavy with traffic. There was an endless procession of carts, their ungreased wheels singing like a madmen's chorale, most of them pulled by thin, wiry men, transporting enormous burdens of cut stone, heavy gravel, bricks fresh from the kiln, coking coal, briquets, limestone, burlap-covered bundles of textiles, iron housings, castings, iron ore, slag, towering pillars of heavy-duty truck tires, wood, cotton, wool, steel drums, saucepans, iron kettles, earthen pots, iron bars, grain, sand, kerosene, night-soil and other loads that I could not recognize under the jute, straw or burlap packing.

Some burdens were so heavy the man could barely haul his cart. Sometimes, one man pulled and one pushed. Sometimes, a donkey pulled and a man pushed, but more often the men with donkeys simply reclined atop their mountainous loads and drowsed as the animal moved slowly down the road. Not all carts were pulled by donkeys and men. An occasional one was horse-drawn or mule-drawn or cow-drawn or bullock-drawn. But men provided the principal motive power.

It was slow work threading our way out of the city and its industrial suburbs, with the streams of traffic coming and going.

Along the road lay rice paddies or millet fields, and just beyond them rose the low silhouettes of textile plants, and in the distance loomed the belching stacks of two big steel mills. Anyang was a growing industrial center, with chemical, textile and tobacco plants, as well as steel. The factories sprawled out into the outskirts.

The carts on the road were the industrial transportation system, bringing to the factories raw materials and taking away the finished product. The factories were crammed with every kind of advanced technology but it was human muscles that made the system run. To be sure, a railroad served the steel mills and chemical plants, but astonishing quantities of raw materials, including most of the iron ore, coal, coke and limestone, were hauled in hand-drawn vehicles.

I saw hardly any gasoline-powered transport on the road and none at all in the countryside. I kept a log of motor vehicles, and in more than 250 kilometers I recorded: two modern buses, their bulk completely filling the road; two tractor-driven harrows, working in the fields; a machine-powered steam shovel and two large trucks at the open-cut iron mine that provided ore for the Anyang plants; and between 20 and 30 two-cylinder garden-type tractors being used to pull carts.

Once we left the tall chimneys of the Anyang mills behind, we drove straight into the days of Thomas Jefferson. This was a land where the internal-combustion engine had not yet been used. No longer was the road paved. It was thinly graveled, and the trains of carts (and the passing of our car) sent endless clouds of dust billowing over the countryside. There was nothing in the landscape to suggest we had not been magically transported into the deep past. Here men and their animals reigned, with no mechanical contrivance more complex than a pump. It was a landscape that had not changed materially, I thought, since the time of Marco Polo. The caravans moved like a slow frieze, and they did not halt at darkness. Of course, the carts' porters pulled off the road for a few hours' sleep. But the animal-hauled ones went on, their drivers asleep, the donkeys faithfully following each other's tails. Sometimes their burden was lightened by huge sails that were hoisted to catch the wind that sprang up at sundown and softly murmured across the darkened fields.

Nor was the century turned back only along the highway. In the fields men and women and children were harvesting a bumper crop of wheat, but not with mechanical aids. No gigantic machines trembled across the land. Here the grain was cut by men and women with hand scythes, then bound in sheaves with a strand of fiber. You could have seen a similar sight in the Plymouth Colony or, later on, in the lands of the Western Reserve as they fell to the plow. This was farming before the days of the McCormick reaper. The sheaves, bound and stacked, were brought by cart to the threshing platform—hard, baked-clay floors, twice the size of a basketball court. There they were flailed by hand or beaten over crude revolving wooden drums to separate the grain from the straw.

In village after village, men and women were tossing the grain high with wooden shovels, letting the wind catch the chaff and separate it from the hardening kernels of golden wheat.

Beside the threshing floor, cottages and houses of straw were being erected, neat and orderly enough for regiments of little pigs, and conical mounds of straw were being covered with a heavy layer of clay which would harden in the fierce Honan sun and create a mud silo to preserve the straw for winter forage.

In the fields, I saw men turning the soil with wooden plows, cutting clean furrows in the dry earth. Sometimes one man pulled a plow and another guided it. Sometimes, in heavy soil, two men pulled the plow. More often than not it was drawn by a cow and occasionally by a horse. Much of the land was planted to grain, mostly wheat, which was in full harvest, golden and hard, at mid-June. The fields were being prepared for a second crop, corn in many places but in others cotton or sweet potatoes.

We passed village after village, some of the houses mud and wattle, but many more of cut stone. (This was Linhsein County, and it is famous for its stone and its stonemasons). Each village was a gauntlet of children, peering from every courtyard, lined up along the narrow street, craning their necks from behind stone walls to see the passage of an automobile with white barbarians sitting in it. The boys ran naked and healthy (those below six or seven) but girls, except for toddlers, wore small diapers.

Alongside the road, and through the fields, flowed water. There were irrigation ditches almost everywhere and, in many villages, reservoir ponds. Here and there across the fields were wells where cows or donkeys faithfully plodded endless circles, drawing the water to the surface. Within the houses, or in the courtyards, women stood over the hard-clay stoves in which great iron basins were inset, cooking for the families of eight, ten, twelve, or fourteen.

As we drove deeper into the countryside, the feeling grew in me that I was experiencing not a prevision of the world's future but a retrospective glimpse into our own American or European past—the world in which men and women labored with their own hands, with a few animals, a few primitive implements—experiencing a life so simple, so integrated with the land, the weather and the plants that its symmetry seemed almost magical. I found myself entering deep into the past, a pleasant past, even a nostalgic past, but not one that seemed to have much relevance to the world from which I came.

But this was not how the Chinese saw Linhsein County. The Chinese saw it, through entirely different pairs of eyes, as a land that had been transformed almost beyond recognition. Only a few years before, this was a land so arid and so barren that Linhsein people used to say: "Water is as scarce as oil." It could not support its population. Drought struck nine years out of ten. People sold their children, and themselves went out to beg, in order to escape starvation. Of 500 big villages, 300 had no water supply. In drought, people walked ten or even twenty *li* (three *li* equal a mile) to fetch their water. Those who had wells sold water by the cup. It was a countryside of gullies and stones. Although its name meant "forest" the mountains were barren and brown, the trees long since chopped down. There was little topsoil and crops averaged no more than 100 catties per *mu* [a catty is one pound, two ounces; a *mu* is about 1/6 of an acre]. Few people were able to grow enough grain to last more than half a year. That meant six months of starvation out of every twelve. The biggest crop in Linhsein County, it was said, was the crop of stones. There was no disease, it seemed, that was not endemic—cholera, small pox, measles, tuberculosis, syphilis, gonorrhea, schistosomiasis. Bubonic plague was not unknown, and, of course, many people simply starved to death. In winter there was neither wood nor coal to heat the huts or to cook the food. In summer there was no shade in which to escape the blazing sun.

That was Linhsein as the Chinese remembered it. What they saw as they now looked across the landscape was fields, well-tilled; irrigation water running through the rills of millet and the squared-off rice paddies; water in ditches through the villages, and happy, splashing children. They saw women, their backs bent, washing clothes in the precious liquid, and across the horizon they looked in awe at an aqueduct that might have graced a Roman countryside. They saw new houses in the villages, built with well-baked bricks from the kilns that dotted the fields. They saw tile roofs, not thatched, and their eyes lighted up at the road along which our car bumped and rocked—a real road. Granted, it was full of holes, granted that dust rose in clouds. Still it was a road, and it led from village to village, and ultimately, to Anyang itself. Even ten years earlier there had been no road, only footpaths that wandered endlessly through the fields. Carts and barrows could move on the paths, but not trucks, or buses or automobiles. Now there was a link with the outside world. People could move back and forth instead of spending their whole lives within the confines of a single village.

The Chinese saw the mud-walled latrines lining the roads and fields, one every 200 or 300 yards. They saw the old men with their carts and shovels painstakingly picking up the droppings from the road. They saw the children, tanned and healthy, bursting the walls of the villages. They saw the skin of the younger children, fresh and unblemished, their eyes clear and bright. And they could remember the suppurating sores, the ulcers on the eyes and mouths, the pus and smell of the disease-stricken children of Linhsein a few years back. They looked to the loess hills and saw new terraces sculpting the hills with mosaic patterns, groves of walnut, apple, apricot, peach, willow and pine trees marching up the eroded slopes of the mountains. They saw the thin blue dust that hangs eternally in the skies over Honan, and measured visibly the difference from the past, when it was not a dust haze but a storm of grit-edged particles that filled the air, wounded the eyes, infected the lungs and blotted out the sun.

This was how Chinese eyes saw Linhsein County. I do not think they saw anything wrong in the throngs of healthy children crowding the villages, although, if they stopped to consider, they must have known that Chairman Mao Tse-tung's birth-control precepts were hardly being carried out. Actually, they were apt to say, "Well, it doesn't make a great deal of difference, because, of course, there is much work to be done and we need every hand we can get for the great tasks that lie ahead." Perhaps that was why, when the young Red Guards were sent down to Linhsein from the city, the village elders quietly urged them to marry village girls and settle down and raise families (even though neither the Guards nor the girls had reached the age the party had specified as being the right one for marriage).

As our car rumbled along, we overtook a beautiful young woman, brightly dressed in a green and pink silk blouse and wearing a big hat of fine straw, sitting astride a handsome gray donkey. My companions smiled knowingly. "She's going home to her mother for a visit, leaving her in-laws. That's how they do it in Honan—wearing their best clothes and riding a donkey." The young woman looked proud and self-assured. Her life in the new Linhsein County was turning out well.

A bit further on, six men and women, sweat pouring from their foreheads, were carrying a litter on which a man reclined in the hot mid-afternoon sun. He was not a landlord, as he might have been in times gone by. He was a patient being taken from the village to the nearest district hospital.

To my eyes, to my American eyes, this was a primitive and picturesque scene, a scene of rural life in a distant Asian region, filled with "color" and strangeness. But to Chinese eyes it was nothing short of a miracle, and, when I understood what Linhsein had been a few years earlier, I could only agree. The transformation had not been achieved without gigantic effort. It was accomplished by the construction of the Red Flag Canal, which brought water from the Chang River on the border of Honan and Shansi Provinces into Linhsein County, where a system of interconnecting channels distributed it to the land. Linhsein people compared the system to the construction of the Great Wall. It involved moving more than 16.4 million cubic meters of earth and stone—enough to build a 12-foot highway from Canton to Mukden. There were more than 2,300 *li* of canals, 134 tunnels and culverts (48 *li* long), and 150 aqueducts 13 *li* long. More than 30,000 people had been mobilized to carry out the construction.

The Chinese eyes that could best see and measure this transformation were those of the people who had lived in old Linhsein.

For example, there was Kuo Chon-ting, a lively grandmother of 46 who came to her husband from a very poor family as a child bride of 14. Now, she was the matriarch of a family that numbered 14, most of them, including herself, members of the Cheng Kuan township people's commune. In the old days, her family was too poor to have a house, and of course they owned no land. They lived by begging, and lodged (when they had lodgings) in a village temple. This was not an unusual family. Now Kuo Chon-ting lived in a village courtyard house, surrounded by family and possessions. Her husband worked in the county seat and her son was a member of the county performing troupe. The son's wife worked in a match factory nearby, and they had three children, two boys and a girl. A second son was a barefoot doctor in the village, and his wife was a member of the commune. They had one daughter. A third son was doing his army service, but his wife was in the commune. They had one daughter. Kuo Chon-ting's fourth child was a schoolgirl of 14. The three generations lived together in three houses around three sides of a large bean-and-tomato-planted courtyard. Kuo Chon-ting proudly showed off her possessions—a mahogany table and two mahogany chairs, two big painted chests, two mahogany sideboards, a sewing machine, a big modern wall clock and a radio.

Was she well off? There was no question about that in her own mind as she told how she went out in the village as a child to beg, of the meanness of the landlords, how they set dogs upon poor people and beat them when they pleaded for a bowl of rice. Life was good now. Better than she had ever imagined it could be. Her family earned 450 to 460 catties of grain per head per year, plus 400 yuan (a yuan is about 40 cents) in cash. And this did not include cash income earned, for instance, by her husband at the county seat, and by her eldest son. She went to her kitchen and showed us enormous earthen vessels, as big as those in which Ali Baba's 40 thieves hid themselves —all filled with grain. She pointed out the lofts over the kitchen and over the bedroom, where more great jars of grain and barrels of flour were stored. In her own terms she was rich. And, while she worked hard with her hands as did all the members of the family (including children), they seemed to have as many personal possessions as had the hated old landlords who had harassed her as a poor beggar child. But, of course, these riches were earned by the efforts of Kuo Chon-ting and her family. There was no ownership of land, no hiring of labor, no sharecropping (with the landlord getting two thirds of the harvest), no moneylending, with the poor peasant paying 50 percent interest or more per month.

Kuo Chon-ting did not talk about the Cultural Revolution. She did not speak of Chairman Mao Tse-tung (although she had his picture on her table). Perhaps I was wrong but it seemed to me that her measure of the Revolution and the Cultural Revolution was in catties of grain, of mahogany chests, of healthy children growing up, of a house to live in, and of freedom from starvation and disease.

I knew that this was not a typical commune. Linhsein was not a typical county. There were many far worse—where water had not been brought to the land. And there were many far better—where natural conditions were not so harsh. On this commune, the average output at the time of Liberation had been 200 catties per *mu*. After the Red Flag Canal was completed the yield was lifted to 857 catties. But this was substantially below the yield further to the south, where there was abundant rainfall and more fertile land. There were 80,000 people in this commune, and they owned 140,000 *mu* of land. Their average income was 130 yuan, 50 fang (a fang is 1/100th of a yuan), per capita per year, of which they got about half in grain and the rest in cash.

In the south, not far from Changsha, I saw the Kao Tang Ling People's Commune, where 17,600 persons worked 18,000 *mu* of land with an average yield of 1,100 catties per *mu*. Their income was 90 yuan per person (not counting what they earned from their own gardens, pigs and poultry) plus 700 catties of grain per head. This was a commune that was considered to be about average. There were others nearby with a yield of 1,500 catties per *mu*. There were some where the yield was as low as 900.

What did the Cultural Revolution mean to the Kao Tang Ling Commune? Not very much so far as I could find out. Here the talk was all of increasing production, of getting better yields, of more efficiency. The Cultural Revolution had sent a few Red Guards to the commune. Some were still there—tolerated rather than welcomed. I do not mean to suggest that the Cultural Revolution was unfelt here, within a few miles of Chairman Mao's birthplace. But it did not press itself forward as a dominant factor in the life of the village.

This seemed to be true at a third commune, by far the richest and most complex one I visited—the Double Bridge Commune, also known as the China-Cuba Friendship People's Commune—about 25 miles outside of Peking. This commune had 38,000 population, 3,600 hectares (a hectare is 2.47 acres) of land, six production brigades and 59 production teams. It was into all kinds of activities—forestry, wheat, rice, vegetables (for the Peking consumers market), soybeans, corn, cotton, grape vineyards, apple and peach orchards, stock farming, dairies, a pig farm, a poultry farm, a stud farm, an insecticide plant, a pesticide plant, a flour mill, a farm implement repair station and a fish hatchery. There probably were other activities that I forgot to list. This was an outstanding commune, which delivered to Peking 10,000 gallons of milk and an average of 125,000 pounds of vegetables daily; 1.25 million pounds of fruit, 6,200 pigs and 40,000 Peking ducks (that is, ducks force-fed to a weight suitable for use in preparing Peking duck) a year. There was some variation in income among members of the Double Bridge Commune, because their duties varied so much. But the average probably ran about 150 yuan per capita, plus 500 or more catties of grain, with this augmented by the sale of pigs and other produce to the state on an individual basis. Here, too, I had the feeling that the goals and aspirations of the farmers and their families were basically material; that the measure of success of the Cultural Revolution, for example, was largely to be found in the extent to which it boosted production and enabled the families to live a better, more comfortable life. They were proud of their transistor radios, their bicycles and their sewing machines. Everyone knew the price of a sewing machine (130 yuan) and a bicycle (130 to 160 yuan). They did not yet have television sets, but they were beginning to think of the possibility of buying them.

It was only when I talked to Chuang Ho-shan, head of the Revolutionary Committee of the commune, that I got the feeling of something other than a material yardstick by which to measure life in the countryside. Chuang had been a school administrator before coming to the commune, and I think his assignment to the commune was connected with the upheavals of the Cultural Revolution. When I asked him about his own personal goals, he talked in terms quite different from those used by the commune members.

"What is the aim of working, after all?" he said. "It is to build up the country, to further the purposes of the Revolution. We must exert ourselves far more if we are really going to improve the country. Even with all our people, there are not enough to do the work. There is unlimited work to be done. . . ."

He had never before worked with a commune and had no special training in agriculture.

"But I know the countryside," he said. At 46, he was a mature man who had taken a role in the Revolution in 1949, and had been in the school system ever since. His family was in Peking, where his wife was a teacher, and he left the commune on weekends to visit her and his 13- and 10-year-old boys.

I asked him what he hoped his boys would do. That, he said, depends on the country's situation. They don't have to worry about jobs. They will graduate from middle school and then spend two years in the countryside or in a factory. Whether they would go on to higher education depended on whether they applied, and whether their applications were supported by their associates and superiors.

He liked his work in the commune. There were not many bad eggs in the group. Seldom did any cases of theft occur. If such a thing happened, the person was criticized and shown the wrongness of his acts.

Really, nothing but very trivial cases occurred. Once a youngster on his way home from work passed by a shed where a production team had stored some fireworks. There was a bundle lying outside. The youngster carried the fireworks home and showed them to his parents.

"You didn't bring home a bundle of fireworks," they told the boy, "you brought home a bundle of selfishness."

The next day the boy returned the bundle.

I asked whether there had ever been any more serious crimes. Had there ever been a murder, or a rape?

Never, he said, at least not since he had known the commune.

What about husbands beating up wives?

Well, there was an instance or two of that, he conceded, but usually it was more a matter of quarreling than fighting, and for cases like that they found that education usually took care of the situation.

What about drugs? He smiled. There was no drug problem. Once there had been an opium problem. But it vanished with the education of the population. The important thing in all cases, he felt, was education. That was why it was so important that the middle school graduates were coming to the countryside for two years before going on to higher schools. Two years of work before going to college taught them a great deal about real life.

Life in the commune, he thought, was going well. It had its drawbacks. The farming was insufficiently mechanized. There were many things that needed to be improved. But people were working well.

"As you know," he said, "our motto is 'Serve the People.' "

I had no doubt that this quiet, serious, thoughtful man was doing his best to live up to the motto. He was separated from his family much of the time, living in the countryside, after having lived a long time in the city. He was, after all, engaged in an unfamiliar task, but he found his work satisfying, and he was, in his modest way, doing his best to improve not only production at the commune but also the life of the commune members. He was, I thought, an excellent example of the selfless official whom Chairman Mao Tse-tung was trying to create, and this, to be certain, was one of the great objectives of the Cultural Revolution.

But what of the commune members at the Double Bridge Commune and the other communes I had visited—those in Linhsein County, and in the Changsha area? I felt no such conviction about their members.

As I sat drinking tea with the old grandmothers, as they showed me their possessions with such pride, as they pointed to their caches of grain and lovingly numbered the members of their families and enumerated the total family income, I could not help thinking that I was getting a peek into a corner of the Old China, rather than the New.

I could see the same grandmothers in the old days, wearing their best black silks, their hair pulled up in a tight bun, sitting in their mahogany chairs beside their mahogany tables, and offering tea to a foreign guest—the same pride in possession, the same accumulation of objects and things, the same cultivation of the basic human traits of acquisition and, let's face it, greed. Where was the difference between old and new? The difference, it seemed to me, lay in two areas. The new acquisitors were sharply limited in the amount of their acquisitions. They could not benefit by their neighbor's misfortunes. They could not squeeze the poor peasants. They had to acquire through hard work and diligence. They could not own land and let it out at ruinous rates. Nor could they lend money in usury. They were certainly curbed. But had they piled up those precious jars of grain for the good of the state? (To be sure, the state did encourage them to accumulate reserves, because this provided a supplementary reserve against war or famine.) Had they bought their mahogany furniture, their elaborate clocks and their stocks of wool and silk because of some new revolutionary urge? Were they constantly thinking of their neighbors and how they could do them good? I doubted that. I thought the gleam of the old devil shone in the eyes of these very Chinese ladies, and I did not think there was very much new about it. One could rationalize their position. One could say that they had suffered so much in the past that it was only fair that they profit a bit now, that they be allowed to enrich themselves a little and lead a more comfortable life. But had we not heard this before? Had that not been the motto of the French bourgeoisie? Had that not been the philosophy of Stolypin when he so successfully utilized the acquisitive force of the middle-class peasants in Russia, and, within a decade, created a remarkably rich, energetic and successful kulak class of private farmers?

Perhaps, it was too early to make a judgment. But it seemed to me that the tendency toward *embourgeoisement* was more plainly visible in the Chinese countryside than the image of a New Chinese Man.

7

Willow Grove

The small plane seemed to hunt its way through the eroded hills and wind canyons of northern Shensi, nosing out of Yenan and the narrow valley airstrip, just as it had back in 1944, when General Patrick Hurley landed and startled Mao Tse-tung out of his natural aplomb by giving a Choctaw war whoop from the open door of his DC-3.

Northern Shensi *is* erosion, endless eroded hills, and low, worn mountains, the sides ravaged by centuries of wind and occasional torrential rains, the land as scarred as the crater of the moon; barren, red, lifeless. One range of hills is identical with another. Only when the plane finally picks out the Yenan valley and slips down swiftly onto the narrow runway beside the boulder-filled River Yen does your eye catch a sudden splash of green—rice fields, tenuously irrigated by water drawn from the river.

In June, northern Shensi lies naked and baking in the China sun, and even more naked and baking than usual in June, 1972, as drought held the land in a copper grip.

Here Chairman Mao finally broke his Long March in 1935. Here, and in nearby Pao-an, his forces rested, consolidated their strength, established a stronghold, 13 years before the Communist regime proclaimed its power in Peking. It was in Pao-an that Edgar Snow spent months interviewing Chairman Mao, Red Army Leader Chu Teh, Chou En-lai and Lin Piao for *Red Star Over China*. And here in Yenan lived the famous American liaison mission in World War II—John S. Service, John Patton Davies, Colonel David Barrett. Here were the great shrines of the Communist Revolution, the huts and caves where Mao and his associates worked out the philosophy and strategy that were to bring their forces victory over Chiang Kai-shek, and leadership of the world's greatest population mass.

Yenan was holy ground to the Communist Revolution. During the Cultural Revolution, a million Red Guards made the pilgrimage here. As I walked the hot Yenan streets, listening to the shaking of the earth and the deep boom as blasting for underground shelters (or quite possibly underground factories) echoed in the valley, looking up at the red-brown hills and the famous pagoda towering over it all, visiting the caves where Mao studied and taught and wrote and husbanded strength for the great battles that lay ahead, it seemed to me like a town of ghosts—not a ghost town, for the streets were lively, there was a bustle of traffic, a big new tourist hotel was going up, factories were being built—but a town where the ghosts of historic figures still seemed to tread the streets: Mao, Chou, Lin Piao, Chu Teh and even, of course, the Americans.

But it was hard for me to catch the spirit of the Yenan days, listening to young guides in the museums rattle off their spiels or looking at the bowdlerized photographs on the walls that often merely showed the tables at which the decisions were made, or the empty stage where meetings were held. The pictures of the participants could not be shown—too many had fallen from favor.

Not until one morning when I drove out of Yenan a few miles to visit the Liu Ling—the Willow Grove—Commune did I feel that I had gotten back to the Yenan of the 1930's, the Yenan of those endless nights when Mao studied and wrote for hours, as a candle glittered dimly in the stone-walled cave.

Liu Ling was not Yenan, but it was a simple community of Shensi caves, hewn in the loess walls of Naopanshan, rising up from the rocky course of the River Nan. Nothing was easy in Willow Grove. Nothing ever had been. Probably nothing ever would be. This was Yenan as Yenan had been, or as close to Yenan as can now be remembered—before the victory of the Revolution began to change the valley, to bring in plumbing, piped water, paved (though roughly) main streets, reliable electric lights and power, factories and industry and a general atmosphere of development. It was easier to imagine Chairman Mao in Liu Ling than in Yenan itself.

But Liu Ling was much more than a spiritual bridge back to the Yenan days of puritan virtue and Spartan simplicity. It was also the headquarters of a brigade of the Liu Ling Commune. Communism had come to these barren valleys nearly 40 years ago. Nowhere in China could I find a land where the lessons of Mao Tse-tung had longer been tested, a region where Communism as the Chinese practiced it had a longer history, and not only could I personally see and examine commune life in the loess hills of Yenan, I could see it also through the impressions of observers far more skilled in China than myself. This very commune had been visited a dozen years earlier by Edgar Snow, and then intensively studied on two successive occasions —in 1962 and 1969—by the Swedish socio-journalist, Jan Myrdal, and his wife, Gun Kessle. Thus, I saw Liu Ling not only with my own eyes, new to China but familiar over a quarter of a century with Communist agriculture in the Soviet Union and every other Communist state in Europe and Asia, but also with the eyes of three knowledgeable foreign observers (as well as the eyes of the Chinese who accompanied me).

This was a help, but I would have traded it all for one quick visit to northern Shensi in the 1920's, before the Long March finally came to an end only a few miles from Liu Ling in 1935. Of course, I could guess what the land had been like. Flying over these hills I was flying over land that reminded me of the Grand Canyon (without any canyons quite so deep or of such striking color) or some of the more desolate reaches of the Dakota Badlands. It was not the kind of place where any American pioneer would have halted his westward trek and attempted to homestead. It was not even a place that might have tempted the tough Cossacks or strong-willed Ukrainian farmers, pushing east past the Urals into the water-parched regions of Turkestan—although, physically, it much resembled northern Turkestan. Snow saw this country in the 1930's and thought it worse blighted than the Oklahoma dustbowl.

"There were very few trees, and it was arid except for swift summer floods and winter snows," he observed. "Its best asset was a fine dry healthful climate. That alone probably explained why poor people could survive in their tumble-down caves, infested by flies and rats (bubonic plague used to be endemic) and scratch an existence from scabby patches of grain planted on slopes sometimes as steep as 30 degrees."

That was the base. That was where the farmers of Liu Ling started when Mao's Red Army, like men from the moon, turned up in their valley in 1935 and gave them a chance to change their way of life.

I tried to keep that image in mind as I followed Brigade Leader Feng Chang-yeh up the hard-clay path that led past the caves that sheltered the Liu Ling school, the Liu Ling machine shop, the Liu Ling granary, the stables and the corral where a dozen horses and donkeys morosely stood; alongside the hill, where new caves were being roofed with a foot or two of red earth; past the upper hill, where 40 men and women were carving out earth for the roofs and, simultaneously, creating a new terrace; on to a hard-clay eminence, swept with dust-laden wind. There an orchard had been planted, and there I could look over the low range of hills at irrigated fields of rice.

Some things I could clearly see without asking questions, without knowing the past of Shensi, without knowing what it had all looked like when Snow was there and when the Myrdals were gathering information for their classic study, *Report From a Chinese Village.*

I could see that the loess soil was rich but desperately hard to work, because of the lack of water, the difficulty of irrigation and the fierce winds that even on that June morning were moving between the hills with a low murmur and with force enough to pick up the dust from the tilled plots around the orchard, exhausting the moisture from the soil as a blacksmith's forge burns oxygen from the bellows.

There were apples and peaches and apricots and plums planted on the shoulder of the hill, and Feng Chang-yeh, his eyes sad and his face graven, said that there was no irrigation for the hill, and every drop of water had to be hand-carried up the 70-foot incline from an irrigation pipe 300 yards distant. Once I had carried pail after pail of water 100 yards from a Russian village well to nurture a 50-foot garden plot. I thought I knew something of the labor invested to turn the desert hill into an orchard.

Of course, it had not been done overnight. The social changes in Liu Ling had come about infinitely more gradually than, for example, the transformation of Russia's agriculture into collective farms by Stalin. Russian collectivization had been rammed through by Stalin's imperious *Diktat* and the party's machine guns, in a period of 18 months, in 1929–30. The cost to Russia was desperate famine, decimation of livestock herds, exile of 20 million peasants, the death of 3 to 5 million people and a blow to Russian agriculture that 40 years had not entirely healed. The scars burned so deep that a traveler to an out-of-the-way Soviet collective or state farm (not the fine, well-run, excellently equipped show farms near Moscow and Kiev) even in the early 1970's could meet a peasantry grim, scowling, sullen, inward-turning in their harsh resentment, never worn away, against the central authority in Moscow. After nearly 60 years of Communist rule, Russia had not created a reliable agricultural base.

But what of China? I could see how different the picture was in studying the record of Liu Ling. The peasants had taken the land and redistributed it to themselves, chasing away the landlords and owners, when the Red Army came in 1935. There was no communizing of the land during those early days. None during the long and peaceful era when Mao Tse-tung presided over Yenan. The peasants farmed their own plots, helped the Red Army, and began to educate themselves and improve their health and sanitation under the urgings of the Communists. They met Mao Tse-tung and listened to him talk about their problems. They knew the Communists, and some of them became Communists. But there was very little Communism in Liu Ling during those years. And they were lean years—one good crop in three years, one failure, one somewhere in between. At least that was the average. There was no orchard, no terracing in those times. Millet was the principal crop, and the peasants were dirt-poor. The chief advantage they had was that they no longer paid rent, and they no longer paid taxes.

It was not until after 1948 that things began to happen here. Even then the pace was gradual—first a labor exchange group in 1949, two years later a labor group for mutual help, then in January, 1954, an agricultural cooperative, a consolidated and bigger cooperative the following winter, called the "East Shines Red" Higher Agricultural Cooperative, which comprised four villages—Wangchiako, Hotoma, Erchuankou and Liu Ling, and finally, in 1958, during the time of the Great Leap Forward, the Liu Ling Commune was formed—according to Snow in 1960, it embraced 59 villages with 1,592 families including about 2,600 able-bodied men and women workers and 65,000 *mu* of land; according to Myrdal in 1962, 57 labor groups, 1,401 households, 5,039 individuals of whom 1,938 were able-bodied, and 360,000 *mu* of land, of which 30,027 were cultivated.

From the time the peasants first took the land into their hands until a fully socialized production system under the commune was established, nearly 25 years had passed. And from that time until I strolled over the loess hills and watched the production team hacking into the red clay, another 14 years had gone by.

Perhaps, this explained the matter-of-fact atmosphere of Liu Ling (and the other communes I visited); the direct, almost blunt, attitude of Feng Chang-yeh toward questions of production and development. He did not seem surprised at inquiries, nor did he seem to feel that he was "on show," that he must put a good face on things or lose status with the western visitors. Of course, western visitors were nothing new to him. He had met Snow and the Myrdals and some others. He had lived in Shensi all his life. He had lived in Liu Ling since 1948 or 1949, and, since 1952, he had been a leader in the community, first of the labor exchange, then of the Wangchiako Agricultural Cooperative, then of the "East Shines Red" Higher Agricultural Cooperative and finally, with the organization of the commune, he became head of the Liu Ling Labor Brigade, which he still led. He was 48 years old, and for the last 20 years, he had devoted his life to the transformation of Liu Ling from a threadbare band of peasants living on the edge of starvation into what he now regarded, with some reason, as an efficient and progressing commune.

The brigade he headed had 10,000 *mu* of land, of which 3,270 were under cultivation. He had a labor force of 284 able-bodied full-time workers. It was a bit smaller than in 1969 when the Myrdals were there. Then there were 161 households with 709 dwellers, of whom 301 constituted the able-bodied work force. There had been a slight but measurable decline in population at Liu Ling since Snow first visited the commune 12 years ago. Income had moved gradually upward over the years, but there had been no spectacular rise—nor was there likely to be one. It was around 80 to 84 yuan per capita per year 12 years ago, and it ran from 80 to 120 yuan now, depending on the individual and the harvest. This was exclusive, of course, of grain and food received in kind.

The important fact about income at Liu Ling was that it was figured on a per capita basis. The family is the basic unit here—as it is throughout China. Feng Chang-yeh had seven members in his family, and his return averaged out about 120 yuan a head. His was a little larger than the usual family. He put the average unit at about six. But, of course, there were others with nine or more members.

What was important to the Liu Ling community was how they lived. When Feng Chang-yeh came here 25 years ago, there were only a few caves, miserable ones, more like hovels than caves. Today almost all the families lived in caves. Actually the word "cave" does not really describe a Shensi habitation. These were firmly built stone and brick houses backed up to the hillside and partially excavated into the hill. Most of the house projected from the clay bank. However, the roof was made of earth—two feet of it—which kept the cave snugly warm in winter and marvelously cool in the desert heat of summer.

The façade of the cave on the village street was a beautiful wooden fretwork, partly open and partly covered on the inside, with oiled paper giving light to the cool recesses. The floors were of stone or hardened clay. Outside the caves was a courtyard area where some families grew beans, corn and sweet potatoes and where each family had a baked-mud pigsty with one or two pigs fattening in it the year around.

For plowing and transport, Liu Ling boasted 185 horses and donkeys; 105 cows were kept for milk, which was supplied to Yenan. There was one tractor. Liu Ling had a blacksmith, and a small machine shop to mend its equipment, and a small electric-powered mill to grind its members' wheat and millet. There were carpenters who skillfully planed logs down with an axe to build the caves, and beehives had been set up near the new orchards (but the bees were not doing too well; the heavy DDT and pesticide treatments sprayed on the crops decimated the hives).

Perhaps, the most striking aspect of Liu Ling was the continuity of leadership and the continuity of growth. There had been little change in the community as the form of administration changed, and virtually no change in the leadership. Even the Cultural Revolution passed over Liu Ling more like a summer thunderstorm than a hurricane. Feng Chang-yeh was no more immune to criticism than any leader anywhere in China. He was said to have followed the line of Liu Shao-chi. (It is more than a little difficult to understand the reason for this criticism, except, as the Myrdals noted, that he had possibly become a bit authoritative in his administration.) But he "saw the error of his ways," and when the Liu Ling Brigade formed a Revolutionary Committee in the fall of 1968, it picked Feng as its chairman. And he was still the chairman, working hard, long hours, doing his best to keep up the tempo of the work, to bring production along, to see to it that each year the people of Liu Ling lived a little better life. And, in this, he had succeeded.

The peasants of Liu Ling did not live as well as those in many other communes. There were fewer sewing machines. There were not so many transistor radios (though more wired ones). But no one went hungry. There was coal or charcoal for the *kangs* in winter, and coal for the cookstoves in summer. The children suffered nothing worse than colds or an occasional bout of chicken pox or measles. There were a few stomach complaints in summer and some bronchial complaints in winter. The youngsters went to school, and each year two or three went from the six-year Liu Ling primary school to the middle school.

The day I was at Liu Ling was the eve of a famous Chinese holiday—the anniversary of the death of the poet Chu Yuan, who lived from 340 to 278 B.C. Chu Yuan was a great patriot in a declining dynastic era. When invaders overran the country, he killed himself by jumping into a river. From that time forward, he had been a national poet and a national hero. Traditionally, the Chinese threw a confection called *tsung-tse* into the river as a sacrifice to Chu's death.

Now, on the eve of the holiday, celebrated on May 5 of the lunar calendar (June 15), the housewives of Liu Ling were busy making *tsung-tse* for the next day's celebration. They had been down to the marshy shores of the River Nan and picked a particular kind of wide-leafed pungent reed. These they were forming into cones and filling with a mixture of sticky millet and dates, to be eaten at the morrow's feast. They sat on wooden stools in their cool caves, mixing the sticky confection in wooden pails while a circle of beady-eyed young children watched, with mouths watering. The children wore simple shifts of cotton, worn and faded. They were barefoot, their faces were dirty and their feet dusty. But they were healthy children, and if not many were fat, at least none bore the telltale protruding ribs of undernourishment.

I was impressed by Feng Chang-yeh. He showed me as much of his commune as he could in a brief visit. He did not pretend that it was perfect. Indeed, I did not think he had any elaborate hopes that it would ever be among those in the first rank. But he knew what had been achieved, and he knew that the achievements were solid. Most of them were due to hard work; most of Liu Ling's small successes were in damming a few gulleys and creating small water reservoirs. The possibilities were limited, but only with water could the land's yields be raised. In the last year or two the commune had dug new wells, and these were a great help. But more were needed, particularly if the program of creating orchards on the hillsides and gradually reforesting the worn loess hills was to be carried on. And this cost money—or work days of brigade members—and with all that had to be done to keep production up, only a limited amount of drilling could be afforded each year.

Feng Chang-yeh knew every foot of Liu Ling. He knew precisely which crops could be raised on each *mu* of land—and so did the other members of the commune. Their land was not planted in great fields and cultivated mechanically. It was cultivated in small strips and subdivisions of fields, one terrace in one crop, and the next in another. They knew by years of experience which crop grew best on which plot. No one came from Peking to tell them they must convert all their fields to corn. No one came from Peking to announce that machine-tractor stations would undertake all plowing and seeding and harvesting operations. No party secretary from the provincial capital suddenly pounced on the Liu Ling Commune and fired all the leaders and chairmen.

And here, of course, was the dramatic difference between the Liu

Ling Commune and any Soviet collective farm I had ever visited. In 25 years I had *never* visited a Soviet collective farm that was directed by a man who had been resident on the farm or resident in the area for 10 years—let alone 20. I had never visited a Soviet collective farm that was not told by the regional center (which, of course, had been told by Moscow) precisely what crops to plant, where to plant them and when to plant them. I had never seen a Soviet agricultural endeavor where the men and women living on the spot were permitted to run their own affairs *because they were known to understand local conditions better.*

Contrary to all of the propaganda I had heard about Chinese "blue ants," and communes in which men and women lived in the same barracks, wore the same clothes, shared the same meals from the same wooden bowls, I found the hallmark of the Chinese commune to be diversity, local autonomy, total adjustment to local conditions, free and easy interchange between the team and brigade leaders and the membership, individual houses, individually farmed plots, individually owned animals and poultry (in addition, of course, to the commune plots), extraordinary diversity from one commune to another, and remarkable absence of interference from Peking and the provincial centers and peasants were free to sell surplus private production on the market.

I don't want to suggest that conditions were idyllic in the communes, or that politics was absent. They were not. And I encountered in some communes a number of experienced political workers who had been transferred into the communes to give better leadership, to ginger up production. But basically, the commune leadership was local, was intimately knowledgeable about the land it was tilling and the crops that were being grown.

What, then, had been added by the Communists? First and foremost, a convenient means for organizing the countryside and the peasant work force for more efficient labor, simultaneous action to carry out the laborious processes of seeding and harvesting. Then, of course, there was the great gift of health through the virtual elimination of epidemic disease; the elimination of the ruinous burdens of taxes and interest; the gradual introduction of better strains of seed and of improved fertilization (utilization under sanitary conditions of human fertilizer and provision of processed fertilizer in ever-increasing amounts); and the provision of technical aid and capital for large-scale irrigation projects that often made the difference between life and death in the arid areas of China.

What about mechanization? I saw hardly a trace of it—either by U.S. or by Russian standards. When I told the Chinese that we utilized less than five percent of our population to grow our food they could not believe it. China still used about 80 percent of hers—and she needed more, not less.

In the countryside, there was a notable absence of the coercive machinery of the Russians. Of course, I did not see more than a fraction of China, and not more than a handful of communes. But there did not appear to be the kind of police apparatus that the Russians employed, and the atmosphere of the countryside (like that of the cities) was notably relaxed and easy compared to Russia's.

It was obvious that the Chinese peasants had not been driven like stubborn cattle into the communes. They had been led in slowly and easily and, if not all had welcomed them, certainly the great majority had—enough so that the others went along.

In this, China seemed to me unique among Asian Communist countries. It was not like Mongolia, where the herdsmen, in so many areas, had been forced against their will to give up their traditional horse-and-sheep economy and go over to the hated grain agriculture, insisted on by the Russians. It was not like North Vietnam, where the slaughter by the poorest peasants of landlords and wealthy peasants, encouraged or directed by the party in the 1950's, had left such deep and aching wounds. Nor was it like North Korea, with its incessant exhortation and omnipresent police apparatus.

I came away from Liu Ling with no feeling that I had visited the Future—the Future either of Asian agriculture or of world agriculture. Indeed, I did not believe that any Chinese would say that the Chinese countryside represented the future. Rather, it represented the Chinese past—the traditional methods of Chinese farming, excellently and efficiently carried out by traditional Chinese peasant families, living, if not luxuriously, still healthily and in comfort, so far as food and shelter were concerned, getting larger yields from their land not by any remarkable new technology but by more efficient application of the old—plus water (from irrigation), plus better seeds (from central experimental depots), plus better fertilization (provided or encouraged) by the central government.

What Chairman Mao had so brilliantly accomplished in the Chinese countryside was to make traditional China work; to end the terrible catastrophes of the old China—the epidemics, the floods, the droughts, the famines. Even in this summer of 1972, north and northwest China was experiencing the worst drought in 50 years. The countryside was turning sere and brown before our very eyes. There had been no appreciable moisture since the heavy snowfall on the day President Nixon visited the Imperial City in February, 1972. And none was expected before the August rainy season. Yet, because of irrigation, because of careful plowing, because of excellent application of traditional Chinese farming methods, the overall loss of crops was minimized. True, the second crop would not be as large as normal. But irrigation and water conservancy saved most of the first.

This, then, was the genius of the Chinese Revolution in the countryside, so far as I could observe it. It left unanswered questions for the future. Chinese agriculture on such traditional terms could be carried out only with enormous labor reserves. China needed every hand of the farm-working 80 percent of her population to plow, to plant, to harvest. And at critical times, not only must all school children, all university students and much of the normal city apparatus, and even factory workers, be diverted on a crash basis to the fields, but also most of her armed forces—and still there weren't hands enough.

What would happen when industrialization of agriculture began? When the tractors began to replace the millions of horses and the tens of millions of bent-backed peasants? This would be the great crisis, the crisis of the second transformation of the countryside. It was still, in all probability, 10 or 20 years distant. It could be carried out only with enormous increases in the volume of farm machinery, of fertilizers, of electric power. But when it came, China's greatest technological revolution would be at hand—the shift of her manpower base from country to city. That would involve the transportation not of tens of millions, but of hundreds of millions, of persons. That would be the greatest transmigration of human beings the world had ever seen. That, to be sure, would be the most striking test of the Chinese Revolution. And it would inexorably occur before the end of this century.

I looked back at Liu Ling as our car moved slowly away from the administration compound. Feng Chang-yeh and two of his co-workers stood at the gate, not waving, silently bidding the foreign visitors goodbye. There was something very competent, very down-to-earth about them. The transition would, to be sure, be a wrench. But somehow I thought the Feng Chang-yehs of China would manage to carry it off. If anyone could—they could do it.

8

Big Red Steeltown

I was reminded of Gary, Indiana, as I drove into the suburbs of sprawling Wuhan to visit the Iron & Steel Company of Wuhan. "Big Red Steeltown" was what the Chinese called it. It was different, of course, from driving south through Chicago, through the Black Belt, past the University of Chicago, on into South Chicago, the Republic Steel mills and Gary. In Wuhan we did not pass miles of Schlitz signs, street after street with the green half-curtains of South Chicago bars, the men leaning idly in the doorways and a few bored whores shifting their weight from foot to foot, waiting for a live one. Instead, we swung down a busy thoroughfare through the old Hankow shopping district, past stores and banks and offices, across a square and into Lu Wu—a wide street, half boulevard, half concourse—leading up to the bridge across the Han River, across a nub of Hanyang and then onto the mile-long new bridge over the Yangtze and down into Wuchang and out a long, long street that finally took us to the suburbs and Big Red Steeltown. It wasn't Gary, to be sure. But there were points enough of similarity.

Chinese Steeltown is big, and dominated by the stacks of the mills, the huge gray bulk of blooming mills, rolling mills, blast furnaces, coke ovens, slag heaps and open-hearth furnaces. The smoke from the plant billows high in the air, and at night, I could see the red glow of the furnaces from my hotel window miles away. This was the second largest steel complex in China, second only to the great Anshan No. 1 works in Shenyang (Mukden). But with a difference. Wuhan was built entirely under the Communist regime; Anshan was the product of years of foreign investment and Japanese operation.

When I talked to Sun Chen-hao, deputy plant director and member of the Revolutionary Committee, I got more echoes of Gary. Sun

Chen-hao was broad-shouldered, heavy-set and balding, with that air of strength and no-nonsense that seems to be tempered in the open-hearth process, whatever the country. Big Red Steeltown was *his* town, and *his* responsibility. It was not just a cluster of factories. It was an aggregate of 65,000 workers, 55,000 of them production workers. With their families, they made a community of more than 200,000 people. Big Red Steeltown had its own housing, its own water and sewerage system, its own transportation and its own police force. It was an integrated enterprise, controlling its own raw materials, mining its own iron ore and its coal, conveying them by its own transport network of trucks and rail lines. Workers got their housing, their gas, their water and their electricity from the Iron & Steel Company; Iron & Steel Company buses took them back and forth between apartment complexes and the industrial site. The Iron & Steel Company had its own network of company shops and service facilities. It maintained its own schools for workers' children, and its own farms for producing food. It was a completely self-contained community and enterprise existing on the periphery of Wuhan but, in many ways, independent of it.

The Iron & Steel Company went into production on September 13, 1959. Sun Chen-hao worked on the construction of the plant from the start, and his life—from the time he was discharged from the People's Liberation Army in 1954—had been devoted to steel.

Wuhan is one of the great cities of China—the fourth or fifth largest, with a population of 2.7 million. It is actually a consolidation of three cities—Hankow, Hanyang and Wuchang—and it had been the scene of a critical struggle in the Cultural Revolution, a struggle in which the Iron & Steel Company played its part.

For a time, Wuhan was controlled by the military commander for Hupei, Chen Tsai-tao, who opposed Chairman Mao's leadership. Wuhan followed its own independent course during the first months of 1967, and in July, a military insurrection broke out in which the Hupei army authorities held prisoner Hsieh Fu-chih, Mao's Minister of Security; and Wang Li, Mao's propaganda chief. They had been sent to the city to try to restore order. It was only after a strong show of military force by Mao's lieutenants that the situation was brought more or less under control.

The Iron & Steel Company was not unaffected by Wuhan's turbulence, which Sun Chen-hao, in words that might have been echoed by Andrew Carnegie or any 19th-century American steel baron, attributed to "extreme left-wing elements and anarchism." The fighting severely curtailed the Iron & Steel Company operations, although only one blast furnace was actually shut down completely. The others were banked, but the fires never went out, and no physical damage occurred. Production, however, was brought to a halt. The fighting in Big Red Steeltown, Sun Chen-hao insisted, was entirely with fists and sticks. No firearms were used.

Soon, however, level heads prevailed. Criticism of leftist tendencies got under way, opposition to Chairman Mao was repudiated, and production began to pick up. Total shutdown occurred for only a few brief periods. Once the worst was over and workers began to understand what had happened, production began to rise, and now, five years later, output was well ahead of all previous records. Morale had never been higher.

To Sun Chen-hao, the Cultural Revolution was only a more or less minor obstacle in the upward course of the Iron & Steel Company, and its ultimate effects, he seemed certain, had been quite positive.*

The Cultural Revolution was by no means to be compared, he made clear, to the blow dealt the Iron & Steel Company by the Russians—a blow that was staggering in impact and from which the enterprise was only now fully emerging. He made no attempt to conceal his bitterness over what he regarded as a deliberate attempt by the

---

* The Cultural Revolution in Wuhan was a much more serious matter than was indicated by the comments of Sun Chen-hao. There were repeated armed clashes in Wuhan from June 4 to July 30, 1967, in which more than 800 people were reported killed. The workers of the Iron & Steel Company of Wuhan were heavily involved, particularly in an organization called the Million Heroes, which was opposed to the Peking Red Guards, and which had the support of Wuhan Military Commander Chen Tsai-tao, who employed the 8201 Division to back them. Chen Tsai-tao for some time opposed Peking's instructions, and when Hsieh Fu-chih, Minister of Security, and Wang Li of the Central Cultural Revolution Committee (who was ultimately purged as a member of the May 16th Group) came to Wuhan to put down the trouble, they were kidnapped, and Wang Li was injured. Premier Chou En-lai then flew to Wuhan to try to settle the trouble. He landed at an outlying airport when he found the Wuhan airport surrounded by the Million Heroes. He feared that he, too, might be detained. At the height of the trouble, the 8119 Division of the PLA, ten gunboats and a number of air force units were concentrated in Wuhan. The Million Heroes seized the Yangtze bridge, halting all traffic, and PLA planes flew over the city, dropping leaflets. In the end, a compromise was worked out that left many of the anti-Red Guard officials still in charge. Perhaps not all the trouble in Wuhan had been ironed out by 1972. In any event, I found a markedly different spirit among Wuhan officials from that in other Chinese cities. They were uncooperative in carrying out projects that had been suggested in Peking and the only sharp argument I had with any officials in China occurred here.

Soviets to sabotage—or even destroy—one of the greatest industrial complexes being built in China.

He had described to me the scope of the Iron & Steel Company—the six mines, four for iron ore, two for coal; the four blast furnaces; the seven open-hearth mills; the coking plant; the sinter-crushing works; the 1150-mm rolling mill; the blooming mill; the heavy-steel rolling mill; the steel-plate mill; the chemical and construction materials subsidiaries; and the visit of Chairman Mao to inspect the first blast furnace, which went into operation on September 13, 1959. We were about to tour the mills themselves when I asked whether the Soviet Union had played any role in building the vast enterprise.

"If you are interested in that," he said, "I will be glad to tell you of our experience, after we have had a look at the plant. First, let us hurry to the mill, because they will be tapping one of the furnaces at 4:30 and I'd like you to see the steel as it pours out."

After a quick look at the fiery river of molten metal, we went back to Sun Chen-hao's reception room, and I heard the story of the Russian experience. His words tumbled out one after the other in a surge of anger and bitterness.

"As you know," he started, "China was a poor country after liberation and we had to launch ourselves into industrial production. We got help from the Soviet people and from Comrade Stalin at that time."

A bit later, the Russians agreed to give China major help in building an industrial base, and among the enterprises for which they promised assistance was a major iron and steel complex at Wuhan. The plant was actually designed, top to bottom, by the Leningrad Designing Institute. The Russians not only provided the blueprints, they sent specialists to assist in construction and production, and they contracted to provide virtually all the equipment needed.

Preliminary work got under way in 1956, and by 1958 all-out construction was in progress. Up to this point, there had been only the most trivial friction between the Russians and the Chinese. Almost all of the Soviet plans had been accepted without question, and the few changes were very minor. The Russians proposed that the open-hearth furnaces be housed in steel structures. The Chinese, acting in accordance with Chairman Mao's injunction to be frugal, favored a reinforced-concrete building. After discussion, a building that was 70 percent reinforced concrete was erected. The original Russian designs called for high walls around each plant. The Chinese could see no reason for the walls; furthermore, they would interfere with ventilation. "Perhaps in Russian conditions such things are needed," Sun Chen-hao said, "but here the walls were completely unnecessary." Finally, the Russians agreed to modify their plans. They proposed a pumping installation to draw water from the Yangtze, which the Chinese demonstrated was not suited to local conditions. So the design was modified.

These changes, Sun Chen-hao emphasized, were not the cause of serious difficulties. They were worked out amicably between the Russians and the Chinese. Most of the problems flowed from Russian ignorance of Chinese conditions. For example, he said, the original design called for a central canteen in the office building where we sat. There was to be a bakery to provide the Chinese workers with bread and buns. The Chinese pointed out that they didn't bake bread. They ate steamed bread and rice. So the plan was changed to provide several mess halls and no bakeries.

In other words, Sun Chen-hao emphasized, the work between the Russians and Chinese went along perfectly well. They grew fond of some of the Russian experts, and the feeling was reciprocated.

Then, like a bolt from the blue, one August day in 1960 the Russians ordered most of their specialists home. Ten days later the remainder were withdrawn.

Sun Chen-hao and his associates were stunned. They asked the Russians why they were leaving. "We don't know why," they responded. "Orders are orders." Some of them wept. But they packed their bags and vanished.

The worst was yet to come. With withdrawal of the specialists, the Russians ceased sending equipment for the mills. Construction was barely under way. The rolling mill was just being started. Hardly any equipment had arrived.

"Khrushchev fabricated a lot of rumors," said Sun Chen-hao. "He was trying to deceive the people of the world, as well as those of the Soviet Union. He claimed China didn't cooperate with the Russian specialists—so they were withdrawn. He said that the Chinese didn't follow the advice of the Russian specialists. But 93 percent of their suggestions were carried out, and only in a few cases did we not agree."

The Russians, he said, deliberately put the heaviest possible pressure on the Iron & Steel Company. They reneged on their promises and refused to supply equipment which they had contracted to supply. Sometimes they provided individual machines but would not deliver control mechanisms. Sometimes they provided the machines but only after delays of two or three or even more years. Some of the machinery never was delivered.

This was a blow that China could not quickly overcome. It meant that, with plants and machines half completed, they had to finish the job on their own. It set back the Iron & Steel Company about five years. Not until 1965 was the damage more or less overcome. Sun Chen-hao believed that the Russians, the "revisionists," had thought that China would never be able to complete the mill.

When the blow fell in 1960, only a single open-hearth furnace was in operation, and only two blast furnaces. The blooming mill was nearing completion.

"All the rest of the plant," Sun Chen-hao said, "was built in the course of the struggle against revisionists abroad (the Russians) and at home (the Liu Shao-chi group)."

It was not easy. The entire heavy-steel rolling mill was redesigned by Chinese engineers, and all of the equipment—every single machine—was produced in China. Much of this task fell to the Anshan works in Shenyang. Many of the machines built for the Iron & Steel Company were the first of their kind ever made in China.

There were other problems. The Soviet plan for the mill was not bad, but it was dominated by the concept that "China is a blank and poor country." The Chinese engineers found that much of the equipment and many of the processes provided by the Russian plan were not the most modern.

"Much of the equipment from Russia which we bought and ultimately installed was, we discovered, relatively backward," Sun Chen-hao said. "For example, in the sinter plant, they gave us machines which they had experimented with and had found not very satisfactory."

The machinery produced extraordinary amounts of dust, and was so dangerous to the health of the workers that the Chinese finally abandoned the Russian equipment and made their own. Some of the measuring devices for the blooming mill proved defective. Some of the automatic controls did not work. All of these were replaced with Chinese machines, often originated by the workers themselves.

One handicap that the Iron & Steel Company was not able to overcome was the siting of the plants. They were not well placed for continuous processing, and the basic location, so far as shipment of raw materials was concerned, could have been better.

But, difficult as the experience was, Sun Chen-hao regarded it as a positive one.

"We were confronted by pressures," he said. "But we did not bow to them. We did all we could to create our own equipment and gradually we managed to turn the Iron & Steel Company into a complex enterprise. We showed that our workers could be ingenious and capable of solving the most difficult problems."

Now, he said proudly, not only did the Iron & Steel Company turn out steel for China, "but also for the revolution of the world"—steel for the Tanzania railroad, steel for North Vietnam and steel for Albania. Steel went to other markets, as well, "but these countries supported us first and it is our duty to help them."

As for the Russians, Sun Chen-hao was grateful: "They are our best teachers. They taught us to do things with our own hands."

For the future, he saw no technical problems that China could not resolve by its own efforts, if necessary. To be sure China would like to learn the best from every country. But if any nation sought to put pressure on China as Russia had, it would fail.

He had unlimited enthusiasm for the work force of the Iron & Steel Company. Their average age was well below 30. One third were in the 18–20 age group, just out of middle school. All had completed middle school, and most had a year or two in the countryside, working on the farms, before coming to the steel company.

The wage level of the plant was very low because of the large number of young men and women working as apprentices. They received 22 yuan per month the first year, 24 the second and 26 the third. Then they went on the regular payroll at 37½ yuan. This meant that the average wage at the Wuhan plant was somewhat below 60 yuan a month (about $26.50). The highest pay of any worker was 108 yuan a month, but engineers drew from 150 to 230. The boss, chairman of the Revolutionary Committee, got 180, and Sun Chen-hao earned 150.

Sun Chen-hao was a married man, and his wife worked in the office of the company. Thousands of husbands and wives were employed together in the plant—in fact, this was more common than not. The Suns had three children. The oldest boy, at 26, worked in a light-machinery plant, having graduated from the light-industry institute in Wuhan. The second boy was 20 and a soldier in the PLA. The girl was 18, and she had gone to the countryside after graduating from middle school. She worked for two years with the peasants before returning to become an apprentice electrician in the repair department of the company's metallurgical plant.

Sun Chen-hao wore a small enamel emblem on the left breast

of his gray shirt. It bore a cameo of Chairman Mao and a slogan in Chinese that read: "Serve the People." This was the motto most often worn by Chinese officials and managers. The words were a quotation from the Chairman.

As Sun looked back on the struggle to create the Iron & Steel Company, he felt that the worst was behind them. He had a confidence that he had not had in the beginning, and it was born of the difficulties that had to be overcome in getting the plant going and surmounting the great crisis imposed by the Russians. The workers had been tempered by what they had been through—both the struggle to create the plant and the struggle of the Cultural Revolution. He felt that they shared the confidence that he had come to feel.

I don't know whether Sun Chen-hao was a typical Chinese industrial manager or not. I visited nine or ten industrial enterprises during my stay in China. Some were heavy industries, like the Wuhan plant and the Heavy Generator Factory of Peking. Some were light industries, like the No. 1 Transistor Equipment Factory of western Peking or the No. 3 Cotton Textile Plant of Peking.

But whether in heavy or in light industrial establishments, I was impressed by the same characteristics. The executives seemed relaxed, easy in their relationship with a foreign visitor like myself, and equally easy in their exchanges with workers on the floor. The contrast between the atmosphere of the Chinese factories and that of most of the Soviet factories I had visited was dramatic. In 25 years of Russian experience, I had probably seen 200 or more plants from Moscow to Khabarovsk. I had seen steel mills, power plants, coal mines, aluminum plants, wood fabricating industries, cement works, electrical equipment complexes, textile combines—I could hardly imagine a Soviet industry that I had not, at one time or another, inspected. I knew Soviet visiting procedures from the outside and the inside. I had seen how carefully swept and cleaned their factories always were, how well dressed the workers appeared, how efficiently the machines performed. I had listened to the director spiel off his accomplishments: The plant had just set new production records. It had overfulfilled the plan by 15 percent. The workers' enthusiasm had reached new heights. Their technical innovations could not be equaled. It was the kind of booster's talk that you used to get from the chamber of commerce of a not-too-flourishing midwestern industrial town. Everything rosy, no dark spots.

And when the questioning began, the director would always be edgy and guarded, afraid that he might somehow let the cat out of the bag and say something that did not fit the perfect picture he had just painted. As he escorted me through the shop I could watch his eye quickly roving over the machines. Thank god they were all working! *Slava boga!* The production workers all had on their clean dungarees. When he paused at a machine I knew that this had been well rehearsed in advance. It was always a pretty, slightly flustered girl mechanic, who quickly went into her patter. Or a veteran worker, his hands horny with toil and honest grease (but his face soap-scrubbed and fresh and his overalls package-new). If I should lag behind a minute and show special interest in a worker or a machine just a little distance off the carefully prepared route-of-march there was visible nervousness—what was the foreigner up to? What had he spotted that was wrong?

In Soviet plants, the atmosphere was always guarded, always defensive, always fearful that some stray word, some sudden question, some glance into an unexpected nook might give the secret of the whole sham away.

Not that the factories were shams. They were perfectly good and quite efficient on the whole. But what went on when the visitor came was a carefully prepared charade. I had gotten to know quite a few Russians over the years and sometimes they laughed shamefacedly over the rigmarole they had to go through when a foreign visitor was expected. Such a hectic time of washing up, of getting new potted plants for the director's office and the employees' lunchroom; new posters and slogans put up on the walls and the old ones carefully scrutinized for any negative comments. The plant and the offices had to be cleaned and swept and sometimes painted. The route of the visit was carefully worked out so that no obsolete or dismal shops beyond cosmetic treatment would be seen. The workers were briefed on what to say (and, more important, what not to say) and those who were to be interviewed carefully rehearsed their lines. The others were sternly warned against talking to the foreigner (usually an unnecessary precaution since he probably did not know Russian). Those who spoke English or French or German were told that it would be a very serious matter if the foreigner should speak to them in one of those languages and they were caught engaging him in conversation.

The Russian visit was always a tense one. The visitor could not help but sense the cross currents of apprehension. If his eye was quick, he not infrequently caught a glimpse of the shop stewards hurriedly running ahead to warn more distant colleagues that the cavalcade was on its way.

In essence, the principles of the visit to the Russian factory had been laid down 200 years ago by Count Potemkin, who used to stage-manage Catherine the Great's visits to the countryside. The visits were preceded by months of preparation so the sovereign would see nothing but progress and good living throughout the land. In the case of one notable tour of Catherine to the Ukraine, Potemkin built whole villages so the queen could see how happy, how prosperous, how contended were her subjects.

I got none of this feeling from the Chinese. They offered a diametrically opposite approach. From the beginning, the plant manager spoke modestly. He outlined the history of his enterprise, sketched its physical scope, listed its employees and products, and then, frankly, began to talk about its defects. The production line was not arranged as well as it might be. The noise in the loom room was too high and had a bad effect on the workers, and they had not yet found a solution to this. The reclamation of scrap material was inefficient. The workers' sanitary facilities left much to be desired. Some of the machines gave them a great deal of trouble and often broke down. They had improved output, but not nearly as much as they should.

Then, with beguiling modesty, the manager would turn to the visitor and say: "Please give us any suggestions you have for improving our work. We know that we are not nearly as up-to-date as we should be. We appreciate your help."

This was not, as I first supposed, mere courtesy—a graceful gesture to the visiting foreigner. The Chinese really meant it. When you had gone through the plant, the first thing they wanted was not compliments but criticism. They wanted to know what was wrong and how it could be done better, and if you had no ideas to propose, they felt let down. On the other hand, if you suggested that the girls handling a sticky tar solvent should wear rubber gloves to protect their hands, they immediately responded. "Of course," they said. "That is a very good idea." If you proposed that they should use soundproofing and acoustic tile in the loom room to reduce the clatter, they said very seriously: "Yes, we are thinking of that. But we believe it would be even better if we can devise a machine that doesn't make so much noise."

Along with this went an ease and relaxation not only of the managers but of the workers. The plants had *not* been specially swept for the foreign guest. That was obvious as you walked down the corridors. They were not disorderly, but the normal working clutter was there. The machines did *not* all work. Quite a few were idle, and the manager made no attempt to divert attention from them. Here and there, a group of mechanics would be laboring over a press or a drill trying to get it back into working order. When I stopped to watch, everyone looked up grinning. The workers had not rushed home to put on new outfits (if, indeed, they had them). They were wearing the ordinary work clothes you would expect to see on factory workers anywhere. Some had dirty faces, and some had dirty hands. It embarrassed neither them nor the plant executives. Nor was there any other sign of tension in the plant. Before the workers in Sun Chen-hao's blast furnace tapped the molten steel, they lazed around, casually drawing on their protective clothing. They stared curiously at the visitors and then went back to their own animated gossip. Walking through the Heavy Generator Factory at mid-morning, we saw clusters of workers here and there, sitting near their idle machines, drinking tea and talking. They cast a casual glance over at the visitor and his escorts and then went back to their talk. No one had run through the plant in advance, warning them to get to their machines lest the foreigner get a bad impression of Chinese efficiency.

The Chinese position was that their factories were *not* as efficient as they would like them to be, or hoped they would be. But they thought that this was normal at the present stage of Chinese development, and that, as time went on, efficiency would improve. They did not conceal the fact that their factories were enormously over-staffed, that the payrolls of every enterprise were at least four times as big as in the equivalent American factory (and probably twice as large as in a Soviet plant). Wage scales were low. The range of pay in the Iron & Steel Company of Wuhan was not an exception. The average pay in the Heavy Generator Factory was 50 yuan a month. The director got 140 to 150, and some workers made as much as 80 or 100 yuan. In the textile plant, the pay ranged from 40 yuan to about 80 yuan, although some engineers earned as much as 180. The country as a whole had a uniform wage scale, industrial workers were classified in eight grades, with pay gradually increasing on a basis of tenure and skill. But it was obvious that egalitarian principles were rigorously applied, and the wage spread between the lowliest worker and the highest-paid specialist or executive was never more than five or six to one, and normally, not more than 50 percent.

There was an intense feeling of communality in the plants. Families worked together and lived together. They lived in factory housing and engaged in the same kind of activities. They knew each other intimately.

In this, the Iron & Steel Company of Wuhan was certainly typical. It was not only a great industrial enterprise; it was a community. When Sun Chen-hao rode back from the plant to his flat in Big Red Steeltown, he passed the queues of people at the large shopping center. He looked down long lanes of tree-shaded streets. The shops were built and run by the company. The streets were paved, and the shade trees and parks were provided by the company. The red buses that moved along the streets were run by company drivers, and the bicycles the workers rode on were bought in company stores. Big Red Steeltown was, in the purest sense, a company town.

But there was, of course, a difference between Big Red Steeltown and Steeltown, U.S.A. Here, as Sun Chen-hao said: "Everybody should be a servant of the people." By this, he meant not only himself but the whole working force of the enterprise. They served not themselves but all the people of China. That was what the company was all about, and, if Sun Chen-hao was to be believed, it was not doing too badly. The plant had just opened up its No. 4 blast furnace—built and constructed since the Cultural Revolution, with the help of more than 200 other factories in Honan and Hupei—all pooling their efforts—and the building would go on. The Iron & Steel Company was not complete. Perhaps, it never would be. There were plans for great new complexes of machine tool and machinery works, expansion of the chemical plant, and many other things. In fact, there was no real limit to the kind of enterprises the Iron & Steel Company would be getting into.

"The Russians were good teachers," Sun Chen-hao repeated with a smile as he waved me goodbye, "and we are good pupils."

9

Life in Wuhan

I was walking down one of the broad streets of Wuhan that led out of the old British concession into what used to be called "the Chinese city." It was a hot day in June, the street was busy with traffic—trucks, buses and occasional automobiles. The shop shutters had been raised, and people filled the sidewalk.

"What is the principal difference," I asked a Chinese friend, "between this street in Wuhan today, and this street before the Revolution?"

He thought a moment and answered: "The flies. You can't imagine what it was like to walk down the street of a Chinese city in the old days. You could hear a humming in the air, strong, like the sound of violins in an orchestra. It was the flies. If you looked down you could hardly see the pavement for the flies. They seemed to form a solid moving mass, up to your knees."

I asked an American who had been in China before the Revolution what the principal difference he noticed today was. "The smell," he said. "You can't imagine the variety of smells in the old Chinese city. All bad. They were so intermingled you could not make out the individual components. But they all went together to make up the Chinese-city smell."

Another friend said that the thing he noticed most was the absence of beggars. Not just mendicants in ragged clothing, but the horrible cripples and mutilated persons, the men without noses, the children with gouged-out eyes, the women with pus running from their dragging breasts, the mothers who thrust their babies at you—babies with watery-blind eyes and open sores at the mouth, the stumps of men who lay propped up along the pavement—waiting for alms, or waiting for death.

And, said my friend, there was that other sight of old China—the coolie who fell in his traces. Perhaps he was pulling a heavy load. Perhaps he was just standing waiting for work. Who ever knew why the coolie collapsed? He lay on the pavement in the hot sun, his ribs like the staves of a barrel, his chest hardly moving, his mouth open and gasping, his face a crater of bones. The crowd passed on, walking around him, no one stopping, no one even looking, perhaps a policeman, his head in a sun helmet, would happen along and poke the body with his long stick. If there was a sign of movement, he would poke again, jabbing and flailing, to make the man rise to his feet. If the man was unconscious, or dead, the policeman shrugged his shoulders and moved along. Finally a refuse cart would come, and the body would be hurled in among the dung and the ashes.

That was the China city as remembered from the days before the Revolution. I looked again at Wuhan—the constant flow of traffic, the air—not clean, but clear. But the pollutants were not flies, germs or human excrement. They were the exhaust fumes of cheap gasoline, the smell of coal-burning stoves and, occasionally, the whiff of industrial gases from the vast factories across the Yangtze River. There were no beggars. There were no mutilated children. The policemen stood at their posts, directing traffic. They carried not long nightsticks but small revolvers on their hips. Coolies still hauled carts, but, thin and wiry as they were, none collapsed, none looked ill-fed or diseased.

It was clear that the problems of Wuhan were not the problems of Old China. But what might they be? Drugs? From all I had heard and seen, I doubted that Wuhan suffered from a drug problem. Traffic congestion? There was some congestion, true. But nothing an American city would have called by that name. There were accidents. I had seen three accidents in Peking—each caused by bicycles. Two of them were bicycle collisions, the third, the crash of a bicycle and a truck. In fact, I had seen two street fights between bicycle riders who collided, leaped from their vehicles and flailed away with bare fists, while a crowd gathered, and eventually intervened and sent the belligerents on their way. What else? I rummaged through my mind for the problems of the average American city—garbage disposal? It didn't seem likely. Street litter? The streets were neat as pins, and so were the sidewalks, the public parks and every open space I saw. Slums and slumlords? Well, there might be slums, but I knew that slumlords had been done away with long since. There might, to be sure, be budgetary problems—that bane of American cities. I did not know how the Chinese cities were financed, and this might be one point of parallel between cities of the United States and those of the People's Republic of China.

On the morning of my last day in Wuhan, I sat down with nine specialists from the Wuhan city government at a round-table session to try and get the answers to those questions. There were two members of the Municipal Health Bureau; two from the Commerce Bureau, which handled every kind of retail trade and service in the city; three from the planning and housing bureau; and two from the Iron & Steel Company of Wuhan, members of a special research unit, concerned with questions of pollution.

Pollution was one problem I *knew* Wuhan had in common with the west. I knew from looking at the skyline the afternoon before from the deck of a cabin cruiser on West Lake, one of the beautiful Imperial lakes of China, that Wuhan's pollution was at least as bad as that of any American industrial city. There on the skyline rose the stacks of the Iron & Steel Company and other Wuhan industrial enterprises, and from them towered plumes of purple-black, brownish-red, and carmine-yellow smoke that festered in the sky for miles and miles. In my hotel room, I had noted tell-tale deposits of soot on window ledges in the morning. Whatever else Wuhan might have solved, it was apparent that it was not pollution.

That the Wuhan officials were ready to concede, although like other Chinese officials in other cities, they did not really seem to perceive pollution to be the menace that we Americans did. There was in their attitude an echo of that sentiment so often found in American paper-making towns, where residents, commenting on the sulphite stench, respond brightly, "That's the smell of *money*." Or, like the residents of Pittsburgh or Cleveland in the early 1900's who engraved on their business letterheads and memorialized on their postcards dramatic clouds of black smoke billowing from their proud new mills, they equated smoke with progress

But, pollution aside, it was apparent that the difference between the Chinese municipal problems of today and those before the Revolution was profound. Tan Tai-chieh, head of the Municipal Health Bureau, called Wuhan before 1949 a city of chronic epidemics—cholera, smallpox, measles, diphtheria, typhoid and typhus. Infant mortality was 200 per 1,000 live births, and the tuberculosis rate ran about six percent.

Each of the foreign concessions—the British, the French, the Japanese and the German—had its own inadequate sewer system, which pumped raw sewage into the Yangtze. There were no sewers for the Chinese city, just open ditches beside the principal streets. "In summer the city stank to high heaven," said Kuan Chih-fan of the City Planning Bureau.

That was the first problem tackled after the Communists came into control, and, by 1953 cholera and small pox had been wiped out, largely through mass inoculation. A "patriotic-sanitation" movement was launched, and a four-pests movement (against flies, mosquitoes, rats and mice). The incidence of typhoid and dysentery dropped radically. Formerly the leading causes of death in Wuhan were cholera and small pox. The city had its last cholera case in 1951, and there had been only one case of diphtheria in 1971. The rate has been brought down to two percent, and infant mortality, Tan said, was now only four percent.

I felt that he was not as precise as he should have been on infant mortality. He said that it varied from district to district, and that, in some areas, particularly on the outskirts of the city, it was considerably higher than four percent. But he had no supporting figures. I concluded that infant mortality was much lower than it had been in 1949, but perhaps not quite as low as he would wish. (A comparable U.S. figure, incidentally, is 21.8 per 1,000, or about two percent—for white male infants under the age of one, as of 1968.)

He put the overall death rate in the city at six per 1,000, but what it had been before the Communists came into power no one could precisely calculate.

Venereal disease had simply vanished with the abolition of prostitution. There was no syphilis and no gonorrhea, and as for the new sulfa-resistant strain of gonorrhea it had not even been heard of.

Not that Wuhan was without health problems. There was still some infantile paralysis, although all children got oral vaccine in the form of sugar-coated pills, distributed through the schools or at neighborhood clinics. There had been several dozen cases of infantile paralysis in 1971 and, despite a similar oral-vaccine program for measles, there were considerably more cases of measles. Most of these occurred in children coming into Wuhan from rural areas where vaccine programs had not yet been instituted.

Tan was worried about encephalitis type-B and hepatitis. There was no effective remedy for either disease, both of which were not uncommon, and although they had been testing Chinese traditional herbal remedies, they had not come up with anything helpful.

They were still working on the problem of mosquito control. DDT had been used extensively, but malaria had not yet been eliminated entirely.

There were other problems—a distinct shortage of hospital beds

—only 13,600 for the city. Tan said this figure provided 4.5 beds per 1,000 residents. But I calculated that if these beds were designed to serve the whole city of 2.7 million the true ratio was only about one-third of his figure. There was not likely to be much improvement in the foreseeable future, since the city budget called for the addition of only 1,000 beds to make up for 1,000 that had been transferred to the countryside.

But the most awesome problem of pre-Liberation—the disposal of sewage—had been resolved, just as it appeared to have been in every other Chinese city I visited. Not only had sewage been eliminated as a source of disease, but in contrast to American practice, it had been put to beneficial use. China, of course, had an historical tradition of using human excrement as a fertilizer. Now, however, the whole process had been sanitized and placed on a scientific basis. The sewage was pumped into fermentation pools and permitted to ferment until it lost any disease-carrying properties. Then it was pumped to the suburbs and introduced into the irrigation system to provide fertilizer for the crops. Human waste from outdoor toilets was collected by the traditional honeycarts and by honey-barges on the Yangtze and deposited into the fermentation pools for transformation into organic fertilizer. Organic garbage from the city was treated in much the same way.

But the problem of industrial wastes was not resolved. Industrial wastes still poured into the Yangtze, particularly from a very large paper mill and from the coke plant of the Iron & Steel Company, which discharged quantities of phenol into the river.

Nor had even a start been made on air pollution. The city had no inspection service, exercised no powers over industrial polluters and, it seemed to me, Tan had never even thought of such an approach until I raised the question.

On the other hand, Wang Hsiu-hui of the Iron & Steel Company's research department had given it some thought, but action was another thing.

"You can see all that smoke still coming from our chimneys," he said with an engaging smile. "The business of our organization is to develop the multiple utilization of waste gas, water and materials. We want to turn harmful things into useful ones, and use all the waste materials we can."

He admitted that not only did smoke pour from the chimneys, but old and inefficient machines in the plants often discharged pollutants within the factories as well as into the city's atmosphere. He singled out the Iron & Steel Company's sinter plant as a particularly bad example.

It was quickly apparent that the main thrust of his work had been to utilize waste products of the manufacturing process and, to some extent, to try to conserve the phenol that was now flowing into the Yangtze. A phenol-evaporation machine had been tried, but it was very inefficient.

As for the sulphur chemicals coming from his stacks, he smiled wryly and admitted there had been no work at all on this. They were hoping to get a lower-sulphur-content coal or possibly to develop a desulphurization process at the minehead.

What, I wondered, had been the effect of massive use of DDT and other insecticides—was there any awareness of the dangerous side effects? Tan shook his head. They were just beginning to work in this area. They were not very well versed in possible side effects of DDT. True, they knew that some insecticides were poisonous, and they knew that some pests had developed resistance to the chemicals. Because of this they were beginning—but just beginning—to try to develop biological methods of insect control.

Actually, as Fan Hsiao-pao of the Commerce Bureau pointed out, they had been brought to a recognition of the poisonous qualities of insecticides by an unfortunate experience. Fan, a bulky, craggy-faced, outgoing man, was in charge of Wuhan's retail trade. Several years ago there had been a serious outbreak of poisoning in the city that was traced to chemical residues on fruits and vegetables. He personally instituted a regulation that no produce was to be sprayed within 20 days of the time it was to be brought to the city for marketing. He had also been working with his produce suppliers—communes near Wuhan—to urge them to develop biological means that would not expose the consumer to possible hazard.

"I'm in a curious position," he laughed. "I distribute both DDT and vegetables."

The fact was that he ran all of the city's food services, including restaurants, and all of the city's retail outlets, except those that sold grain and clothing. He was in charge of all hotels, baths, barbershops, department stores, clothing factories, laundries, cleaning establishments and purveyors of household utensils.

"I sell everything but machine tools," he added. "I sell farm implements, pesticides and fertilizers."

And he had problems—problems of complaints from customers,

particularly those who found services for repairing clothing, patching shoes and renting tools inadequate. He was constantly looking for new and better ways to help his customers. He kept his stores open around-the-clock near big industrial plants where workers often were on a three-shift basis, and he had opened special 24-hour shops near railroad stations so peasants and others coming to the city could always be served.

But his customers complained that they had to stand in line and wait too long and also that the supply of some items was not equal to demand. They complained about the attitude of the clerks—either they were rude and quarrelsome, or they did not make an effort to satisfy the customer.

This, he acknowledged, was wrong. The whole purpose of the retail system was not to make money. It was to serve the workers, peasants and soldiers.

But the problem of supply was a serious one. It was an old saying in Wuhan that as soon as snowflakes were to be seen in the air, the prices of vegetables soared. He had tried to encourage the communes around the city to expand their production so that there would be enough food for all without radical rises in prices. And he had increased storage capacity so that the supply of goods could be regulated. He tried to hold prices down. Part of this was accomplished through a state subsidy to the peasants so that they were not dependent entirely on the purchase price of their foodstuffs.

"Every year," he said, "Wuhan city has to spend a few million yuan to subsidize the peasants in their production of vegetables."

One of his biggest problems was short supply of certain consumer items that were in great demand. For instance, he could not get enough TV sets. These sets sold for 300 yuan and up. He got about 2,000 a year. Another critical item was watches. He received 40,000 a year, to sell at prices ranging from 40 yuan for a cheap variety to 90 to 120 yuan for better-quality watches. He got 40,000 to 50,000 bicycles a year, selling at 130 to 190 yuan. That was enough to meet demand. But his supply of sewing machines was short.

One reason why Fan had such difficulty in keeping sufficient stocks of consumer goods on hand was the heavy influx of peasants who came to buy goods not available in the villages. The impact of their buying power depleted his stocks. The peasants did not earn large sums of cash; the average income per peasant was well under 100 yuan (about $44) a year. But with their large families, this might total 500 or 600 yuan, and it could be supplemented by cash sales of produce. The purchasing power seemed miniscule by American standards, but when matched against small supplies of consumer goods (2,000 TV sets, 40,000 watches, 40,000 to 50,000 bicycles per year in a city of 2.7 million population) it had a very powerful influence. Hupei is a province of 33 million population. Of course, only a small fraction of these people came to Wuhan to make their purchases. But even at the rate of 10,000 to 20,000 a day over the year, the numbers run to staggering totals.

The problem of maintaining a supply of goods that would meet ever-rising demands was one of the most serious facing the officials of Wuhan.

I could not but be curious as to how Wuhan confronted problems of this kind—what kind of forward planning was done. After all, it was a community of 2.7 million people and it had grown at an extraordinary pace—more than tripling in size since 1949, when it numbered 970,000 population. How had the city managed to cope with such an influx?

"Is there advanced planning?" I asked.

The reply came from Kuan Chih-fan, director of the planning-housing bureau—a title that indicated that planning and housing in Wuhan were almost synonymous. Wuhan's plans were part of the country's fourth five-year plan, which was in its second year. The city now had 35.6 million square meters of building space, of which 14.2 million square meters were designated for housing. There had been a 214 percent increase in housing since 1949, when the total was 6.7 million square meters.

That is to say, while the city's population was tripling, its housing was doubling. It did not take much arithmetic to demonstrate that this had to be the most critical problem in the urban area.

"We still do not meet the people's requirements," Kuan said very meekly. Nor did there appear to be an indication that the city was going to be able to overcome the huge deficit. The building program was limited by the funds available under the government's overall plan, and for the remainder of the current five-year cycle, that is, until 1976, not more than 450,000 square meters per year would be built within the city proper.

I asked whether this would keep Wuhan level with the normal population increase. The plan, said the city officials, called for no increase in population.

"But you have tripled your population in a little more than 20 years," I observed. "How is it possible to bring this growth to a sudden halt?"

The answer was not very satisfying. In effect, what the officials said was that it was national policy to stabilize the population at its present level or at an only slightly higher one. The plan did not call for further expansion of Wuhan. Instead, it called for the creation of satellite cities outside of Wuhan. Already a number of small cities were springing up outside the larger city and its suburban limits.

Did this mean, then, that Wuhan's great industries were not going to expand any further? What about the Iron & Steel Company? I knew that it projected substantial expansion and growth. Was this not true of the remainder of Wuhan's industries?

The officials nodded their heads in agreement. It was true that the Iron & Steel Company was continuing to grow, but perhaps not quite as fast as previously. It was true, of course, that the growth of the industries would require more workers, and this would mean more facilities. Already the task of providing housing was being divided between the city and the industries, with the city providing about one-third of the apartments and the factories building the remainder.

I asked what was being done to provide the city with more electricity. No one had any figures on that. It was handled by another department.

I turned to a question that had already troubled me—the question of hospital facilities. The figures provided by Tan indicated that these facilities were less than adequate at the present level. What was being done about increasing them to meet future needs? It turned out that about 80,000 square meters of construction per year was programmed, not even enough to overcome the present deficit.

What was being budgeted for sports facilities and theaters? I asked. Nothing, it seemed. Last year the opera house had been rebuilt, but no other entertainment or recreational facilities were currently planned.

There may have been a number of reasons for the small construction program, but the principal one was the limited state funds available for these purposes. The city did not have funds of its own for capital construction. Where the state made the money available, construction went ahead very rapidly, as in the case of the Wuhan sewer system. Before 1949 the total of sewers in the city was 36 kilometers. By 1953 the new unified system for Wuhan was completed with state funds—560.6 kilometers of integrated pipes, plus 44 pumping stations and four large-scale treatment plants. Moreover, two large drainage systems had been built in the suburbs to eliminate marshes and areas subject to schistosomiasis. There had been 400,000 *mu* of such areas before Liberation. Now only 20,000 *mu* were left.

All this had been accomplished because the state had incorporated the projects in the state plan and had advanced the needed capital funds.

The picture of Wuhan now seemed fairly clear to me. The city had accomplished miracles in transforming the life of its people—in eliminating disease, malnutrition, poverty and illiteracy, and in providing a clean place to live that was fairly well stocked with consumer goods and minimally supplied with recreational facilities. It had built great industries and had provided some housing. It was not plagued with many of the problems that beset the over-abundant life and economy of American cities. It had turned its sewer situation from a harrowing danger to a remarkable asset. But—like American cities—Wuhan was faced with a critical problem so far as growth was concerned. I did not for a minute believe the uneasy assurances of the officials that, by some miracle, Wuhan would stop growing. It might slow down a bit. It was not likely to triple in size again in the next 20 years. But I had yet to see a Chinese city that was not growing rapidly. If all of Wuhan's industrial managers continued to project increases in capacity and output, Wuhan was bound to grow. And judging from the record, it did not seem that the city was handling this key dilemma with much more foresight than the typical American city. Nor did the reasons seem entirely alien. The American city was constantly bumping up against lack of capital—whether from local or federal or private sources—to build new housing at the rate at which the old deteriorated. Wuhan had the same problem. It did not control its own capital budget. It could—and undoubtedly would—make recommendations for increases in capital expenditures and hope that they might be included in the government's five-year plan. But if the funds were not advanced (and thus far the government was clearly falling far behind needs) the city was as powerless as New York City or Chicago to build the apartments needed to house the ever-increasing total of residents.

I don't know the name of the Mayor of Wuhan, and my request to meet him had been turned down. He was too busy, the officials said, to receive an American correspondent. I was sorry about that. I thought I could have told him a few things about John Lindsay's problems in New York that would have struck a not unfamiliar note.

10

Four Pretty Maidens of Sian

In all of China I don't believe I could have found four prettier girls than Chao Kuo-sen, 23, with soft black hair, delicate limbs, a quiet smile, a maroon silk blouse and a new wristwatch; Peng Hsiang-chun, 23, with a perfect almond-shaped face, deep brooding eyes, a supple figure and pale green blouse; Wang Li-ping, 24, a little fuller than the others, cheeks glowing red, speaking in a soft musical voice and wearing a red blouse; and Wang Li-chu, bright brown eyes, and looking more like an elfin of 11 than a mature 24.

We were sitting in the rehearsal hall of the Song and Dance Ensemble of Sian, after a concert, talking with the members of the company in which the girls were the leading dancers, the prima ballerinas, and I was asking about their lives. Each had joined the company as little girls, usually at the age of 11 or 12. All had liked dancing from the time they could skip about. They had danced with the other children in primary school, and then, because they were good at it and liked to dance, they had applied for admission to the Ensemble ballet school.

Black-haired Chao Kuo-sen joined the school in 1960. She had danced in school performances in Hopei province where her family lived, and, when they moved to Sian, she auditioned for the ballet. First, she had to pass an exam in Chinese literature, then she came to the company for a personal interview. She was asked what she liked to do, why she wanted to enter the school and how she had gotten interested in dancing. She had to pass a physical examination, an examination of her personal appearance and a test of her ability to dance and sing. After all this, she won admittance to the school. Tuition was free. She, like the other students, lived in a dormitory and visited her family only on weekends. She worked hard, but there was nothing she liked better, and now she had reached the top. She was a leading member of the company and danced in *The White-Haired Girl*, one of the most popular ballets. She danced the role of the White-Haired Girl in the opening episodes, while the Girl's hair was still black. Two other girls shared the role, one dancing the numbers in which the Girl's hair turned gray and the other in the last sequence, when her hair was white.

The story of the other three girls was almost identical with that of Chao Kuo-sen. Each had entered the school in 1959 or 1960. Each had loved dancing from the time she could toddle. Each came from a similar background. Peng's father was a worker in the Honan Opera Troupe of Sian. Wang Li-ping's parents were factory workers. Wang Li-chu's mother worked in a factory, and her father in the countryside. Wang Li-chu had a younger brother and three younger sisters, all of whom were interested in dancing and singing and who performed in an amateur group attached to their mother's factory.

Long before I had come to China, I had heard much of the new morality of China's youth—of the puritanism of Chinese society, the absence of prurience, the de-emphasis of sex, the purity of relations between China's young boys and young girls, the abolition of arranged marriages, the end of child marriage and the institution of late, very late, marriage. Scotty Reston had come to China a year earlier and reported that it was a "sink of morality," and I had seen enough of China to begin to echo that opinion. Certainly, there was little evidence that Chinese women sought deliberately to attract male attention. They dressed—with the rarest of exceptions—in rather baggy trousers and loose blouses that concealed their figures and caused their breasts to disappear so completely that I began to think Chinese female anatomy actually *was* different until I went to the ballet and found that the dancers had beautiful figures, just as lovely as any of their western sisters.

What, then, was the truth about China's youth? Had China changed that much? Certainly in China's past sex had played a spectacular role. The Chinese courtesan and the beautiful concubine were celebrated figures in all Chinese classics. Their role in China's history had often been dramatic, even in recent times.

Walking the streets of the Chinese cities, I had seen no sign that sex even existed. There were few illustrated posters—whether exhorting the people to do their best to plant rice or simply advertising a movie. None indulged in any bodily display. True, there were posters of handsome heroes and heroines of ballets like *The White-Haired Girl* or *The Red Detachment of Women* but the context in which they were shown—going forth to battle, struggling against oppressors, conquering deadly enemies—was not exactly like the movie posters in Times Square. Beautiful girls and handsome young men danced in the ballets, and sang in the operas, but even old-fashioned romance seemed far from their minds. There were no close-ups, no clinches, no warm and lingering embraces, no kisses. The high point of a boy-girl relationship was likely to be, as in *The White-Haired Girl*, the moment when the girl was presented with her own rifle by the boy.

This made it plain enough that, so far as the government was concerned, there was an official morality, a kind of Boy Scout-Girl Scout atmosphere that was encouraged and advanced by the party propagandists.

But how did it work out in the individual lives of Chinese boys and girls? How particularly did it work out in the lives of these four beautiful girls of the Sian ensemble? I asked Chao Kuo-sen whether or not she was married. No, she answered with a laugh. She was not married and she had no intention of marrying soon. She wanted to concentrate on being a dancer as long as she could. As a matter of fact, she said, she did not intend to marry until she was 34 or 35. At that age, she thought, she would probably be too old to dance. Then it was time enough to get married. What about boyfriends? I asked. Chao Kuo-sen blushed and turned around to look at a dark-haired young man in the orchestra who played one of the traditional Chinese instruments. Yes, she said, she had a boyfriend. He was the young man in the orchestra. So I asked Peng Hsiang-chun the same questions. She, too, did not intend to get married until after she was 30. She wanted to go on dancing, and later she wanted to become an instructor. Did she have a boyfriend? Yes, indeed. He was a dancer in *The White-Haired Girl*, taking the role of one of the wicked landlord's stooges. Wang Li-ping set 30 as the minimum marriage age. "At least not before 30," she said. "Maybe later." She also had a boyfriend, a musician in the orchestra. Wang Li-chu offered an identical pattern. Marriage at 30, a boyfriend in the dance ensemble who danced the role of a guerrilla scout in *The White-Haired Girl*.

So here were four beautiful girls, each insisting she would not marry until after 30, each with a boyfriend with whom she danced or worked. What did it mean? Did these young people actually keep their distance? Did they intend to have no warmer relations than an occasional handshake until they were 30? I did not have the courage to put the question bluntly, to ask outright what the basis of their "friendship" was—was it entirely platonic or did they follow the American example and sleep with each other before marriage? Each girl had blushed deeply when I asked about a boyfriend. Each was obviously embarrassed by the question. But the rest of the company did not seem to be. They nodded and giggled in a way that made plain that the attachments of the young couples were common knowledge and wholly accepted. I asked one other girl these same questions. She was Cheng Tsai-tsoi, a bit older, a former ballerina who was now a teacher. She was married—but she had not married until she had quit dancing. She was now 32, and she had a baby girl, two years old. She had, in fact, done exactly what the four younger girls had announced they intended to do—she had deferred marriage until her active dancing career was ended.

It was difficult to interpret the evidence of the four Sian maidens. But I had one other clue. I had met another lovely Chinese woman, a bit older than the Sian girls, Chen Yunanchi, an actress from the Shanghai drama theater. She had come to the United States only a few months previously with her American husband, Gerry Tannebaum. The couple met in Shanghai while she was acting in the theater and he was working for the China Welfare Association of Madame Soong Ching-ling. Yunanchi had told me about their courtship—how delicate it had been by American standards. They met once or twice by chance, and then one night Gerry waited for her at the backstage entrance of the theater. They walked down the street and went to an ice cream parlor. After that they continued to meet and take quiet walks in the Shanghai streets. But, of course, Yunanchi's theater friends quickly became aware of what was going on. They came to her and urged her to stop seeing Gerry unless the two were absolutely determined to marry. And some even tried to persuade her not to see Gerry, regardless of their feelings for each other. "This kind of thing simply wasn't done," Yunanchi explained.

In other words, if a young woman like herself, or like the Sian girls, went out walking with a young man, it was an extremely serious matter—acceptable if the couples planned to marry, but regarded as "loose and light" conduct if it was a mere flirtation or a casual affair. And if it was casual, the consequences could be serious. Your companions in the company (or the office or the factory or the commune) would speak to you seriously, warning of the immorality of your conduct. If you persisted, there would be group meetings, the collective would "struggle and criticize" in an effort to turn you from your erroneous path, and you might even lose your job.

In the light of Yunanchi's story it seemed to me that the boy-and-girl friendships of the Sian girls had to be serious ones; they must be predicated on eventual marriage. Otherwise, they would not have been tolerated in the close context of the Sian ensemble. But, even so, the nature of the relationship between the boys and girls was not clear, nor did I, to the end of my stay in China, find absolutely conclusive evidence on what role sex played in such boy-and-girl friendships.

Several weeks later I met a group of young Chinese-Americans at Changsha—10 or 11 young university students, mostly from the Pacific Coast. All but one were western-born, of Chinese parents from Kwangtung Province, the Canton area. They had been doing graduate study in Hong Kong, improving their knowledge of Cantonese, and now they were embarked on several weeks of touring China. Some had visited relatives in Kwangtung—grandparents, uncles, aunts, cousins. The youngsters looked and acted like any group of American college students—the girls in short skirts, halters, blue jeans, indifferent blouses, sneakers, no bras or very loose bras, long manes of hair; and the boys in jeans, jerseys, long hair and scrawny beards. Wherever they went in China, they created a stir.

Except for a few notable experiences, they were thoroughly enjoying China, but they, too, had been impressed and baffled by the high morality and purposefulness of the young Chinese they met.

"Wow!" exclaimed Candy Chin, a San Francisco State student from Salinas, "they really mean it!"

Candy meant that the Chinese were completely and totally asexual so far as relations between boys and girls were concerned. One day, she said, she was walking down the street in Canton with another young student, John Hsu, from the University of California.

"John had his arm around my shoulders," she said. "It didn't mean anything, it is just John's way. I heard one of the Chinese on the street say, 'Wow! Look at that couple! Do you see what they are doing!' "

Of course the Chinese did not actually say "Wow!" That was Candy's word. What the Chinese said was "*Ay-yee!*" But it meant the same thing, and it meant that the Chinese were startled and shocked to see a boy walking in public with his arm around a girl. Candy was confident that young Chinese did not approach sex as did American youngsters. In fact, she felt sexual relations played no part in the life of the Chinese students. She believed they practiced total abstinence.

John Hsu had the same opinion. He believed that the Chinese meant it when they said they did not touch each other until marriage, which in the cities seldom seemed to occur until the very late 20's.

He felt that the whole Chinese approach to life so subordinated sex and so sublimated it that there could be no real comparison between the mores of young Americans and young Chinese. The Chinese were kept busy from early morning until late at night in intense and physically exhausting activities. They rose at six or before and spent some time in calisthenics. They devoted half or a third of their time in grueling work in the countryside or in factories. Whenever there was a spare hour, they engaged in group activity—lectures, athletic competitions. They had no time for sex and no energy for it.

Another youngster had not been satisfied with the answers the Chinese offered on questions of personal relations. They giggled and smiled so much when any questions were posed that she decided to walk in the streets at dusk to see for herself how young people behaved; whether under cover of darkness there was any physical contact.

"You know," she said, "it is not correct to assume that they don't have feelings for each other. You just watch them. There are a lot of them who walk together on either side of a bicycle. That means something. And then, if you watch closely, they will touch shoulders from time to time. Shoulder touching is very big. But if they actually walk together and hold hands that means they are about to get married."

Her view was supported by one of the young American boys. "You mustn't draw too many conclusions just from what you see," he said. "I talked to some of my relatives about this. They laughed the way Chinese do and said, 'Oh, you Americans, you ask such funny questions.' But when they got serious, they said that, of course, boys and girls and men and women in China fall in love and show their feelings for each other—only they just don't make any public display of them."

Ta Ling-wong, a graduate of Otis Art Institute in Los Angeles, felt that the de-emphasis of sex made for a much more relaxed atmosphere among Chinese young people, and that the relations between Chinese boys and girls were stronger and better than those between American boys and girls. "It's not so competitive," she said. "There's not so much pressure to pair off as we have in the United States."

One girl suggested that the lack of public demonstrativeness, the shy behavior of both boys and girls in China, the modesty of their dress and their conduct had nothing necessarily to do with the Cultural Revolution. "Take the young people in Hong Kong," she said. "Of course, there are hippies and kids who just ape what they see and hear in the movies and TV. But look at all the others—the ones from better families. They don't go out unchaperoned and they are almost as shy and modest as the kids in China."

The Chinese-American youngsters had raised one question with Chinese students that led to a total cultural gap. This was homosexuality. I don't know how the issue came up, but I think that it must have arisen from the American side. I cannot imagine a Chinese boy or girl asking a question about homosexuality. Perhaps it was mentioned by the Americans in connection with a discussion of women's liberation, another topic on which the Chinese seemed very puzzled by American attitudes. But raised it was. The Americans told their Chinese friends about the homosexual movement in the United States, about gay liberation, the political rallies and the demonstrations, and about the role of lesbianism in the women's movement. The Chinese were deeply shocked—offended is probably a better word. They simply did not know such things existed, and they did not like to talk about them. They found it hard to believe that the Americans were serious when they spoke of the increasingly active political role being played by both male and female homosexuals in the United States, and about the support being given by liberal and radical movements to their cause.

There was, they insisted, nothing like that in China. Perhaps, they conceded, there might be a few isolated cases of homosexuality, but certainly those involved persons suffering from a disease, and they must be treated as being ill, and cured of their abnormality. Speaking for themselves, they had never heard of any such cases.

I spoke of homosexuality with one or two older Chinese. Their reaction was similar to that of the young people, but not so violent. These were men who had been adults before the Revolution, and they were completely aware of homosexuality. But they simply dismissed it as a factor in China today. "There is no such thing," one of them said. "Our society is too healthy for that."

My feeling was that these were the reactions of a Grundy-like society that sought to impose the conformity of the "good" over the "bad," and in which the total resources of that society—propaganda, the official apparatus, the close sense of community and comradeship

—were rallied to create a common social profile. Obviously, there was no place in this for homosexuality. It did not even need to be mentioned. It was patently in contradiction to the principles of Chinese society.

Yet I could not help wondering. No decree and no insistence on conformity could eliminate deep physiological and psychological tendencies within human beings. A universal attitude that there *could be* no such thing as homosexuality did not eliminate it. Especially not in such a country as China. One had only to turn to the classics of Chinese literature to quickly perceive that male love for males and female love for females was a constant and accepted element in Chinese society from the dimmest recesses of history. The Chinese classics made little or no distinction between the love of a man for another man—or, more often, the love of an adult man for a handsome boy—and the love of a man for a handsome woman. In fact, judging from the literature, such relationships seemed to be very common and involved no social opprobrium. True, that literature largely dealt with the wealthier or noble classes, but there was no evidence that homosexuality was not recognized, accepted and practiced by all classes in China.

That being true, I could not help but wonder how lasting the current attitude of amazement, horror and revulsion against homosexuality was likely to be. It seemed to me to be cosmetic rather than basic. It obviously did not mean that there was no homosexuality in China. It simply meant that—for the present—there was no overt homosexuality, because Chinese society not only declined to permit any manifestation of homosexuality but even to admit the possibility of its occurrence.

The young Chinese-Americans were a little shocked, on their part, at what seemed to them to be the rigidity of Chinese attitudes toward this aberration. But they were chary of making final judgments. They had been in China only ten days, and the mass of impressions had almost overwhelmed them. They were honestly divided as to the genuineness of the "purity" of Chinese youth. But they were not divided in their impression of the spirit of Chinese young people, which, they felt, simply represented the spirit of Chinese society in general.

"You know," one said, "we had heard so much about China from our parents—about the poverty, the disease, the terrible conditions under which people lived. And then we came here and met the people. Gee—it was terrific!"

What impressed them was the spirit of fellowship, the spirit of working together, not for some personal aim, but for the common good. One for all and all for one. Chinese young people, they felt, were working for Chinese society, for the Chinese nation, not for an individual goal. They helped each other when they got into trouble. In school, instead of each trying to outdo the other, better students tried to aid those who could not do so well.

"Of course, we know things aren't perfect here," one girl said. She had visited her aunt and uncle and had met her cousins. Her relatives had seemed upset by her visit. They shied away from questions, talked in whispers or sat silent. "They just seemed paranoid," she said. Probably, she thought, they had been through some bad experiences and were afraid that more difficulties lay ahead.

"That's why I'm reserving my judgment about China," she said. "But not about the young people. They *really* seem to mean it. I've never met people like them."

I found cynics among some foreign observers in Peking. They refused to believe that Chinese conduct was as antiseptic as it seemed. And they told stories and anecdotes to support their view. One diplomat who had served in Peking for a long time said that he knew the Cultural Revolution was coming to a close when he began to see so many young Red Guard girls pregnant. I thought this might be a bit of foreign prejudice, but a Chinese friend said that it was certainly true—many of the young girls did, in fact, get pregnant during the turbulent days when all of young China was on the march from city to city and village to village. "The young people were together all the time," he said. "There really wasn't any discipline. It just happened."

Another foreigner told of a British businessman, long resident in China, who was spending a few days in Peking. One evening he came out of his hotel and looked for his car. It was there but the chauffeur, a young woman, was absent. He spoke a little Chinese and asked the other chauffeurs where she had gone. They laughed and smirked and said they didn't know. But the smirks aroused his suspicions. He went around to the back of the hotel and there he found his chauffeur thoroughly occupied in the back seat of a parked car with another chauffeur.

"I think there is more going on between Chinese boys and girls than foreigners ever imagine," this man said. "I sometimes walk in the parks at night and there are quite a few couples in the shadows and on the benches. If they aren't there to make love, I don't know what it is that brings them together."

I, too, walked the streets and strolled the parks. I never saw any public intimacies. In fact, I never saw a couple walk hand in hand or arm in arm. Only rarely did I see a man and woman sit together on a park bench. Invariably they sat some distance apart and were engaged in a conversation that did not look at all personal. Once, on a park bench in a remote corner of the Imperial Gardens, I saw a young couple sitting close together—the remoteness and the closeness of the couple suggested affection. I can't add any more than that. Driving in Peking, Shanghai and other large cities at night, I often saw people on foot, sometimes in little clusters. So far as I could tell from a glimpse, the clusters were invariably all-male. I did see, once in a village near Anyang at about 10 o'clock in the evening, four or five boys and girls strolling together. They had no shovels or rakes or hoes, and did not seem to be either going to the fields or returning from them. They seemed, indeed, like an ordinary group of young people out for a stroll. But they did not hold hands or put their arms around each other's waists. They walked along, a fair distance separating each girl from each boy, exchanging banter and occasionally singing songs.

The Chinese officials with whom I raised the question accepted without reservation the fact of the purity of young Chinese men and women, indeed, their physical virginity. All things considered, I concluded that the evidence supported that view, although there were bound to be some backsliders. Certainly the evidence supported it, so far as the city young people, the intelligentsia, the students, the activists and the idealists were concerned. Whether the mores of the young factory workers and the young peasants in the fields were as pure, I did not know, but there was some reason to suspect that there were more violations of the code among them. There was, for example, the sheer overwhelming presence of an extraordinary number of babies and children in the villages, the obvious youth of the mothers and the large number of pregnant girls to be seen in the countryside.

But this did not really weigh too much against the validity of the basic code of the Chinese Revolution and its impact upon Chinese youth and society. The impact differed sharply, however, from that of the Russian Revolution on Russian young people. The Russian revolutionaries were as idealistic as the Chinese youth. They were sternly moral individuals, but at the same time they stood strongly for full sexual freedom as part of the liberation of women from the prejudiced codes of the old society. Men and women, in the view of the young Russian revolutionaries, must be perfectly free to choose whether or not to have sexual relations. It was an individual decision, and no one had a right to impose his will or his prejudice upon any other individual. True, this gave rise to considerable controversy. The advocates of "free love" and removal of all inhibitions on relations between men and women ultimately collided with the more conventional views of Vladimir Lenin, who felt compelled to pronounce the verdict that "love is *not* just like a glass of water" as it had been proclaimed to be by, among others, Alexandra Kollantai, who insisted that if a man and woman felt like having intercourse, it had no more significance than drinking a glass of water. Lenin was more old-fashioned than that. But hardly as old-fashioned as the framers of the moral code of the Chinese Revolution. The Russian Revolution produced a sexual release in Russia that flourished with abandon and did not begin to wane until Stalin's regime and Stalin's imposition of legal and moral strictures which, in reality, were designed to produce a rise in the Russian birth rate by turning Russian women back to *Kuchen und Kinder*.

Not so the Chinese Revolution. From the Yenan days, the Chinese army was taught never to molest women, and to be as pure in their sexual conduct as the young people of China today. In fact, it seemed to me that the moral code that was professed by Chinese society and by which at least a considerable portion of that society lived, was precisely the moral code that Mao Tse-tung proclaimed for his troops during the Long March. And this, I had no doubt, was no accident. For if the Cultural Revolution had one principal aim so far as Mao was concerned, it was the revival of the moral and spiritual values of the simple days of revolutionary struggle.

So far as the present generation of Chinese youth was concerned, so far as the beautiful young ballerinas of Sian were concerned, it seemed clear that Mao had succeeded. The evidence was overwhelming that Mao and the Cultural Revolution had, indeed, turned China into a "sink of morality."

11

A Bull Session

It is one thing to create a generation of young people of remarkable moral qualities but it is quite another to apply those principles to the kind of problems that life may impose.

I could see as I traveled around China how the young people interacted, say, in a factory, in a school, or out in the commune. There they led a collective life, strongly motivated toward a common goal. They worked together, lived together, studied together. They helped each other and, within the limits of their understanding, tried to solve common problems. They struggled to aid their country in its enormous projects of growth and development, and they fought, as best they knew how, against those they perceived to be their country's enemies at home or abroad.

Of course, they were products of an intensely homogeneous environment. They were, after all, all Chinese (almost entirely by race), all Han, all of the same stock, all emerging from much the same environment, all subjected to the same cultural heritage and, with the coming of the Revolution, all strongly integrated into the party's aims, ideals and aspirations.

A mixture of idealism and strong motivation did not necessarily produce positive results. After all, great tragedies have been precipitated in the world by idealists whose motives were of the highest. Cromwell's men were idealists, but they wrought great harm while they thought they were doing good. The same was true of the leaders of the Spanish Inquisition. And the ideals of the French Revolution led straight to the tumbrels of the guillotine. Idealism in itself is no guarantee against injustice. It was apparent to anyone who listened to the story of the Cultural Revolution that idealism had led some of China's young people into wildly anarchistic confrontations. It had been the mainspring of aggressive and compulsive attacks which had little or no rational motivation on individuals and institutions. There had been moments (and more than moments) when young people had plunged into paroxysms of xenophobia—into attacks on individuals simply because they were foreign, or were thought to be tainted by foreign culture or foreign aims. Houses had been attacked, and objects of art hurled to the streets—just because they were *foreign*.

Neither idealism nor even the highest patriotic motivation was, I thought, necessarily to be equated with wisdom or justice or knowledge.

I badly wanted an opportunity to sit with a group of Chinese youngsters and engage in a free-wheeling conversation that might give some clue not to their motivation and ideals but to how, given the ideals, they reacted and responded to ideas and stimuli of various kinds, including those outside their normal ken.

The opportunity came at Tsinghua University—a rare opportunity, because Tsinghua, having been at the heart of the Cultural Revolution, was strongly under the influence both of the Revolution and of the post-Revolution national reintegration of aims and objectives.

There were nine young people in the group I met in a big breezy room on the second floor of the administration building, the very building that had been the headquarters for one faction of the Red Guards at a time when the university was the scene of armed conflict between two bitterly hostile Red Guard groups. Several Tsinghua faculty members were present, but they remained silent for the most part—intervening only occasionally, when they could no longer restrain themselves.

The ages of the young people ranged from 20 to 25. Two were members of the armed forces, a navy youngster and an army youngster, but all were studying at Tsinghua, mostly in the engineering departments, and some in very practical specialties, such as machine tool production. Tsinghua had always been China's leading science-engineering university, but since the Cultural Revolution it had introduced a number of simplified courses designed to turn out not theoreticians in high-energy physics or optics, but mechanical engineers and practical factory technicians. Most of the youngsters were taking those practical courses, and they had entered the university only in the last year or two. It had been closed down until 1970, and thus far, against a pre-Cultural Revolution enrollment of 12,000, only 4,800 had been admitted.

The youngsters sat in a semi-circle in deep armchairs, with me in the center, and as the discussion became heated, they would scribble furiously on pads of paper, then excitedly read their statements. Around the circle they were:

Chiang Yun-ching, a quiet, gentle, 25-year-old girl specializing in machine tool production. She sat very thoughfully during the two-hour session and only once intervened with a tentative statement.

Nieh Shing-kuo, a very talkative, very opinionated, 22-year-old boy who reminded me of the young Komsomol propagandists I had encountered in Russia. He had a longish face which grew animated as he argued his points. Like Miss Chiang, he was a machine tool specialist.

Fan Sheng-li, a 23-year-old boy, specialist in electrical engineering, quiet, dark and thoughtful. He followed the discussion closely but seldom spoke.

Chun Pao-chin, a dark, animated 22-year-old girl, who grew impassioned and even fierce as she angrily argued her points. She was specializing in boiler making. She talked a lot, often interrupting her comrades by simply raising her voice and talking until she drowned the others out.

Ch'im Chin-hua, a very pretty 24-year-old girl, specializing in machine building. She smiled sweetly whenever she had something to say.

Shan Han-yuan, 23, a dark, very shy boy, specializing in English. After a year and a half, he was able to carry on simple conversations with only a trace of an accent. After the bull session, he lost some of his shyness and used his English quite freely to point out sights to me as we climbed up to the college tower for a look at the campus.

Wei Tung-tse, 23, a computer specialist. He was serving in the navy and came in after the discussion had got under way. Never during the two hours did he open his mouth.

Kuo Jui-shing, Wei's 20-year-old friend from the PLA. The two arrived together. Kuo spoke a lot and always from a strong ideological viewpoint. Both young men wore their uniforms.

Chang Shuang-chiao, 23, an electronics student. She wore glasses and liked to give ideological speeches, often interrupting her fellow students to speak her mind. She came in about half an hour after the session had been under way.

There were occasional remarks by Professor Chien Wei-chang, a rocketry specialist who once studied at Caltech and who played an important ideological role at Tsinghua. He had been severely criticized early in the Cultural Revolution but emerged as a strong spokesman for the post-Cultural Revolution ideology. I thought—possibly unfairly—that he had many of the self-serving tendencies of the recent convert who is determined to demonstrate that he is more Catholic than the Pope. Once or twice Ma Wen-chen, an ordinary worker who was a member of the university administration and the Revolutionary Committee, intervened, and so did Tsao Yu-chien, a pretty, black-pigtailed girl, who had been a member of the Red Guards and had stayed with her faction until the closing weeks of the struggle.

None of the youngsters had ever met or spoken with an American before, although a delegation of American students had visited Tsinghua a week or so earlier, and some of them had friends who had met the American students. I spoke in English and they in Chinese with our remarks being interpreted back and forth by Yao Wei. When Professor Chien intervened, he sometimes spoke in Chinese and sometimes in English.

I began by saying that I knew the students had never had any personal contact with American students and I wondered what kind of impressions they had of them. What I was really trying to do was to get some notion of the picture of American young people that might have filtered through to them from the press and what they might have heard from family or friends.

There was a significant pause. The students glanced at each other, then several began to scribble in their notebooks. Presently, Chun Pao-chin, one of the most furious of the scribblers, spoke up, reading from the notes she had just made:

"We have heard about the students' movement in the United States from the papers and we sympathize with their struggle. Some of my comrades met some American students when they were here a week or so ago. We think they have contributed to the cause of friendship between the two countries."

There was another pause and then Ch'im Chin-hua said: "We strongly support the American youth in their seeking for the truth."

Again there was a silence, which I did not break. Finally, Nieh Shing-kuo, also reading from notes, said: "What impressed me most from reading in some newspapers and from what my comrades who met the Americans told me is that the American students hold such good views and are very much against the war in Vietnam."

That seemed to exhaust their ideas about American students, so I took another tack and asked whether they had ever heard about the drug problem in the United States.

Again Chun Pao-chin was the first to respond: "I've read something about youth and drugs. I feel this is a bad habit and very harmful to health and a very bad phenomenon. It is a social problem which is caused by the environment in the United States and I hope that use of drugs will not increase in the future."

I interjected: "Has anyone in this room ever heard of any of his friends using drugs?"

The youngsters looked at each other, giggling a little and shaking their heads negatively, and Chun Pao-chin said: "I've never heard of any of my friends using drugs, and I have never heard of anyone in China using drugs."

Professor Chien Wei-chang observed that when he was a student in the old days, some of the students at the university smoked opium.

"Chiang Kai-shek," he said, "issued an edict forbidding the smoking of opium, but since he was one of those profiting the most from opium, it didn't stop anything. After Liberation we did away with opium smoking."

Tsao Yu-chien added that the only way she knew about opium was "from seeing opium pipes in an exhibition hall."

"I have a friend at the No. 3 hospital attached to the Peking Medical College," Nieh Shing-kuo observed. "That's the hospital which serves this district and we go there when we are ill. My friend said that when President Nixon was here one of his doctors paid a visit to the hospital and asked whether there was anyone there using drugs and how we treated people to cure them. That's the first time I ever heard of people taking drugs and I found it very queer. If drugs are bad why do people use them?"

I said I thought this was a very good question—one that had troubled us greatly in America, but that the reason for taking drugs apparently had nothing to do with whether they were good or bad for you.

My next question had to do with rock and roll. I asked whether any of them were familiar with American rock and roll. This provoked general laughter. They all started talking at once, replying that they had never heard rock and roll. In fact, the very idea seemed to be hilarious. Several, however, said they had heard the name, rock and roll, but not the music.

"Would you like to hear rock and roll?" I asked.

Again Chun Pao-chin cut in first: "We haven't heard it, but we've heard that it is played not only in the United States but also in the Soviet Union. It is played on the Soviet broadcasts that are beamed to this country."

Nieh Shing-kuo added: "We like to lead a lively, vigorous and militant life instead of listening to some soft kind of music."

I could not resist asking the students how they could possibly know that rock and roll wasn't militant music if they had never heard it played.

Nieh Shing-kuo responded: "Before the Cultural Revolution, art and literature were fields dominated by the revisionist line of Liu Shao-chi, and at one time they propagated bourgeois music, and we feel that it is not in conformity with our aims and does not reflect our life. We think that music must also have some ideological content."

Kuo Jui-shing, the PLA soldier, came in during the discussion of rock and roll and now he joined in: "We lead a very full and vigorous life. We get up at 5:30 every day and play ball games, sing revolutionary songs and engage in athletics. We don't think bourgeois music and dances are in conformity with the needs of student life."

Clearly this was a subject about which almost all of the youngsters felt strongly. The very idea of rock and roll seemed to constitute a threat or a challenge to the way of life to which they were devoted.

Chun Pao-chin, more and more excited, exclaimed: "We are using our spare time to learn our own revolutionary plays and operas. We feel that learning from the revolutionary heroes and heroines helps us to study and work better for the cause of revolution and for the cause of the whole world."

Nieh Shing-kuo said: "We feel that the literature and art of one specific country has a lot to do with the use of drugs, and with our revolutionary art, we don't need anything of what we have heard about the art of some revisionist countries. This kind of thing does not play any role in the life of our people and only makes people degenerate."

I had been a little puzzled at the strength of the feelings that erupted over rock and roll, and surprised at the remark that rock and roll was beamed into China by Moscow. Now, with Nieh Shing-kuo's remarks, I saw the context in which the youngsters had placed rock and roll. They did not, as I assumed, think of rock and roll as specifically American. In fact, they did not seem to think of it as American at all. Instead, they saw it as Russian, as one of the manifestations of the hated revisionists (just another code-word for Moscow). They hated rock and roll not because it came from America but because they thought it came from Moscow and had been encouraged by the traitorous Liu Shao-chi.

Kuo Jui-shing made clear this deep feeling against any kind of art that was alien to China or alien to the revolutionary cause—and specifically to all art and music that originated in Russia.

"I feel," he said, "that any art or literature always serves a particular class, and the art and literature of our country serves the proletarian class. From what we hear from Soviet broadcasts, the content of their art is so far-fetched as to be ridiculous. What they are propagating is the development of people's individualism. This is designed to serve their own purposes—not to serve the interests of revolution. That's why their ideology needs remolding."

I decided to see if I could press home to the youngsters the basic implication of their replies—its clearly chauvinistic content.

"In other words," I said, "you don't want to hear what you haven't heard. To me that sounds rather chauvinistic."

There was dead silence. I did not really believe the young people had taken in the full implications of what I had said, and this was confirmed when Chun Pao-chin observed in a very sulky but very firm manner: "Nevertheless this is our view."

I was not willing to let it drop at that. What, I asked, would they think if they had asked me whether I liked Chinese opera and I had responded that I didn't want to hear Chinese opera because the only kind of music I liked was Wagner?

"What do you think of that?" I asked.

Again there was deep silence. This discussion was leading the young people out onto ground on which they felt insecure. No one, it was obvious, had ever suggested to them that there might be something wrong with the idea of listening only to their own music. When the youngsters remained silent and nonplussed, Ma Wen-chen, the worker member of the Revolutionary Committee, interposed: "Our approach to music and art is that it has always served a particular caste."

And for the first time Shan Han-yuan spoke:

"If you ask me whether I have heard rock and roll, well, I have not. But before the Cultural Revolution, there was a revisionist line in music and films. We even had western movies showing in Peking. That kind of thing would not be suitable for Chinese youth today."

Professor Chien Wei-chang added: "The Socialist system is different, and rock and roll music is not compatible with the Socialist system."

The question was getting down to whether or not rock and roll was part of the Socialist way of life; if it was not, it should not be heard. In other words, I thought, only books not on the index were to be read, lest the purity of the system be jeopardized.

Chang Shuang-chiao spoke up. She said that she came from Tientsin and had been a worker before she had come to Tsinghua University.

"Music and art and opera," she said, "should first of all be Socialistic. They must reflect the life of the worker. We like revolutionary operas because they reflect ourselves. We do think of other music sometimes. I mean foreign music. We play the *Internationale*, for instance, and that was written in Europe, and we like international music from Korea, Albania and Vietnam. This also serves the cause of Socialism. I have not heard rock and roll music but judging from the name, we need no such music. It would not serve the workers and peasants. It is much more outlandish than our music. I don't want to impose my view, but I was a worker. *On the Docks* is a new revolutionary opera. I like it. It depicts the workers and I myself was a worker. After hearing the opera, I work harder for the cause of the revolution and the whole world. We had bourgeois music before, and now it would only have a corroding effect."

It seemed to me that her attitude was polymorphous perverse—that is, that the workers wanted to see and listen only to entertainment about themselves as workers. It was an even narrower, even more naïve view than had been expressed by any of the others.

I tried another tack.

When he was in Peking, I said, President Nixon had seen the revolutionary ballet, *Red Detachment of Women*. He liked it very much and praised it in his remarks on returning to the United States. Now it had been shown to the whole country on American television.

"Mr. Nixon," I pointed out, "is not a proletarian, and the United States is not a proletarian country. Shouldn't we enjoy your art? Why do you think you would not enjoy ours?"

Again there was a substantial pause before Chun Pao-chin, having written out her response, read it: "It all depends on how you like music. All peoples have the same aspirations, and everyone wants liberation. As for the question of Mr. Nixon liking the ballet—maybe he liked it from the artistic point of view. That he liked it from the political point of view is improbable."

Kuo Jui-shing joined in: "I'm very happy to know that *Red Detachment of Women* has been shown in the United States. Now the American people can know the struggle of the Chinese people through that film. Whether President Nixon really understood the ideological content—that is another matter. The purpose of the ballet is educational. He may have liked the ballet from the artistic point of view, but I don't think he could have understood the educational purpose of it very well."

There was an implication that underlay my question which I did not think they clearly grasped. Or perhaps the implication was too sharp for them to handle. First, how could President Nixon have missed the "educational" point of the ballet? And second, if Americans could enjoy the artistic aspect of Chinese productions, why could not Chinese enjoy the artistic side of American productions? It did not seem likely to me that I would get very far in trying to explore that ground, so I turned the conversation in another direction.

"Mr. Reston," I recalled, "said that you are the most moral and puritanical people in the world. Is it true that you don't have dances?"

There was a wild outburst of giggles. All of the boys and girls looked at each other, laughing and chattering. Finally one said: "What kind of dancing does the question refer to?"

"I was referring to any kind of dancing," I said.

Ch'im Chin-hua replied: "That's not true. After all we have all kinds of activities—singing, dancing, opera, ballet. We put on our own performances. We have our own dance group."

Yes, I said, but do boys dance with girls?

That brought on a general outbreak of crosstalk. There was much jabbering and some giggling. Finally Ch'im Chin-hua said: "Yes. Boys and girls do dance together. But this is all in group dancing. Folk dancing."

Well, I asked, is there any girl here who has ever danced with a boy, or is there any boy who has ever danced with a girl?

This produced an explosive chorus of "noes."

"Okay," I said, "suppose you were visiting the United States at the invitation of some American students and suppose they asked you to go to a dance—what would you do?"

The question cast a pall over the youngsters. They looked puzzled and embarrassed and no one hurried to respond. Finally Chang Shuang-chiao said very slowly and, somewhat sadly: "I'm sure our American friends would be polite enough not to make us do what we don't want to do."

Kuo Jui-shing broke in to say: "I don't think you can unify all dancing. All countries have their own ways, and when we go to the United States we can dance in our own way."

Then Chang Shuang-chiao continued: "Contact between the American and the Chinese people will eventually expand. Your ping-pong team was here and had a very friendly reception, and our ping-pong team was equally well received in the United States. I am sure you won't expect us to do things that we are not accustomed to."

The question upset the young people so much that I was sorry I had asked it and hastily changed the subject. With what foreign culture, I asked, were they familiar, outside that of their close friends and allies, Albania, Korea and Vietnam?

Kuo Jui-shing replied: "Cambodian. Prince Sihanouk has composed many songs. We sing them and we have seen the Cambodian dances."

If you had a chance, I said, to go abroad what countries would you like to go to?

Chun Pao-chin leapt in to answer with enthusiasm: "Oh, the Socialist countries first, of course—Albania, Korea, Vietnam and Cambodia."

Any others? I asked.

There was a rather long pause and then Chun Pao-chin, a bit reluctantly and probably out of politeness, said: "Well, of course, America."

Chang Shuang-chiao said: "If we have a chance, we would like to go to many foreign countries to learn from them their strong points. We like to learn from the peoples of other countries. First of all, I would like to go to Albania. I have heard so much about it and how it has been carrying on the struggle for so long. We know the American workers and students are carrying on arduously, and we would like to learn from them."

It seemed to me that I had tried the patience of the young people enough. My questions had constantly gone against the grain of their habits of thought and had, often, been deeply disturbing. It was time to put the shoe on the other foot.

"I've asked too many questions," I told them. "You have been very nice and answered them all. Now, do you have any questions that you would like to ask me?"

This seemed to be wholly unexpected. Silence hung in the air for half a minute. Then Chun Pao-chin spoke up: "After the United

States student delegation came back to America from visiting here, what did they write about China?"

I was terribly sorry, but I could not answer that question. I had been away from the United States for a long time and the students must have returned to the U.S.A. during my absence.

Professor Chien spoke: "That long-haired American ping-pong player who was here—what did he write or say when he got back from China?"

I told him that Cowen had been ecstatic and had talked so much about China, appeared so often on television, and had been interviewed so often, that he had become very famous.

Fan Sheng-li asked how American students lived, and I replied that they lived not entirely unlike Chinese students. They had dormitories, and lived on the campus, just as Chinese students did. Perhaps they did not study quite so hard as the Chinese, and certainly they did not spend all their spare time on athletics.

"They like to listen to rock and roll," I said, "they go to dances, drive around in their cars with their girls. But they are also very much interested in political and social questions, and they are very active in causes like the Vietnam war, racial equality and the like."

"You mentioned equal rights," Chang Shuang-chiao said. "What do you mean by that?"

Equal rights for blacks and whites, I explained, equal rights for Puerto Ricans, Chicanos, Indians and other minorities. Equal rights for women, students, prison inmates, equal rights for anyone who was discriminated against. I did not have the heart to say that one of the important student causes was equal rights for homosexuals. I simply did not know how I could explan that to them.

Nieh Shing-kuo: "I've heard that the crime rate among youth is very high in the United States—is this true, and what is the reason for it?"

I said that, to my regret, it was true and that the principal cause was the drug problem. Addicts, I pointed out, were mostly young, and they needed $100 to $200 a day to buy drugs, and they got it by robbery, burglary and even murder.

It was evident that the students no longer were asking questions just out of politeness. Their interest had been engaged and they were asking questions now for information.

Nieh Shing-kuo continued on the drug question, asking whether

I thought the drug problem could be solved. I said that I felt it could, that it was largely a matter of economics.

"Take the profits out of drugs," I said, "and the problem will begin to wither away. That's why many in the United States believe that drugs should be given free to addicts to end the commercial motive. Now billions are being made in the drug traffic."

Chiang Yun-ching now spoke for the first time, asking in a quiet, almost bewildered, voice: "But don't the young people know that drugs are bad and dangerous? Why do they take them?"

I thought that was a hard question to answer. But I added that I thought they took drugs, at least in part, because it was a kind of cult and, in part, because they started taking them on a dare and then, in part, simply because the pushers persuaded them to try it "just once."

Nieh Shing-kuo spoke up a bit primly, observing: "We are very sympathetic to this problem but we think it is the result of the social system."

I conceded that the social system was always at fault in any problem, but that I thought in this case it was really an aberration of our social system.

"What," Chang Shuang-chiao asked, a bit slyly, "do you think of the social system?"

"I am a very strong supporter of the social system in America," I replied. "I think that, on balance, it does far more good than harm. It has built up a great country. Of course, it has bad defects. The drug problem is one. But, on balance, the system does far more good than harm."

"But the majority of your youth take drugs," Chang Shuang-chiao insisted. "This is very bad."

I responded rather strongly, warning Chang not to get the problem out of proportion. It was not a majority of American youth that took drugs—not by any means. In New York, I said, with a total population of perhaps 15 to 18 million in the metropolitan area, I doubted that there were as many as 300,000 addicts. That, I said, was far too many. But it was not a majority, or anything like it.

"But," persisted Chang, "it will get bigger and bigger."

"No," I said, "no, it won't. We aren't standing idly by and letting the problem grow. If we have any strength in our system it is that of continuous self-criticism. We look for our defects and we struggle to correct them. Sometimes it takes a long time. It has taken a long time to end the war in Vietnam and to change our policy on China. But we do change and we will lick the drug problem in the end."

Kuo Jui-shing said that he had read in the Chinese papers that there was a workers' movement and a student movement in the United States.

"What are its demands?" he asked.

My answer both disappointed and shocked the students. There was a workers' movement, I said, and its principal demand was for higher wages and shorter hours. Wages were already quite high (I did not dare say how high compared to Chinese wages), and the working week was often as low as 32 hours. But the workers still wanted more money for less work. The students, on the other hand, generally backed political and social demands. They wanted an end to the war in Vietnam and equal rights for all Americans. These were the kinds of causes that aroused their enthusiasm. On the other hand, the workers' demands were largely economic. There was, unfortunately, little sympathy between the workers and the students and, even more unfortunately, the workers, more often than not, were hostile to the students.

At that point the questions from the students seemed to have run out, and the bull session came to an end. I did not know how much the students had learned from it, but I knew that I had a better understanding of the results of the Cultural Revolution than I had gotten from any other discussion in China.

So many things were now clear. The students, to be sure, were idealistic. To be sure, they were strongly motivated—by motives of patriotism, service to their country, service to their fellow countrymen and, at a somewhat greater range, service to the cause of revolution (although this was quite plainly a cloudy concept that did not really seem to go much beyond support for those countries closely allied to China—Albania, Vietnam, Cambodia and North Korea). They were obviously chauvinistic, without really understanding the nature of their chauvinism. So far as culture was concerned, their definition could hardly have been narrower. It recognized only that culture which was deemed useful to the Revolution or to Chinese patriotism. The idea of more general culture was alien, and seemed to them threatening. They were ignorant of conditions beyond the frontiers of China, and only weakly interested in learning about things that did not directly touch them. They had no hostility toward the United States, but no special curiosity about it. The Soviet Union was another thing. They were violently hostile to Russia and to anything that even in the periphery of their knowledge seemed to be identified with it—rock and roll, for example. Their mores and morals fitted the pattern I had already seen, a code as rigid as that of the Puritans. Not only did they not indulge in activity that might bring boys and girls into close physical contact —they did not even like to talk about such a thing. It was an embarrassment just to think about dancing two-by-two.

There was, I thought, no further question. The Cultural Revolution and the Yenan ethic had indeed produced a notably moral generation. But it had, at the same time, produced one which, by my standards, was almost pathetically naïve, often dangerously chauvinistic, intellectually incurious and uninformed almost to the point of illiteracy about matters that did not relate closely to their lives and their country's interests.

There was, I thought, both strength and peril in the profile of young China that these young people presented. Of course, it might not be typical. And, of course, the impression had probably been distorted by two or three of the more politically articulate of the young people. But taken all in all, it was an image, I thought, that carried formidable implications. Puritanical morality had not always provided a formula for either political stability or benevolent intercourse among nations. What its meaning might be in Chinese terms, the world has still to discover.

12

All Men Are Brothers

Li Chien-chang, professor of Chinese literature at Wuhan University, is a distinguished gray-haired man whom I judged to be about 60 years old. He was dressed in a very neat dark gray tunic, on which he wore a gleaming Mao button, and gray trousers, and he spoke softly and hesitantly, choosing his words carefully, like a man picking his way across a bit of difficult terrain.

I had asked him to tell me how his teaching had changed since the Cultural Revolution. He was a specialist in the Chinese classics, and I was interested to know precisely what effect the turbulent Cultural Revolution had had on literature and writing.

I already had some grasp of the impact of the movement on the character and attitudinal thinking of the Chinese intelligentsia, but I wanted something more specific. I wanted to know, in chapter and verse, how Professor Li taught his subject before, and how he taught it now.

The Chinese classics, I knew, played a critical role in the Cultural Revolution. In many places, the works had been denounced by Red Guards and even burned. Publishing houses had stopped publishing such great books as *Water Margin* (better known to Americans as *All Men Are Brothers*), *The Dream of the Red Chamber* and *Monkey*. But now—at least in small quantities—the classics were again being put out.

Before speaking with Professor Li, I had listened to a lecture by one of his students, discussing *All Men Are Brothers*. It was given to a class at Wuhan University that included at least a dozen PLA men, most of whom looked considerably older than the usual college student.

The lecturer spoke with almost military precision. He quickly drew on the blackboard a functional diagram that was supposed to represent the main forces contending in the novel, then plunged into his thesis, which, essentially, was a warning against accepting at face value the slogans and aspirations of Sung Chiang, the novel's main character. Sung, leader of a peasant rebellion, fought under the slogan "Rob the Rich to Give to the Poor." But, in the end, the lecturer said, he betrayed the peasants, just as Li Hsui-cheng had betrayed the peasant cause during the T'ai-p'ing rebellion against the Manchus in the 19th century and, in fact, just as Liu Shao-chi had betrayed the cause of the Chinese Revolution only yesterday.

The reason for this, said the lecturer, was that Sung Chiang was raising the rebel flag not in behalf of the peasants but in behalf of himself. He wanted to make himself emperor. His character was exposed by his conduct. He had gone to the capital and there had not only had relations with a prostitute but got into contact with the ruling dynasty—this was just the beginning of his betrayal.

The speaker analyzed the novel in political terms, emphasizing that social conditions had been ripe for revolt, which was why so many people followed Sung to the Liang Shan Mountains. But Sung's leadership was not capable of producing victory because of the defects in his character and philosophy. In fact, this had been the history of peasant uprisings of which China had had so many. Always the leadership was defective. Why? Because the leaders came from petty official or landlord backgrounds. They did not have the class basis that was the only real guarantee of success. Sung Chiang should not, therefore, be presented as a patriot just because he fought enemies from abroad and sought to bring down a corrupt ruling emperor.

How, I asked Professor Li, did the lecturer's presentation of *All Men Are Brothers* differ from what he would have told his classes before the Cultural Revolution?

A bit haltingly, Professor Li began to speak.

Before the Cultural Revolution, there had been an erroneous line in education. Personally, his world outlook had not been thoroughly remolded. He presented wrong ideas in his lectures and had not acted in accordance with Chairman Mao's teaching, which was to adopt a critical attitude toward classical literature.

During the Cultural Revolution the masses criticized his erroneous methods. It was not true that the classics had been burned generally. Those were only isolated instances. Most of the classics were still on the shelves of the libraries, unharmed. Of course, their publication had been halted. But the publication of almost everything had been halted. And, besides, the classics had never been published in very large editions.

"We must respect the classics," he said. "The question is, how should we study them?"

The principal tool in examining them must be historical materialist theory. They must take what was good from the classics and criticize the bad. After all, these were works of a feudal society and were bound to contain dregs as well as healthy parts. In the editions now being published, each book contained a preface that told the people the correct attitude to have toward the classics.

Before the Cultural Revolution, Professor Li had presented Sung Chiang as a totally positive character. He made no class distinction between Sung Chiang, with his individualistic aspirations, and the peasant uprising. The peasant uprising must be evaluated positively, but Sung Chiang, in reality, had betrayed its cause.

"We must always understand the mainstream," he said very seriously, "and not be misled. There is a big difference between the lectures I gave previously and these I give at present."

During the Cultural Revolution, many students had written Big Character posters criticizing Professor Li's attitude toward *All Men Are Brothers*, and he had come to feel that they were correct.

"However," he added, a bit wistfully I thought, "large amounts of research are yet to be done. We are just at the beginning. What we have done already in analyzing *All Men Are Brothers* is far from enough."

In other words, it seemed to me, what the Cultural Revolution had done was to put primary emphasis on the socio-political content of the great Chinese masterpieces, whereas previously study of them had proceeded on more or less conventional literary and stylistic lines.

This analysis was supported by a second professor of classical literature, Professor Liu Ta-chieh at Fu Dan University in Shanghai.

The main point to be made about *All Men Are Brothers*, he said, was to show how history had been shaped by the various peasant uprisings. This was what gave feudalism its form in various dynasties, and the book presented an excellent exposition of the inevitability of peasant uprisings caused by the landlord and the bureaucratic class.

"In China," he said, "the motive force in history has been the peasant uprising."

First, an analysis must be made on an ideological basis, and only then could the artistic content be dealt with. "We feel," he said, "that all these classics represent great achievements in artistry. But we must make the necessary analysis to let the students see how vicious was feudal society. We must compare the old and the new and teach our students to hate feudal society more and love our new society more."

Professor Liu was a dean of Chinese classical literature. His principal field was *The Dream of the Red Chamber*, which he had studied, lectured upon and written about for 40 years.

"Before the Cultural Revolution," he said, "I over-emphasized the love theme of the *Red Chamber*. Now this is all changed. In accordance with Chairman Mao's teaching, I am emphasizing the dialectical side of *Red Chamber*, applying the principles of historical materialism."

He now understood the historical background of *Red Chamber* as he had not before. Because of his personal world outlook, he had put the love theme first.

Now, the main theme he emphasized to young people was opposition to feudalism; how the landlord and ruling class had exploited the laboring people and how the broad masses of the working people had lived in poverty. He showed his students the dark side of feudal society and how bad the conditions that prevailed under it were.

In the past, he had treated the love theme in the book as a kind of anti-feudalist motif. But this really was not correct. In the end, Chia Tao-yu, the main character in the novel, became a monk. How could he possibly struggle against feudal society in such a way—by becoming a monk? Professor Liu's old idea was very erroneous. In fact, you could tell at once by the title of the book that this could not be a positive work. Its main thrust was that the world is like a dream, and that, of course, meant the book did not look toward the future. To take *Red Chamber* on its own terms meant to take a negative attitude toward the future. It served no educational purpose. The outlook of the writer was steeped in feudalism and thus, he could not help but write a work in which he showed that the hero could do no more than love women and become a monk. Nevertheless, the author's exposure of the landlord class and the dark life of the peasants had great historical significance.

The fact was, said Professor Liu, that the "four villians" of the Cultural Revolution had, in part, used classics like *The Dream of the Red Chamber* and *All Men Are Brothers* to disseminate their own anti-Mao line.

I had never heard of the "four villains." They were, it turned out, Chou Yang, one-time deputy minister of propaganda, and for a long time the virtual arbiter of Chinese cultural affairs; Hsia Yen, a deputy Minister of Culture, a playwright and an important figure in the film world, adapter of three films that became targets of the Cultural Revolution—*Early Spring in February*, *A Chiangnan in the North* and *The Shop of the Lin Family*; Tien Han, a playwright and chairman of the Union of Dramatists; and Yang Han-sheng, a writer and Vice-Chairman of the Writers' Union.

Before the Cultural Revolution, Professor Liu said, the Chinese literature department had carried out the line of Liu Shao-chi. They had given their students "book knowledge behind closed doors." Their work was divorced from reality and from Chinese politics. Many students changed sharply as soon as they got to the university. They became influenced by the Liu Shao-chi line and separated from the working class. They worked for personal goals, rather than class or social goals.

Chairman Mao, he said, had given a whole set of instructions for the teaching of the liberal arts, but, due to the influence of Liu Shao-chi, they had never been carried out. Now, since the Cultural Revolution, they were trying out those ideas experimentally. For instance, they had for the last two years taken the whole of society as their laboratory. They were using two methods. Students read actual literary works and then went out into the field to see how the book compared with reality. This was where the "four villains" came in. The students took works written by them and went back to the sources to see how the novels compared with the real conditions about which they were written.

For example, he said, there was a work by Hsia Yen about indentured laborers in a Shanghai textile mill owned by the Japanese before Liberation. The students went to the factory described by Hsia Yen, talked to the workers and learned how their situation had been distorted by Hsia Yen. In the end, both the students and the workers benefited.

The second kind of literary activity was even more pragmatic. The students went to factories and farms and worked alongside the workers and the peasants. Then they wrote up their experiences, and the accounts were published in newspapers and broadcast by radio stations. The students formed close links with the media, and the media sent them out to make investigations and write reports.

Sometimes, they wrote criticisms. When *Red Lantern* was published, the students wrote criticisms for the newspapers. When *On the Docks*, a revolutionary opera, was performed, students went out and applauded it. On the 90th anniversary of the great revolutionary writer, Lu Hsun, the Maxim Gorky of China, they wrote articles about him.

"In the old Chinese literature department," Professor Liu said, "the situation looked very dead. The new department is very lively. We write and do so many things."

Lin Ching-shu, one of the students in the Chinese literature department and a former worker in a textile factory, supported Professor Liu. Last year had been the 100th anniversary of the Paris Commune, and she had studied about it. Sometimes she had trouble, because the place names sounded to her like the names of people. But she had gotten over these difficulties because the teachers and students helped her. Many of them had been better trained than she, but now she had read Marx's *The Civil War in France* five times, and had come to understand the importance of art and literature to the proletariat. There had been 60 newspapers in Paris, 30 of them against the Paris Commune, and only 12 on the side of the Commune. The Commune had failed. The lesson was that it was important to have the power of the newspapers in the hands of the proletariat so as to create "our own proletarian opinion." She had written about that. In fact, she had written eight articles, and some of them had been published in the Shanghai newspapers. In the old Chinese literature department, she said proudly, even if you had stayed in it for many years, you never would have studied *The Civil War in France*.

Lin Ching-shu was one of many, many workers and students who were linking personal experience and study, and publishing the results in newspapers or broadcasting them by radio.

One Sunday morning I went to the offices of the newspaper, *Wen Wei Pao* in Shanghai, the newspaper that had made its columns available to Chairman Mao Tse-tung when he was unable to get any other paper to publish a criticism of *Hai Jui Dismissed from Office*. (It was this article that marked the opening of the Cultural Revolution in November, 1965.)

Wen Wei Pao had played a leading role in the Cultural Revolution. It had carried on the struggle for Chairman Mao's viewpoint. Nowhere in China, I thought, could I get a better sense of what the Cultural Revolution meant when translated into actual writing. I had not during my stay been able to meet any professional writers, poets or playwrights. To suggestions that I should talk with them in order to understand what the Cultural Revolution meant in cultural terms, the reply was: The writers were very busy with their new works, works that were being written in accordance with the principles of the Cultural Revolution. It was not yet time to talk with them. The first works would not appear, in all probability, before autumn. After that it would be a different thing.

Because of the role of *Wen Wei Pao* in the Cultural Revolution, and because of the newspaper's long and cherished literary reputation, I asked the editor, Fan Yo-ten—an angular, dour man with an unexpected dry wit—what the paper had been doing in a literary way. It turned out that it published at least one literary work a week, as well as frequent articles of criticism.

"We publish lots of works," he said, "novels, poems, essays. We publish articles by amateur writers, workers, peasants, soldiers, party workers and intellectuals. Often these are articles about how they have studied Marxism-Leninism and the thoughts of Chairman Mao in order to direct their work in practice."

What, I said, are some of the outstanding literary works you have printed lately?

The literary editor of the paper, Ho Chien, a thin-faced, nervous woman whose husband formerly had been a university instructor in political economy but who now was engaged in party work in a factory, answered the question. She wore a coal-gray patterned silk blouse, decorated with a Mao button, and her hair was cut in a short black bob. As she spoke she toyed constantly with a pale-green scarf.

There had been lots of good things, she said. Short stories, essays, poems. Some dealt with agricultural or industrial production, some with army affairs, but all were designed to show the change in the mental outlook of people, how new leaders were being trained and how intellectuals had been tempered by their experiences in the countryside.

What, I asked, are some of the literary works you have published? This question seemed to fluster her a bit. She exchanged looks with Editor Fan and then, apparently reassured, went ahead.

Well, she said, the most recent issue of the paper with literary material was the July 1 issue. That was the anniversary of the founding of the Communist Party, and the whole of page four (it was a four-page paper) had been devoted to poems by workers, peasants and soldiers telling of the great changes that had occurred since the founding of the party. The page was illustrated with a woodcut of the building in Shanghai where the First Party Congress was held.

What else had been published lately?

There had been some short stories in the last two or three issues. One, called "The Secret of Yenan," was about a girl whose father and mother were old revolutionaries. She was born in Yenan but brought up after Liberation. She wanted to carry on the Yenan spirit by going to the country to serve the people. The purpose of the story was to educate Shanghai's young people in the spirit of service to the people. It had been written by a young man, Hua Tung, who had contributed only once or twice before.

This year, 1972, was the 30th anniversary of Chairman Mao's talks at the Yenan Forum on art and literature. Because of this, *Wen Wei Pao* and the Shanghai *Liberation Daily*, with which it was closely associated, had issued a call to the people of Shanghai to write for the papers. They had gotten more than 10,000 articles in two months. This apparently was one of them.

Another outstanding short story published by *Wen Wei Pao* was called "The Making of a Zipper." It was the story of a very young apprentice in a zipper factory, who paid no attention to the quality of his work. An old worker kept telling him of the importance of making zippers, but he didn't listen. Finally the old worker took the young man to a department store and got him to work as a salesman at the zipper counter for a few days. He waited on a lot of customers and listened to their complaints about the bad quality of the zippers. Thus he began to understand the importance of making good zippers, and he went back to the factory and started to turn out high quality products.

The zipper story, Ho Chien said, was written by a worker. It had been sent in over the transom.

The paper not long ago had published the first act of a play by Chiao Ku-san, the leading writer for the Anhwei Opera Troupe of Shanghai. It was called *Collecting Cinders*, and it dealt with economy in production and the practice of frugality, as urged by Chairman Mao. Chiao Ku-san had suggested that Ho Chien come to rehearsals of the play. She had gone, liked it very much, and put it into the paper.

Another work had been written by the collective of the Shanghai Fishing Company. It was about two fishing boats, Nos. 457 and 458, which had suffered no accidents for five years because the crews had employed Chairman Mao's philosophical work, *On Practice*, as a guide to their navigation procedures. She had asked the workers to send her a copy of this work after someone called it to her attention.

An article of which the paper was very proud was called "Looking for Water." This had been written collectively by a hydrological team in Shanghai. It told how they had gone to the high mountains to drill wells in a region where there was thought to be no water. After studying Chairman Mao's *On Practice*, they had struck water.

In her next issue, she was publishing the experiences of the grass-roots organization of the sulphuric acid workshop of the Wu Ching chemical factory in studying Marxism-Leninism and the thought of Chairman Mao. Another article that would soon be published dealt with Chinese traditional medical pharmacology, written by a worker in the pharmacological industry.

I asked about literary and dramatic criticism—was this also done by amateurs, or was there a regular staff? The answer was: both. There had been recent criticisms of the opera, *On the Docks*, and the cantata, *Song of the Dragon River*.

What new plays had been presented?

Recently there had been a new short play called "The Sound of the Needle under the Shadowless Lamp." I thought that this might be a detective thriller, but my guess was wrong. It was the story of a young doctor employing acupuncture anesthesia, a young doctor who was dedicated to the people and to science.

Another new theatrical presentation was what was called a "comic dialogue." This genre was satiric dialogues about contemporary events. It was a form that had traditionally been very popular in China but had been suspended since the Cultural Revolution. Now it was being revised—very successfully. The new production was called *Removing Mountains*.

The paper frequently published reviews of new dances. Recently there had been reviews of a performance called *Fighting During the Autumn Harvest*, which dealt not with the Autumn Harvest Uprising which Chairman Mao led in 1927, but with the yearly struggle to get in the rice and wheat.

What about novels? I asked. You have mentioned none whatever. Haven't any been written?

Ho Chien looked again at Editor Fan and then at several of her colleagues. Finally someone made a suggestion and she nodded her head. Yes, there had been a novel published fairly recently. It was called *Battle History of Hung-nan*, and it told of the struggle in the countryside during the period when agricultural cooperatives were being established, in 1951–1952.

The paper did not pay for any of the literary efforts it published. Instead, it gave the writers what they called "souvenirs," since presents were frowned upon as a possible kind of bribery and a relic of the old society. The "souvenirs" took the form of books or stationery or writing materials. Sometimes, they were works by Marx or Chairman Mao. Newspaper staff critics, of course, were on a regular salary. Ho Chien's salary, for instance, was 74 yuan a month, and this seemed to be fairly typical.

I wondered where the suggestions came to Ho Chien for articles by obscure factory workers. Did they arise, by chance, in the Propaganda Department of the Shanghai Revolutionary Committee? Well, she said, the Revolutionary Committee didn't submit articles on its own. Sometimes the Propaganda Department did. But usually, they encouraged others to write. She and the editors worked in close contact with the Propaganda Department and the paper was, of course, the organ of the Shanghai Revolutionary Committee.

The literary picture now seemed complete. Literature had been harnessed firmly to the cause of the Revolution, to the achievement of the goals of the Revolution, to the deepening of perception on the part of the people of the ideals and objectives that had been spelled out by Chairman Mao. Literary quality took second place, and might even be ignored. The important thing about the medium was the message. The classics had been integrated into the same system. They were made to demonstrate the evil of the old and the blessedness of the new. As for contemporary literature in the western sense, there was none.

I could believe that *Collecting Cinders* and "The Making of a Zipper" might arouse enthusiasm among the workers, and even cause them to do their work better. But they were nothing more than thinly disguised production manuals. If this was art, Henry Ford was Michelangelo.

Nor was this definition of art applied solely to writing. The message of the ballet was revolutionary vigilance, revolutionary sacrifice, hatred for the old and support for the oppressed. I could not well judge Chinese music, but I noticed that the scores of *The White-Haired Girl*, *Red Detachment of Women* and *The Yellow River*

Cantata were so simple that children of nine and ten had no difficulty in giving virtuoso performances. I had been to the only contemporary art exhibit that seemed to be open in Peking. It was made up of photo-like paintings of irrigation systems, steel mills and hydroelectric stations. I had seen its duplicate at the Tretyakov in Moscow in 1949 at the peak of Stalinist Socialist realism. My opinion was not unique. I heard enthusiastic foreign supporters of the Chinese regime mutter about the abysmal quality of contemporary Chinese painting and sculpture. I had no reason to doubt that the same judgment applied to music, theater, drama and fiction (if there was any fiction currently being produced, which seemed dubious). Chinese Pop Art. There was no other word for it. Propaganda on a crude level, deliberately placed at that level because that was deemed to be the level of the Chinese peasant and worker.

But did this really make sense from the viewpoint of the Chinese Revolution? Was it possible to raise the level of culture, and the ethical aspirations of a people by lowering "art" to the commonest denominator that could be found? I had argued this point in Communist countries before. In Russia, particularly, where the Lumpen bureaucracy was constantly trying to depress the level of artistic performance on the contention that the masses could understand and appreciate nothing better. But was this not, in reality, an invidious view of the masses? Was this not, actually, the personal view of gray bureaucrats who had never read a poem or stood before a Raphael or a Da Vinci, who had never lost their soul to Anna Karenina, and had never seen the Venus de Milo? So it seemed to me. I did not believe that true revolutionary purpose in China, or in any country, could be served by debasement of cultural ideals.

China was a nation of 5,000 or 6,000 years of cultural achievement, the most magnificent tradition in the world. This was to be seen at every hand—in the glory of the Forbidden City, with its infinitely expandable quadrilaterals; in the perfection of the Ming tombs; in the divinity of the artifacts newly taken from the tombs—the wondrous jade armor and the gold and feather headdresses. No people in the world had created greater art than the Chinese. Was this nation going to turn its back on that and settle for *Collecting Cinders*?

The more I thought of it, the more certain I was that they were wrong who believed this was the highest achievement, the end result of the Communist Revolution and the Cultural Revolution. It seemed to me that evidence to prove the case lay at hand—specifically, in the outburst of Chinese archeological excavation, the opening not only of the Ming tombs but the great finds at Sian and Changsha and a dozen other places. All of these were being hailed by China's propaganda press as the finest flower of the Cultural Revolution. Photographs of the treasures were posted everywhere, and the artifacts themselves were displayed in marvelously tasteful exhibits, opening up all over the country, just as the political museums were shutting down to extricate the relics of Liu Shao-chi, Lin Piao and all the others who had been cast out of Communist heaven.

It was as if there was a direct intent to bury the memory of the anarchical attacks by Red Guards on China's cultural treasures during the wildest days of the Cultural Revolution; to demonstrate to the whole population—the masses, the intellectuals, the party elite, the workers, peasants and soldiers—the vast richness of China's cultural heritage.

If I was right, the mainspring of this could be only one person, Chairman Mao. To be sure, I had no doubt that he had also encouraged the production of pop art, pop plays, pop novels, pop poems. All this was in the same category as the exemplary tales for children that filled the American school books, magazines and literary caskets of 1870. This kind of thing was designed to instruct and inform, to enlighten the dimwitted and the barely literate.

But behind it, or so it seemed to me, loomed an entirely different vista—a vista leading toward a new golden era of Chinese culture. I could be wrong. The chance could be missed. The emphasis on the beauty and the treasure of the past might be a passing phase.

Yet, I did not think so. My conviction deepened as I studied what seemed to me the most powerful evidence of the true direction of Chairman Mao's thought. Chairman Mao seldom appeared to his people. His appearances had grown more and more rare. But in 1972 he received a succession of distinguished foreign visitors—President Nixon, Madame Bandaranaike of Ceylon, Foreign Minister Schumann of France, and others. He received them all in the cluttered study of his office behind the red walls of the Imperial City. He did not bother to have anyone neaten up the room. In fact, it was far too cluttered for that. He sat in the same overstuffed chair where he spent so many of his days. He greeted each guest with the tables about him piled high with papers and books, and, behind him, the wall was a solid bookcase. What were these papers? They were Chinese classics, every one of them; the ancient books of China, bound in the traditional way, stack upon stack of them and, by his arm, the ones that he himself was reading, folded back in places, peppered with book marks, and on all the other tables, more piles of the classics.

I had lived long enough in Communist countries to know that nothing happens there by accident. Or hardly anything. And certainly the chief of a Communist country never permits his photograph to be taken, let alone published, without deep thought as to its symbolic and political content. Mao's picture of his classic-cluttered study was published in every Chinese paper and magazine. Not once, but again and again.

Chairman Mao deliberately chose to have himself photographed not perusing *Collecting Cinders* or even "The Sound of the Needle under the Shadowless Lamp." He was portrayed surrounded by the cultural wealth and tradition of China.

When Premier Tanaka of Japan visited Mao, he was received in the same book-lined study, and the Chairman handed to the Premier a parting gift—a six-volume edition of the most ancient classic of Chinese poets, Chu Yuan, the very poet whose feast I saw being prepared in the caves of Yenan. Chu had drowned himself, thrown himself into the river, in 278 B.C. But first he had written his great work, *Li Sao*, with its lines to his Emperor:

> High God in Heaven knows no partiality;
> He lives for the virtuous and makes them his ministers
> For only the wise and the good can ever flourish
> If it is given them to possess the earth.

The message was perfectly clear and was intended to be. China was moving forward on the lines of her great traditions. There might well be a transient flurry of pop art. But after a while—and we must remember that China moves on a different kind of time than we—she would push forward, as Professor Li put it, on the main stream, the stream that had never halted in 5,000 years. But which had often been interrupted.

"...if the people of two countries want friendship with each other and exchanges—how can we oppose it?"

—*Premier Chou En-lai*

A sunny day in Tien-an Men Square
at the gates to the Forbidden City.

Crossing the border in
People's Republic at Shum C

万岁

中华人民共和国万岁
LONG LIVE THE PEOPLE'S
REPUBLIC OF CHINA!

Some of China's Eight Hundred Million
—or is it One Billion?

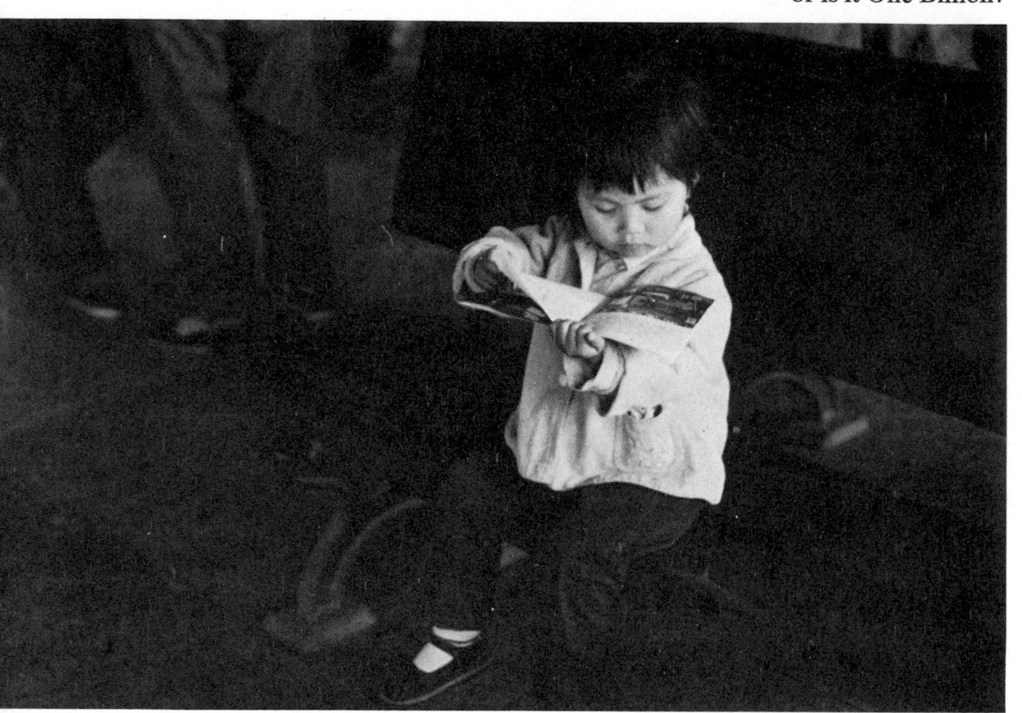

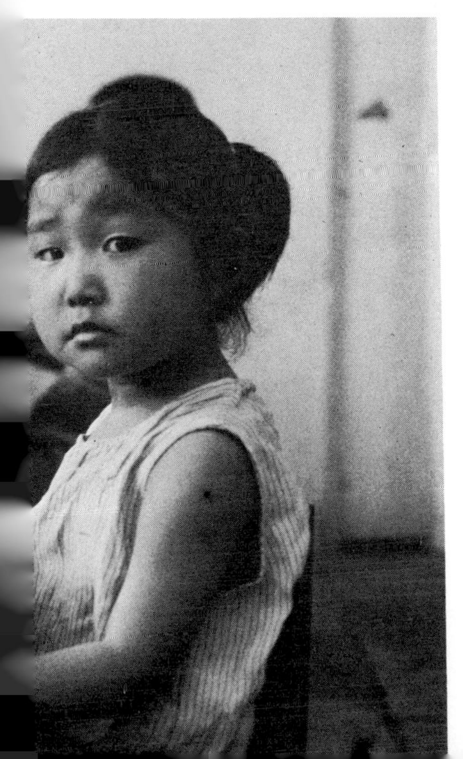

万岁

摄影部

团结起來 爭取更大的胜利

ACUPUNCTURE—

probably nothing in New China has aroused more American curiosity and interest. In Peking's Friendship hospital acupuncture anesthesia is now used for a very large percentage of operations. These photos were taken as a 29-year-old woman was operated on for the removal of an ovarian cyst.

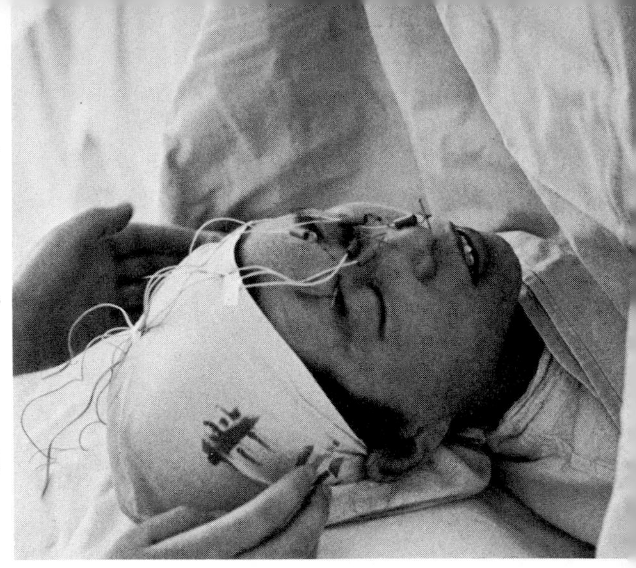

The young woman is prepared for operation; acupuncture needles are inserted in her nostrils and eyebrows.

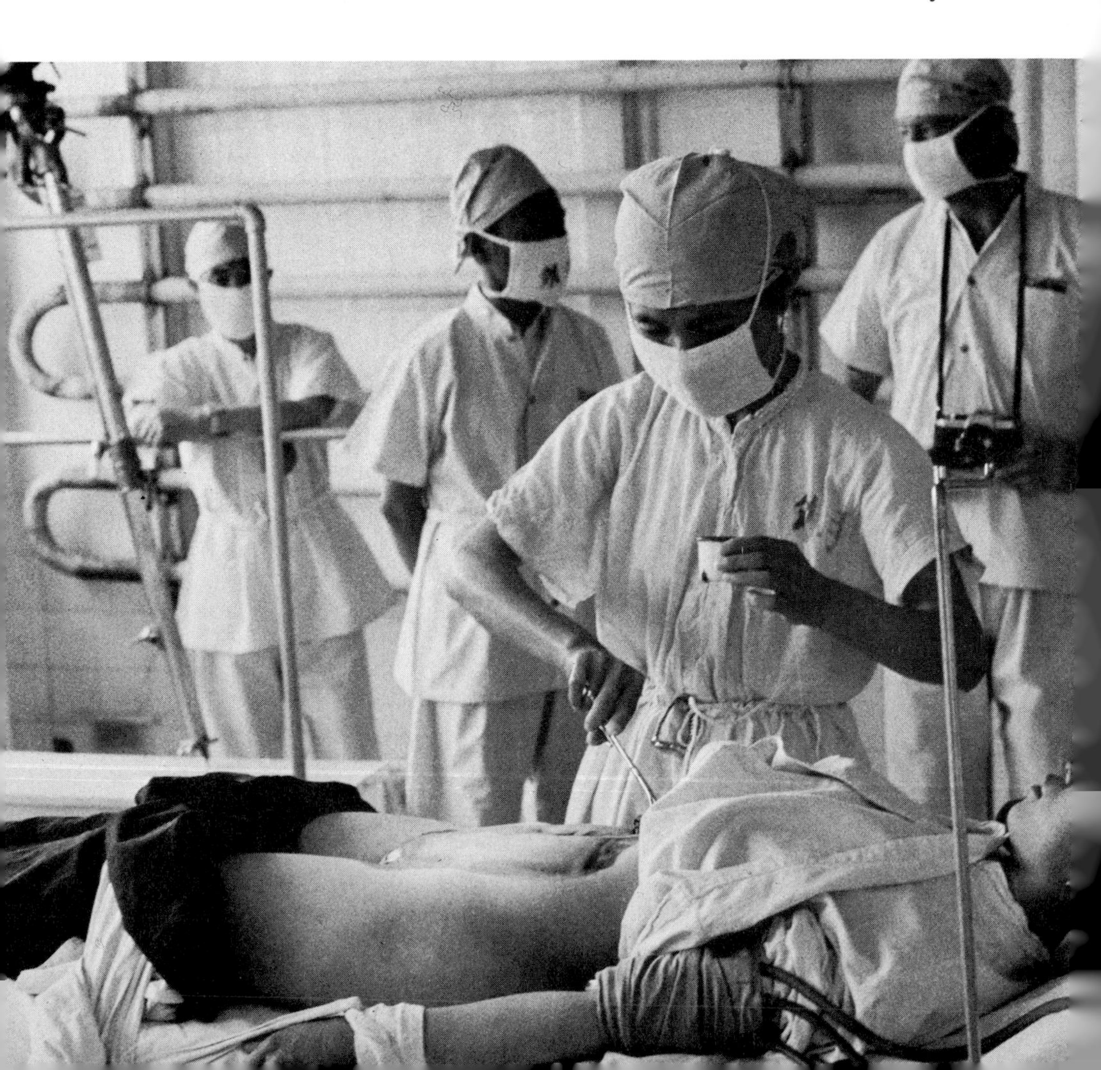

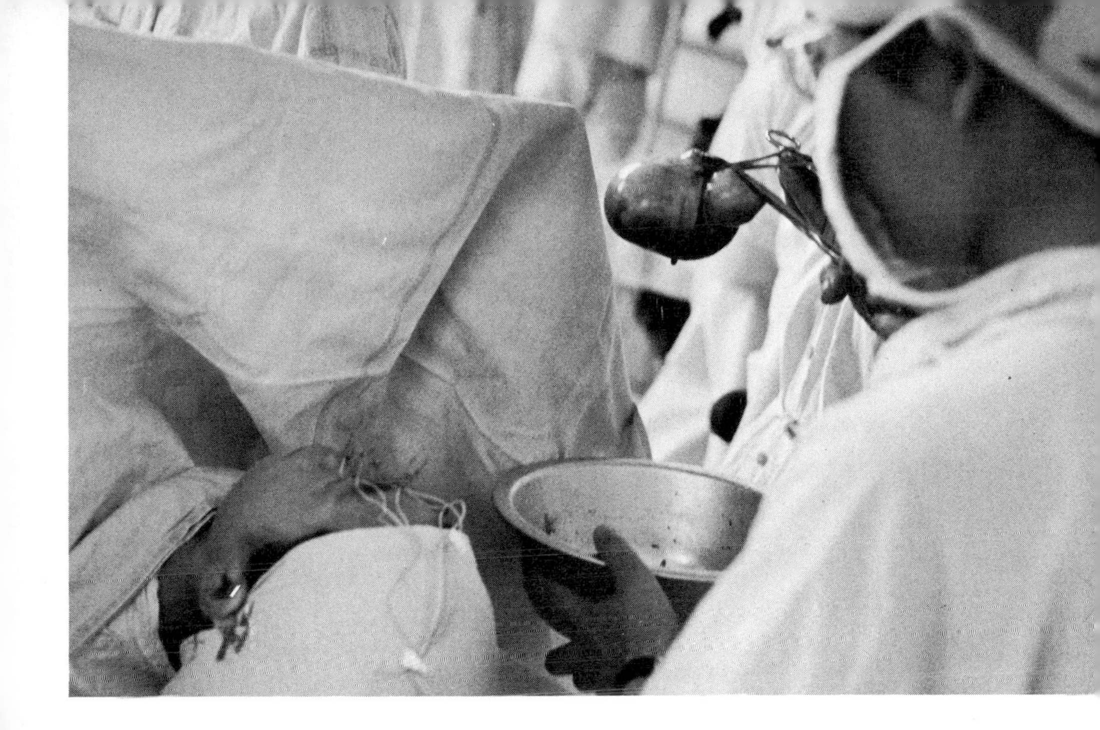

Dr. Wong makes the incision of the abdomen; the young woman says "it feels like a feather has passed over my abdomen." (Above) The cyst, nearly as large as a grapefruit, is removed.

(Over) Linhsein county—once "water was as scarce as oil." Now the Red Flag Canal has brought irrigation, fertile crop lands and terraces.

Life on the commune is simple but healthy. Dams provide water, man provides most of the labor and the horse is prized. (Below) A Chinese "barefoot" doctor.

The blacksmith is an important man in the Liu Ling (Willow Grove) Commune a few miles from Yenan where Mao Tse-tung and his supporters made their headquarters for many years.

Preparing *tsung-tse* of sticky glutonous millet and date
at Liu Ling to celebrate the 2,096th anniversar
of the death of the Chinese poet, Chu Yuar

Harvest time in Linhsein coun
(Opposite) Winnowing the gra

沿着毛主席的光辉
'五七'道路乘胜前进

men at May Seventh school outside of Peking, singing the Song of the Pig Breeders.

"I'm more than 60 years old but I consider that my remolding is only beginning. I am determined to continue my remolding, filled with revolutionary vigor."

—Professor Sung Chiang-ching, Wuhan University.

The bull session at Tsinghua University. Left to right: Chiang Yun-ching, Nieh Shing-kuo, Fan Sheng-li, Chun Pao-chin, Ch'im Chin-hua, Shang Han-yuan, Wei Tung-tse.

The bull session: Chang Shuang-chiao, Kuo Jui-shing, Professor Li Chien-chaing, Tsao Tu-chien, Ma Wen-chen, interpreter.

New students at Tsinghua University in their dormitory. All of these girls are studying machine and tool building. This building was badly damaged in fighting between the Red Guards during the Cultural Revolution.

Wang Li-ping, Wang Ti-cho, Chao Kuo-sen, Ching Tsai-tsoi–the four ballerinas of the Song and Dance Ensemble of Sian.

"In the political field it is not easy to find persons like Mao Tse-tung who can combine the theory of Marxism-Leninism with practical Chinese revolutionary experience..."

–*Chou En-lai*

"It is very hard. It is not easy to find a leader like Mao Tse-tung. There are not many people like him. We are all his students but we cannot do as well as he."

—Chou En-lai

"I am a Prince. I am not a proletarian. I am a bourgeois. I cannot be a Communist. I confess, Madame, I have not any Communist culture. I have read only Mao Tse-tung..."

–Prince Norodom Sihanouk

Jade armor linked with gold forms the burial dress of Prince Chung Shan,
Han dynasty nobleman of 2,000 years ago.

Stones from Peking's Great Wall taken down to form foundations of labyrinthian anti-nuclear shelter system underlying city.

From 1936 to 1945 Mao Tse-tung lived in Yenan and
his home was this cave hollowed from the loess hills.
At left his antechamber, at right his study.

The mile-wide Yangtze river at Wuhan where Chairman Mao Tse-tung swam on July 16, 1966 to demonstrate his strength and vigor as the Cultural Revolution gathered force.

Yenan—the mountain fastness in northern Shensi where Mao and his followers found refuge after the Long March. In background the famous Yenan pagoda. Foreground right, a large new tourist hotel is under construction.

Nine- and ten-year-olds at target practice.

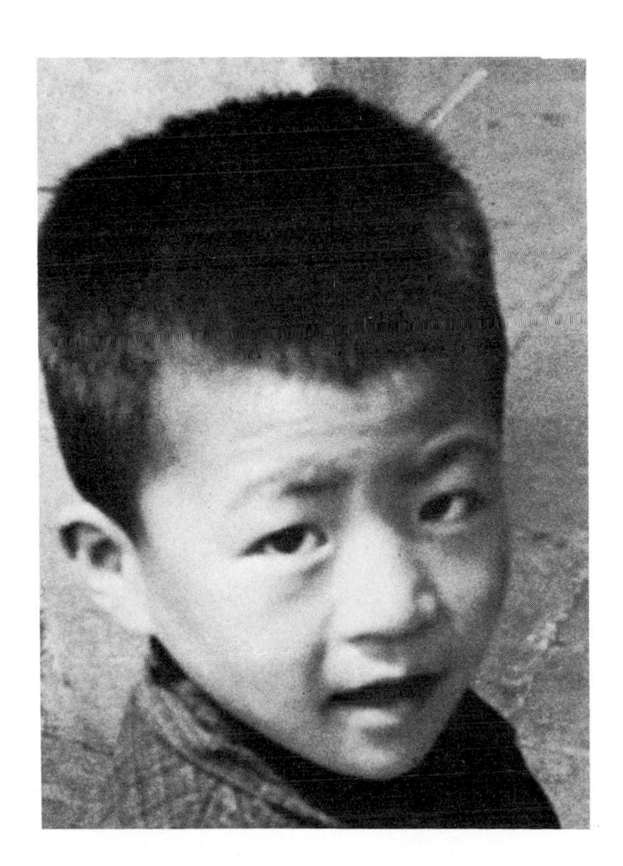

angsha Normal School
. 1 where Mao studied
a boy and returned
er as a teacher. It is
l in use.

"The Americans were so open, so kind, so generous. My father thought that Southerners were just like Chinese. Why did I go to school in America? My father made me."

—Mme. Soong Ching-ling

The Wuhan Iron & Steel Co. is China's second largest. Designed by the Russians its construction was delayed and hampered by the pullout of Soviet experts.

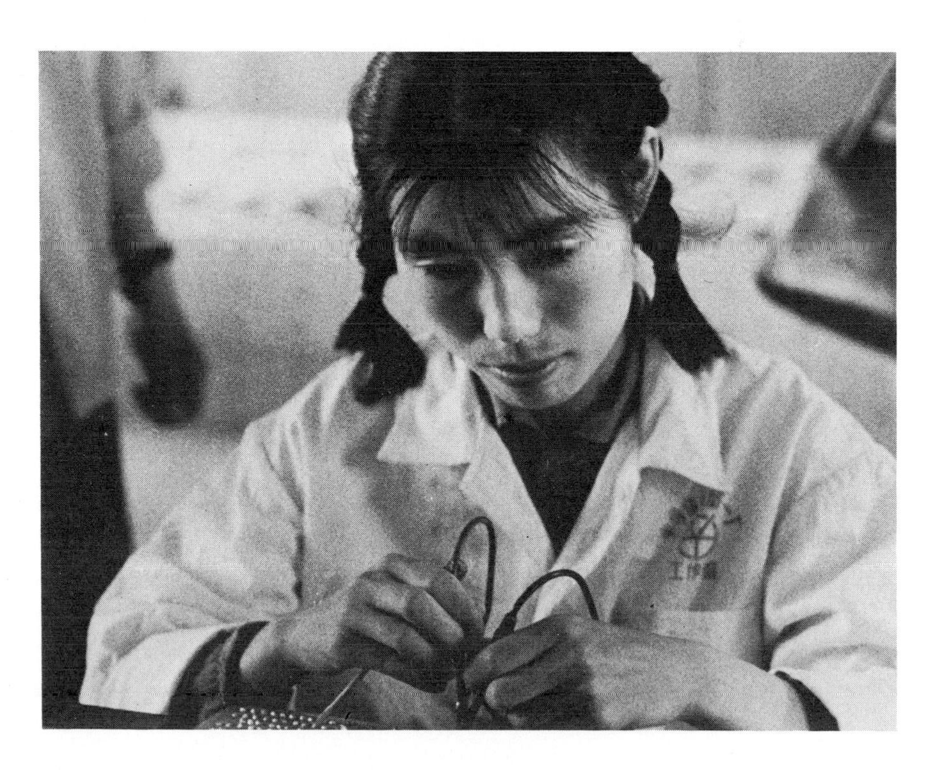

"I think it is quite natural and quite all right to educate people with the spirit of hating the target of our struggle, the USA—don't you?"

–Premier Kim Il-Sung

Kim Il-Sung University–
the tallest building in
Pyongyang.

Kim Il-Sung's birthpl
at Mangyongc

Massive bronze statuary groups composed of
hundreds of individual figures flank the
heroic Kim Il-Sung statue in Pyongyang.

Reciting names, birth dates and death dates of The Revolutionary Family of Premier Kim Il-Sung.

Chang Dok Pyon is chairwoman of the Chongsan-ri collective farm, one of the best in North Korea.

Premier Kim Il-Sung has visited Chongsan-ri collective farm to give on-the-spot-guidance 62 times through 1970 as Mme. Chang points out.

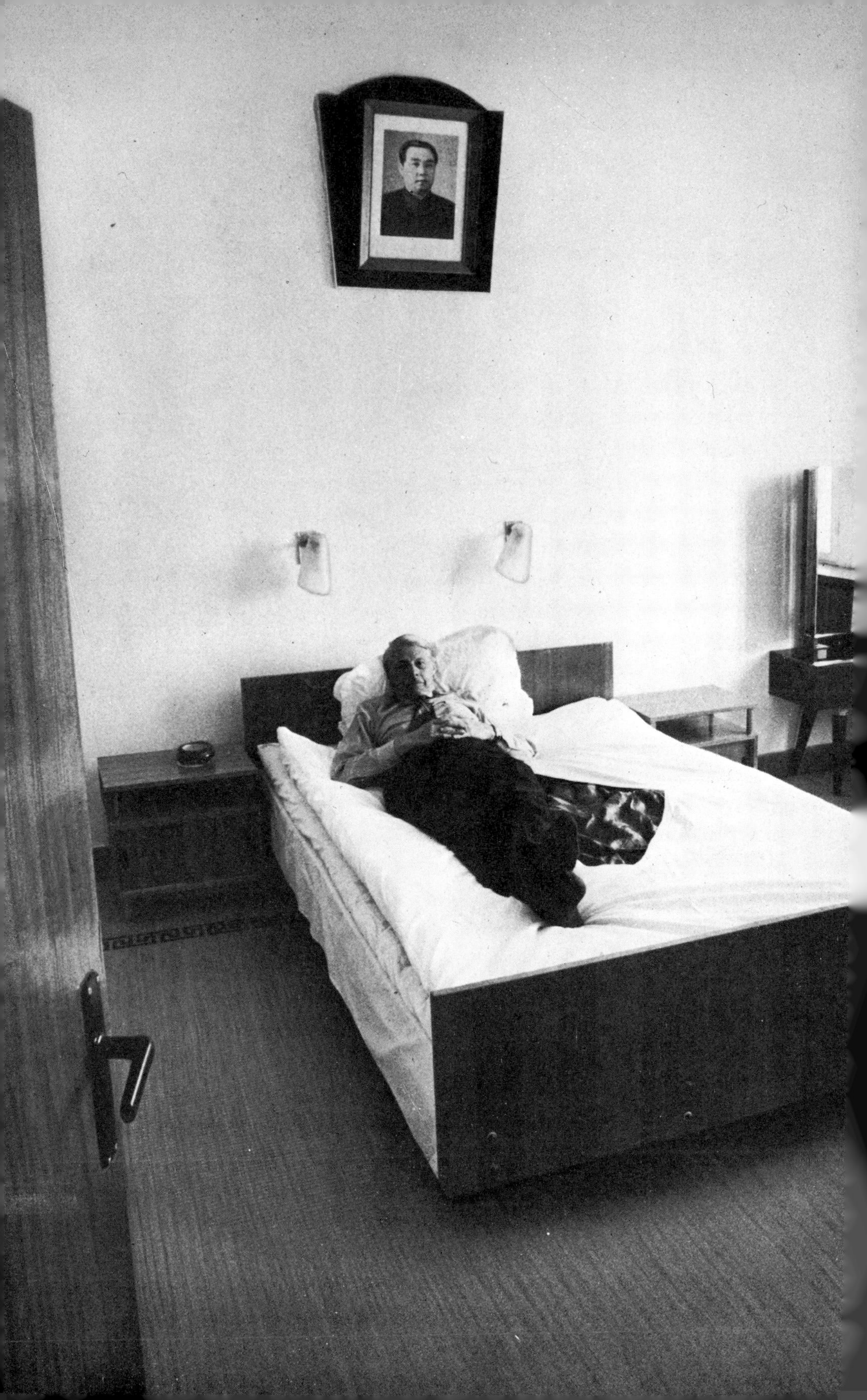

13

China's Millions

The most important fact in the world today may well be a statistic. In fact, two statistics: China's population and the rate of its growth.

The figures are a secret. I know no other way of stating this. To be sure, the Chinese government and its officials use population figures, state them, refer to them and repeat them. But the question is—do these figures really reflect the total number of people in China and do they realistically describe the rate of growth?

I do not believe they do. Wherever I went in China, I asked questions about population, about the birth rate, about the rate of growth, about population control and birth control, about the size of families. I did not, of course, come up with a general population profile of China. But almost all of the evidence I gathered supports the view that China consistently understates her population, and understates its remarkable, continuing rate of growth.

The story of China's population is a long and complicated one, but it is desperately important. China, by any calculation, is the world's largest nation—whether her population is placed at 750 million (the figure that has been used in Peking for several years), 800 million or 850 million (which is used by many foreigners), or approaching 1 billion (as I suspect).

There was never a Chinese census before 1949, only estimates based on tax collections and random samplings (although these go back to the second century B.C.). Estimates gave China a population in 1949 of about 550 million. An official census of 1953 gave mainland China a total of 575 million, and in 1957 China officially estimated its population (including Taiwan) as 656.6 million. For the next ten years, Chinese officials used the figure 650 million in almost all of their pronouncements, although Mao Tse-tung, in 1964, told Edgar Snow that he believed China's population was then 680 or 690 million. In a speech on March 11, 1966, Lin Piao used the figure 700 million, and in February, 1968, at Lanchow, reference was made to 750 million at an official meeting. A series of provincial statements issued in 1966–67 gave a total population of 712 to 713 million. Another series of provincial figures issued in 1972 gave a total for 1970 of 697.3 million—15 million less than four years earlier.

The disparities between these figures are so glaring that it is obvious that one of two things must be involved. Either Chinese officials actually don't know the country's population, or they are deliberately seeking to confuse.

American demographers have struggled with this problem for years and, not surprisingly, have come up with a variety of estimates. Dr. G. Etzel Pearcy, geographer of the State Department, estimated in 1969 that as of January 1, 1966, China's population had reached the level of 760.3, 800.3 or 894.5 million—depending on which of several growth factors was applied. John S. Aird, of the U.S. Bureau of the Census, projected a low estimate of 754 million and a high of 793 million for 1968. He believed that the 1953 Chinese census understated her population, and that all subsequent calculations based on 1953 were likely to understate the total. A 1970 U.S. Census estimate put China's population at 871 million, and a 1972 United Nations study suggested a figure of 786.6 million.

There has been almost as much confusion over the rate of population growth as there has been about the total. Growth, of course, depends on the ratio between birth and death figures. Chinese officials have given different figures for the rate of increase. In 1960, Premier Chou En-lai told Edgar Snow that two percent was the "average" figure. The rise between 1953 and 1957, according to Chinese official figures, was 2.3 percent per year. On other occasions, figures as high as 2.2 were used by the Chinese and sometimes as low as 1.8. In 1963 Chou En-lai put the Chinese birth rate at 30 per 1,000 (or three percent) and said it must be reduced to 7 per 1,000. An Indian specialist calculated the birth rate in 1959 at 40 per 1,000 and the death rate at 12 per 1,000. The United Nations calculated China's birth rate in 1971 as 33.1 per 1,000 and the death rate at 15.3 per 1,000.

The Indian specialist, S. Chandrasekhar, put infant mortality in 1959 at 50 per 1,000 live births. In 1957 Dr. T. T. Fox reported in the British medical journal *Lancet* that China's infant mortality was only 22 per 1,000 compared to 25 per 1,000 for London. The figure in the United States in 1972 was 19.8 per 1,000 live births. The figure was 12.9 in Sweden; 16.4 in France.

Victor and Ruth Sidel visited Shanghai in 1971. They are medical specialists in Baltimore. They were told that the birth rate in Shanghai was 7 per 1,000 in 1971. This must be compared with 17 per 1,000 for the United States as a whole, and 25 per 1,000 in ghetto areas of the cities.

The birth rate is perhaps the most critical figure, and the diversity of the reports—if nothing else—tends to arouse doubts. It has been apparent, of course, that China's death rate has been declining in spectacular fashion recently, as a result of widespread hygiene and gigantic public health efforts.

Visitor after visitor has attested to the success of the public health effort—the transformation of unsanitary conditions in the cities and streets, the elimination of flies and the end of epidemic diseases. It was not, of course, literally true that, as one traveler reported, "there are no flies in China." There were. I established this to my own satisfaction by keeping a log of each fly I saw in nearly six weeks. The total was 52, not counting a few mosquitoes, a few gnats, four brown ants and four small unidentified bugs I found in a hotel bath tub. Nineteen flies were logged in a single locale—the Double Bridge Commune outside Peking, most of them in the horse stalls. That figure doesn't seem unusual, but the fact that I went to other communes and saw not a single fly, not even in pig pens, is.

Of course, this achievement has not been attained without cost. It is not entirely the result of individual fly-swatting campaigns. It is mainly due to the most intensive drenching of the land in DDT that I had ever seen, or hope to see. You almost needed a gas mask to get through hotel corridors and public buildings late at night, after the DDT sprayers have done their work.

The scent of the spray lies over China like a blanket. Two months later, I still hadn't got it out of my nostrils. On a Saturday night in Shanghai, they even supplemented the customary DDT ministrations by burning in every block a canister of a chemical similar to DDT that spread over the city in clouds. It was designed to rid the city of any remaining mosquitoes. That was done at least twice a summer all over south China.

The process is effective. The land has been cleansed of all mosquitoes and almost all flies. The public health results are incomparable. But with it has gone very large numbers of China's birds and bees (I was constantly amazed at how rarely I saw a bird) and the ultimate cost of introducing such fantastic quantities of chemicals into the natural food chain could hardly be calculated. A similarly effective chemical campaign against rats and mice virtually eliminated these pests—along with most of the cats and dogs.

But Chinese public health authorities feel that the price in future reckonings is small when placed beside the savings of lives that has been achieved. I would not argue with them.

But it has been the very success of this remarkable campaign that throws substantial doubt over the validity of the Chinese population figures, because the elimination of disease has so radically lowered China's death rates. Unless the birth rates have been cut even more radically, the population can only rise—steeply. If China's population was increasing at a rate of 2.3 percent per year (as the official figures indicated) between 1953 and 1957, this would mean that the net increase per year, calculated on the 1958 official figure of 646.3 million (without Taiwan), would have been on the order of nearly 15 million a year. If by 1960 the rate of growth had dropped to two percent "on the average," in the words of Premier Chou En-lai, China would then, as a result of the compounding of the earlier figures, still be growing at the rate of 13 million per year. The total in 1960 would have reached about 675 million, and, unless there was a further radical drop (and the .03 of a percent drop in two years which Chou's statement implies is a fantastic drop!), the total by 1964 would have been in the neighborhood of 730 million rather than the 680 to 690 million reported by Mao Tse-tung to Edgar Snow. By that time, the annual increase would be up to 14 million per year and pushing 15 million.

If the same two percent rate of increase continued to 1972, the total would be well over 850 million, and the annual increment would now be running at over 16 million a year.

All of this, of course, is speculation. If the Chinese population increase has been brought down to the Japanese rate (the world's lowest), it would be only one percent a year, and the totals would be correspondingly smaller. But no one—not even the Chinese—has claimed a figure anything like that low. The latest United Nations estimate of the current rate of increase is 1.78 per cent.

The actual data I collected in China are a random sampling—very random. But in almost every case they suggested higher birth rates and larger population increases than the official estimates.

Take one characteristic sample: the Fang Sheng district of Peking. This area has a population of 52,980, divided into 14,136 households, or families. There are 22,808 working people in the area;

16,260 students or pupils; 7,762 retired persons, disabled veterans, persons too old or too ill to work, elderly housewives, etc. And 6,142 children under the age of seven, that is, pre-school. This means that in that single (and apparently typical) area of Peking, 11.6 percent of the population were children born within the last seven years. This makes an average of one baby, or pre-school child, to every two households. If the pre-school children are grouped with the school children, they constitute 42.3 percent of the population—an extraordinarily high percentage of young people, one that, obviously, is influenced by a high, vigorous birth rate, and one that will contribute to maintaining a high rate of reproduction.

What is significant about this population profile is that it is a city profile—the biggest city, and the city where the government's intensive control programs have presumably had the most striking results. I visited a number of families picked at random by the Fang Sheng Street Committee—or, more probably, selected because they were thought to be typical or outstanding. It supported the picture of big, vigorously growing families. One was a family of nine, another of seven (these were extended families, with a grandmother as the central figure). There were children in every courtyard. This was in old Peking, and almost all the housing is courtyard housing. There were ten primary schools serving the area, four day nurseries and one boarding nursery—another indication of the substantial numbers of children.

Of course, one Peking neighborhood is not necessarily a clue to all Peking neighborhoods, and 52,980 people are a small sample of the city's estimated 7 million, but I was assured that it was, in fact, a typical Peking district—nothing at all unusual about it. If the percentages for Fang Sheng neighborhood are actually typical, it would mean that, of the 7 million population, Peking would have about 3 million children and youngsters of school and pre-school age. The youthfulness of China's population means, of course, that a startling percentage of young women are in or approaching child-bearing age, which inevitably means a further population surge.

Another bit of evidence: Without exception every city or community for which I obtained figures has undergone a spectacular rise in population in recent years. Sian, the capital of Shensi Province, had a population of 400,000 before 1949. It now numbers 1.4 million, and there are another 1 million in Sian County—a metropolis of 2.4 million in all. The province as a whole has had a comparable increase from 13 to 14 million to 21 million. Obviously, this cannot be entirely attributed to the natural birth increment. There has been very substantial migration into Sian for many reasons—development of industry, deliberate expansion of the city, and a vast construction program—possibly with a view to making it an alternate government center in case Peking should be destroyed by nuclear bombing.

In Sian, the officials offered a figure on the rate of population increase. They said it was 20 per 1,000 per year for the province as a whole—that is, 230,000 to 280,000 per year. I could make nothing of this figure. The province's population had increased more than 50 percent in the past 20 years, and the city's had nearly quintupled. I did not think that growth of such magnitude could be turned off like a spigot. Possibly the officials meant a birth rate of 20 per 1,000. In several widely dispersed communities I was given the 20-per-1,000 birth-rate figure. My guess was that this was the official target and that the officials were dutifully repeating it.

For example, in the Double Bridge Commune outside of Peking—a community that had grown from 20,000 in 1958 to over 38,000 at present—I was told that the birth rate was 20 per 1,000 and that there was an annual population growth in the commune of 600 to 700 a year. If the population grew at the rate of 20 per 1,000, it would be increasing at a minimum of 760 per year right now. Judging by the number of children in evidence, it seemed to me that the commune leaders must be offering a statistic that was official rather than actual.

The picture of rampaging city growth was one I encountered wherever I went in China. Anyang had a population of 90,000 to 100,000 before 1949. Now it was 300,000—up threefold. Chengchow was 150,000 in 1949, 600,000 now—up fourfold. Linhsein County had 410,000 population before Liberation, 700,000 now. Wuhan had 970,000 in 1949. It was up to 2.7 million now. Changsha was below 600,000 before Liberation and over 800,000 now. I did not get the pre-Liberation figures on Shanghai's total population but it was given as 10 million now, a little more than 5 million in the city, and a little more than 4 million in the suburbs. An indication that Shanghai's population was as young, vigorous and reproduction-prone as that of Peking was given by statistics showing that of the 10 million, 3.5 million (more than a third) were students and pupils. This compared with 1.2 million industrial workers and 1 million workers in shops, hospitals, offices, etc.

If Shanghai's pre-school population followed the pattern of Peking's, it would number about 1.2 million, bringing the total school and pre-school population in this city of 10 million to 4.7 million. I was so amazed by the Shanghai figure of 3.5 million school children and students that I made the Shanghai officials repeat it three times. They laughed at my astonishment but admitted that it was a very high percentage: they thought that it might be the highest school and student population in the world. I was not inclined to disagree, and later comparison, of course, disclosed that the Shanghai figure of 35 percent students was not too different from the 30.7 percent in the Fang Sheng district of Peking. By contrast, in 1972 about 28 percent of the U.S. population was registered in educational institutions from kindergarten to graduate school.

There were a couple of localities that did not show such a spectacular growth trend. One was Yenan. Its population when it was the seat of Communist power in the late 1930's and 1940's had been 70,000. It was now 50,000. But, of course, there had been a great drop when Mao Tse-tung and the Communist hierarchy moved away, taking with them the PLA forces. Actually, Yenan was growing even more rapidly than some of the other places I visited. Its population was up 10,000, or 25 percent, in the last two years—again, obviously, due to heavy in-migration.

The city of Suang Kan, near Changsha, was said to have a population of "over 300,000." It had had a population of "under 300,000" about five years ago. Honan Province was said to have a population of "over 50 million" now. About five years earlier the population had been estimated at between 40 and 50 million.

The most detailed big-city-population data I obtained came from Wuhan. This, it is to be recalled, was a city of 970,000 estimated population in 1949, which had mushroomed to 2.7 million. The officials gave the birth rate as 16.14 per 1,000 and said that infant mortality was 4 per 1,000. The overall death rate was given as 6 per 1,000, implying that the growth rate was now 10 per 1,000 or only about 27,000 per year, a phenomenally low rate. Unfortunately, I felt something less than confidence in the Wuhan statistics. The officials said, for example, that infant mortality was higher in some areas of the city than 4 per 1,000, particularly in the suburban areas, but they did not contend that in any areas it was below 4. This suggested to me that the 4 per 1,000 figure could not be accurate. My skepticism was strengthened by other circumstances. They said that infant mortality had been 200 per 1,000 before

Liberation—a figure that was credible. However, previous studies of infant-mortality rates (notably that of S. Chandrasekhar of the Institute of Population Studies at Madras) had given it as 50 per 1,000 in 1959. A drop from 50 to 4 was hardly credible, and the figure was only a fifth as large as the one for infant mortality in the U.S.A. Moreover the reported Wuhan birth rate was lower than that of the U.S. in 1970, when our figure was 18.2 per 1,000.

What particularly caused me to be skeptical of the low rate of increase was my inability to obtain comprehensive data on how the birth rate had been reduced. Wuhan officials said that their principal weapon was propaganda through districts and organizations—urging families to pay heed to family planning and birth control. They mobilized the masses and held rallies and discussions, and technical instructions were given to the populace. But when I asked for details—how many birth control clinics had been established, which contraceptive means were most popular, how many intra-uterine rings were installed per year, how many vasectomies were performed, how many condoms distributed, and the method of distribution—I got only vague answers.

There appeared to be no contraceptive clinics, as such. Such advice was passed along through other institutions, existing neighborhood clinics (but not through the schools). As for contraceptive devices, "research was being conducted." Very few sterilization operations had been performed. They were not popular with men. The intra-uterine ring was the most popular device, and, in general, more women used contraceptive devices than men. The pill, however, was not popular. Women didn't like it. The one they used was the 20-day-a-month pill (other officials called it the 22-day pill). After strong pressure from me, a reluctant estimate was made of 70,000 to 80,000 uterine rings installed per year, but the uncertainty of the official who gave it suggested that he may simply have been grabbing a figure out of the air. No figure was obtainable on condoms. The only information anyone seemed to have was that condoms were sold, not distributed free, and could be bought for two feng (about one cent) apiece.

It seemed curious to me that officials who had the birth rate figure precisely down to the last decimal (16.14) could be so imprecise on all of the underlying data.

If birth control and family planning were being given the high priority they must have had to achieve so spectacular a drop in reproduction, the officials, it seemed to me, would have a great deal more data readily at hand. I could not help recalling that in an extensive discussion with the Fang Sheng Street Committee in Peking, the question of birth control never arose. True, I had asked no questions about it, but the workers of the committee spoke, *in extenso*, about all their important activities—health problems, clinics, mothers' care, children's care. But not a word about family planning. Here again, if the subject had high priority, it would have been natural for the Fang Sheng workers to mention it.

To my surprise there is no birth control propaganda carried on in the schools. Ma Wen-chung, a pleasant-faced, quiet man who headed the Revolutionary Committee directing the 31st middle school in Peking, put that very bluntly to me: "Sex is no problem for us. As I understand the question, this is more a social problem than one of the schools."

If there was any sex question, he insisted, it was not a matter for the schools to handle. They had no birth control clinics; they did not advise girls about pills; even their hygiene classes did not put any special emphasis on the anatomy of sex, venereal diseases or similar topics.

The hygiene courses, he said, were to help the children build their bodies. There were no special courses on sex. Contraception was not a matter for those of high-school age. It was an adult question. He came from the old society and he knew that in that society it was natural for children to have affairs and for pregnancies to occur. But now all that had changed. Any youngster who had an affair, or any girl who got pregnant, would be despised, and the whole of society would be against such conduct.

When I asked him how the problem was dealt with in the adult world, he said: "Late marriage and social education." And, in fact, there was a mass of evidence along these lines. I had heard no talk whatever about family planning at the Double Bridge Commune. They said they had a 20 per 1,000 birth rate, and when I asked whether they could absorb the natural increase in the commune they said that was no problem. In fact, they needed more hands to do the work because of lack of mechanization. I did not think that this attitude would lead to a very sharp cutback in reproduction.

I had much the same experience at the Cheng Kuan People's Commune in Honan Province. Here I met with the leaders of the Ta Tsai Yuan (Big Truck Farm) production brigade. This brigade comprised 310 families with a population of 1,624. Before Liberation, there had lived on the same land 180 families with "over 700" population. In other words, this little segment of Honan Province showed the same riotous growth as did almost every other part of the country, an increase of just under 150 percent in 22 years. When I noted that the population seemed to be increasing, the villagers agreed, but quickly added that "now we are going in for family planning and propagating knowledge about it." I asked Dr. Yuan Chang-chi, who ran the brigade clinic, what was being done in specific terms. He said that he distributed two kinds of contraceptive pills, the one-a-month kind and the 22-a-month kind. After much pressing, he estimated that 80 to 90 women used them. I could not calculate precisely what percentage of the child-bearing population of the brigade that might cover. At a minimum, there must have been one woman of child-bearing capability per family, which would mean less than 30 percent coverage. But if the families I visited were typical (and I had to assume they were), this ratio was much too high. One family had 14 members, including four nubile females. The other was a family of six, with two women of child-bearing age. So, just as a guess, if the figure of 80 to 90 was correct (which again I doubted), this didn't provide coverage of more than 10 to 15 percent of the women of child-bearing age. As for the intra-uterine ring, the doctor said "quite a few use them" but added that the problem with them was you had to have workers to insert them. I did not think many were in actual use. He dismissed the condom as "not popular." So far as visible evidence was concerned—the commune, like every village I saw in China, was bulging with children. In every village I saw pregnant women and nursing mothers in every crowd.

At the Kao Tung Ling Commune outside of Changsha, there had been 3,300 families in 1958. There were 3,900 now, with a population of 17,600. No one could remember the 1958 population figure. In the Shang Li brigade, which I visited, there were 670 families with 3,200 people in 1958, and 780 with 3,800 at present. If these figures are correct, there were 4.78 members per family in 1958 and 4.88 per family today. In other words, no reduction in family size. In fact, the reverse. They are worth noting only because the commune officials contended that they had cut back population growth to 1.5 percent per year. How this can be possible at a time when actual family size remains the same, or increases, is beyond understanding. A possible explanation is that each year the commune releases 50 to 60 young people to work in the city. This may produce a technical retardation of population growth for the commune, but it would not be reflected in China's population as a whole. The officials put the average size of families in the commune at four to five (which fits the figures), but said that some families ran up to as many as ten members. The families of the commune leaders, I found on questioning, usually numbered five.

But it was when I got into the mechanics of population planning that the vagueness set in. This was a question, they said, which was handled at the production-team (the lowest unit of organization) level. They did not use posters or lectures or movies to propagate birth-control information. One person in each brigade was supposed to be in charge of "such matters." What methods were used? The uterine ring was not. Abortions were rare. (This was a general tendency, I found. Abortions are technically available to women, but I could find no evidence of a widespread practice of abortions. To the contrary, there was an obvious negativism toward abortion—almost, if not quite, an open prejudice.) "We don't encourage abortions here," said Li Ping-kui, the party secretary of the Shang Li Production Brigade. He said the condom was "quite popular," but had no notion of what percentage used either the pill or the condom.

There was, although never mentioned by officials, a basic factor (outside of traditional prejudice) working against radical population control in the countryside. Not only were more hands needed almost everywhere, in view of almost complete dependence upon labor-surplus methods rather than machines, but there was a direct economic motivation for a family to have many children. Production returns were divided in the communes on a per capita basis. The family with six or seven children had a substantially higher return than one with only two or three. And, contrary to all propaganda, the family was the essential unit, the building block of the communal society of the countryside.

It was also apparent, the more I talked with Chinese officials, that the government's chief weapon in population control was not, really, mechanical birth-control technique. It was late marriage, a deliberate device to take women out of child bearing for a number of years at their period of greatest fertility. I had seen this in the cities where, among the current generation of party officials, intellectuals, students, members of the intelligentsia, it was working. It seemed far more the rule than the exception that city young people were deferring marriage and child bearing far beyond the normal period. In the city, the suggested minimum age for women was 28 and for men 30. Whether this campaign was having as much effect on industrial workers and their families I did not know, but the sample families I interviewed at industrial establishments seemed to be limiting offspring to two or three. I had the impression they were marrying a bit earlier than the officials and the intelligentsia.

But China was 80 percent rural. City reproduction rates are always lower than rural in every country in the world, and the reproduction rate of peasants coming to the city is always radically lower than that of their country cousins. There are many reasons (outside of official propaganda): cramped housing, lack of economic benefit from large families, urban problems in caring for children, city social pressures, etc.

If, as it seemed to me, China had made a definite inroad on her reproduction problem in the city, this was only the tip of the iceberg. The problem remained in the rural areas, with 80 percent of the population. And it was precisely in the rural areas where, so far as I could discover, the population was continuing to reproduce at a rate well over the official goals set by the government.

For example, while city girls were discouraged from marrying until 28, in the country the age was set (by party propaganda) at 23 to 24, and 25 for men. Thus, country girls were going into reproduction four to five years ahead of their city sisters—yet country girls already were bearing a wildly disproportionate percentage of China's babies. These babies, thanks to the tremendous breakthroughs in public health, were surviving. They were not dying, as their predecessors had, at the rate of 200 to 300 of very 1,000 born. This was where the population problem centered, and the mild and feeble efforts of the country's officials did not seem likely to bite deeply into it.

In fact, after I had put my notebook and pencil away and was sitting in a quiet, relaxed, general conversation with Li Ping-kui and the other leaders of the Kao Tung Ling Commune, they virtually agreed. "It is a very hard thing," one said, "to change old habits. It can't be done overnight." I discovered in further informal conversations that it had proved virtually impossible to root out in the village the traditional tendency to marry off girls as soon as possible and to have as many children and grandchildren as possible. Not even the advent of the Red Guards into the villages had ended that. In fact, not a few village elders had persuaded young male Red Guards from the city to marry their village daughters, to settle down, raise families and become part of the community. I was delighted to discover that Chairman Mao agreed with this assessment. In December, 1970, Edgar Snow congratulated Mao on the great progress which had been made in the past five or ten years in birth control. The Chairman gently chided Snow. He had been taken in. No such great progress had been made. In the country, women still kept having children until they produced a boy. If the first was not a boy they tried again and again and again. Pretty soon there were nine children and the woman was 45. Maybe then she would stop trying. It was going to take time to change that attitude.

What did all of this add up to? I thought that, in general, it supported the view that China's population continues to grow at a rate substantially greater than the officially conceded rate. What size her population now is, I don't know. But I think that China's leaders do know, or can come very close to establishing it. For one reason: Two commodities in China are rationed—rice and cotton textiles. This is a national rationing system, based on individual and family cards that specify in detail the numbers and names of the individual recipients. It provides complete control figures for all city and town populations. The rural areas are totally organized in communes, and each commune has an accurate, up-to-the-minute register of every household and the number of members of each family. The two figures, added to the number in the armed forces, provide a total that cannot be far from right. I raised this point with some Chinese officials. They conceded it was valid, but said some commune figures might not be accurate because people might be slow to remove the names of those who have died, reducing their family's rations and per capita shares in the commune. That could be true, but considering the degree to which Chinese, by the sheer fact of the enormous population of the country, are inevitably aware of each other's affairs, I doubted any significant distortion occurred.

I do not know why the Chinese government has been reluctant to make accurate population totals and growth rates public. It is possible that, in some fashion, the subject is slightly embarassing because of the long-standing Marxian contention that population control is not necessary. This thesis was evolved by Marx in a quarrel with Malthus in the 19th century. Malthus predicted that the world would ultimately drown in its own surplus population. Marx took the view that the world could always feed itself if only Socialist methods of distribution were introduced. Thus, the employment of radical measures to limit population have always been suspect among classical Marxists. This ideological contradiction, indeed, for a time, caused the Chinese to introduce no family planning methods after they came to power. But practical considerations inevitably won out.

It might be that, since the figures would reveal an inexorable upward course for China's population, they are embarrassing because they expose the relative lack of population control. However, the Chinese tend to be admirably frank in admitting mistakes and failures, so this seems rather unlikely.

A more critical reason is that the precise figures for Chinese population and growth would cast a penetrating light on China's general policy, and her foreign imperatives in particular. The population totals provide the best estimate as to China's economic and military potential. The growth rate discloses what those potentials are likely to be in the future. If, for example, the figures show (as I believe) that China's population will cross the 1 billion mark* before the end of this decade, they would also reveal that shortly after the year 2000 there would be 2 billion Chinese in the world, that is to say, about one-third of the world's population. Numbers like this have *never* been encountered in the history of mankind. China is already almost equal in manpower to the United States, Russia and India combined —the next three largest states in the world.

When one begins to calculate the effect of this population mass on world affairs, one enters an arena of relative strengths and disproportionate ratios that is staggering. The weight the Chinese carry in the world today is great. But that which they will carry tomorrow is titanic.

There is one country in the world that reads the Chinese figures with horrible fascination. That is the Soviet Union. For, while China still feeds her population well (and even accumulates large reserves of foodstuffs), the day will come when even the achievements in introducing irrigation, modern fertilizers, pesticides and high-performance seeds will not be enough. China will need more land for her millions, and the Russians possess possibly 1.5 million square miles of territory that once was China's.

In other words, China's precise population and rate of growth is a military secret of deep significance. That, I imagine, is why the Chinese are reluctant to give the world the precise numbers.

---

* The Joint Congressional Economic Committee in 1972 estimated China's population would total 1.32 to 1.33 billion by 1990.

14

The Cure of The Thousand Needles

When I first visited Mongolia in 1959, there were 30,000 or 40,000 Chinese in the country, but so far as any contact was concerned, I might as well have been in Timbuktu. Even when my Mongol hosts introduced me to Chinese who were working as specialists in the factories, they held aloof and unsmiling. Not once did a Chinese offer me his hand.

One morning I was taken to see a new hospital in the heart of Ulan Bator that had been built with the technical assistance of Czechoslovakia and equipped entirely with apparatus from Eastern Europe. Passing through a large ward, we arrived at a small laboratory where I was introduced to a doctor who turned out to be Chinese. To my surprise, he greeted me with a smile, put out his hand and invited me into his office. He was the resident acupuncturist. He proudly showed me a chart on the wall with hundreds of points in red and blue, indicating the places on the body for the insertion of needles, then he waved to a cabinet where I saw, gleaming in the bright morning sunshine, his "thousand needles." Wouldn't the American visitor like a demonstration? I gulped and beat a hasty retreat. I had heard only vaguely of acupuncture, and I had no intention of subjecting myself to the "cure of the thousand needles."

I knew that acupuncture was practiced in Russia, along with some forms of Chinese herbal medicine, and I had always classified it in my mind with other Russian medical oddities—the ancient art of cupping, the application of leeches, the use of powdered reindeer antlers to restore sexual powers, rhubarb and ginseng as aphrodisiacs, and folk remedies much too arcane even to try to understand.

But by the time I came to China, in 1972, my attitude had changed from skepticism to deep interest. I had heard (as who had not) that acupuncture was being successfully used in China, specifically for anesthesia, and quite possibly for other purposes. I was eager to see for myself.

One day Charlotte and I were taken to Friendship Hospital in Peking, not far from our hotel, the Chien Men. That was the district hospital for the Chien Men region, and its director was Chang Wei-hsun, a former American. Dr. Chang had been born in Los Angeles, had interned at Los Angeles County Hospital after graduating from medical school, and had then studied at Children's Hospital in Boston, Peter Bent Brigham and Bellevue. His specialty was pediatrics. He had sailed for China on the eve of the proclamation of the Communist regime. In fact, he was on the Pacific when he heard the announcement on October 1, 1949, that Mao Tse-tung had taken power. Since 1958, he had headed the pediatrics department at Friendship Hospital and in recent years he had become its director. Friendship was a large, modern hospital with 600 beds, serving 2,000 to 3,000 outpatients. It had 14 clinical departments and 575 medical workers, including 270 doctors. It had been completed in 1952 by the Peking municipality. A nursing school was attached, and it maintained a mobile medical team for service to the countryside adjacent to Peking. Both western and traditional Chinese medicine were practiced, but much more western than Chinese.

Dr. Chang was a rangy, graying man, a bit on the thin side. He smoked one cigarette after another and spoke easily, with his accentless Los Angeles intonation, and he was obviously a bit regretful that he had to devote so much time to administration and so little to pediatrics.

On the day of our visit, hospital doctors were performing four operations with the use of acupuncture anesthesia, and that was what we had been invited to watch. There were about a dozen visitors in all, including two retired Chinese-American doctors from Honolulu, a German woman surgeon and a group from the British Embassy, including Mrs. Anthony Royal, wife of the British Minister of Trade, who was visiting Peking.

Friendship Hospital had been employing acupuncture anesthesia for only about a year and, in fact, Dr. Chang explained that the technique was a very recent development. Acupuncture as a means of treating disease had been used in China since at least 400 B.C. But its use to replace conventional anesthesia in operations dated back little more than ten years to experiments that were first undertaken in the No. 1 People's Hospital in Shanghai. The success of this hospital led to experiments elsewhere—the Liuchow Tuberculosis Hospital in

Kwangsi, the No. 1 Tuberculosis Central Hospital in Shanghai and the Shanghai No. 2 Medical College.

Research into acupuncture had been stimulated during the Cultural Revolution by the emphasis Chairman Mao placed upon the legacy of traditional Chinese medicine. But the decision whether or not to employ acupuncture was one for the individual hospital and the individual surgeon to make.

The operations at Friendship Hospital, we learned as we donned white hospital gowns and gauze masks, were for the removal of an ovarian cyst in a 29-year-old woman; the removal of a senile cataract from a man of about 70; a hernia repair on a 30-year-old man; and a thyroid operation on a 24-year-old woman.

We met the patients before they were taken into the four adjoining operating rooms. Each seemed cheerful and alert. Dr. Chang said they had had no sedation of any kind, nor did I note any sign of it. The surgeons had told their patients about the procedures that would be used, and I saw no trace of apprehension in any of them. The young woman whose ovarian cyst was to be removed was wheeled into the main operating theater and transferred to the operating table and lay there in her white surgical gown, just like any pre-surgery patient in an American hospital. Instead of an anesthetist, the acupuncture nurse sat at the head of the table with her needles and acupuncture panel. Deftly, she inserted seven small gleaming points of steel that looked a bit like sewing-machine needles. The needles went into the nostrils of the patient and just above her eyebrows, apparently penetrating to a depth of only a few millimeters. Each needle was attached by a fine electric wire to the panel, and was rotated electrically instead of by hand (as had been done when the technique was first started). The nurse at the panel was able to adjust the speed of the needles, and that regulated the degree of stimulation. Slow speed, less stimulation. High speed, more stimulation. As I watched the needles gently twitching, the girl's face remained calm and peaceful, no sign of pain or apprehension. The nurse had instruments not only to control the vibration rate of the needles but to monitor pulse, blood pressure and respiration. For 20 minutes, while the surgeons, Drs. Fang and Wong, scrubbed and prepared for the operation, the acupuncture needles twirled, inducing, as Dr. Chang was quick to note, analgesia, as it is properly called, not anesthesia. Occasionally, the nurse gave the young woman a sip of tea from the spout of a small brown porcelain teapot. The room was filled with spectators, craning their necks to try to get a look at the patient. Several of the British visitors had 16-mm and

8-mm movie cameras, and they climbed chairs and stepladders for a better angle. The patient showed no sign of being disturbed by all this. Nor was there the faintest sign of tension or nervousness in her olive face.

When Dr. Wong finally made the abdominal incision with a quick sure stroke of her surgical blade, the nurse asked the girl if she felt any sensation. "Yes," she said, "it feels as though someone has passed a feather across my abdomen." The operation proceeded rapidly.

Occasionally, I darted into the other operating rooms to see how patients there were progressing. Only two needles were used for the cataract operation, one adjacent to each ear, and in 15 minutes the operation was completed. I had seen cataract operations in the United States under local anesthetic. There seemed to be no difference in the technique except that the Chinese used acupuncture instead of novocain. Later, the opthalmologist, Dr. Ma, confirmed that. He said there was no difference whatever. However, he preferred acupuncture because, with novocain, there was a slight clouding of the tissue. With acupuncture there was none, so that you could see exactly what you were doing. He now used acupuncture in 90 percent of his cataract cases.

When the ovarian cyst was finally removed—after about half an hour—it proved to be nearly as large as a grapefruit. The nurse had been giving the patient occasional sips of tea. Now she asked the girl if she had felt anything. The girl said yes. It felt as if something had been pulling deep inside of her, and then as though a great weight had been removed. But there was no pain.

I talked to the young woman as she was wheeled from the operating room. She was as quiet and relaxed as she had been before the operation. There had been no pain at all, she said, with a little twinkle.

Later, Dr. Wong said she had been employing acupuncture for about a year for most of her gynecological operations. However, where there were major adhesions, she preferred a conventional anesthetic. She felt there were certain problems that had not been entirely overcome in the use of acupuncture. Sometimes, analgesia was not complete and the patient might feel some pain. Also, almost every patient complained of a kind of visceral discomfort when an organ or a tumor was removed. It was a curious kind of pulling sensation. Everyone felt that it was unpleasant. Occasionally, a patient complained of dizziness.

However, she had found acupuncture very useful in almost all kinds of surgery in her practice—removal of the uterus and Fallopian tubes, ovarian operations, intra-vaginal operations and Caesarean sections. And, of course, the greatest boon was the absence of post-operative effects from anesthesia. The added strain on heart and lungs was eliminated entirely—an important factor, especially with older patients. Dr. Wong did not use acupuncture in childbirth. That was a natural process, and the only instance in which acupuncture might be used there was for the relief of pain if the contractions were particularly strong. Then a few needles might be employed, and this did not interfere with the natural-birth process. Dr. Wong estimated that she used acupuncture now for about half of her surgical cases. Doctors in the eye, nose and throat department said they used it for about 60 percent of their operations.

One of the most spectacular and successful uses of acupuncture was in brain surgery. Dr. Chang said that when they first started experimenting, they used 40 needles and 23 nurses in carrying out a lobotomy. Now a single needle behind the ear was all that was used, and about one third of their brain operations were performed with the use of acupuncture. Surgeons doing abdominal operations liked acupuncture, because they could ask patients to cooperate. For instance, when a hernia was sewed up, the patient could be asked to cough and the doctor could instantly test whether there was any weakness in his repair work. Acupuncture was being widely employed in dentistry, and here, the surgeons said, they often did not use needles. Merely pressure on the nerve points. It was being employed experimentally and successfully in veterinary practice. There was only one group of patients on whom acupuncture anesthesia was not yet being generally used—children. The surgeons had no ready explanation of why it was not used with children. They simply said that in that area, experimentation was still in progress.

Physicians reported that when long operations were performed, the effects of analgesia sometimes began to wear off before the operation was over. They were experimenting to see what could be done about that. One approach was to decrease stimulation after starting it at a high rate, then to increase it toward the end, when the effects begin to wear off.

The attitude of Dr. Chang was reserved rather than exuberant about acupuncture. He displayed some concern about the head-over-heels enthusiasm that acupuncture reports had aroused in the west. His associates emphasized that they were still not certain as to the exact mechanism that caused acupuncture to work, although they felt that it must be a form of analgesia working through stimulation of the autonomic nervous system. But, they emphasized, much more experimental work had to be done before the underlying principles could be established.

The operations we witnessed were quite similar to a series witnessed by Dr. E. Grey Diamond and Dr. Paul Dudley White during a trip to China in September, 1971. Dr. Diamond witnessed three operations—two thyroid cases and a stomach ulcer case—at the Kwangtung Provincial Hospital at Canton; and four more—for frontal lobotomy, a cataract, a pulmonary tuberculosis lesion and an ovarian cyst—at the Third Teaching Hospital of Peking Medical College. The procedure in these cases was virtually identical to that followed in the four operations we witnessed. In some of the cases Dr. Diamond studied, the patients were given mild sedation the night before the operation, and some had light anesthesia as well as acupuncture.

Dr. Diamond was told that acupuncture anesthesia was routinely employed in eye, ear, nose and throat operations, in Caesarean section, in many brain operations and in limb surgery and dental work. It was used in abdominal surgery except for heavily muscled patients. In those cases, it was said not to provide sufficient muscle relaxation. The Peking Medical College had run a series of 4,900 acupuncture anesthesias, and the Canton hospital had done about 1,500. Each said that the technique had been successful in more than 90 percent of the cases in which it was used.

Medical service was not free in the hospital—although the charges were reasonable by American standards. The young woman whose ovarian cyst was removed would pay 15 yuan (about $6). The cataract bill was eight yuan; the hernia repair, six; the thyroid operation three. All of the patients would pay one yuan a day for hospital care, in addition to the cost of the operation, but general medical service was free to workers, state employees, teachers and educators, and students. Peasants, however, had to pay one yuan a year (about 40 cents) for medical services. The state reimbursed the hospital for the disparity between patient's payments and actual costs. Much of the disparity arose from the treatment of peasants sent to the city for attention and unable to pay at the regular rates.

There were in the Chinese health services a good many more women than men doctors, but all were paid at the same rate. In the group we met, the pay ranged from 120 to 156 yuan a month.

The remarkable success with acupuncture had spurred a general investigation of the use of the technique for all kinds of diseases. But here the western-trained Chinese physicians obviously were filled with caution. They recognized that some effects attributed to acupuncture might be due to the power of suggestion, and they warned that too little was understood of the manner in which the needles affected the nervous system to arrive at intelligent answers. This, of course, did not prevent many foreigners in Peking from embracing acupuncture as a miracle cure. And I met not a few diplomats who said their headaches, insomnia, colds and arthritis had been relieved. I even encountered a lady who was certain that acupuncture had cured her barrenness and enabled her to conceive a child.

One area of use of acupuncture in which the Chinese reported success was in the treatment of certain forms of congenital deafness in children. Here, they said, they had had a substantial number of cases in which totally deaf children were enabled to hear. But they added quickly that they did not know the reason for this. Presumably it related to the stimulation of the nervous system by the needles.

Acupuncture was not the only miracle of Chinese medicine. The Chinese had also perfected what they regarded as a very advanced technique for the rejoining of severed limbs. Dr. Chen Chung-wei, chief of the orthopedic department of the No. 6 People's Hospital at Shanghai, who perfected the method, demonstrated it to us. He was a big, broad-shouldered, self confident man, one of the few Chinese I met who bandied the name of Chairman Mao about in every other breath, and who emphasized the important role Chairman Mao's thought had played in his achievements.

Dr. Chen's technique did not differ essentially from that used by Dr. Ronald A. Malt in September, 1962, to restore the severed pitching arm of Little Leaguer Everett Knowles at Massachusetts General Hospital, but Dr. Chen had gone several steps further. He not only sewed on hands and arms that had been severed, but also fingers. He claimed a record of 95 percent recovery of function in 94 cases of severed limbs and hands carried out up to the end of 1971, and equal success with 151 patients whose fingers have been sewed on since 1963.

The finger operation is much more difficult and complex than the limb, hand or foot, because there are so many fine veins and arteries in the finger, each of which must be individually sutured. Not infrequently, Dr. Chen was confronted with a case in which three or four fingers had been cut off. The physical strain of sewing back three or four fingers was enormous. An operation, Dr. Chen said, might require up to 15 to 20 hours. The suturing of the fingers required very small needles and sutures. Much of the work had to be done under magnification in order to see the tiny vessels and the materials with which he worked. Once the fingers were successfully sewed back, regeneration of nerve connections proceeded at a regular and predictable pace, a few millimeters a week until, finally, after two or three years, sensation had been restored to the whole hand.

Dr. Chen had only one patient in the hospital at the moment. He took us up to the ward where she was convalescing. Her hand had been severed and resewed and was still in a cast. Patients had to stay in the hospital for several months after the operation. Additional corrective surgery was often needed, and there was an elaborate program of orthopedic exercises to restore the muscle functions and make certain that the hand would be restored to useful functioning.

Then we met two patients who had been completely cured. I never had two such iron handshakes in my life.

The first was 26-year-old Liu Tse-fang, a young woman in a Shanghai automobile-spare-parts factory. Her hair was bobbed, she wore an apple-green silk jacket and she had a grip like a blacksmith. Her fingers—four of them—had been cut off by a lathe. Her co-workers picked up the severed fingers and rushed her to the No. 6 Hospital. Now she was back on the same job, earning 50 yuan a month. She was not married, but had a boyfriend. "The party and Chairman Mao gave me back my hand," she said. "And now I'll do more for the Revolution."

The second patient was Fan Ken-far, a carpenter working for a construction outfit. He cut off four fingers with an electric saw. Two had dangled from his hand when he arrived at the hospital. Dr. Chen asked: "Where are the other two fingers?" The factory workers looked around the saw and finally found the fingers where they had been flung by the machine and rushed them to the hospital. After ten hours of work Dr. Chen got the fingers all back on.

Fan was 41. The accident had happened in August, 1967. He had his job back; his hand was stronger than ever (he almost crushed my hand in a friendly demonstration of his strength), and he was confident that had he lost his fingers before the Revolution, he would now be a beggar unable to earn his living.

One of the technical problems that Dr. Chen had solved was that of preserving the fingers during the hours required to sew each one on. He did this through refrigeration. The fingers were kept at a low temperature but above freezing, and the blood was replaced by a saline solution. As he completed sewing on one finger, the next would be removed from the refrigerator and brought to the operating table.

Dr. Chen's techniques were being taught to other hospital teams in other Chinese cities, and patients were flown in to No. 6 Hospital from the countryside—sometimes from hundreds of miles away, by special plane. Dr. Chen was confident that his technique was superior to that employed anywhere else in the world. He conceded that the first operations might have occurred in the United States (although he was inclined to take priority here, as well). But he did not believe that anywhere else had such a volume of operations been performed, or so great a backlog of experience accumulated. On this, I was rather inclined to agree. I did not think that there existed in the United States surgical teams prepared to work 10, 12, 15 or 20 hours to restore severed limbs or fingers. It was true that occasionally such operations were performed in the United States. But they were unusual, and I could not help wondering whether this might not be, at least in part, because of the extraordinary cost that such continuous skilled surgery involved. Were we in the United States as prepared as the Chinese to devote thousands of dollars of surgical time to the task of putting back hands, limbs and fingers? Perhaps, in the military surgery of the Vietnam war. But not as a regular run-of-the-mill service in New York or Chicago. We were more inclined to accept the result of the amputation and try to care for the handicap by means of prosthetic devices. Here there might very well be a contrast in value systems between China and the United States, with measurable consequences. Certainly there was nothing in Dr. Chen's technique that could not easily be duplicated in the general hospitals of American cities—provided they were prepared to pay the price in money and personnel.

American surgeons had already visited Dr. Chen and studied his techniques, just as American doctors had witnessed the use of acupuncture anesthesia. I was certain that within a very short time, possibly not longer than a year or two, acupuncture would be in experimental use in the United States, and probably in general use within another year or two.

Beyond that lay other interesting possibilities. The Chinese were engaged in a comprehensive examination of their traditional herbal medicine to try to discover what principles underlay the use of these age-old remedies. This was going forward hand-in-hand with an inquiry into acupuncture as a curative method. The Chinese pharmacology had been built up over 5,000 years of a civilization's existence. Stripped of superstition, it could hardly fail to contain wonders that would enrich and prolong human life. The first fruit of the new friendship of China and the United States might well be humanitarian.

15

Island of Tranquility

The mahogany table was sprinkled with white camellias, and the chandeliers caught the crystal glasses in a thousand facets. The silver was burnished, the china from Limoges, the men wore white jackets and the women wore jewels with their *décolletage,* or their Cambodian *sampots.* Fans softly moved the humid air. Occasionally, in the distance, there was a sound like thunder, and the crystal goblets gently tinkled. The thunder came and went like heat lightning on the August prairie. Our host smiled quietly. "Pay no attention," he said, "it's only the bombing in Zone D. It goes on like this almost every night, and night after night." Our hosts laughed a gentle Cambodian laugh, and we went on to talk of other things. The year was 1966. The place was Svay Rieng, about eight miles from the South Vietnamese frontier on Route Nationale No. 1.

It was pleasant to visit Cambodia then, pleasant but a bit strange. All around, war raged. The bombs fell eight miles away. The great forests along the frontier burned and smoldered in the napalm. Earlier that day we had ridden by jeep deep into the jungle north of Svay Rieng to the border posts of Cambodia where, it was alleged, the Americans had bombed very recently. I saw the smashed buildings, the bomb-scarred forest, and village residents told how the low-flying planes had come over. Others told of American artillery that crashed across the border. Fortunately, the only casualties had been cows. War raged along the Cambodian eastern frontiers. Here were the sanctuaries of the Vietcong. Bloody fighting went on day by day. To the north on the Laotian frontier, the sound of American bombers echoed night after night and day after day, as hundreds of tons of high explosives were dropped to interdict, it was said, the Ho Chi Minh Trail. Nor was the western frontier quiet. Sometimes Thais came across the line and attacked the Cambodians. Sometimes the Cambodians retaliated.

But in Svay Rieng we ate from Limoges plates and drank from crystal goblets that vibrated pleasantly in the distant thunder. At Angkor Wat each night, beautiful Cambodian dancers performed the ritual dances—the dances that were carved in bas relief on the walls of the ancient capital. And in Pnompenh life was idyllic. The food was good at the Hotel Royale, the best French food east of Paris, it was said. Prince Sihanouk was busy. He had a passion for making movies and had mobilized the whole of Cambodia's air force to take part in the latest production. He himself wrote the script and directed and produced the movie. His daughter, Princess Bopha Devi was the heroine, and his cabinet ministers had been dragooned into taking roles. The picture ran for six hours, and members of the *corps diplomatique* had to sit through the whole performance. A cut version, running only 3½ hours, was being prepared for the festival at Cannes.

Cambodia was, as her ruler proclaimed, an "island of tranquillity" in a sea of danger. She was not at war and, if war raged on her doorstep, if there was violation of her neutrality in the frontier areas by Vietnamese and Americans, if there were clandestine arms and supply shipments through Cambodia to North Vietnam, if Cambodian middlemen bought American supplies in the huge black market bazaar on Route Nationale No. 1 and some of these eventually made their way north, if Prince Sihanouk was engaged in an eternal balancing act, now expelling the Americans on charges they were plotting with the CIA to assassinate him, now proclaiming China Cambodia's No. 1 friend, now pouting at the Chinese and beginning to warm up to the Americans again—if all this was going on in a Graustarkian kind of way—still Cambodia was not at war. She was, indeed, an "island of tranquillity." If her economy was a baroque combination of greedy private enterprise, official corruption and state socialistic enterprises—at least it could be said that the people, by and large, were as content as they were beautiful. Life was easy and unstrained in Cambodia. No one starved. The rice and the fish were plentiful.

Not much disturbed the ancient Cambodian way of life, except the schools, the hospitals and the sanitation Prince Sihanouk had introduced. There were some shoals of dissatisfaction amid the tranquillity. Certainly the upper classes missed the lush days of American aid, the huge American establishment, the high rents and high prices and easy dollars. It was getting hard to obtain spare parts for their Mercedes, and gasoline was rationed. But compared to what went on beyond Cambodia's borders, it seemed like heaven. Never had I found a people that lived a life so compatible with nature, who had adapted themselves so beautifully to their environment. They were simple people, beautiful people, pacific people. They had never—at least not for a thousand years—been good warriors. They were no good at the competitive rituals of the modern world. But they had no need to be. They were isolated and protected from it—isolated and protected, everyone conceded, by the tightrope versatility of Prince Sihanouk. He was not a king—he had abdicated his throne. He was, he insisted, a prince. He ruled, he insisted, as a democrat. There were political parties (their principles did not bear looking at too closely) and a parliament. But everyone knew that Prince Sihanouk was it. He ran Cambodia, and whatever else he may have done, he kept it out of the second Indochinese war while everything else on the peninsula went up in flames. It was no mean achievement. No one really understood how he did it. Foreign diplomats sometimes cursed him, often said they despised him, but in the end, had to admit admiration for his genius.

In 1966 Cambodia was the only bright spot in Southeast Asia. It was not easy to visit. One of the ways in which Prince Sihanouk protected his country was to control access very carefully. He was particularly strict against newspapermen, and strictest of all against American newspapermen. But I was fortunate enough to spend three weeks there with Charlotte, and they were three idyllic weeks. It seemed to me then that since Sihanouk had managed his balancing act so well and had kept Cambodia out of war so long, there was no reason why he should not succeed until the end—whenever that might be. (I assumed, of course, in those times, that the war might eventually be brought to an end.)

My first intimation that this might not be true came in January, 1970. I happened to be in Paris dining with an Asian friend whom I had first met in Cambodia in 1966. During dinner he was called to the telephone. He returned to the table shaken. "It's the damnedest thing," he said. "You know Sihanouk is in France for his annual cure. I've just been talking with one of his men. There's been a curious political development, and he may be out. It's hard to believe, but he may never go back to Cambodia."

I could not have been more shocked. I had not seen any signs of Cambodian internal crisis. But in this, it appeared, I was mistaken. There had been growing trouble, largely economic, which was causing sharp political repercussions.

Even in 1966, Cambodia's economy was not robust, but this made little difference to the peasants who comprised 90 percent of the population. They lived on their rice and fish, and if manufactured articles were in short supply, they hardly cared. Not so the upper class and the bureaucrats. They were caught in an inflationary spiral. Sihanouk's austerity and control of export-import trade prevented the upper classes from making the profits they were accustomed to. The army was getting restive. It was short on modern equipment. It couldn't get parts and ammunition for the weapons it had gotten in the halcyon days of U.S. aid. There was no graft or kickbacks to be pocketed in getting supplies, as they now were, from the Chinese.

This fed back into parliament. Sihanouk in November, 1969, confronted a serious loss of support. There was a series of angry rows; Sihanouk was defeated on some critical issues, and finally, in a huff, he decided to abandon Pnompenh and go on his annual pilgrimage to France to take the cure. His thinking, I gathered, was that if he left, his enemies would fight among themselves, and he would be able to return, take advantage of their disarray and come back stronger than ever.

But events did not move as the Prince calculated. Or moved more swiftly than he anticipated. The full story of the complex maneuvering has not yet been untangled. Even Premier Chou En-lai, during a dinner meeting in Peking, asked Richard Dudman of the *St. Louis Post-Dispatch* and me what we thought *really* happened in Cambodia —whether it was a CIA plot, as Sihanouk officially insisted, or what. We were not, I am afraid, able to enlighten him very much.

My own belief is that if the Prince had hastened back from Paris instead of going to Moscow and Peking to try to line up support, Cambodia might still be an island of tranquility. But, of course, that was not to happen. As Sihanouk rode out to Sheremetovo Airport in Moscow with Premier Kosygin on his way to Peking, having failed to get the backing he wanted from the Russians, the Soviet Premier quietly advised him that news had just come in of a *coup d'état* led by Lon Nol. The Prince was out. From that time, he had lived in Peking, generously supported by the Chinese, still the head of the royalist government, but head of a government-in-exile, quartered in Peking, dependent upon Chinese generosity to maintain his entourage, communicating with his countrymen by radio broadcast, his chief connection with Cambodia maintained through the Khmer Rouge, the Cambodian Communist movement, which, when he ruled in Pnompenh, he had done his zealous best to suppress.

It was an incongruous situation. The Prince was supported by Peking while the Lon Nol government was backed by the United States, and, such is the dialectic of Peking-Moscow, retained the diplomatic support not only of Moscow but of the whole Soviet bloc, with the exception of iconoclastic Rumania.

If the spectacle of the prim and puritanical Peking Communists supporting the once eccentric, pleasure-loving and individualistic Prince seemed odd, it did have its political *raison d'être*. It clearly played a major role in Peking's long-range strategy for Southeast Asia and the less well-developed nations in general.

I had long been in communication with Prince Sihanouk, and one morning after I had arrived in Peking, Charlotte and I were invited to meet with him. The Chinese had put at his disposal the former French Embassy in the old Legation Quarter of Peking, on one of the narrow, tree-shaded lanes close to the Forbidden City. Our taxi pulled up before a great, red-painted gateway, set in high old walls, where three PLA men maintained a guard post. The taxi was not permitted to enter, but they motioned us to walk in. We found ourselves in a spacious park with a long, curving road leading through well-kept lawns, with islands of flowers, to a big brick house, a typical 19th-century mansion. To one side, a ping-pong table was set up under some chestnut trees, and there were deck chairs scattered around for spectators. Another PLA man was on duty at the entrance. He motioned us to wait, and soon a Cambodian aide emerged to lead us up a sumptuous staircase to the second floor, where Prince Sihanouk greeted us. He was wearing an immaculately tailored gray, narrow-pin-stripe suit, a deep red and dark blue figured silk tie, a white shirt, a gold tie-clasp and black shoes. He looked trim and handsome (perhaps his diet in China was less Lucullan than in Pnompenh), and he was obviously delighted to see us. I had missed him by two or three days during my trip to North Korea, where he had spent a month as the guest of Premier Kim Il Sung. After his Korean trip, he had gone off for a couple of weeks' travel in Northeast China, visiting the big industrial cities of Manchuria; the next week he was leaving for his first tour of Europe and the west since establishment of the government-in-exile, visiting Rumania, Albania, Yugoslavia, Algeria and Mauritania.

He led us into a drawing room decorated with a very large blown-up photograph of himself and Chairman Mao. A beautiful bowl of flowers—red, white, and yellow roses, white peonies and red and yellow straw flowers—stood on a center table. There was a large picture of the famous new bridge across the Yangtze at Nanking, done in mother-of-pearl; a cabinet of Chinese objects of art to one side; a pale, very beautiful taupe Chinese rug on the floor; a dozen gray slip-covered armchairs; and on a table to the back of the room, some Cambodian silver-work dishes and a large stack of presents, brightly gift-wrapped and ribbon-tied.

The Prince put Charlotte at his side and began a monologue that hardly needed any questions from me, directing his remarks and attention to Charlotte. He talked, as always, with animation, throwing his hands out in supplicating gestures, raising his eyes to the heavens, his face mobile and his animation by no means diminished. I knew that this was going to be a very busy week for him. He was seeing Dudman the next day, meeting an English correspondent the day following, and was going to spend the weekend, or much of it, making a documentary film with the French correspondent, Jean Lecouture. Perhaps this added to his exhilaration.

He plunged into his story, and I found it fascinating. In Asia, he said, when countries are not Communist, their armies inevitably are rightist. This was the case in Cambodia. He used to tell Lon Nol (who was his commander-in-chief) that neutrality was the only policy that would save Cambodia. The Prince had been criticized because he refused to join the Free World and the anti-Communist crusade. All the other Southeast Asian countries had joined in, even Indonesia under Suharto, the Philippines, Malaysia and, of course, South Korea. His army criticized him for not signing up.

Well, he had refused. Not because he was anti-American. He was not anti-American even now. He loved the American people and the American policy of independence. But geography had placed Cambodia in a very hot spot.

"Observers said," the Prince declared in English, with an outgoing gesture of his arms, "that I liked to walk a tightrope. Yes, Madame. But how else could we do it?"

He had told his army that if they accepted sophisticated weapons from Washington and a large American subsidy, they would not be happy very long, because soon they would be engaged in the war in Vietnam. If you accepted things from Washington, you had to pay the price. And the price, he warned them, would be their death.

He had been compelled to leave his country to take the cure in France—if he did not go on a compulsory diet for two or three months each year he got too fat. It was not a question of appearance but one of health. He spent two months in France, and while he was there, the government in Pnompenh organized manifestations against the North Vietnamese Embassy and the Vietcong in Pnompenh on the question of sanctuaries. (He did not make reference, I noted, to the fact that he himself had issued some blistering statements against the North Vietnamese and the Vietcong in the weeks before he left for France.)

As for the sanctuaries—they existed. He had had no real choice in that question.

"Understand, Madame," he said, his face earnest, "I had to close my eyes somewhat about that."

But the Pnompenh politicians had their national pride and their independence, and they wanted to wipe out all the North Vietnamese and Vietcong sanctuaries.

Well—how had it all worked out? He pulled a newspaper clipping from his pocket, a UPI dispatch by Kate Webb ("Who was once captured by our forces and then freed."). It told of the Cambodian Communist forces occupying another 2,000 square miles of Cambodian territory.

"You see," he said, "President Nixon didn't intend to do this, to turn the territory over to the Communists, when he supported Lon Nol."

He clasped his hands together and turned his eyes down.

"I say this," he said, "not with pride but with humility. It is only Sihanouk who can reunite Cambodia. The rightists say that I am a traitor. But you will see, Madame, that the war will intensify, and Cambodia will be more and more destroyed, and the population will suffer, unless I am permitted to go back and establish peace and unity and neutrality."

He said that China supported his concept of Cambodian neutrality. His "old and dear friend, Chou En-lai," did not interfere. Chou wanted neutrality for Cambodia. China did not want an ally. A non-neutral Cambodia would be a threat, rather than an aid, to stability in Asia. China supported his cause not in order to Communize Cambodia but to help Cambodia return to neutrality and non-alignment.

North Vietnam had given the same pledge. After the war, Cambodia and Vietnam would be close friends—but not allies.

"No one wants to satellitize Cambodia," he insisted. "No benefit will come from satellitizing Cambodia. Only more trouble."

He had been asked why he was in the Communist camp if what he was fighting for was non-aligned status. Well, suppose Switzerland had been oppressed by the Soviet Union. Wouldn't Switzerland ally herself with other countries to oppose the aggression? Belgium had done just that in World War I.

Most of Cambodia now had been liberated. In effect, Lon Nol

controlled only Pnompenh. When the Prince had been running things in Pnompenh, the CIA and the Pentagon considered him an enemy of the Free World and a supporter of Communism. But who was working for Communism now?

"I think," he said with a wry smile, "that President Nixon is a better agent than I am. Washington is a better agent for Communism than Mao or Ho."

I asked him if he could have seen President Nixon when he was in Peking. He said Chou En-lai had tried to arrange a meeting, but Nixon refused. Then, after the Shanghai communiqué, Chou En-lai took a plane and briefed Premier Pham Van Dong and himself on what happened between the Chinese and the Americans. (Sihanouk had been visiting in Hanoi during the Nixon visit.) The Prince said he had received a warm letter from his old friend Senate Majority Leader Mike Mansfield when Mansfield was in Peking, promising him continued support. Once again, Sihanouk was absent in North Korea at the time of the Mansfield visit.

President Nixon, he concluded, was still insistent on trying for a military solution in Southeast Asia. But this was foolish. The longer the U.S. supported Lon Nol, the more of Cambodia would be taken by the Communists. Perhaps all of Cambodia. Yet it was not too late to save Cambodia from Communism, because both China and Hanoi wanted him to return and set up a neutral country. And the Cambodian Communists agreed that Cambodia should be a neutralist popular democracy under the Royal flag and the Royal Constitution of 1947.

Of course, after Liberation, it would not be Sihanouk who would be the real master of Cambodia. It would be the Khmer Rouge. But they planned to let Cambodia remain a kingdom, with themselves in a cabinet that would include non-Communist members. But, since the Communists would lead the army, they would, in fact, have the power.

I wondered whether the Prince's philosophy had changed since he had come to live in China. After all, many had regarded him as something of an Asian playboy, what with his movie-making, song writing and an often sybaritic way of life.

The Prince grew serious and thoughtful. The number-one problem in Cambodia was corruption. The men who made the coup against him claimed he was corrupt. But it was actually they who were corrupt. If he had been corrupt he could not stay in China.

"The Chinese are the purest, the least corrupt, really puritanical people I have ever seen," the Prince said with earnest intensity. "If you meet them you can see that they like me. They will say that I am a prince, but that I am worthy of the confidence of my people."

He quoted a Cambodian diplomat as saying that Cambodia had grown a hundred times more corrupt under the Lon Nol regime.

"It is not my Communists who are corrupt," he said, emphasizing his words with a gesture of his hand. "They are 100 percent pure. I am a prince. I am not a proletarian. I am a bourgeoise. I cannot be a Communist. I confess, Madame, I have not any Communist culture. I have read only Mao Tse-tung, but many of his ideas are not Communist. They are just Asian and patriotic. I love him truly. I have never read Karl Marx or Engels or Lenin. I have not read one line of them. I do not like them. I do not like Marx and Lenin. I like Mao Tse-tung, not as a Communist but as an Asian philosopher and a patriot."

His thinking, he said, had not changed since coming to China. But if his country was to have a chance, it must not be corrupt. It was necessary to take from the Communists their cleanliness and freedom from corruption. He felt that the Cambodian Communists offered this hope. His was not entirely a government-in-exile. There were 11 ministers in the liberated zones, and they were popular. They were intellectuals. They were educated. They were poor. They were not rich.

"In Pnompenh," he said, "the ministers have their Mercedes-Benzes and their luxury villas. In the liberated zones, the ministers live with the peasants and eat with them."

He expressed love and affection for the Khmer Rouge. He admitted that when he had been in Pnompenh he had believed in men like Lon Nol, not in the Communists.

He talked of the corrupting effect of American military spending on other Southeast Asian countries—Thailand, for example, where the government and army leaders grew very rich and the masses very poor. There was no equilibrium. To stabilize the Third World there must be some just distribution of wealth. He did not mean Communism. He did not mean just one class. He was a Buddhist, and Buddha himself had stood for social justice. To develop Asian countries, corruption must be ended. You could see this in the Philippines, in Saigon, in Bangkok and in Vientiane. The United States was the number-one corrupting power. Russia didn't give one percent of what the U.S. did to underdeveloped countries. Now in Cambodia, for the first time, there was a chance for honest government with the Khmer Rouge. His views had not changed because of his residence in Peking. He was a non-Communist, but now Cambodia had an army almost like the Chinese. It was honest, and it was loved by the peasants.

He again emphasized that he was not anti-American. The only obstacle to good relations was U.S. support of Lon Nol.

"The U.S. planes bomb us every day and night," he said. "The U.S. is represented in Cambodia by napalm and bombs. For the people, the U.S. means just that (he pointed to the sky)—the killing of people and not the destruction of armored units. I do not want to be an enemy of the U.S.A.—even my Communists want to normalize relations."

He did not think there was much chance for a coalition between Lon Nol and his government. Paris, and even Moscow, had suggested that. But Pnompenh and he were in agreement on this question; both were against it. In the long run, the Lon Nol government would be wiped out. He was very patient. He saw no possible result but victory. There must be a new government, not necessarily a Communist government but one that was new in spirit and non-corrupt. Lon Nol and his supporters would go to France. They had money in Swiss banks. They were rich. Some of the Saigon ministers were planning to do the same thing.

He was opposed, also, to a new Geneva conference. Some foreign powers had suggested this—France, Russia and Britain—Cambodia was opposed and had asked China not to agree to a new Geneva conference (actually, China was just as opposed as Cambodia).

The Geneva meeting of 1954 had merely set the stage for the second Indochina war by the partition of Vietnam into two parts. A new conference would create three Vietnams—one north and two south. It would divide Cambodia. He would have Angkor Wat and Lon Nol would have Pnompenh. There would be an East Laos and a West Laos. This would simply create conditions for the third Indochina war.

"It would, Madame," he said, rolling up his deep brown eyes, "be merely the entre'acte."

He could see no solution but the acceptance by the United States of the seven-point North Vietnam program. There would be no question about the prisoners. Of course they would be returned. This would mean the fall of Lon Nol. It would be good for Cambodia if the United States disengaged in Vietnam. He could not imagine the U.S. getting out of Vietnam and continuing to support Pnompenh just for the sake of Lon Nol's beautiful eyes.

"He has beautiful eyes," said the Prince sarcastically, "but not beautiful enough to attract President Nixon."

War might continue in Laos, thanks to the intervention of Thailand. But he doubted it. The best troops in Laos were the Meo tribesmen trained by the CIA, but there were few of them who survived. The majority of the fighters now came from Thailand. If the American mercenaries disengaged, then Prince Souvanna Phouma and Souphanouvong, the two contending cousins, would come to an agreement. After all, despite their feud, Souphanouvong was still Souvanna Phouma's vice-premier.

Everything, in the end, depended on President Nixon. He had said he must avoid a bloodbath in Saigon. But what did he think he was doing every day? Every day there was a bloodbath in North and South Vietnam, in Cambodia and Laos. What was a bloodbath? It happened every day in the rain of American bombs. The President said he didn't want to suffer the first American defeat in history. But Indochina didn't want to defeat the United States. It just wanted to defeat its local enemies like Lon Nol. They were the enemy—not the U.S.A. Indochina wanted to resolve its own problems. It wanted peace and re-establishment of relations with Washington. Cambodia and Hanoi and the Vietcong all wanted, one day in the near future, to have friendly and diplomatic relations with the United States. No one had any intention of humiliating America. They wanted to be good friends with the American people. But President Nixon continued to interfere in their affairs.

"If he continues," the Prince declared solemnly, "he will achieve defeat for the United States. It will not be our work but the work of President Nixon. He has to choose. Now we can achieve peace in honor and in friendship. I do not pretend to be more intelligent than President Nixon, but it seems to me that his policy is not right."

He said that his Cambodian forces were armed, in large part, with weapons purchased from corrupt members of the Lon Nol government—American arms—M-16 rifles, rocket launchers, ammunition, medical supplies, even American uniforms. They could buy anything they wanted. All they needed were dollars, and these, thanks to the generosity of the Chinese, they had. Real American dollars printed in the U.S.A., not fake ones. They had far more American than Chinese weapons. It was very convenient because it was difficult to transport Chinese weapons. They had to depend on North Vietnam for transport, and North Vietnam couldn't deliver more than 30 or

40 percent of the weapons provided to the Pathet Lao and Cambodia by the Chinese.

But with American weapons close at hand and readily available for dollars, the problem was easily solved. Lon Nol and the Americans handled the transport. Most of the purchases were made at big trading bases within 50 kilometers of Pnompenh.

"We get all these weapons directly or indirectly from President Nixon," he said. "You know it is just a tragicomedy. But not to the people. They are losing their arms, their legs, their eyes and their lives."

The Prince talked a bit longer. He became nostalgic about America. He had driven four times from New York to San Francisco and back. He loved the country and the highways and the Howard Johnsons. He had no hatred for America. He loved Americans and their folklore. Of course, he loved China as well. He had written many songs about China—the most famous was "Nostalgia for China," which he wrote in 1965. Very recently he had written a new song that he called "Long Live China and Long Live Chairman Mao." He had written the song while he was touring northeast China. He was in Harbin when he finished it. The song had been published already by the *People's Daily*, and the Chinese liked it very much. Premier Chou En-lai wanted all the Chinese students to learn to sing it. He had tried very hard to write revolutionary songs. But it didn't work out. They always came out somewhat sentimental. He just could not change.

The Prince rose. He gave us a collection of his songs to take back to America, with his warmest greetings. His eyes melted as he spoke, and there was a tear, I think, in the corner of his eye. He was sentimental. He had been talking for a long time about his country and the complicated dilemma in which it found itself.

It was, I suppose, self-serving talk in some ways. Yet, it seemed to me that most of what he said made very good sense.

The Prince might be a tightrope walker. And he was in China with the most difficult of prospects ahead of him. Even if he got back to Pnompenh, he would not be the master he had been in the past. The Communists would have won that right by force of arms. It would be their victory—but one to which he had contributed not a little. The Prince's standard might be a little tarnished, but the Cambodian peasants listened to his broadcasts with regularity and devotion.

What the Prince had done was to paint a picture of the future of Southeast Asia as China was beginning to envisage it. It was a picture that seemed to me to make good sense not only for China but for the

United States. It was predicated on defusing the Southeast Asia theater, the Vietnams, Cambodia, Laos, Thailand and all the rest. It would provide a neutral buffer between the two worlds, the gradually emerging Chinese sphere, and the gradually contracting American one. Best of all, it carried a real chance of peace in that anguished world.

There was pathos in the position of the Prince. He was not a Communist. He was not a Marxist. The whole dialectical method was alien to his Cambodian spirit. His balancing act had finally come to an end—but perhaps it had to end. Perhaps it was beyond the power of any individual, even one as subtle, as clever, as sensitive in his intuitions as the Prince. But his motivations in the past had been right, so far as Cambodia was concerned. He *had* made it an "island of tranquility" in a turbulent world. Now that tranquility was gone. It would never be the same again. The vision of Cambodia, the lovely dancers stepping down from the bas reliefs at Angkor—we would not see that again in our time regardless of whether the Prince and "my Communists" or Lon Nol and his American backers won out. The land had been ravaged. I knew what had happened to Svay Rieng, that quiet and elegant border capital where the crystal had tinkled so gently to the percussion of American bombs. Long since, the tinkling had ended, American bombs had crashed down in all their terror. Svay Rieng and every city and village of Cambodia now knew America by our fiery symbol from the skies. We had brought the American way in Asia to Cambodia.

The Prince now sat in his magnificent residence in Peking or traveled across the world, seeking somehow to bring an end to this horror. I could only hope his efforts would succeed. Whatever regime he and his Khmer Rouge might establish in Cambodia, I hardly believed it could be worse than the reality that we Americans had imposed upon that infinitely pleasant land.

But it was worth remembering that if the Prince returned to rule over his beloved Cambodia, it would be a Cambodia that owed a heavy debt to China, a heavy debt to North Vietnam, and it would be a Cambodia in which the power was actually wielded not by the Prince but by those men whom he called "my Communists." The Prince was, I thought, sincere in saying he hoped for friendship with the United States—and that Hanoi hoped for friendship, too. But it would be—when, if and as it came into being—a friendship far different from that of the United States and Cambodia in the past, for over it all would loom the visible shadow of China.

16

Entering the Hermit Kingdom

On December 4, 1950, the last American units pulled out of Pyongyang. A cold wind was driving from the north, but it was not yet snowing. There was a constant rumble of heavy explosions, and great columns of orange-red smoke stood over the city. General Walker had ordered all bridges, power plants, airports and warehouses destroyed, and millions of dollars in food, ammunition and stores had been set afire. Days are short in Pyongyang in December, and the troops had instructions to be on their way well before nightfall. Already the 25th Division, which had been holding north of the city, was falling back to the south. The last British tank unit pulled out of Pyongyang shortly after two in the afternoon, and minutes later, U.S. engineers touched the electric detonator, and the bridge across the Taedong River rose into the air and then dropped with a deafening crash to the bed of the stream. By the time the sun slipped into the sullen cloudbanks and early dusk fell over the unhappy city, the last Americans were well on their way to Seoul.

Pyongyang was the capital of the Democratic People's Republic of Korea. It had been held by the command of General Douglas MacArthur since October 20. Now, 45 days later, the battered city, heavily bombed by the Americans before its capture, savagely demolished by the retreating North Koreans, and again devastated by the retreating Americans, was about to fall back into the hands of Marshal Kim Il Sung and his recent Chinese allies. Ahead lay weeks and months of tactical and strategic bombing which, by the time the Korean ceasefire was initialed in 1953, would leave Pyongyang a broken field of rubble, twin in horror and devastation to Coventry, Stalingrad and Dresden.

Before the advance skirmishers of the American 1st Cavalry entered Pyongyang on October 20, 1950, no American had set foot in the North Korean capital since the founding of the Republic in 1948. Nor, in fact, had any Americans been permitted to enter Pyongyang since August, 1945, when the Soviet Red Army swept down in its victorious war's-end offensive, smashing the Japanese and occupying Korea up to the 38th Parallel in accordance with the Yalta agreements. And, if you wished to go back of that, you found that from Japan's victory over China in the Sino-Japanese War of 1894, Americans had gradually been squeezed out of Korea, particularly after the formal Japanese annexation in 1910.

So it was that when an Ilyushin-14 plane of the Korean National Airways touched down at a temporary airport, an hour's drive northwest of Pyongyang, just after 9 P.M., May 12, 1972, and two Americans—myself and John Lee of the Tokyo office of *The New York Times*—stepped out in the darkening spring evening, we were making history. We were welcomed by two beautiful six-year-old Korean girls, dressed in the long national *chima* in pastel red and blue, handing us bouquets of salmon-colored gladiolas, then drawing up their arms in flathanded full salutes that would have done a British sergeant-major proud.

We were the first non-Communist Americans to come to Pyongyang in the 24-year life of the North Korean regime; the first to set foot on North Korean soil since the end of the Japanese regime in 1945; the first since long before the outbreak of World War II. I never could find out when the last American newspaperman had visited Pyongyang. It was an event so far back into history that all trace had been completely lost. I guessed that no American newsmen had been in Pyongyang for close to half a century.

In my journalistic career, I have not infrequently had the good fortune to be the first correspondent to visit a sealed-off country. After Stalin's death in 1953, I was the first American in two decades to visit the remote reaches of Siberia. I was the first American to visit Albania after World War II (in 1957), and probably the first to see that unhappy little mountain kingdom since Mussolini's cowardly legions took it over in the mid-1930's. I was the first to get back into Bulgaria after the Americans had been expelled at the height of the cold war, and the first into Rumania at the same time. I broke the ice in Outer Mongolia in 1959, and penetrated Burma and Cambodia in 1966, when both were off-limits to U.S. newsmen. And I was first into Hanoi in 1966. But never, in a lifetime of breaking down barriers, had I experienced the sensation of entering a country which for *half a century* had been locked against Americans.

The truth is that Korea did not win its ancient title of "the hermit kingdom" by chance. Historically it had resisted relations with western nations more fiercely than any other country of the Orient. Europeans had opened up trade with China in the 17th century, and by the 1840's, under the shattering influence of the Opium War, intercourse had become a *fait accompli*. Japan had been "opened" by Commodore Perry in 1854. But not Korea. The hermit kingdom fought all attempts at western contact. Missionaries were slaughtered. Trade ships burned. Shore parties attacked. In the end, it was Korea's neighbors—the Russians, the Chinese, the Japanese—who by stealth, treachery, trickery and armed force pried open the Korean clam. And even they had no easy task. The Japanese occupiers *never* subdued the Koreans. After 30 years of annexation, Japan imposed her rule only with force—one policeman to every 400 Koreans—savage reprisals, executions, tortures, imprisonment, exile, mutilations.

The Korean heritage was hatred, paranoic xenophobia, violent nationalism, an emotionalism that had no equal in any other Asian state.

This is history, but it must be recalled (and while in North Korea I kept reminding myself of this history) if anything about today's North Korea—the attitudes of her people, their intransigence, their suspicions, the extremism of their propaganda, and the sheer dogmatism of their prejudices—is to make sense.

I am at home in every Communist nation of Europe and Asia. I have met almost every Communist head of state and hundreds, if not thousands, of Communist officials, journalists and diplomats. Since World War II, I have spent much of my time in the Communist milieu. I think I know their psychology and the way they treat the visiting press as well as anyone.

But never have I experienced anything like North Korea. When I first penetrated eastern Siberia, I sometimes found a secret police detail of 15 to 20 men assigned to watch (or more literally to surround) me as I made my progress through the streets of the cities. They accompanied me to and from outdoor privies and occupied all the berths around mine on the Trans-Siberian Express. In Albania, on occasion, not only was I barred from a factory to which I had been officially invited, but representatives of the Albanian Foreign Office, as well, were not permitted entry. On my first trip to Outer Mongolia, I was installed in a government guest house far outside Ulan Bator, and not permitted to walk the city streets or even to go with my escorts to a watchmaker's shop to get a new crystal for my watch.

I mention these examples because they were unusually restrictive. But they pale before the restrictions of North Korea. In 16 days of interviews, sightseeing, visits to factories, schools, kindergartens, a university, theaters and museums, I only once walked alone on a North Korean street—and then only for about 150 yards—before a panting interpreter, in extreme agitation, ran up to accompany me. I never once spoke with a passing man on the street—or woman or child. I never spoke with a peasant in the field or in his cottage and only once visited a peasant's cottage. (He and his family were conveniently away for the day, working in the fields.) I never spoke to a worker in a factory with the exception of an occasional group that had been so rehearsed in their performance as to be laughable. I had the remarkable experience of walking through a chemical plant for half an hour without even *seeing* a worker, so carefully had the itinerary been laid out.

I never visited a worker's apartment. I never visited a store. I never ate in a restaurant. The only commercial institutions I saw were the international desk of the post office and the foreign-exchange counter of the state bank. I was housed in beautiful government guest houses in which there were often no other guests, houses surrounded by walls and barbed wire with Tommy gun carrying sentries at the gates and military barracks adjacent, where reserves "to protect the foreign visitors" were on hand. In some cities the chauffeur of the car was a high security officer. In other cities he was a low-ranking officer. I obtained almost no statistics on national production or the national economy. All of them are secret. In fact, a lady alderman even refused to say how many people lived in her district of the city. "It has not been announced," she primly insisted.

It is a land where blood revenge is glorified—specifically in an opera *The Sea of Blood*, written by Premier Kim Il Sung himself—and in songs sung by children in kindergarten; where hatred—hatred for Americans—is officially and stridently encouraged because, as the Premier put it to me, "without educating our people in this spirit (of hatred) we cannot defeat the U.S., which is superior in technology."

It is a land where autarchy and national self-sufficiency are carried to the point that neither tea nor coffee is drunk. (North Korea has only a tiny tea production.) Instead, apple pop is the national beverage, because North Korea has more apples than she can possibly consume or export.

It is a land where chauvinism and xenophobia are so strong that you will almost look in vain in the historical museums and the government propaganda for mention that the Soviet Red Army liberated North Korea from the hands of the Japanese at the end of World War II. The feat, instead, is attributed to the "Korean Revolutionary Army," a military organization that did not exist at that time, led by Marshal Kim Il Sung, who bore no such title for many years to come.

As if to square the circle, official accounts of the Korean War do not mention, or mention in only the most peripheral fashion, the intervention of the 1 million Chinese troops that turned the tide after General MacArthur had driven Kim Il Sung back across the Yalu. In the North Korean official version, the war ended not in a stalemate but in a dramatic *Korean* victory over the shattered, humiliated, broken American "imperialist" forces.

It is a country in which children in the crèche are taught that the greatest glory is to be a soldier, and no fate is finer than to die for the Korean fatherland. I do not suppose that in any country since Bismarck's Prussia has the profession of arms, the supremacy of the military, and the cult of the uniform been raised so high. Certainly, I know of no other country where children of six and seven stage tableaux and dances in which they act out savage battles against the enemy (sometimes Japanese, sometimes American), accompanied by such songs as "Let's Mutilate the Americans."

Nor can I conceive of any other people deliberately taking a full day to drive an American visitor deep into the countryside, 100 kilometers or more from Pyongyang, to show him a museum dedicated to American "atrocities" purported to have been committed during the Korean War—a chamber of horrors, filled with photographs of women with their breasts torn off, corpses with stakes driven into their mouths or genitals, prisoners being beheaded, mutilated corpses, blood-stained clothing, knives and pincers supposedly employed in these terrible crimes. Sweet-faced young Korean girl guides eagerly recite one tale more monstrous than another. In every instance in which specific data on the perpetrators of these horrors could be established, it was plain that the putative villains were not Americans but Koreans from the South.

To place these "American" acts in a logical framework, an elaborate historical infrastructure has been constructed which Pak Yun Il, the lean and ascetic Savonarola who is Director of the Atrocity Museum at Sinchon, explained in detail. The foundation for American aggression against Korea, he assured me, was laid down on February 2,

1845, when Senator Pratt of New York, speaking in the U.S. Senate, declared: "The time has come to stimulate the eagerness of our merchants and seamen for riches and markets in these countries which have been kept undiscovered from ancient times."

The country Senator Pratt had in mind, said Pak, was the ancient kingdom of Choson, that is, Korea. From January, 1865, to 1876 the Americans "invaded" Korea on 13 occasions, Pak said; but unfortunately he was able to provide only a few details of these early anti-Korean acts, with the exception of one that is well-known to every Korean school boy and girl. This was the appearance in the Taedong River on August 15, 1866, of the American vessel, the *General Sherman*. This ship was sunk just outside Pyongyang by a band of Korean patriots, who used fire boats to set the ship ablaze. All of the "American aggressors" perished in a fiery death, thanks to the efforts of a Korean named Kim Ung U, who organized the patriots and sank the American ship. The name of Kim Ung U is one of fame and glory in today's Korea, for he is none other than the heroic great-grandfather of Premier Kim Il Sung, a man who might be called the great-grandfather of the Korean Revolution. I did not meet a single Korean who was not amazed to learn that I had never heard of the *General Sherman* and the long struggle of the "American imperialists" to carry into fruition the "aggressive schemes of Senator Pratt."

No detail was too small for incorporation in the Sinchon chamber of horrors. The only mention of the American missionary effort in Korea (which, in reality, struggled long and hard to aid the Koreans against the Japanese) was an anecdote about an American priest who was said to have found a Korean schoolboy stealing apples from his orchard and branded the child on the head with the word "Thief," written in sulphuric acid. Americans were said to have plundered Korea in 1945, carting off its industry and seizing its mines and factories. A million Koreans were alleged to have died at American hands, and Kim Il Sung was quoted as saying: "The crimes committed by the Yankees far surpassed those committed by the Hitlerites." The museum preserved the ancient allegations that the United States conducted germ warfare in Korea and displays "infected insects"—cockroaches, tadpoles and others beyond identification—supposed to have been dropped into the Korean countryside to spread disease and death. Another exhibit shows photographs of a Communist Party official who is said to have been skinned alive. The skinning knife is shown beside the photograph, but no skin. The skin, I was told, had been burned.

The museum received 350,000 visitors a year, largely school children. I asked Pak what was the reaction of the children to what they saw.

"The boys are strongly filled with hatred for the U.S. imperialists," he said," and ready to fight to the last against them."

What, I asked, was the philosophy of the museum?

We are taught, he said, as follows: "U.S. imperialists are the sworn enemy of the Korean people. They have repeatedly invaded our country since the intrusion of the *General Sherman* in 1866."

It seemed to me that the museum was fulfilling its function brilliantly.

There is no easy way to sum up North Korea in a phrase or a revealing incident. The chauvinism, xenophobia, nationalism, hatred (both natural and stimulated), suspicion, hostility to Americans (and generally to all foreigners and perhaps most strongly to Japanese), the natural arrogance and independence, the "feistiness," as they would say in Indiana, all of these qualities are coupled with natural grace and warmth, overwhelming hospitality, a sense of pride and dignity, intense dedication to the work ethic, a surpassing patriotism and love of country, patience, endurance and purposefulness.

When I tried to put down words that would characterize Korea, I began with adjectives like Prussian, Cromwellian, Stalinesque, Othello-like, militaristic. But then I halted. For how to couple these traits with a flambent passion for flowers, a love for trees that is almost druidic, a genius for the creation of beautiful parks and gardens hardly matched by the Japanese, a dedication to the welfare of all Korean children, and particularly the younger ones, a dance tradition of beauty, a taste for sports extravaganzas and grandiose public entertainments, a remarkably Victorian family life, excellent modern architecture, and an obvious liking, among supposedly fierce revolutionary cadres, for secluded country estates, goldfish ponds, white-jacketed stewards, fine German motor-cars and excellent Japanese wristwatches?

It is obvious that North Korea is far too complex to be summed up in a word, but about one thing there could be no doubt. No more fiercely independent country could be imagined. You did not have to spend much time in North Korea to recognize that whatever its origins in the complex ending of World War II, it was not, and could never have long remained, anyone's puppet—not Russia's, not China's and certainly not Japan's or America's. I had seen fierce nationalism in other Asian countries—notably in North Vietnam—and to only a slightly lesser extent in Burma. But nowhere was it as fierce as in Pyongyang, so fierce as to be almost aggressively provocative. It was not difficult, in the light of this national mood, to understand the intractability of the Panmunjon negotiations, the difficulty in bringing the Korean War to an end, and such spectacular crises as the *Pueblo* incident.

But there was much more to North Korea than national pride. When the battered Americans hastily fell back south in December, 1950, after blowing up the Taedong bridge, they left behind a city of less than 400,000, a city where by the time the armistice was signed in 1953, only three buildings were still standing—two small department stores, and the city hall. The North Koreans estimated that about 420, 000 bombs fell on the city, a little more than one bomb per inhabitant. In the country as a whole, 28 million square meters of housing were destroyed, and 3,700 industrial enterprises. Much farm land, particularly rice paddy areas, was destroyed through the blasting of dikes and the destruction of irrigation systems and canals.

The morning after I landed in Pyongyang, I was driven through the city in a mint-fresh, gray Mercedes-Benz 200, which had only about 625 miles on its odometer. The bridges across the Taedong River (there were three in place of the prewar one) were fine, double-arch steel and concrete structures. The city was bisected by broad, handsomely paved boulevards, lined with shade trees, interspersed with frequent parks, decorated with fountains, and acres of flower beds and pleasant walks.

I looked over the city from the pagoda atop Mount Moranbong beside the Taedong River. The skyline was dominated by a 600-foot radio and TV tower with a 400-foot viewing platform and, I believe, a restaurant, much like the Tokyo tower—but not yet open. The tallest building was the 22-story No. 3 Building at Kim Il Sung University. There was an enormous sports complex, with a 70,000-capacity stadium, an indoor sports palace, several eight- and ten-story office buildings and hotels, a block-long railroad station and a striking new complex of government buildings and offices, as well as an older complex centering around vast Kim Il Sung Square, where demonstrations and parades were reviewed. Most impressive of all was a new Museum of the Korean Revolution, two blocks long, positioned on a height overlooking the city. Centered on the broad plaza before this structure rose an heroic 60-foot solid bronze statue of Kim Il Sung, mounted on a towering pediment, floodlighted at night, and visible for miles outside the city.

I looked in vain for any sign of war damage. This entire city, now boasting a population of more than 1 million, had been built since 1953. It had been built by hard and industrious labor. North Korea is not a rich country. It lay in ruins in 1953. True, it had help from the Soviet Union and from China. (It is impossible in the present state of North Korean chauvinism to establish exactly how much but it probably totaled about $5 billion.) Basically, the job was done by the North Koreans themselves, in primitive, back-breaking toil. And they were still toiling.

I arrived at the peak of the rice transplanting season. Driving in from the airport long after dark, I saw bands of men and women, sometimes students, sometimes adults, marching along the highway, to and from the fields. Everywhere I went in North Korea, the fields were filled with men and women from first light to nearly midnight. Everyone was working. Field after field was filled with North Korean army men, their uniform pants rolled up to their hips, working side by side with the back-bent women, to get the precious crop re-set. There is a six-day work week in North Korean factories, but after work and on Sundays, the workers "volunteer" for additional chores—working in the countryside or laboring in the parks and on city construction sites.

The results of this toil could be seen everywhere—in the truck-filled streets of Pyongyang, lined for the most part with monumental buildings, many of them in that unhandsome Soviet style that characterizes the boom cities of Siberia: Sverdlovsk, Novosibirsk or Khabarovsk—or in the countryside, where the land is cultivated even more intensively than in China, and with substantially more mechanization. To be sure, for the most part North Korea still cultivates rice by man and woman power. But in one 100-kilometer stretch of highway enroute from Pyongyang to Sinchon, I kept tab of mechanical equipment at work in the fields. I counted 36 tractors and bulldozers in the 100-kilometer stretch.

One of the finest collective farms in the country is the Chongsan-ri collective in the Pyongyang area, a farm that has been visited no less than 62 times by Premier Kim Il Sung. The chairwoman, Chang Dok Pyon, is an efficient, handsome woman in her mid-40's, with a quiet voice and composed face who wore a green silk blouse and a black velvet skirt. She is a graduate of the national management school, and she clearly knows farming. Her husband was killed in the war, and her 23-year-old son went straight from high school into the Korean army in order to "get revenge on the enemy," that is to say, the Americans.

This farm, with about 650 families and 1,000 working members, cultivates 1,200 hectares of land of which 655 are in rice, 250 in non-paddy crops, 200 in orchards, and the rest in vegetables and sericulture. They have 50 28-horsepower tractors, 24 75-horsepower tractors, five 15-horsepower machines and 13 garden tractors. They also have eight trucks. This is a far higher degree of mechanization than I found on even the finest Chinese communes, and the level would exceed that of most Soviet farms. With this equipment, the average Chongsan-ri farmer earned 3,500 won (2.2 won to the dollar) per family last year, plus seven tons of rice. The farm employs chemical weedkiller so that no longer must the peasants manually weed the rice. It used 1,760 pounds of chemical fertilizer and 25 tons of manure per hectare and would soon be putting a ton of chemical fertilizer on every hectare of rice.

With the introduction of mechanization, the farm was constantly reducing its labor force and sending the surplus peasants into industry. Its peak peasant labor force had been 1,700. So far, 500 had been sent to industry and it was hoped to cut the force in half in the next two years.

To be sure, Chongsan-ri is no typical farm. It is a pacemaker model; but what Chongsan-ri does today will be done by the other North Korean farms tomorrow. By intensive application to agriculture, North Korea has managed to achieve one of its most critical autarchical, chauvinist goals—it has become self-sufficient in rice and other foodstuffs—no mean feat, since, traditionally, the north was industrial and traded its manufactured goods for the rice of the south.

But if Chongsan-ri is a model, nonetheless, the other collective farms of North Korea follow its pattern. The national average of mechanization is stated to be 1.5 tractors per hectare, which is about the same as at Chongsan-ri. In two or three years there will be three or four tractors per hectare. All of this machinery, of course, is produced in North Korean plants—tractors, cultivators, harvesters, and trucks. In fact, the country is said to be 98 percent self-sufficient in machine tools, and, having seen a sampling of the machine tool and machinery industry, I am inclined to think this boast is not far from the truth. North Korea was 80 percent agricultural under the Japanese, but now the percentages have been almost reversed. By 1956, 34 percent of national production was industrial. In 1972 the figure had risen to 74 percent.

I managed to collect a few figures on industrial production but there was no way of checking their reliability.

In speaking to the Fifth Congress of the Workers Party of Korea in November, 1970, Premier Kim Il Sung gave several production estimates for the year 1970. He estimated electric power at 16.5 billion kilowatt hours. This, according to a chart at the Pyongyang Industrial and Agricultural Exposition, is supposed to rise to 28 to 39 billion kilowatt hours by 1976. He put coal production at 27.5 million metric tons and steel-ingot production at 2.2 million metric tons. Steel output—according to figures posted at a stadium display for President Barre of Somalia, should rise to 3.8 to 4 million by 1976. The Premier gave cement production as 4 million metric tons in 1970, and fertilizer at 1.5 million. The Industrial Exposition gave 1970 fertilizer production as 1.3 million tons, and said the 1976 goal was 3 million. The Premier offered no figure in 1970 for textile production, but the 1968 total was estimated by American specialists at 227 million meters. The Industrial Exposition put 1972 production at 400 million meters, and the stadium display put the 1976 goal at 500 to 600 million.

Assuming that these figures are reasonably correct, they give North Korea the third largest industrial plant in the Far East, third only to Japan and China—a very distant third so far as Japan is concerned, but a remarkably close third to China when you realize that North Korea has a population of only 14 million compared to China's 800 or 900 million. The fact is that on a per capita basis North Korea is the most intensively industrialized country in Asia, with the exception of Japan.

Premier Kim Il Sung now calls North Korea an "industrial state," and the term is apt. North Korea is said to turn out in 12 days what required a whole year in 1944. Its industrial plant has grown 30-fold in that period. The machine tool output of 1949 is now turned out in five days. Machine tools are even exported to Czechoslovakia. The manager of the impressively efficient Chollima Rolling Stock Plant at Wonsan, Yon Sung On, told me that he was now shipping freight cars to the Soviet Union (for use on the Siberian railroads), to Mongolia, to Poland and Hungary, having created sufficient capacity to supply all of North Korea's own needs as early as 1962. Not one of the plant managers I met was willing to give me production figures. "They have not been announced by the government," each man explained, often with a frown of suspicion that the question should even be put.

But the secrecy was in dramatic contrast to the obvious efficiency and productive capacity of the rapidly expanding North Korean industrial establishment. The enormous Ryongsang Engineering Works, the largest of its kind in North Korea, at Hamhung—a port that was flattened during the Korean War—was built on the site of a small factory that the Japanese had used to make spare parts for nearby chemical plants. It had been converted by the North Koreans to farm machinery production but was destroyed in the Korean War by savage bombing (about one bomb per square meter). In 1954 it reopened, making knives and forks from scrap steel and metal wheelbarrows. Today it turned out more than 100 kinds of large machines, including 3,000-ton presses, 6,000-ton presses, 200-millimeter boring machines, 400-millimeter boring machines, 3,000-ton compressors and 8-meter turning lathes. No production totals for the plant had been released, but it employed just under 5,000 workers, and in recent years had recorded 30 percent gains in production per year, with up to 20 percent increases in worker productivity. In April, 1972, it had already reached the level of production planned for 1977.

These figures may seem vague or dry, but they conceal a tremendous technical and industrial achievement. North Korea does not yet produce the most advanced and sophisticated machinery, but she turns out products that are fully competitive with those of most Soviet factories, and superior to those of most Chinese plants. She now ships machines to half the countries of Asia and the Middle East, and clearly is headed toward becoming one of the major supply sources for the Third World.

Any visitor to the Hamhung-Hungnam area on North Korea's eastern seacoast is instantly aware that he has come to an advanced industrial complex. He sees the same endless vistas of industrial smokestacks against a rugged backdrop of mountains that he might see in the Urals, and over it all, because of atmospheric inversion, hangs a pall of smoke and smog worse than any in Los Angeles or Tokyo. At 11 A.M., as I drove out to the Hungnam fertilizer plant, smog lay so low and thick over miles of countryside that I could not even see the tips of nearby plant stacks. The area was permeated with the heavy smell of phenol. The fertilizer plant stacks were belching orange-red smoke which the director identified as nitrogen dioxide and sulphur dioxide.

This is one of the greatest industrial concentrations of Asia, but because of strict security classification, I got only vague indications of the names and sizes of plants. But it is the principal North Korean chemical and synthetic center, and a major heavy-metallurgy and machine-building complex.

Korean workers enjoy a pay scale somewhat higher than Chinese, but substantially lower than Russian. The average pay in the Ryongsang engineering plant is 90 to 100 won a month. The director earns 180.

The average pay in the Chollima rolling stock plant was 90 to 110 won a month. At the Hamhung woolen textile mill it was 90 to 120 won. The textile work force is largely female. Due to increased productivity, the work force has in the past few years been cut from 3,000 to 2,000. At the Hungnam fertilizer plant, the average worker's pay was 110 won and the director got 250.

The directors of North Korean enterprises describe them as paradises for workers. My own feeling was that some American managers would consider them even more paradisical. Yon Sung On, the stocky 48-year-old director of the Chollima plant, described the chief role of the union as the increase of production. As a result of its efforts, he was able to overfulfill his production plan by 36 percent in 1971. He had no labor problems. In fact, he could not recall ever having had one. I asked whether his men ever showed up late for work, drank too much, or indulged in absenteeism. He looked at me in utter astonishment. His workers never drank too much, always got to work on time and never failed to show up. What about plant disputes—did the trade union step in to protect the rights of the workers? Yon laughed uproariously. That was ridiculous. He had never heard of a dispute in his shop. Work was carried on without argument or trouble. He knew such things occurred in Capitalist countries, but not in North Korea. Here, it was all one big, happy family. A worker might occasionally fall behind in his norm, but then his comrades would help him to speed up, and with "proper education" no one would lag behind.

I asked what he did when he fired a worker. Never in his years as manager had he let a man go. Workers were sometimes shaped up, but never discharged. Did they ever get dissatisfied and go to another job? Well, once in a while, he said, there were transfers, but even this was rare. If a worker wanted to leave, he had to have the director's okay and then the director would negotiate with another plant for a job. But it didn't happen often. Perhaps a fisherman might get assigned to an engine shop and would like to go back to a more congenial task.

Since the workers were masters of the country, the state, he said, was responsible for looking after them and seeing that each got into the proper niche.

He had no trouble getting skilled workers because the "power organs" (by which, I supposed, he meant the party) sent him all he needed from the technical and trade schools. There was no competition between industries for workers and no raiding of each other's personnel. No one provided better wages or working conditions in order to lure the best men to work for him. There was no petty theft or any other crime. Once in a while there might be an example of shoddy workmanship or spoilage. But then the workman was "educated," and it didn't happen again.

All this and a wage scale in which the average was 90 to 110 won per month at 2.2 won to the dollar.

The pace of work in the North Korean factories was much brisker than in Chinese factories, and I thought efficiency was higher than in most Russian factories. Presumably, I was taken to see the best—not the worst—plants, but this is customary in all countries. It is only fair to emphasize that the best in North Korea is very, very good by standards prevailing in other Communist countries, but it would be wrong to suggest that Korea has the efficiency and productivity of Japan.

However, the same traits that can be seen in North Korean kindergartens, schools, universities and other educational institutions—that is, diligence, hard work, discipline, quickness, manual dexterity, orderliness and concentration—can be seen in the factories.

And this was true even though my visits often seemed a bit like a poor scenario out of an old Keystone Cop comedy, with security men racing around corners to prepare the workers in the next shop for the oncoming visitors; our route marching down corridors still wet with hasty sweeping; plants in which hasty placards had been lettered and painted to make certain that the American visitors would get the optimum dose of anti-American propaganda; and where little work teams (often composed entirely of plain-clothesmen hastily dressed in painfully new coveralls) approached the visitors to hector them about the sins of American imperialism. The Vinalon plant of Hamhung was outstanding in this respect. Vinalon is a synthetic textile made from limestone and coke. It was invented by a Korean, Dr. Li Sung-gi, in 1938, under the Japanese occupation, and has been produced in both China and Japan. It is the darling of North Korea's textile industry because North Korea produces no cotton but has lots of limestone and coke, and this synthetic perfectly fits the nation's autarchical profile. Here I encountered two groups of workers.

The first was made up of half a dozen pretty girls in the spindle room who came up to John Lee and me and pretended they didn't know who we were. "I never saw men so tall as you," one said. "Who are you?" I asked her to guess. She said she couldn't. I suggested we might be men from the moon. She said there weren't any men on the moon. I said there had been some there lately. She then "guessed" we were Americans and added, "If I hear that some man is an American I don't like it, which you can understand because I am from South Korea." She added that all Americans were liars. Then she went on to tell how she had been separated from her family since the war. Her workmates listened with wide eyes and open mouths as the dialogue went on. Each of them wore a pretty red kerchief and a blue apron, and each carried a small wrench in her hand. When John asked if they were going to use their wrenches to attack the U.S. imperialists, they broke into a fit of giggles that I thought would never end. The second group of "workers" was not quite so amusing. It was half a dozen men with remarkably clean faces, caps and dungarees hastily smeared with Vinalon wool. We encountered them at the packing shed, and throughout our conversation, two sad-faced workers (apparently the actual packing squad) continued their labors, occasionally craning their necks to watch the show.

The opening line from one of these men was: "All Americans are liars." I asked him if he had ever met an American before. He said no, but he knew they were liars. He then said: "Is Nixon still blowing his war trumpets?" I asked him if he had not read in his newspaper that Mr. Nixon was presently in Moscow negotiating with Mr. Brezhnev. This disconcerted him a bit since, of course, the North Korean press had reported nothing about the Moscow summit. I finally ended the confrontation by telling them that if they continued to talk, their production quota would fall below the norm. One man, however, grabbed me by the hand and would not let me go until he delivered his prepared lines. Meantime, the other "workers" were violently objecting to having their pictures taken.

After this incident, one of our North Korean escorts said with portentous emphasis that I might find it very unpleasant if I walked out on the street and the people discovered that I was an American.

When I retorted that I had no fear whatever of the North Korean people; that they seemed good, fine people to me and that I would walk among them without fear, he retreated a bit but continued to insist that people all over North Korea would talk as sharply and ask as many unpleasant questions as the "workers" in the factory. I said I'd be glad to conduct a sidewalk poll of North Korean opinion on the United States. But, of course, this never came about.

I could not refrain from contrasting, for the benefit of my North Korean host, the difference in attitude I had encountered in North Vietnam—a country engaged in a desperate and active war with the United States—and the attitude evinced in Pyongyang.

For, as I noted, not once in Hanoi had I ever been hectored by a Vietnamese about the conduct of the United States. Not once had a North Vietnamese come up to tell me that "all Americans are liars." Not once had it been suggested that I might be in danger if I walked in Hanoi's streets as an American. And, in fact, I had walked all over Hanoi without guide, censor or guard, simply by myself, at a time when American bombing raids over the capitol were a daily occurrence. I do not think, I am sorry to say, that my remarks had much impact.

But these propaganda shenanigans could not take away the basic fact that North Korea under Kim Il Sung's leadership had accomplished something amazing. In the 20-odd years since it was left flat on its back by the Korean War, it had become a remarkably efficient and productive country, self-sufficient in food and capable of conducting a substantial export business in manufactured products and machines. And all this while rebuilding her cities in excellent style, turning out more than 300,000 housing units a year, creating a technical engineering base of specialists and technicians said to number 500,000, establishing a first-class educational system and creating one of the toughest, best-disciplined, best-equipped military forces in Asia. It could not have been done without major aid from Russia and China and the other Communist countries. But this aid came to an end at least ten years ago. I presumed that the North Korean army was still dependent upon Russia for its air force replacements and improvements, and at least somewhat dependent on the Chinese for artillery and ground materiel. But no information whatever in the military field was to be obtained from the North Koreans.

So far as I could observe—from the distance at which I was kept from ordinary people—they were well-enough fed, well-enough housed and well-enough clothed. Their urban pay scale was not high, but housing cost only 1.5 percent of their pay and included water and electricity. Peasant housing was built free-of-charge, and there was no rent. The price of rice was subsidized by the state, and rice was resold at a low price (80 jung per kilo) to the consumer. There were no signs of visible poverty, no inflation, no beggars, no evidence of epidemic disease. I do not know whether, as the North Koreans constantly insisted, their standard of living was higher on the average than in South Korea. I suspected it was, so far as the peasantry were concerned, because the peasantry in the North had been given many monetary advantages in order to encourage food production. So far as workers were concerned, it probably was a standoff as regards material conditions and the standard of living—clothing, housing, working conditions—was markedly superior to that of China—even to Peking's. And it was at least as good as in western Russia and probably considerably higher than in Siberia.

I was never able to resolve the dilemma of the attitude of the average North Korean toward the United States. I strongly doubted that he was as hostile as my official hosts insisted, or as their conduct (to isolate me from North Koreans for my own protection) suggested. My guess was that, in reality, the North Korean, like his Russian cousins, had long since been bored by the anti-American propaganda, and the barrier between myself and the ordinary North Koreans was designed to keep me from perceiving this, and also to keep the North Koreans from seeing that Americans did not have horns. I did not believe that the ordinary North Koreans were so objective in their attitude toward the Japanese (and quite possibly the Russians and Chinese). For these were their immediate neighbors, and so far as the Japanese were concerned, there were bitter and recent memories which time had not yet wiped out.

I presumed that most North Koreans were proud of their country, but I did not really believe that all North Koreans felt, in the words of a song often rendered by kindergarten choruses: "We have nothing to envy in the whole world." Or that they truly believed another schoolgirl's favorite which I heard at one program after another: "Birds are flying to us after hearing our happy song."

17

In The Bosom of The Fatherly Marshal

At precisely 10 A.M. on the morning of May 26, I stepped from a silent elevator in the sleek, new, white-marble building that houses the Premier's offices into a blaze of klieg lights, whirring movie cameras and exploding flashbulbs, to find a heavy-set, broad-faced, broad-shouldered, broadly smiling man in an impeccably tailored, gray-drill tunic and trousers, putting forth a hand of welcome. It was Marshal Kim Il Sung of North Korea, the man whom in the past two weeks I had heard called a thousand times "our respected and beloved leader." In fact, I had never heard his name mentioned without these adjectives. Every interview had begun with a tribute to "our beloved and respected leader." Every conversation opened with a reference to "our beloved and respected leader." Every newspaper article, no matter what the subject, opened with the ritual reference. Pick up a magazine and thumb its pages. Each page began with "our respected and beloved leader."

At every factory, farm, school or kindergarten, I had been taken first to the rooms set aside to his cult. Every institution had displays dedicated to him. The Chongsan-ri Collective farmers showed me a room to which I was admitted only after removing my shoes. Here was the very chair in maroon velour where Kim Il Sung had sat, the podium from which he had spoken, a sand table model of the village showing the houses (26) he had entered in his many (62) visits. Outside the adoration room stood the very willow tree under which Kim Il Sung once sat and conversed with the villagers.

In Hamhung I had the privilege of staying in a hotel room Kim Il Sung once visited. There was a plaque dedicated to the event, and his picture on the wall above my bed, the very bed, I had no doubt, on which he had rested his ample frame.

I listened to four-year-old children in a crèche sing to the accompaniment of the teacher's melodeon, "A Very Small Hut In Mangyongdae," with its verse:

> This is the house where our leader was born;
> We wish to visit this house. This is the house where
> The fatherly Marshal was born
> And lived with his parents;
> And we wish to follow the example of the Marshal.

I had watched a dance by the children, celebrating their new school clothes. It ended with them giving thanks to the Marshal for his gift of the clothing. They sang the refrain: "We are happy," bowing and holding up their arms in homage to the Marshal's portrait hung high over the stage.

And, in fact, I had visited Mangyongdae, the little village outside Pyongyang where the saga of the Marshal began with his birth on April 15, 1912, now a vast public park, visited by some 1.3 million a year, including 2,000 foreigners. Here had been preserved the slender locust tree that Kim Il Sung had climbed as a boy, when he was trying—but failing—to catch a rainbow, an event memorialized in children's verses and innumerable paintings. Here had been preserved the comfortable cottage where his family had lived since about 1850, when his great-grandfather got a job guarding a local landlord's private cemetery and received a little compound of well built mud and wattle huts in compensation. It was here Great-Grandfather Kim Ung U was living when the famous *General Sherman* steamed up the Taedong River, just a stone's throw away, and from here that he rallied the patriotic Koreans to burn the vessel and destroy the hated Yankee invaders.

Here lived Kim Il Sung's grandparents, Kim Bo Hyon and Li Bok Ik, both now revered as revolutionary patriots. The grandparents lived on in the house until after the triumph of their grandson in 1945, continuing to work as peasants, and when Kim first came to visit them a few days after Liberation, they asked how they could invite him to sleep on the simple straw mats that covered the floor (preserved as a precious relic to this day). To which Kim bravely responded: "I used to sleep in the mountains on beds of leaves when I was fighting the Japanese. Now, it is wonderful to sleep in my own house."

Here at Mangyongdae had been retained the family portraits: in one room the great-grandparents, the grandparents and Kim's uncles and cousins (all now revealed to have been leading revolutionaries); in another, the portraits of Kim Hyong Jik and Kang Ban Sok, Kim's father and mother, both honored figures in the revolutionary movement, and Kim's brothers, only one of whom now survived. Here were preserved copies of Kim's father's poem "Green Pine Trees on Namsen Hill," with its epic line "I'll be unyielding while restoring the country, even though I am torn to pieces." And the wooden plows, harrows, cultivators and rakes used by the family, as well as the yellow bowl from which the future Premier ate his rice.

All of these treasures were displayed within the grounds of a flower-planted park, with great vistas leading up to a hill overlooking the Taedong, with a distant view of Pyongyang and the site of the sinking of the *General Sherman*. Here, also, was the sand wrestling pit, where Kim used to try his strength against fellow schoolmates, at first unable to best them, but finally learning how to conserve and apply his strength and win victory.

I had been told how, after Liberation in 1945, his countrymen came to Kim and asked permission to create a national monument at Mangyongdae, and how he had resisted their pleas, saying, "We have more important tasks to accomplish." Only after the country was well on its way to reconstruction did he yield to the importunities of his well-wishers and consent to the building of this monumental reservation. Here were preserved no end of mementos—the guns his mother gave Kim and a comrade; the two revolvers handed over to his wife by Kim's father, with the injunction to give them to his son with the message: "Though you might be torn to pieces and your bones turned to powder, you must fight to restore the fatherland." There was also a boy's slingshot just like the one Kim once fired at a Japanese soldier. Mangyongdae is called by the North Koreans "the place of 10,000 views." On the day I visited the site, it was a bower of bougainvillaea, lilacs—very pale and in their last days—marvelous yellow primroses, grape arbors, strawberry patches and a profusion of roses and myrtle.

Of Kim's mother, the museum's director, Li Yong, said: "She is the mother of us all." In fact, an official pamphlet is called "Mrs. Kang Ban Sok, Mother of Korea." Of the Premier's family, the director added: "This was a patriotic family," an obvious understatement in terms of the family's achievements as recorded at their birthplace. But only when I visited the new Museum of the Korean Revolution, dedicated on April 24, 1972, the anniversary of the founding of the Korean Revolutionary Army (just nine days after Kim Il Sung's 60th birthday), was I able to savor to the full the achievements of what North Koreans call, their voices touched with awe, "the Revolutionary Family."

Never in any Communist country had I encountered a phenomenon like this. Even in Stalin's heyday, his cult was firmly centered on his own person. Only intimates knew much about his family, and they often paid for their knowledge with their lives. None of the other Communist chiefs had been surrounded by a "revolutionary family." It is true that most of Lenin's family engaged in revolutionary activity and even played a certain public role in the early Soviet days. Their careers have been recorded, more or less, in Soviet history. But there was no deification, even while Lenin was being raised to god-like status.

The "Revolutionary Family" and its heir, Kim Il Sung, constituted something quite different. One day I was attending a first grade class in Pyongyang when a little girl got up and began to recite, shouting like a squad leader calling on his men to storm a machine gun nest. What, I asked in some trepidation, was the little girl doing? She was, I was told, reciting the names of the Revolutionary Family, together with their dates of birth and death and a few salient achievements.

The best way to describe the new Museum of the Korean Revolution is to say that a complete tour of all the rooms takes four days; a quick tour requires two and a half. I took a quick-quick tour. I spent a little more than half a day and saw only about one-third of the 95 rooms, which contained 4.4 kilometers of exhibits. I suspect the building is the largest single structure in Asia. It is 210 meters long and covers 240,000 square meters. The plaza outside is decorated with a bronze statue of Kim, and two massive sculpture groups, 23 meters high and 50 meters long, incorporating 238 individual figures of workers, peasants, revolutionaries and soldiers. The inner décor of the museum is accented with stainless steel; the miles of carpets are blue and red; and the rooms, so far as I was able to inspect them, were dedicated almost entirely to the life, the times and the achievements of Kim Il Sung.

The story began with the Revolutionary Family and the episode of the *General Sherman*. Then it examined, with excruciating detail, the career of Kim Il Sung. This started in the third room of the hall and was still in progress when I finally broke off the tour. By this time, the story had been carried down to the opening of the Korean War.

Here had been preserved: the ladder that Kim Il Sung used when he went down to a conspiratorial cellar for a secret revolutionary meeting in Manchuria in 1927; a rather battered six-shot automatic revolver given to him by his mother; a scale-model of a house where secret meetings were held in 1932; Kim's pistol used in the early 1930's, lying on a cream colored silk kerchief against a red velour background; the cigarette holder Kim gave to a guerrilla in September, 1932; many of his fountain pens; a mockup of a snow-covered cabin where Kim once stayed (with pine scent sprayed into the room to increase the realism); pocket watches; shoes; sweaters; Tommy guns; mess plates; all the paraphernalia of a lifetime of guerrilla activity—field telephones, copies of his orders, maps, pamphlets and writings—room after room of them; dioramas of famous battles (in one a blue jay sings happily of his joy at greeting Kim; deer come out to meet him, flowers bloom and tears flow from the cheeks of the common villagers); charts; sand tables. But no word of what Kim did during World War II (presumably he was in the Soviet Union); only a casual reference to the Soviet troops who liberated Korea. (They are described as fighting side by side with Kim's Korean Revolutionary Army.)

It is an impressive display. Not all the rooms, I believe, were open at the time of our visit. The general public had not yet been admitted, and the last eight or ten rooms were hastily lighted and opened for us, heavy with the smell of paint, sawdust and shavings on the floor, and exhibition cabinets not yet completely in place.

Amid these artifacts were two of great simplicity. One was a gold ring, displayed in Room 14. It lay on a small cushion covered with lace. It was a present from Kim to Kim Hauk Fu, a woman guerrilla. The date apparently was 1936. In the next room, largely dedicated to materials on the precursors of the Communist Party of Korea in the late 1930's, another simple gold ring was displayed—a present by Kim to Kim Juang Suk.

I do not know the story that lies behind the simple gold band presented by Kim to Kim Hauk Fu in 1936. All that the serious young girl interpreter at the museum, employing her schoolroom English for the first time, could—or would—say was that Kim had given the ring to a woman who was a brave guerrilla comrade. She must have been more than that, and I think she was, in fact, Kim's first wife. I would guess that she was killed in one of the dangerous skirmishes in which Kim's guerrillas were constantly involved during those days.

I make that assumption because I know that Kim Juang Suk,

whose golden ring is in the next room, was Kim's wife. She, too, was a guerrilla fighter, joining Kim's tiny force as a member of the Children's Corps in 1932 or 1933. She rose through the ranks and began to be dispatched on trusted and important missions in 1937 by Kim Il Sung. She had met him for the first time in the spring of 1936 and was immediately transferred to his personal detail and, in the words of a reminiscence written by a friend, "after that, under the personal leadership of Marshal Kim Il Sung, Comrade Kim Juang Suk grew up as a fighter faithful to him." In 1939 she was a member of Kim's personal bodyguard and saved his life in a fire fight with Japanese soldiers, throwing her body in front of Kim while she shot a skirmisher about to fire on him. Kim Juang Suk died about 1947 or 1948, and Kim has since married an extremely pretty woman in her early 40's, Kim Song Ae, who now heads the Woman's Union of North Korea.

In the outpouring of writings about the Revolutionary Family, there is no identification of any of these women nor their relationship to Kim. Nor is there any reference to Kim's children (he has, I was told, a considerable number), nor to his relationship to Kim Yung Ju, his brother, a member of the Politburo, and the man whom most North Koreans assume has been designated as his successor.

There are, then, certain limits, the exact lines of which are difficult to precisely define, that govern the cult of "our beloved and respected leader" and the "Revolutionary Family."

The South Koreans have long made much of the fact that Kim Il Sung is not the name of the boy born in 1912 at Mangyongdae. Kim actually was born Kim Song Ju (the name means One Who Becomes the Pillar of the House). His name was changed—or so his official biographers say—about 1930, when he became very active in the guerrilla movement. He was first called Comrade Il Sung (One Star) or Comrade Han Byol. He, thus, was known as the morning star or guiding star that would lead the Korean people out of darkness. Later, he was named Comrade Il Sung but different characters were used. These meant, according to his official biography, "Sun" and "Attainment."

That was done, the biography adds, "in the hope that he would become the bright sun of Korea, as so great a leader of the nation like him could not be compared merely to the morning star."

The South Koreans have contended that, in fact, there was another Kim Il Sung, a more famous guerrilla leader, and that Kim simply appropriated his name.

But this, of course, misses the point completely. Because, whatever his name, there can be no doubt that Kim did become, and in fact *is*, both the morning star and the sun of Korea. Regardless of how much fiction and hyperbole have been mixed into his biography, regardless of the unadulterated and nauseous personality cult, the fact remains that North Korea *is* in a sense Kim Il Sung, and, like it or not, it is not conceivable as a modern state without him. He is the man who has given North Korea its form and substance. He is responsible for its élan, its philosophy, its national psychology, the shape of its economy, the sharpness of its chauvinism, the independence of its foreign policy, its aggressive attitude toward all great powers, and its isolation from the world in general. He is responsible for the excellent new modern architecture of buildings like his office and the Museum of the Korean Revolution, as well as for the heroic statue of himself and the huge sculpture groups that decorate the museum's plaza. He it is who selected North Korea's most original art-culture form—the stadium display of massed-card panoramas, a ritual that makes the card displays at American football stadiums look like kindergarten performances. In these Korean folk festivals, 20,000 young people, equipped with eight colors of cards, run through upwards of 200 evolutions, creating block-long mosaics dedicated to the life and achievement of "the fatherly Marshal."

Western visitors may smile at the Museum of Natural History in Kim Il Sung University, completely filled with exhibits presented by the Premier—his fine hunting shotgun, his excellent Irish setter (stuffed and mounted), the pet black bear (also stuffed) which he kept at home and which was killed by an American bomb during the war; the fish (mounted) which the Premier caught in Supung Lake in 1958 and which naturalists have been unable to classify; the large eel (preserved in alcohol) which the Premier presented on August 5, 1961; the great boar which he gave on March 15, 1972, having received it as a gift from a peasant; the albino sea cucumber which he caught in Korea's inland sea; and the "pheasant of two sexes" (which seems to have both female and male characteristics) which he shot on February 3, 1963.

Foreign visitors may well be reminded of the legend of the loaves and the fishes when they hear that each student at the university got a piece of roasted bear meat after the Premier presented the school with a 420-kilo black bear, which he had shot in February, 1971.

The university was founded under Kim Il Sung's driving leadership in 1946, just a year after he returned to his homeland. It now has

10,000 students, 5,000 correspondence students, 3,000 professors and instructors, a library of 2 million items, which includes, to be sure, the complete collected works of Kim Il Sung, as well as 50,000 volumes from the Premier's personal library. Vice-Rector Sun Ho Hung piously noted that "our students call him our fatherly leader," echoing the sentiment of Moung Suk Kim, ideological director of the Children's Palace, who simply said: "Now all our children are living warmly in the deep bosom of our leader, Kim Il Sung."

The visitor to the Children's Palace learns that the Premier has visited the institution again and again. A plaque records that six times he has inspected the shop where youngsters are taught to drive and maintain trucks, and each visit is recorded by date. A plaque in the elevator of the Mangyongdae State Hatchery quotes him as saying: "In order to improve the people's living standard, it is essential to produce more eggs at a lower price"—a task the hatchery has achieved by turning out ten million eggs a year. The manager of the Vinalon factory says that the Premier selected the site of his new plant, and the vice rector of the university admits that two new school lunchrooms were built after the Premier had a taste of the school food and found it lacking.

The Premier has told the peasants where and how to plant their rice, and has laid down the edict that "fertilizer is rice and rice is Communism." The North Korean national radio starts at 4:55 every morning, and the visitor may know no Korean, but he quickly becomes accustomed to the Premier's name, chanted over and over again. Nursery-school children sing "The Song of Marshal Kim Il Sung," and their walls are plastered with exemplary tales from the Marshal's childhood—how he fired his slingshot at the Japanese; how his mother made him swear to take revenge on the Japanese; how his father swore him to patriotism; how the 14-year-old Kim walked 1,000 *li* in the dead of winter to return to school in his native country; how he crossed the Yalu River to join his father in Manchuria, determined not to return to Korea until it had won independence.

Kim is a man who has invented his own quasi-Marxist patois—the "Chollima Movement" (the name comes from a legendary Korean phoenix-like bird) to inspire production; the "Juche principle" (the name is almost untranslatable but symbolizes Korean independence and self-sufficiency), the "Taen" method of management.

It is quite impossible to walk a hundred feet in North Korea without encountering his name or his personality in some form or other—in sight or sound or touch. The impact is staggering, because there is no other name or personality that is *ever* mentioned. I left North Korea without knowing the names of any other high officials—no generals, no cabinet ministers, no Politburo members. To be sure, you will occasionally find a name or two in small print in the listings of those present at receptions. But more often than not, when the Premier appears on the podium to review a parade, he is seen in the photograph to stand alone. Or there may be a few individuals scattered in haphazard fashion across the page, with great gaps between one and the other. These are the handful the Premier thinks worth publishing; the other faces have simply been painted out. The photograph of my meeting with the Premier showed only three persons—the Premier, John Lee and me. The little, rather inefficient, interpreter who sat between the Premier and me had simply been snipped out. This threw the perspective a bit out of gee, but the Premier obviously saw no reason to honor the interpreter by publishing his picture. Snip. He vanished.

This, then, was the man whose hand I found outstretched to mine on the morning of May 26, as the cameras whirled and clicked. His presence at the elevator was startling. Indeed, my reception was a bit surprising. The evening before, I had gone through a fearsome wrangle with my North Korean hosts, who accused me of being hostile and unfriendly. In fact they wound up some time after midnight declaring that "instead of apologizing for the barbarous conduct of the American troops in Korea," I had been offended when the North Koreans expressed their just wrath and indignation. My attitude was permeated, they said, by suspicion and distrust. After this post-midnight denunciation, I was a bit dubious about whether the Premier would want to receive me. But, as it turned out, he did. And on few moments' notice. It was immediately apparent that he had matters considerably more important in mind than the quarrel between our North Korean hosts and their unusual guests.

The Premier is a big man, accustomed to dominating the scene. He led the way into his large reception hall, motioning me to go ahead, then stepping forward himself. He walked with a rather slow, rolling gait that instantly reminded me of Stalin when he walked onto the platform at the meetings of the Supreme Soviet. The cameras continued to grind as we seated ourselves, and he turned to me with a quizzical smile and said: "You wrote me many times asking to come here. It is now ten years since your first application. What are these questions that you want to put to me?"

Then, before I had more than a chance to express my pleasure at finally getting to North Korea, he launched into a frank but somehow good-natured defense of his anti-American policy, insisting that, since the United States might "pounce" at any moment on his country, he had to maintain the highest degree of preparedness, and that "the most important thing in war preparation, in my opinion, is that we educate our people in the spirit of hating the enemy." North Korea made no effort to conceal this, because with such a powerful foe as the United States, the only way she could win was by mobilizing every reserve.

"Therefore," he said, with a satisfied air, "I think it is quite natural and quite all right to educate people with the spirit of hating the target of our struggle, the U.S.A. Don't you think so?"

He added that he didn't think it was right to halt or conceal what he called the "anti-American education" of his people just because I was coming to the country. To which I quickly agreed, assuring him that I wanted to see North Korea as it was.

The Premier laughed and chuckled as he spoke, often turning to his colleagues for support of his statements, and he obviously enjoyed his exposition of North Korea's hate-America policy. Whereas his colleagues meticulously said that the objective of North Korean hatred was the American "imperialists," the Premier bothered with no distinction and simply spoke of the Americans as being North Korea's enemy. He wore large horn-rim glasses and smoked occasionally, drawing his cigarettes from a green paper packet. He pulled one leg up under him in his big leather chair as he talked, and swayed a bit from side to side. The Korean word for "yes" sounds like "yeah," and he often ended his sentences with a "yeah," drawing in the word almost like a sigh. Although his face was moon-like, as he talked it lit up with frequent smiles, and his eyes sparkled. It was obvious that he enjoyed talking, and he was a good, impressive speaker, gesturing with little circles of one hand, or holding it up with all four fingers and thumb extended, to emphasize his points. He invariably used his left hand for these movements.

When the photographers retired from the room—after about four minutes—very neat stewards served coffee. About half an hour later, they brought tea; at the close of our conversation, they brought in port wine and the Premier offered a toast in which he said simply: "We recognize the American government is not the American people. We want to have more American friends."

Our conversation lasted three hours. What did the Premier discuss? Most of the time, and most important, he talked about his desire to reunify his country, and, perhaps most poignantly, he expressed his philosophy as the leader of a small country surrounded, as he saw it, by larger and hostile countries. North Korea, he said, would never appear as a mendicant in the presence of nations, no matter what their size, that adopted a hostile policy toward her.

"The smaller a country," he said, "the greater the confidence and self-respect it must have. Small countries live on self-reliance and self-respect. Without self-respect, how can we live? How can we turn the right cheek when we are hit on our left cheek? We do not want to go to heaven like that."

Here, I thought, was the very essence of Kim Il Sung and of the North Korean spirit. The smaller it was, the weaker it felt, the more belligerent and aggressive it would appear to the world and to its neighbors. The Premier had many words for America—none of them very friendly—although, in the end, he did concede that the time might be coming for some very small exchanges. (He wondered why they should invite Americans to North Korea if all of them were going to be as offended as I was by their vigorous anti-Americanism—a sensible question, it seemed to me.) But what he was really interested in was anything that might get the American forces out of South Korea, not, it seemed to me, so much because their presence bothered him as Americans, but because he thought they were holding South Korea back from a move toward *rapprochement* with the North.

This *rapprochement,* the reunification of the two Koreas, was his principal theme. I did not then know, of course, that his brother, Kim Yung Ju, had been conferring with Lee Hu Pak, chief of the South Korean Central Intelligence Agency, right there in Pyongyang only a fortnight earlier, and that Vice-Premier Pak Sung Chul would leave Pyongyang for Seoul three days later to continue the conversations that would result in the July 4, 1972, announcement that North and South Korea had agreed to begin steps toward the ultimate reunification of the two countries.

But the Premier convinced me (and I had already been more than halfway convinced) that, in fact, reunification was the number-one objective of Pyongyang's policy. He insisted that he believed it possible to reunify the country without the South's giving up its democratic Capitalist system, and without the North's giving up its Communist government and Socialist economy. What was needed was direct one-to-one conversations without interference from any third powers—particularly not the United States. But no interference was wanted or needed from any other countries—not Russia, not China and certainly not Japan. First, they could achieve some practical steps —resumption of mail service, compassionate visits on both sides, trade and steps toward economic development and cooperation. He favored mutual exchanges of parliamentarians, scientists and political figures, and common talks by all on common problems. This had been begun in the Red Cross talks then in progress at Panmunjon and must go forward. North Korea had no intention of imposing Communism on South Korea, and no intention of invading South Korea, and no fear that the South would impose Capitalism on the North.

I asked the Premier whether he envisaged the creation of separate social systems within one country, somewhat after the fashion that the National Liberation Front had suggested in Vietnam—that is, that Hanoi would continue its Communist system, whereas the South would have non-Communist government and private trade, at least for a period of some years.

That, said the Premier, was his general idea. He was not specifically familiar with Vietnam, but he saw no reason why there should not be a "confederation" of North and South Korea with a Supreme National Committee which would consult on and discuss matters of common national concern while the underlying different social systems continued in both North and South. He emphasized the benefits that would flow from economic cooperation—obvious benefits in view of the traditional concentration of the North on heavy industry and the South on light industry and agriculture. And he pointed to the great economic benefits each side could achieve by a lessening of their huge expenditures for arms.

The Premier pointed out that the Shanghai communiqué of the U.S.A. and the People's Republic of China spoke of support for North-South Korean contacts.

"We clearly remember all the speeches made by President Nixon in China," he said. "What interests me most is that Nixon said the world should not be divided, and countries should not be divided, when he looked up at the Great Wall of China. So I am watching with great interest what channel his words will take in practice."

Everything the Premier said confirmed my impression that among North Korea's patriots and chauvinists he stood first. He believed that this was the only policy that would insure the survival of a small state in a complex and dangerous world. He was surely no Soviet puppet, and I was fascinated in reading back through his published speeches to find that his move toward independent policy had come much further back than I had thought—not long after Stalin's death. Up to that moment no more docile, obedient satellite (judging from his speeches) could be found. But Stalin had hardly entered the great mausoleum on Red Square in 1953 when Kim began to break away and chart a course of independence; to speak of Korea's national heritage; to inveigh against those who routinely copied from either Russia or China; and to emerge, within a few years, as the most skilled "balancer" in the Communist world, beholden neither to Russia nor China, often hostile to one, never kowtowing to either.

Kim set forth his nationalist Korea-for-the-Koreans principles in a remarkably frank speech on December 28, 1955, to his party propagandists and agitators.

"To make a revolution in Korea," he said, "we must know Korean history and geography and know the customs of the Korean people. Yet many of our functionaries are ignorant of our country's history and so do not strive to discover and carry forward its fine traditions. Unless this is corrected, it will lead, in the long run, to the negation of Korean history.

"Once I visited a People's Army vacation home where a picture of the Siberian steppe was hung. That landscape probably pleases the Russians. But the Korean people prefer the beautiful scenery of our own country . . .

"I noticed in a primary school that all the portraits hanging on the walls were of foreigners, such as Mayakovsky, Pushkin, etc., and there were none of Koreans. If children are educated in this way, how can they be expected to have national pride?

"There can be no set principle that we must follow the Soviet pattern. Some advocate the Soviet way, and others the Chinese, but is it not high time to work out our own?

"The point is that we should not mechanically copy forms and methods of the Soviet Union. . . . In learning from the Soviet Union, there is a marked tendency just to model after the external form. Once *Pravda* puts out a headline 'A Day in Our Country' our *Rodong Sinmun* carries the same title 'Day in Our Country.'

"To love Korea is just as good as to love the Soviet Union. . . ."

My visit, I learned very quickly, had coincided with a deep chill in North Korean-Russian relations. It was not only that North Korea no longer gave Russia credit for her liberation. The North Koreans were ostentatiously critical of the Soviet Union, blaming Moscow for its hostile policy toward China, for "splitting the camp," for attempting to dominate small powers—the whole litany. North Korea was equally hostile toward Japan, speaking of Tokyo with the venom acquired during the long, long years of occupation. Their hostility toward the United States was worn on their sleeves. Only China among the great powers was viewed with friendliness, obviously the result of the first coup in Premier Chou En-lai's post-Cultural Revolution foreign policy—his successful visit to Pyongyang in March, 1969, which brought North Korea out of a balanced position of quasi-hostility toward both Moscow and Peking and into the China orbit. How long this might endure no one could well judge. But it was plain that Chou En-lai had welded as firm a bond as he could, and was going to substantial lengths to maintain it. The lengthy visit of Prince Norodom Sihanouk just before my visit to North Korea was part of an assiduous Chinese policy designed to create and maintain a community of interest between North Korea and China and China's friends. I had no doubt that China had encouraged Kim to undertake his new and radical step—not only to move toward *rapprochement* with the South, but to begin to unfreeze his long-hostile relations with the United States.

Despite the harassed nature of my visit to North Korea, it was perfectly clear that my presence was an event of dramatic importance to the Premier. He was not going to permit any quarrel between his underlings and myself to deflect him. My trip to Pyongyang was to be followed almost immediately by that of another American correspondent, and there were more American visits to come. This was, in effect, the North Korean counterpart of the Chou-Kissinger policy. Where it would lead Kim and North Korea could not yet be forecast. But that it would lead out of isolation had already been made certain by my very presence, and this was to be confirmed by the July 4 North-South announcement. I wondered whether the North Koreans had not deliberately picked that date with due regard for its significance. American Independence Day. I hardly thought it was accidental.

This, then, was the great new adventure on which Kim Il Sung was leading his country. Perhaps he was motivated by concern for his military budget as the South slyly insisted. Perhaps he was pushed in this direction by Chou, who saw in *rapprochement* yet another slap at Moscow and a strengthening of the anti-Moscow coalition.

But it seemed to me that the overriding motivation was Kim's own, and that it sprang from the deep sources of Korean nationalism that had already driven him so powerfully in reconstructing his country, in insisting on its entity and in so fiercely and jealously guarding its prerogatives.

For, with all the maudlin propaganda, the garrulous and gratuitous nonsense of the Kim cult, there lay behind it a monumentally astute and visionary statesman. I had no doubt that Kim Il Sung was as ruthless a leader as the Communist world could boast. I had not the slightest question that his police force fulfilled his every will, and that there was an underlay of terror in the country which went into its remarkable discipline. But I also knew that Kim's fantastic cult was not a cult without a content. That is, it was not simply a cult for the gratification of an astonishingly egocentric individual (although he certainly was that). The cult had a conscious purpose. The childhood history of the Premier was employed to strengthen the moral fiber of the young, who were taught to work hard, study hard, be brave, be self-sacrificing, be strict with themselves and their associates, be patriotic, be hyper-patriotic, be dedicated to their country, to its independence, to be willing to give their lives in fighting its enemies and ready for any hardship in making the country stronger.

The youngsters were given an almost Prussian discipline. Day and night I had seen them parading the towns and cities, arms swinging, striding in a kind of Asian goosestep, husky, determined, going to work in the rice fields or marching to the stadium to engage in mass gymnastics, saluting any passing Mercedes in Pyongyang or any car in the provinces, on the automatic assumption that the passenger must be someone important.

The songs they sang, the games they played, the lessons they studied involved a complex and even subtle intermingling of the virtues ascribed to Kim Il Sung and the duties in the life they were being brought up to lead.

Once the young people reached late adolescence and were moved along the conveyor belt into industry, or the armed forces, or whatever task the state deemed necessary, the "military-industrial" facet of the Premier's propagandized personality took over.

Now they learned, as in a catechism, his leadership devices—the Chollima goals, the Juche principles, the Taen methods. Stripped of ideological verbiage, most of these concepts turned out to be hardheaded common sense. And when you perceived this, the Premier began to come through as an uncommonly practical, extraordinarily energetic man, who not only devoted his personal energies to building his country from a backward Asian heritage into a modern industrial state but who had put his personality into the service of innumerable legends which had been woven into the warp and woof of the country's social, economic and political system.

Without the driving force of this ego-directed man, I questioned whether North Korea could have survived the terrible blows of the war with the United States, or the worst struggle of all, in the Premier's own recollection, that of rebuilding the country after 1953. Certainly North Korea would never have been turned into today's well-oiled, carefully, articulately, intensely hard-working, rapidly expanding industrial society without his leadership.

The task had been made harder by the Premier's fanatical determination to make his country an autarchy, dependent upon no one. To be sure, he had had to obtain military aid and materiel from Russia and China. So far as I could observe, he needed Russian help to provide reinforcements and replacements for his trigger-ready air force. (In my seacoast visits, I noted Mig-21 overflights along the coastal waters almost every 20 minutes.) I supposed he could probably provide the arms needed for his ground forces, although there might be some dependence on China. But if that was true, there was never a public word of recognition of the fact. Certainly his suppression of the truth about China's aid in the Korean War, and about the Red Army's role in liberating Korea was designed solely to magnify Korea's own sense of national prestige and strength.

The reunification of his country might well be a more difficult undertaking than any he had yet tackled. But, on his record, I was not going to write off his chances lightly. On April 15, 1972, the Premier celebrated his 60th birthday. Traditionally in Korea, 60 years are a man's life span. This was the significant milestone in Kim's life. It should mark the end of his active career. But there seemed no indication that the Premier had decided to step aside on this traditional date. In fact, a new slogan was being popularized throughout North Korea. It celebrated the long life and vitality given by the regime. It was: "Let's celebrate the 60th birthday at 90!"

18

Vietnam—How Many Years?

The first thing I was taken to see when I arrived in Hanoi on the eve of Christmas in 1966 was the Museum of the Revolution, and the first exhibits I was shown dealt with the wars and triumphs of the Vietnamese people—wars against the Chinese, the Mongols and the Mings. I was introduced to the great national heroes of Vietnam—to the sainted sisters, Trung Trac and Trung Nhi, who drove the Chinese from the Vietnamese land at the start of the Christian era, 40 A.D., (and had become a cult that was the special preoccupation of Mme. Ngo Dinh Nhu, sister of the ill-fated Ngo Dinh Diem); to Than Hung Dao, the great Vietnamese warrior of the 13th century who three times beat off the assault of the Mongol hordes that had seized the Dragon Throne; and to the Vietnamese heroes who fought off China's Ming Dynasty and then graciously provided the Chinese with horses so they could make the long journey back to Peking.

"We would do the same for the Americans," said the museum director a bit wistfully.

Vietnam and China. It was as tangled a history as the Asian continent had spawned—a record of combat and struggle, tradition and enmity, whose roots had struck down well before the start of the Christian era. Again and again the Chinese had thrust southward. Again and again the fierce warrior peoples of Vietnam repulsed the attacks of their northern neighbors. Or so they now remembered the history. But I could not help noting that when the struggles began, the Vietnamese inhabited regions north of Kwangtung Province, north of Canton. And now they lived a thousand miles south, on the Vietnamese archipelago. Something—and I was inclined to think it was the inexorable pressure of China's mass—had gradually shifted the Vietnamese to the south.

I did not have much opportunity in my brief bomb-spattered interval in North Vietnam to pursue the saga of Vietnam and China. But, in intervening years, I came to learn a great deal more about the story from both sides. Vietnam, fiercely independent as it was, actually was suffused in China's cultural overwash. Her language, her governmental system, her mandarin caste, her religion, her art, her mores, all of these (muted, to be sure, by the tradition of Annam and Cochin-China) were intimately linked to China. The interaction of trade, politics, war and religion had forged bonds almost too complex for analysis.

The Chinese had done something more. They had aroused deep in the Vietnamese ethos that same wariness, caution and fear that was to be found in most of the smaller peoples who lived on the fringe of China's enormous periphery. Vietnam had always lain within the shadow of Chinese power. For centuries Vietnam paid tribute to China. Certainly Vietnam now remembered this tribute as being nominal. But that was not the view in Peking. All of the archipelago was considered by Peking to be part of her subject domain, and this view had been held not alone by the Chinese emperors whose reign came to an end in 1911. Maps published in the early years of Mao's Communist regime still displayed Vietnam as part of China's "lost" empire.

Ho Chi Minh was influenced by four cultures, and possibly five—Vietnamese, French, Russian, Chinese and, peripherally, American. I do not know which foreign culture weighed the most, but I think it was Chinese. Ho was a member of the Chinese Communist Party before he founded the Vietnamese Communist Party, and he came to Canton during the exhilirating early days of the Chinese Revolution, quite possibly making the trip with the great Russian revolutionary, Mikhail Borodin, sent out by Lenin to help Dr. Sun Yat-sen. Certainly Ho knew China better than any country other than his own. What was true of Ho was true of many Vietnamese.

I have been told by more than one Hanoi official that—in the long run—they fear China (because she is so close and so powerful) much more than they do the United States, which is distant, and eventually, they feel certain, will tire of the long and profitless war. Indeed, this bias was clearly indicated by Ho when Vietnam emerged under his leadership as an independent entity at the end of World War II. He feared China because she was close. He feared France because he knew she would attempt to regain her colonial suzerainty. But the United States was distant and democratic. He had seen the Statue of

Liberty in New York harbor on his seaman's journeys, and he had, like many young nationalists, read of the American Revolution. Thus, in August, 1945, when he came to draft the new Vietnamese Declaration of Independence, he asked the young Americans of the OSS (precursor of the CIA) mission in Hanoi to provide him with a copy of the Declaration of Independence so that he could incorporate its words into the preamble of Vietnam's constitution. The embarrassed young men had no copy of the Declaration, but Ho was not thwarted. Relying on memory, he opened his Declaration with these words:

"All men are created equal. They are endowed by their Creator with certain inalienable rights, among these are Life, Liberty and the Pursuit of Happiness.

"This immortal statement was made in the Declaration of Independence of the United States of America in 1776. In a broader sense, this means all the peoples have a right to live, to be happy and free . . ."

So Ho proclaimed in Hanoi on September 2, 1945, and he continued:

"We are convinced that the Allied nations which at Teheran and San Francisco have acknowledged the principles of self-determination and equality of nations will not refuse to acknowledge the independence of Vietnam.

"A people who have courageously opposed French domination for more than 80 years, a people who have fought side by side with the Allies against the Fascists during these last years, such a people must be free and independent . . ."

I have no doubt that Ho was moved by American eloquence, but I also believed he was inspired by *Realpolitik*, the normal policy of the small, weak power looking for a strong protector far enough distant so as not to be likely to become a menace.

My belief is strengthened by the fact, revealed in the "Pentagon papers," that in the following two years, Ho on eight occasions wrote, cabled or sent special messages by envoys to President Truman trying to enlist American support and aid on almost any terms. He even proposed an American trusteeship over Vietnam on the model of the Philippines. (He was remarkably impressed with what he regarded as American magnanimity and disinterestedness in granting the Philippines their independence.) No reply did he ever receive. Instead he was led inexorably down the path of new conflict with France, and by the time he defeated the French at Dienbienphu, the Americans, his heroes, stepped in to replace them. Small wonder that he used to ask his American visitors in the last years of his life: "Tell me—the Statue of Liberty—is it still standing upright? Or has it been turned upside down?"

The Chinese, far better than the Americans, understood and appreciated these nuances of Vietnamese psychology. They knew their own history, and in discussing the Vietnamese question, Premier Chou En-lai was at pains to point out the fierce national urges of the Vietnamese which led them to fight war after war against the feudal dynasties of China. In the end, peace came to the two countries—when the Chinese ceased their invasions. But then came the French, and, as Chou noted, the French occupied Vietnam for 100 years—but the Vietnamese never gave up, never ceased fighting.

The Chinese are far too sophisticated politically not to understand that, as a small power on their periphery, Vietnam inevitably will strive for balance, will strive to find another power that can be counterpoised against China to help to insure Vietnamese independence.

It is only within this context that the true nature of the relationship between Hanoi and Peking could be understood.

I was in China in June, 1972, when Henry Kissinger flew in after the Moscow conference to meet with Premier Chou En-lai, to give him a summary of the Soviet-American understandings and, once more, to try to solicit China's aid in bringing the Vietnam War to a conclusion.

I did not see Dr. Kissinger during his visit in Peking, but I did meet with Premier Chou just 48 hours before Kissinger's arrival. The Premier utilized the evening, in part, as a dress rehearsal of remarks he would be making to President Nixon's adviser. He left no shadow of a doubt that, come what may, China would go on backing Hanoi and the Provisional Revolutionary Government (Viet Cong) in the south. And more. He made it equally clear that he would never again put pressure on Hanoi to accept an international settlement of the war patterned on the model of the ill-fated Geneva Conference of 1954, in which he participated. In fact, he said, the Geneva Conference was a sell-out of North Vietnam, because the United States declined to abide by its provisions, and the late John Foster Dulles (who had refused to shake hands with Chou at Geneva) was, as has been made clear in the "Pentagon papers," preparing to violate the Geneva agreement even before the ink was dry on its paper. Never again, Chou said. He felt himself personally responsible for urging the Vietnamese to go along with the agreement. He would not be party to any similar effort in the future. The only solution he would back would be one that Hanoi and the PRG were prepared to offer, presumably along the classic lines of their well-known eight-point proposal.

What this meant was that unless President Nixon and Dr. Kissinger were prepared to get rid of President Thieu, there would be no real and lasting peace in Vietnam.

Premier Chou—and every other Chinese official with whom I talked—emphasized that, while this was *their* position, they would not guarantee that the Soviet position was the same, or would remain the same in the future. I did not think these doubts were entirely prejudiced by the well-known antagonism of the Chinese toward the Russians. I think they felt there might be a point at which Russia would be willing to trade out Hanoi in return for concessions by the United States in Europe or the Middle East—that is, in regions that had more significance and importance to the Russians.

What lay behind China's suspicion of Russia was the geography of the situation—China was near, and Russia was far away.

There was logic in the Chinese view. I had seen the relative disinterest of the Russians—even those in Hanoi—in the plight of the Vietnamese. Vietnam could hardly be further from the parameters of Russian security interests. I had long been certain that had it not been for the Sino-Soviet confrontation, the Russians would long since have traded off their Vietnam position for large-scale wheat or machinery sales by the United States.

Not so the Chinese. China was certain to be concerned over the fate of Vietnam, even if her relations with Russia had been the best; even if Vietnam was all capitalist, instead of being divided. China's interest in Vietnam was identical with America's interest in Mexico. Vietnam was China's neighbor protecting her southern flank. China could not help but possess a constant and unchanging interest in events on the Indochina peninsula.

In 1970, Premier Chou En-lai made two moves of great international significance that were hardly noted in the West. In March, he went to Pyongyang and cemented Chinese-North Korean relations. This move secured China's northern flank. It helped to insure the security of Manchuria and Peking. Russia could still attack, to be sure, but she could not carry out a pincers movement with the collaboration of North Korea (as, I suspect, Stalin once thought of trying against Mao). North Korea, as China's ally, extended Russia's potential front and created the theoretical threat of a blow from North Korea at Russia's Maritime province and her great naval complex at Vladivostok and Nakhodka. No student of Japan's strategy against Russia in 1904 could afford to take this lightly.

The second coup came when Chou moved with extraordinary swiftness and subtlety to take advantage of the American "incursion" into Cambodia and the Pnompenh coup against Prince Sihanouk.

Premier Chou convened a conference in south China (the exact locale has never been revealed), attended by Prince Sihanouk, Premier Pham Van Dong of North Vietnam, representatives of the PRG and Prince Souphanouvong of Laos, with himself as a host. What emerged was a de facto alliance between the Indochina participants. China pledged her full backing to all, and all four agreed, in effect, to collaborate against the United States and to make no separate peace. North Korea, unrepresented at the meeting, adhered to the declaration, and China's guarantee was extended to her.

This was no mere propaganda move, although most U.S. specialists seemed to regard it as such. It was viciously attacked by the Soviet Union, which refused to recognize Sihanouk and continued to maintain diplomatic relations with the Lon Nol government (and has continued to do so to this day). Moreover, Russia has insisted that her eastern European allies take the same line. Only Rumania has refused.

To China this meant two things. First, she emerged as the paramount backer of all the regimes in Indochina arrayed against the United States. In doing so, she stole a march on the Russians. The move was not only of some value in protecting China's southern flank but precluded the Russians' strengthening their position on China's border, if the United States at long last pulled out of the war. More important, it drew Hanoi markedly closer to Peking than to Moscow.

For the future, it offered a preview of the arrangements China envisaged when, as, and if Southeast Asia tensions should ever relax—that is, the creation along her southern periphery of a group of states, nominally neutralist but definitely tilting in her direction and not in the direction of any hostile power.

When President Nixon visited China in February, the Russians directed heavy propaganda at Vietnam, the main burden of which was that China was about to sell out Hanoi. But the moment the Shanghai communiqué was issued, Premier Chou boarded a plane and flew to meet Premier Pham Van Dong and Prince Sihanouk, in order to assure both that there had been no sellout.

I could find no evidence that the crisis of 1972 brought on by the North Vietnamese land offensive and President Nixon's naval blockade and hyper-escalation of the air war had produced any basic change.

Peking diplomats believed that the Hanoi offensive was a byproduct of a Russian effort to undermine the Chinese in Vietnam by outpromising them. They traced the operation to the visit to Hanoi of President Podgorny of the Soviet Union in November, 1971. Podgorny promised Hanoi the arms and equipment needed to turn the tide on the land. This hardware was deployed in the spring offensive. There was a suspicion that the Chinese did not think the offensive well-advised or well-timed. In principle the Chinese favor guerrilla operations, rather than order-of-battle engagements, and the timing of the attacks could not but be embarrassing in the context of the Chou-Nixon *rapprochement*. The Russians were probably well aware of these potentials. Whether there had been argument or conflict within the North Vietnamese government over the offensive no one was prepared to say, but based on what I knew of the ongoing arguments within North Vietnam as early as 1967 over guerrilla versus "main force" engagements, it seemed to me that there must have been dispute, and it might well have been the Russian purpose to cause a cleavage in the Hanoi Politburo.

The Hanoi offensive was launched with spectacular consequences —first, tremendous successes for the North Vietnamese army and then, just as I was going into China in May, President Nixon's radical escalation of the air and naval war. This raged throughout my visit in China. There were immediate rumors in Peking that the Chinese had lifted their embargo on the shipment of Soviet supplies overland across China and were permitting rail routes to be substituted for the blockaded sea access to Haiphong. But this, I was assured on the highest authority, simply was not true. There had, in fact, been absolutely no change in the ground rules. The Chinese honored their existing commitments, but they did not modify their restrictions. What they did do, of course, was to emphasize to the Vietnamese and the Americans privately that their support would go on unshaken. I have no doubt they immediately set about to make good any loss of supplies that Vietnam might suffer as a result of U.S. blockade and bombardment.

Le Duc Tho, the Vietnamese Politburo member charged with negotiations with the United States, passed through Peking the day after I spent the evening with Premier Chou En-lai. There was instant speculation that he would meet with Dr. Kissinger. But he did not. He went back to Hanoi before Kissinger arrived.

I had a long conversation in Peking with a European diplomat intimately concerned with questions relating to China, the United States and Vietnam. He told me that President Nixon first raised the question of a Vietnam settlement when he met with President de Gaulle in February, 1969, suggesting that de Gaulle take some steps that might lead to a successful negotiation. Again, when de Gaulle came to Washington for the funeral of President Eisenhower, President Nixon raised the question, suggesting that he wanted to get entirely out of Vietnam and hoped to take some small steps toward normalizing relations with China.

These revelations seemed completely consistent with remarks made to me by Mr. Nixon in a private conversation in late October, 1968, shortly before his election. He said then that his first action as President must be to resolve the war in Vietnam. If it were not on its way to resolution within six months, it would become "Nixon's war." Without bringing the war to an end, he would be paralyzed in taking any other actions either at home or abroad. He said that he wanted to begin the process of establishing a relationship with Communist China. He did not give this project number-one priority. But he did wish to get it under way—for several reasons. He was well aware of the urgency of the Sino-Soviet conflict, and he felt, quite frankly, that it would be impossible to lay a firm basis for peace in the world if we did not establish a relationship with Peking.

Obviously, the President had gone forward successfully and skillfully to lay the foundation for a new China relationship. But—and this seemed to me the crux—he had not acted on his initial impulse to move with equal deftness to bring the war in Vietnam to a close. Somewhere along the line, and possibly the decision had not come until just before his November, 1969, speech, he had opted out of negotiation and settlement in favor of something that had come to be known as "Vietnamization"—that is, pulling out U.S. ground forces but continuing the war with Vietnamese troops and U.S. air and naval power.

I could not agree when the Peking diplomat offered the following scenario of the President's intentions: first, to change U.S. policy toward China; second, to bring the Soviet Union into the picture (as the President had just done at Moscow); and third, to initiate direct efforts to end the Vietnam War. This the diplomat did not think would be as difficult as many thought. For instance, the Russians had given his government a private memorandum indicating that they would support the creation of an independent non-aligned regime in the South that would be non-Communist and remain non-Communist for a long time. He thought the Chinese favored this, as well.

I said that I believed that both Russia and China would support that solution. Furthermore, I felt sure that the North and the PGR would support it. Indeed, it followed, point-by-point, the program for settlement of the war that I had brought back with me from Hanoi in January, 1967—*more than six years ago.*

Again and again and again, the Viet Cong or the National Liberation Front or the PGR—the names changed with the years but each represented the same thing—had announced this as their program. Again and again and again, the North had agreed that it would support an independent, non-Communist, neutralist South, where private enterprise would continue, and the government would be made up of all elements in the population, with one exception—President Thieu and his small clique.

But, as I pointed out in Peking, that was precisely the sticking point. That was what the deadlock was all about. The United States would not give up Thieu. It would not agree to any government in which he did not participate, and every proposal we made was predicated on this proposition. That being so, what good was it if everyone else was ready to settle—Hanoi, the PGR, China, Russia—the whole world?

It seemed to me that President Thieu was stronger than ever—at least in part because the North's offensive had so clearly shown that he was incapable of defending his regime without U.S. air and naval power. If he couldn't make it on his own, and we insisted on keeping him in power, the only force capable of doing that was America.

So, I told my friend in Peking, I fear the war is not really going to be settled by Dr. Kissinger, nor by President Nixon, nor by anyone else. It may just go on and on. I winced as I said this, because I remembered what Premier Pham Van Dong had told me in the presidential palace in Hanoi so long before. He was speaking in a quiet voice, which I could still hear, speaking softly, and with just a touch of irony. He was talking, of course, about the war—a people's war, he called it, and he said that people's wars were of necessity long wars.

"That's why we are preparing for a long war," he said. "How many years would you say? Ten, twenty—what do you think about twenty?"

I remembered the inward shudder that ran through me. He was, I suddenly realized, speaking in utter, cold candor. Vietnam was prepared to fight ten years more. Or 20 years more. After all, I should realize that. They had fought the French for 100 years. And the Chinese for centuries. I thought then of the American youngsters on the battlefield (this was light years before the demonstrations, the confrontations, Johnson and Rusk and McNamara and Westmoreland still riding high), the deaths, the suffering, the Vietnamese children I had seen in the hospitals, the babies without eyes, the old women who sat, doddering, their minds loosened, their sanity simply whisked away by the bombs, and I said, a bit wanly, well, wouldn't this be a good year to stop the war?

Pham Van Dong took no notice of the remark whatever. He went right on:

"What I used to tell our friends is that the younger generation will fight better than we—even kids so-high. They are preparing themselves. That's the situation. I'm not telling that to impress anyone. It's the truth. That's the logical consequence of the situation. Our Vietnam nation is a very proud nation. Our history is one of a very proud nation. The Mongol invaders came. They were defeated the first time, the second time and the third time. Now, how many times does the Pentagon want to fight? So—how many years the war goes on depends on you. Not on me."

I could not then have believed that five years later I would be sitting in Peking, that the United States and China would have buried many of their major differences, that these great transitions could have occurred, and the war in Vietnam would still roll on, and even now, as I sipped tea with my diplomatic colleague, that American planes would be tearing the Indochina heavens asunder, dropping new thousands of tons of bombs to totals that had long since made World War II look like a prep-school exercise.

My mind turned back to those conversations in Hanoi in January, 1967. I had never reported publicly the full text of what Premier Pham Van Dong had said to me, because there was a passage or two that he wanted kept off the record. In one, he had outlined a simple and direct sequence that could have placed the war immediately on the path to solution—and, in fact, it was the very path that was ultimately followed by President Johnson 15 months later, with his March 31, 1967, partial bombing halt. The North Vietnamese Premier told me in words that were tactful but crystal-clear that if the United States halted the bombing, Vietnam would respond with an appropriate gesture. But, alas, when I got back to the United States and suggested to the White House that I believed it would be useful to tell the President what I had learned in Hanoi, Mr. Johnson found himself much too busy. His response was identical with that which my colleagues, the late William C. Baggs of the *Miami News* and Harry S. Ashmore, former editor of the *Arkansas Gazette,* encountered when they returned from the North a couple of weeks later. The President declined to see them, with the remark: "Y'all know I just can't see *everybody* that comes back from Hanoi."

In all fairness, I did pass my information on to Dean Rusk. But he didn't think it amounted to much.

I had had a slight argument with Pham Van Dong about American peace moves. I pointed out to him that Mr. Johnson had said he was ready to go anywhere at any moment, if it would advance the cause of peace. The Vietnamese Premier gently chided me. He said he thought he knew a little more about that than I did, because he knew things that had happened that I didn't know about. He then apologized in advance for saying something he thought might hurt my feelings and which, on later reflection, he thought he should not have said and thus asked me to delete it from my interview. "You know, Mr. Salisbury," he said, "I am very sorry to have to say this, but your President Johnson is a liar."

Sitting there in Peking on a beautiful early July day, with the sun streaming in, hot and humid, through the open window, a cup of fresh and fragrant tea on the table before me, an impeccably tailored, impeccably educated diplomat of years of experience sitting with me, casually chatting about the logic of the Vietnam situation, I could not help being flooded with a feeling of utter despondency. How long, indeed, would the war go on? What answer, now, might I offer if Pham Van Dong once again posed that simple question: "How long shall we fight—ten years, twenty years?

19

The Legacy of Genghis Khan

On the day I visited the 31st Middle School of Peking, most of the boys and girls were spread across the assembly grounds, doing calisthenics in the hot sun. A physical-culture instructor stood on a raised platform and barked commands as the youngsters flung their arms over their heads, leapt in the air, bent to the ground and ran in place. Beyond the grounds I noticed a high stone barricade, heavy cut stone, neatly stacked and about ten feet high. It extended all along the outer perimeter of the grounds.

In talking with the school's Revolutionary Committee. I asked whether they, like all the other institutions I had visited in Peking, had constructed an air-raid shelter. Certainly, they said, hadn't I noticed the piles of stone on the far side of the school grounds? These had come from the great wall of Peking. Students and faculty had helped demolish the wall and bring the cut stone to the school by cart. Now it was being used to reinforce the walls of the deep underground shelter system the school was building.

Ma Wen-chang, a pleasant-spoken, plain-faced man in dark-blue tunic, chairman of the Revolutionary Committee, said it had been no easy task to take down the wall. It had been marvelously well built. But, beginning in 1969, it began to come down. The whole city turned out to work. It was not easy to get the great stone blocks out without damaging them, especially for people not skilled with their hands. Teachers and students worked side by side. The task was used to instruct the pupils not only in physical labor but in changing times. The wall had been put up to defend the medieval rulers of China; it was taken down to defend the plain people of China.

"Everybody has worked on this, because when the enemy sends his planes, they will not spare any organization in the city," Ma said. "It is quite an arduous task, but at the same time it is a good opportunity to teach the students to be prepared."

He said that the work reminded them that countries still existed that harbored no love for China.

"When the bombs come, they will make no distinction between students and teachers," he said. "As long as there is imperialism in the world, we will keep on digging, because bombs keep on improving and the air-raid shelter system must be improved."

One could not stay passive in such a situation, he said, or as a high official in the Foreign Ministry put it more succinctly: "With 1 million Russian troops on our frontier, we have no alternative."

The Chinese shelter program must be one of the greatest construction enterprises the world has seen. It makes the building of the Great Wall seem like a primitive undertaking; yet the Great Wall dwarfs any building project I have ever seen. The shelters are invisible to the casual passer-by. But they are everywhere. Literally. Not just in Peking, but in every Chinese city we visited—north—west—south—east and center. Travelers we met reported seeing them under construction everywhere. Construction began at a hysterical pace in the autumn of 1969, when everyone in China felt that a Russian nuclear attack might occur at any moment.

That was the year, 1969, of the almost continuous border clashes between Russia and China. The fighting started on the Ussuri in March and continued at intervals until autumn. It included very serious clashes on the Ussuri, the Amur and, most seriously of all, on the Sinkiang-Kazakhstan frontier, in August, 1969. The critical nature of the situation was conveyed by the sudden and dangerous escalation of military deployment along the 7,500-mile frontier that separates China on the one hand and the Soviet Union and its close ally, Outer Mongolia, on the other. Charlotte and I visited Outer Mongolia in late spring and early summer of 1969 and found ourselves set down in the midst of Soviet military preparations so hectic and concentrated that little or no effort at concealment was attempted. We saw Soviet sappers laying high-fidelity communications systems; Soviet engineers emplacing directional-guidance systems for missiles; troops constructing missile bases and launching platforms in the mountains south of Ulan Bator; and everywhere armor, aircraft and personnel arriving in impressive numbers.

There could be no doubt of the seriousness of their purpose. Nor were these preparations confined to Mongolia. They were in full swing to the south and east of the Soviet command headquarters in Khabarovsk, and to the west, where a new Soviet command had been established at Alma Ata to coordinate operations along the frontiers of China's badly exposed westernmost province of Sinkiang and—who knows?—quite probably against Tibet. Before the summer ended, some 800,000 Soviet troops had been concentrated against China, their deployment following the pattern of the successful August, 1945, blitz by Marshal Rodion Y. Malinovsky against Japan's Kwantung army, then occupying Manchuria and North China. Soviet military spokesmen had begun openly to discuss a repetition of this exercise against the People's Republic of China, Moscow spokesmen were hinting at the use of nuclear weapons, and the Kremlin distributed a circular letter to all Communist parties of eastern and western Europe, warning of the possibility that it might be forced to strike against China.

The two nations teetered on the brink, and pulled back only when an extraordinary diplomatic effort was set in motion by the funeral of Ho Chi Minh. Acting under the emotional impact of Ho's last testament, which called for an end to the division in the Communist world, the other Communists persuaded Moscow and Peking to make one last effort. Premier Kosygin flew to Peking en route home from Hanoi to Moscow. (His invitation was delayed by the Chinese until he actually had left Hanoi. He received word of it when his aircraft landed at Dyushambe, Tadzhikistan, to refuel, whereupon he flew all the way back—2,500 miles—and landed in Peking.) The Premier was received by Premier Chou En-lai at the Peking airport, and, in a waiting room, they met for three hours and agreed to make one more diplomatic effort to settle their differences.

The two countries began a new round of bilateral talks in late October, 1969. Three years later, they had yet to agree on an agenda of what to discuss. The crisis, while significantly pulled back from the brink of nuclear warfare, was no closer to resolution three years later.

The Chinese view of what that meant was encapsulated in their nuclear shelter program. It had been launched in the dangerous days of September, 1969. Almost everyone in China engaged in the task in those perilous weeks. What was then done in Peking was to dig a network of shallow five- or six-foot tunnels in every *hutung*, in every courtyard, adjacent to every apartment house, factory and office. Some of the tunnels led to larger communal shelters. A few of them connected with the Peking subway system then being dug at a depth of about 30 feet. Some led nowhere. They were primitive. They afforded no protection against direct hits or near-misses by conventional bombs, and none against nuclear blasts within a quarter-mile. About all that could be said was that they gave a portion of the population a chance to survive a Hiroshima-style attack (that is, one or two or three nuclear bombs on the sprawling area of Peking.) They would have been useless in any concentrated assault. Crash programs were launched in all other cities of China, with priority, naturally, given to work in north China, Manchuria, northwest China and the big cities of central China—that is, the most likely initial targets of Soviet attack.

Once the primitive shelter system had been completed, a new and much more complex task was undertaken—the creation of an underground city beneath Peking, capable of protecting the entire 7 million population from concentrated nuclear attack. This is the system that is now under construction. It is designed to incorporate deep tunnels from every neighborhood of Peking—25 or 30 feet deep—leading from neighborhood to neighborhood and enabling residents of a section attacked by nuclear bombs to make their way safely to an undamaged part of the city. I saw entrances to these tunnels in almost every street and courtyard. Often the original shallow trenches were used as the entryway to the deeper tunnels. It was those deep tunnels that were being shored up with the stones from the city wall. But not alone with these stones. In every neighborhood in Peking, I saw hundreds of pre-stressed concrete arches piled along the roadsides, ready to be put into place in the tunnels. There were stacks of steel girders and great mounds of brick and stone piled at almost every turn.

A new and much deeper subway line was being dug at a depth of 60 feet or more in a great circle around the city. The tunnels lead ultimately to this subway line. Each station on the new line was being built to accomodate large numbers of refugees. The new tunnel network was equipped with electricity, water, food and medical stocks, and ventilation systems. I did not inspect the tunnels myself, but Professor John Fairbank of Harvard and his wife, Wilma, visited one in the courtyard of the house where they had lived in Peking in the late 1930's. Other foreigners had seen the tunnels and shelters in other parts of the city.

In Shanghai, the area under what once was the race course, the gathering place of the smartest foreigners in pre-revolutionary Shanghai, had been turned into one of the city's biggest shelters. The further south I went in China, the less intensive the work on the shelter system seemed to be. Obviously the authorities feared attacks in those regions near to Siberia and Mongolia more than in the more remote regions.

In some respects the Peking shelter system resembled that built at Stalin's orders in Moscow in the late 1940's, when he feared an American nuclear attack. That system centered on the Moscow Metro, a very deep subway that had been built with extremely large stations, which were used as air-raid shelters during World War II. In fact, the Mayakovsky station of the Moscow Metro was used by Stalin and the government as their main shelter.

Stalin constructed a series of new radial links to the Metro, particularly in the central part of Moscow. These radials served no transportation purpose, but they provided a huge chamber where tens of thousands of Muscovites could take refuge. The system was equipped with an underground power supply, water, ventilation and air locks like a submarine, so that individual segments could function even if others were hit. Comparatively deep shelters were built adjacent to apartment and office buildings, and I had seen their ventilator hoods throughout the city. I doubt that other Russian cities were similarly protected, and I had never seen any shelter networks in the Siberian cities, although all of Siberia was equipped with radar and electronic warning systems.

I could not estimate the time, manpower, steel and other materials, and funds that have been poured into the Chinese effort. I guessed that it was on a scale that must have set back the national economic plan by at least a year or two. The program had not been taken into the villages. Obviously, the feeling was that the villages were not likely to be the target of nuclear assaults. Instead, the villages had been strengthened in hopes of making them self-sufficient in the event communications and distribution of supplies were crippled by a Soviet blitz. The peasants had been encouraged to set aside reserve stores of grain and rice. I saw many peasant huts literally bulging with great earthen jars in which the grain reserves had been stored. The brigades and communes were encouraged to maintain stocks of food and materials. Each village was trained in self-defense and guerrilla tactics. In case the centers of the country were destroyed, the villages and countryside would go on fighting.

The Chinese felt they had no chance to match the Russians in nuclear weaponry. Nonetheless, they had expanded and improved their nuclear armament and rocketry. U.S. intelligence sources credited them with 150 to 200 nuclear weapons, including a preponderance of hydrogen bombs. The Chinese had intermediate ballistic missiles with the capability of hitting almost any target in Siberia, from Novosibirsk to Vladivostok, and some of the Urals industrial locales as well. The range of these missiles was estimated at 2,500 miles. The medium Chinese missile had a 1,000-mile capability. They had test-fired 3,500-mile missiles, which would enable them to reach most of the Russian targets in the west, including Moscow and Leningrad. But they were under no illusions so far as their ability to deter the Russians. They knew that the Soviet nuclear missiles were targeted on their principal cities, and that sophisticated Russian equipment would probably destroy most of China's nuclear capability before it could be launched.

Thus, the only way in which China could survive, the only tactic that gave them a chance of fighting Russia, was to seek to preserve as much of the urban populace as possible and prepare the countryside for the kind of protracted warfare that had bled the Japanese so grievously.

The Russians, of course, had not stood still during the three years since the crisis of September, 1969. Most important, they had not reduced their garrisons on China's border. In Outer Mongolia, they had built new concrete runways and permanent housing for their planes. They had sunk their missiles into concrete silos. They had constructed a permanent communications system and built barracks and repair facilities for their armored detachments. And, most significantly in the Chinese view, they had continued their troop build-up until they now had well over a million men on China's frontiers.

The International Institute for Strategic Studies estimated in May, 1972, that the number of Soviet divisions facing China had risen from 30 to 44 in 1971—meaning that the Russians had about one-quarter of their strength in position in the east. By September, 1972, U.S. intelligence sources in Washington reported that three new mechanized Soviet divisions had been posted to the China frontier, and that the total of Soviet divisions now stationed adjacent to the border had reached 49—nearly one-third of Soviet armed strength. The Russians were embarked on a major redeployment that included large-scale military exercises in Outer Mongolia and the eastern Siberian regions close to China.

In these conditions, there could be no talk in Peking of friendship between China and Outer Mongolia, for Outer Mongolia was

Russia's staunchest ally, as well as an important Russian base for attacking China. I knew from my last conversations with Mongolia's Premier Y. Tsedenbal in 1969 that his hostility toward the Chinese was as fierce or fiercer than the Russians'. He contended that as soon as Mao founded his regime in 1949, he called on Stalin to turn Mongolia back to China. Stalin refused, and for that reason—if no other—Stalin's statue still stood in a prominent square in Ulan Bator, the only Stalin statue remaining in the whole Soviet-dominated bloc. Tsedenbal contended that Chinese armed forces had on several occasions penetrated into Outer Mongolia and remained there for considerable periods of time before they were persuaded to retire. And I knew that there had been angry confrontations between the Mongols and Chinese over the operation of the Peking-Ulan Bator-Moscow Express. There had even been an occasion when Chinese and Russian-Mongol forces of division strength had drawn up at the frontier during a confrontation over charges that the Chinese were using the train to disseminate anti-Soviet propaganda.

I did not get a chance to visit Inner Mongolia. This is a border area where, it was said, the Cultural Revolution was still in progress. It was, in a word, sensitive, either because the region had not completely emerged from the tensions of the Cultural Revolution or because it was a frontier zone—or both.

I had long known from my many visits to Outer Mongolia that a strong spirit of pan-Mongolism pervaded all of the Mongol peoples—now divided into three groups—the 1.3 million Mongols of the quasi-independent Outer Mongolia, the 800,000-odd Buryat Mongols who inhabit the Buryat Autonomous Soviet Socialist Republic in the U.S.S.R. and the 1.5 million or more Mongols who lived in China's Inner Mongolia. The hostile atmosphere offered little hope that the Mongols would get far with their dreams of uniting in a Greater Mongolia. Inner Mongolia had been subjected to a heavy infusion of Han Chinese, partly as a result of the building up of its important cities industrially, and partly, no doubt, as a result of a deliberate Chinese security policy. The result was that the Mongols had become a minority in their own country (there are now 17 Chinese for each Mongol).

The Russians, in propaganda broadcasts and pamphlets, contended that the Chinese had committed genocide and were deliberately trying to exterminate the Mongol populace of Inner Mongolia. But they offered no evidence in support of their charges. The fact was that, until the frontier between Inner and Outer Mongolia was firmly sealed ten years ago, the Outer Mongols greatly envied the Inner Mongols because Chinese policy was so much more relaxed than that of their own Russian-influenced government. For example, the Inner Mongols had retained their original Mongol script, and their newspapers and books were much sought after in Outer Mongolia. Perhaps most important of all—the Inner Mongols had the traditional crypt where Genghis Khan was supposed to be buried—an object of enormous Mongol veneration. The Chinese had permitted them to continue their cult, whereas the Outer Mongolia government, under the chauvinistic influence of the Russians to whom the very memory of Genghis Khan was anathema, had been obliged to denounce that greatest of Mongol heroes.

As for the Russians, I had not spoken to a single Russian since the crisis of 1969 who was not infused with hatred for the Chinese. Even poets who were often antagonistic to their government's line, men like Yevgeny Yevtushenko, and scientists like Andrei Sakharov, stood with Moscow on the question of China.

What lay at the root of this violent and seemingly irrational antagonism? I had asked that question again and again of Russians. They attributed it to the "madness" of Mao Tse-tung, the danger of a crazed assault by the Chinese at any moment, the impossibility of conducting rational conversations with Peking. It was difficult to get them to define specific issues. They immediately began talking of insults, of Chinese efforts to undermine Russia in the Communist world, or international rivalries like the competition to be the prime influence in Vietnam, or the kind of rivalry evidenced by Russia's support of India on Bangladesh and China's support of Pakistan. To me, this seemed evidence of disagreement, not its cause.

To be sure, there was the territorial question that had been raised by China. China had pointed out that vast areas once subject to Chinese suzerainty—eastern Siberia, the maritime provinces, virtually all the area east of the Ussuri and north of the Amur as far west as Irkutsk—had once been Chinese. All of this had, by one treaty or another and sometimes without a treaty, fallen into Russian hands. The same was true of Soviet Central Asia. And, of course, there was Mongolia, which had been subject to the Dragon Throne since the 12th century, when the Mongols seized and occupied it. Until 1911, Outer Mongolia had a vassal relationship to Peking. But with the Chinese Revolution of 1911 and the disintegration of China, Imperial Russia had wooed Mongolia away, and to this day the Communist Russians maintained the same relationship.

China had suggested a meeting to rectify the frontiers and redress some of these injustices. They made plain that they did not expect Russia to return the whole 1.5 million square miles that the czars had managed to grab, but they wanted Russia to acknowledge that the areas had been seized under unequal treaties and unfair duress. Then, they said, we will be glad to sign a new treaty that would leave most of the land in Soviet hands. The question had come up as far back as 1954 when Nikita Khrushchev made his first trip to Peking. But Khrushchev angrily refused even to discuss it, and this in essence, had been the Soviet position ever since.

That was the most concrete question in dispute between the two countries. That was the question the Sino-Soviet Commission, which had been sitting in Peking since October, 1969, would ultimately discuss, if it ever agreed on an agenda. But, so far, there had been no agenda, because the Chinese proposed that before discussions got under way, each side withdraw its forces from the vicinity of the disputed areas. The Russians refused to agree, because such action would be tantamount to admitting that the areas were, in fact, in dispute, which they insisted was not true.

I tried to get an explanation from the Chinese as to why the quarrel had flared with such incredible ferocity. It seemed to me that the passions, the intransigence, the belligerence, the emotions evoked (particularly among Russians when the word China was mentioned) had to be rooted in something deeper and more flamboyant than any issue publicly mentioned. I knew, to be sure, that race feelings were involved, particularly on the part of the Russians, who often referred to the Chinese as "monkeys," a traditional word of contempt. In fact, many Russians insisted the Chinese were not really human. They made remarks about their yellow color and their slant eyes that reminded me of the columns Arthur Brisbane wrote for William Randolph Hearst in the heyday of the "yellow peril." I knew the Russians confused the Chinese with the Mongols, deliberately or inadvertently, so much so that when Yevtushenko wrote an angry anti-Chinese poem, he climaxed it with a reference to the famous Russian defeat of the Mongols at Kulikovo.

The racism of the Russians was epitomized by an apocryphal story told of Ambassador Tolstikov on his arrival in Peking. Tolstikov, formerly the Party Secretary in Leningrad, was known for his extreme anti-Semitism. When he disembarked from his plane at Peking airport and looked about at the welcoming officials, he remarked: "Damn you Jews—now you have slant eyes."

French Foreign Minister Schumann talked to the Russians about their fear of China in the course of President Pompidou's visit to Russia in 1970. He said to one of the top Soviet leaders: "How can you fear a country which has a steel production of only 1.2 million tons?" The response was that China's steel production was constantly growing. Moreover, the Chinese had maps that showed Soviet Central Asia in a different color from the rest of the Soviet Union. There was no doubt, the Russian official said, that there would be trouble sooner or later. An important English statesman who discussed the China question with the Russians was convinced that the Soviet general staff regarded China as the main threat, far more dangerous than the United States. He felt that Soviet interest in reopening the Suez Canal was linked directly to a desire to be able to quickly shift naval strength from the Black Sea and the Middle East to the Far East and Chinese waters.

An American scientist expressed surprise to two Russian colleagues—both of them men noted for their outspoken opinions, and neither of them a party-liner—that neither of them seemed to believe it possible to resolve peacefully Russia's differences with China. Both insisted that the situation with China was exceptionally dangerous; that China's economic condition was bad, and that Mao's only hope of holding the country together was through war. The ideological struggle, they said, was ruthless and both felt that the Chinese might turn to arms to try to solve their difficulties. When the American said this kind of reasoning reminded him of what cold war leaders like John Foster Dulles were saying about Russia 20 years ago, both Russian scientists said with great solemnity: "Well, you people were right."

This was not the only evidence of the influence of the late Mr. Dulles's influence on Soviet policy. In 1970, Party Secretary Brezhnev launched a project for an Asian "defense pact." He wanted to get the nations of Asia to join with Moscow in a pact directed against possible Chinese aggression. The project apparently had the tacit support of India, but never attracted general Asian interest. Brezhnev quite clearly was advancing Russia's bid to inherit the protecting role that he suspected President Nixon was beginning to relinquish under the "low-profile" policy. The Chinese, noting the similarity of the Brezhnev proposals to Mr. Dulles's SEATO and CENTO pacts, promptly suggested that the ghost of John Foster Dulles seemed to have taken up residence in the Kremlin.

All of this, I thought, showed passion and emotion. It told me that the quarrel had passed over that barrier that separates the rational from the pathological. But it still told me nothing of the core quesion that separated them.

I put the question to a very high-ranking, very articulate Chinese.

Well, he said, the Russians insist that they are right and that everyone must agree with them. When they let a fart they expect you to say it smells good, and if you don't, they consider you disloyal and suspect.

He said that a discussion had arisen at one of the meetings of the Sino-Soviet Commission concerning my book, *The Coming War Between Russia and China.* The Soviet representative attacked the book, saying that it was an imperialist provocation, a deliberate effort to sow seeds of trouble between Moscow and Peking. Actually, the book appeared almost simultaneously with the first meetings in late October, 1969, between the Russians and the Chinese. It was designed to analyze their quarrel and present the background of the positions of the two sides, in an effort to arouse the American public to the danger that would flow from the two countries actually going to war. It attempted to view the quarrel with objectivity, but it aroused Russian ire because it revealed my belief that the danger of attack existed basically on the Soviet side, which was acting in the most provocative manner toward the Chinese.

The Chinese representative told the Russian that his idea was simply ridiculous. Did he intend to suggest that the conflict between two great powers had been stirred up by a journalist's book? How could the Russian take the view that the problems between two countries as large as Russia and China had been instigated by one journalist? It didn't make sense, because very serious questions were at issue. The Russian refused to accept that view. He continued to contend that the trouble had arisen through provocative reporting.

I suggested to my Chinese friend that part of the problem lay in the fact that Soviet foreign policy was not very different from czarist foreign policy. I doubted that there was anything in Soviet foreign policy with which the czars would have disagreed, particularly with Soviet policy in the Far East. Three-quarters of a century had passed, but Moscow's view of Russia's imperial destiny had little changed from that of Nicholas at the time of the Russo-Japanese War. That delighted my Chinese companion. He felt that I was right, and said that was why the Chinese insisted on calling the Kremlin leaders "the new czars." I said that the phrase was most appropriate, but it made the

Russians very angry. Yes, said the Chinese, when we call them imperialists they really denounce us. They go through the roof. But when we call you imperialists, it is very different—you don't even get angry. I suggested that name calling didn't bother us very much. We had been called so many.

I mentioned another factor in Soviet policy that I thought was of particular importance, so far as China and the east were concerned—the emergence of the Soviet military as a major element in Soviet decision making. I pointed out that, up to very recent times, the military had not had much influence in Russia. The party kept them firmly under control. This had been true under Lenin and was continued by Stalin even during World War II—somewhat to Russia's disadvantage. After the war, Stalin downgraded the military severely, sending great war heroes like Marshal Georgi K. Zhukov to rusticate in obscure provincial commands. But in recent times, the military had begun to play a more and more direct role in policy, participating in Politburo discussions. I felt that the marshals—or some of them—had strongly supported a military solution of the Sino-Soviet conflict. My friend agreed, but added that, in spite of everything, China really would like to improve state relations with Russia, but that it was very very difficult.

When I asked him why he thought the Russians had moved in the direction of open antagonism toward China, beginning in the mid- and late 1950's, the official had no answer. In fact, he made no attempt to explain. He merely shifted the conversation to another topic. I felt that I really was not much closer to the root of the quarrel unless, basically, it was because they were both great powers, and they happened to be neighbors sharing a great continent.

Regardless of how the quarrel started, and my own feeling was that there were personal strands that ran back to the Mao-Stalin quarrels of the 1920's, there was no question that it was here to stay. That was the opinion of every Chinese I met. It was shared by every foreign diplomat with whom I talked in Peking. One diplomat said he had been struck with the good manners and the dignity with which the Chinese maintained their side of the quarrel. The Chinese spoke in relatively soft tones, so far as propaganda was concerned, and they treated the Russians with diplomatic correctness. They had even taken the chief Soviet negotiator, Leonid F. Ilyichev, on a trip around the country. I asked a Chinese diplomat about that. He laughed. The Russians told such lies about what conditions were like in China, the

Chinese thought it would do no harm to let Ilyichev see what the country was really like. Ilyichev was the third Russian commissioner in three years. They did not last very long. It was a grueling assignment, and even the durable Ilyichev was said to be in poor health.

I was told of an incident that had occurred in Peking in 1969 at the height of the Sino-Soviet crisis. A vast Chinese crowd assembled outside the Soviet Embassy (the only one of the European powers to retain its great compound), and remained there chanting and shouting, day after day. The Russians had invited the departing French ambassador to a farewell luncheon. On the appointed day, the French telephoned the Russians. They thought the party might have to be cancelled because of the demonstrations. Not at all, the Russians said, directing the diplomats to drive to the compound and enter through the Commercial Counsellor's gate, which was not besieged. The whole Peking diplomatic corps made its way out to the Soviet Embassy, entering the appointed gate and sitting down to a perfect lunch. The caviar was the best gray beluga, the vodka was chilled Stolichnaya, the service was perfect, and only distantly, from behind the thick draperies, could the chanting of the Chinese be heard.

At the end of the luncheon, the guests retired to the drawing room. There they were served liqueurs by white-gloved attendants who passed around silver trays. In the center of each tray was a pair of binoculars through which the guests might, if they desired, get a closer glimpse of the canaille besieging the front gates. "I felt for a moment," said one of the diplomats, "as though I were back in Peking during the Boxer Rebellion, lunching in the embassy of His Imperial Majesty, Nicholas II."

There had once been a time when the Russians and the Chinese had embraced each other (and the common cause of revolution) as true comrades. It seemed to me that it would be an eternity before that spirit was felt again.*

---

* Late in 1972, border fighting was again reported on the Kazakhstan-Sinkiang frontier in westernmost China.

20

A Roving Discussion

When we flew into Sian on a scorching June afternoon after several days in Yenan, we found a message from Peking. The Foreign Office wanted us to return immediately. Because it was so important that we get back promptly, and because China's plane service is not entirely reliable—plane cancellations, delays of one, two or more days are quite frequent—we were asked to board the evening train at Sian in order to be certain of being in Peking the following evening.

There was no explanation of why we must cut short our visit to northwest China, but I thought I knew the reason. In fact, this was a message I had been awaiting with some impatience. It meant, I felt sure, that we were about to meet with Premier Chou En-lai. I knew from the experience of other Americans that this was usually the way it happened. You were called back from the very ends of China, sometimes just as you were about to leave the country, and returned to Peking for a meeting with the Premier.

On the train ride back, a long journey across the dust and desert of Shensi Province, then into the slightly less-brown Shansi and finally through the ever-greener fields of Hopei—I talked a bit with Yao Wei, our pleasant traveling companion, about Chou En-lai and the remarkable role he had played in his country and the world. I had long regarded him as the most brilliant statesman of his age. He had held the world's attention for more than 30 years and had stood at the center of China's affairs for another ten. I knew all the conventional facts about Chou—his early entry into the revolutionary movement, his studies in France, his long and close association with Mao Tsetung forged in the terrible days of 1927 and Chiang Kai-shek's bloody slaughter of the workers of Shanghai and of Communists whenever he could get them into his hands. In those days, like all those who came to lead the Chinese Communist movement, Chou was a military man, a leader of guerrilla movements, a tough-minded strategist of civil war, and as skillful a tactician as China had produced. He had come back from France in 1924 to lecture at the famous Whampoa Military Academy on tactics. He was then 27, and his life and the Chinese Revolution had already become so intertwined that their strands could never again be picked apart.

I had seldom met an American who served in China during World War II who had not known Chou. During much of that time, Chou was stationed in Chungking as chief of the Communist liaison in the Nationalist capital. Every American diplomat and correspondent knew him. Of course, some had known him earlier, but not many, except those few like Edgar Snow who made their way through the lines to penetrate the Communist strongholds at Yenan and Pao-an. An even smaller band had known him before Yenan, principally in the years 1924–1927, when collaboration between the Communists and the Kuomintang, carried on with the blessing of Dr. Sun Yat-sen and Lenin, was still in being. Of that early group, few had survived. I had known only one American from those days, Anna Louise Strong, who in the last years of her life finally made her way back to Peking, where she died in 1970 at the age of 84. I had known (although only rather casually) one other personality of that era—Mikhail Borodin, the famous Russian revolutionary who had been sent by Lenin to Canton to assist Dr. Sun and who stayed on until the 1927 debacle, when he fled for his life, taking with him in his small entourage Anna Louise Strong.

Neither Anna Louise Strong nor Borodin was a very good source for Chou's early revolutionary years. Borodin had relatively little contact with Chou in those days (and even less with Mao Tse-tung who, moreover, formed an intense dislike for him) and the impressions of Miss Strong were heavily overlaid with those of later meetings and, in addition, the personality on which her interest was focused almost exclusively was Mao Tse-tung.

Nonetheless from Borodin, Anna Louise Strong and others who had been in China during the early revolutionary times, I had long since formed what I can only describe as a romantic concept of Chou. I was familiar with Chou's picture in the early days and in the Yenan period, in which he appeared as a slender, dark-haired, almost aristocratic young revolutionary, with high cheek bones and a secret twinkle in his eyes, as though he knew a great many things that you didn't, and didn't mind letting you see this—although, of course, he had no intention of sharing his secrets. Diplomats of the war period in Chungking, not only Americans but such worldly-wise and worldly-weary figures as Sir Archibald Clark-Kerr (later Lord Inverchapel), spoke with enthusiasm of Chou's skill, knowledge and attractiveness. Old China correspondents recalled with pride their conversations with Chou, leaving me envious, since I met Chou only once (at the Soviet reception I have described previously) and, while he had put on a virtuoso performance on that occasion, I had no chance for any contact more personal than shaking his hand in a reception line of a hundred people.

None of this had inhibited me from carrying on an intensive, but, alas, one-sided, correspondence with the Premier. I had written him at regular intervals for many, many years, beginning with the proclamation of the Communist regime in Peking in 1949. Since that date, I had sent him a communication—written, telegraphic or verbal via the good offices of some visitor to Peking—on the average of once every three months. I hesitated to count how many these might be. Most of the letters and messages had, of course, been addressed to the project of a visit by me to China. But not all. Occasionally, I cabled him for a statement of China's policy on some urgent question. I never had a response from the Premier, although occasionally a friend would return from Peking with word that Chou was aware of my interest and that at an appropriate moment I might expect an answer.

These were some of the thoughts that ran through my mind as the train made its smooth, comfortable but slow progress back from Sian to Taiyuan, back to Yutzu and then up through Chengting and Paoting to Peking. I reminisced with Yao Wei about Anna Louise Strong, telling him how she had written her publisher in New York a year or two before her death, asking him to send her a kind of hairnet that she could not get in Peking, and how he had sent her a lifetime supply—a gross, I think. And Yao Wei told me how Anna Louise's doctor forbade her to eat more than one piece of chocolate a day and how, when her secretary was ill, Anna Louise found the cabinet where the chocolate was hidden and ate up a month's supply.

Back in Peking, the Foreign Office declined to say why they had recalled us, except that it was something important. I took that as confirmation of a meeting with the Premier and, after waiting through the next day under strict instructions to stay in our hotel rooms, or if we went out, not to go far, and be sure to leave word where we could be found, we got a message at about 5 P.M. that we would be dining with the Premier at 6:30 P.M. By this time I had learned that the other participants in the dinner party (on the American side) would be Professor John Fairbank and his wife, Wilma; Professor Jerry Cohen of Harvard Law School; Jeremy Stone of the American Federation of Scientists and his wife; and our friends Richard Dudman of the *St. Louis Post-Dispatch* and his wife, Helen. The Dudmans had been summoned back from Manchuria. Cohen and the Stones had been in Canton, about to leave the country, when word came to return to Peking. This, I knew, was the way it was done. Apparently the Premier's time was so precious that it was difficult to arrange a schedule and be certain that it could be kept, until the last moment.

At 6:15 Ma Yu-chen, the brilliant English-speaking director of the correspondents' section of the Foreign Office Information Bureau, picked us up, and we drove to the Great Hall of the People, the grandiose structure in Tien-an Men Square, opposite the gates to the Imperial Palace. This is the setting for all of China's state receptions, and there, in one or another of the 20 great rooms dedicated to the 20 provinces of China (including Taiwan), Chou En-lai almost every evening was to be found receiving a group of Americans like ourselves, presiding over a diplomatic reception, or, as on several occasions in the last year, dining with Henry Kissinger. We waited a moment on the plaza outside the great door until all the guests were assembled, then in protocol order, with the Fairbanks at the head, we entered to find Chou in his familiar, beautifully tailored gray tunic, decorated only with the small maroon enamel badge carrying a cameo of Mao, and the slogan "Serve the People," at the door to meet us. His face was darker than I had expected, and his great inky eyebrows gave him a Mephistophelean appearance. He pumped my hand until I wondered whether he intended to let it go, repeating several times how delighted he was that I had finally come to China, and how sorry he was that it had taken so long, because he had been aware that I had wanted to come for a long, long time. Beside him stood Nancy Tang, the Radcliffe alumna whose face became famous when she interpreted for Chou and President Nixon, so deft and so quick with her interpretation that I almost ceased to realize that two different languages were being spoken.

In the reception room were the Chinese guests: two vice ministers of foreign affairs, Chiao Kuang-hua (who represented China at the first and second General Assembly sessions of the United Nations to be attended by Peking) and Chang Wen-chin; Ko Po-nien, former Ambassador to Denmark and an important figure in cultural exchanges; Chou Pei-yuan, Vice-Chairman of the Revolutionary Committee of Peking University and his wife, Peng Hua, Deputy Chief of the Foreign Office Information Department, and several lesser dignitaries.

There was a little fluster over picture taking. Chou said: "How shall we do this—by families or in a group?" It was decided to take a group picture, so we climbed onto a gleaming nickel, three-tiered platform, set up before a three-dimensional painting of a Chinese mountain-scape, and the photographers went to work. Chou stood in the first row with the Fairbanks beside him. His face looked healthy and freckled, and he was obviously vigorous and spry. He seemed not too different from the Chou I had last seen at Spiridonovka House in Moscow in 1954. When we walked into a vast reception room, led by the Premier, I noticed that he was wearing brown leather sandals. He walked with an easy gait, slightly thrusting his feet ahead of his body. I imagined it was a gait that had become customary on the Long March, and I fancied that, even now, he could start out on the trail in the morning and end up at nightfall fresh and unwearied.

The reception room was too big for cozy conversation. Chou sat in the center, and we grouped ourselves around him in a big semicircle, sitting in wicker armchairs that were wonderfully comfortable, but just too narrow for my note-taking arm. I was using a new Sian-purchased notebook, with a crimson plastic cover that squished and crumpled, making my task miserable. There were 16 of us in the circle, with John Fairbank on one side of Chou and Nancy Tang on the other. Other interpreters and aides had chairs in a second semicircle. We sat around an enormous taupe rug of Chinese design; the curtains were heavy maroon velour; the woodwork light birch, and the walls covered in pale yellow silk.

John Fairbank opened the conversation on a reminiscent note, recalling that they had last met in 1946 at dinner with Yeh Chien-ying, now China's top military man. The Chinese sang military songs and Chou beat time on the table with his chop sticks. The Fairbanks sang Chinese civil war songs. This brought a chuckle from Chou. "I don't remember that very clearly," he said. "I don't think that I sang very much."

There was a bit of small talk. I reminded the Premier of the only other time I had seen him—at Spiridonovka House, when he told the Russians that it was about time they learned to speak Chinese. Chou laughed. "You wrote many reports about the Soviet Union," he said, "and in the end you could not go back."

This was not entirely true, but I had encountered increasing difficulty in getting a Soviet visa in recent years.

Chou offered cigarettes to his guests. All of the Americans declined. Almost all of the Chinese accepted. The contrast amused Chou. He said he had heard that Americans printed on their cigarette packages a warning that smoking was dangerous to life. He doubted that this was true. Many Chinese leaders had lived very long lives and smoked a lot. (He might have mentioned himself and Mao Tse-tung in this category but did not.) Winston Churchill's grandson had been in China recently and told him how Field Marshal Montgomery had tried to persuade Churchill to give up smoking and drinking. Churchill had replied: "Look, I'm ten years older than you; I have lived to a ripe age and I smoke and drink and see no reason to give it up."

Chou suggested that perhaps a joint scientific inquiry might be launched by American and Chinese scientists to see whether there was, indeed, a connection between smoking and cancer. Jeremy Stone quickly offered the collaboration of the American Federation of Scientists, and Chou asked whether they combined practice and science, "as Chairman Mao has done." Stone said they had, indeed, but that in China they combined theory and practice best. "You have done better than we have," Stone said.

Chou rejected this sharply. "Really?" he said. "You really think that? I don't quite believe it." He said, however, that it was not easy to find persons like Mao Tse-tung who could combine the theory of Marxism-Leninism with practical Chinese revolutionary experience.

"It is very hard," he mused a bit sadly, shaking his head for emphasis. "It is not easy to find a leader like Mao Tse-tung. There are not many people like him. We are all his students, but we cannot do as well as he."

To my astonishment, a few weeks later I read an article by one of the evening's participants in which he speculated that Mao might be suffering from cancer. He arrived at this speculation by putting together the recurrent rumors about Mao's health and the juxtaposition of Chou's remarks about cigarette smoking, cancer and Mao. I confess that I could not follow this reasoning. I saw nothing in Chou's comment that linked Mao with cancer—quite the contrary, in fact.

The conversation went on in a somewhat desultory fashion. Chou expressed regret that Jerry Cohen's wife had not been able to be present (she had been in China but had returned to Japan to look after their children), but pointed out that families do provide problems.

Professor Yang Chen-ning, a physicist at State University of New York at Stony Brook, on Long Island, had arrived in Shanghai that very day. It was his second trip. He had been to China the year before. He had not been able to bring his wife, who was the daughter of a well-known Kuomintang general, because they had small children, and they could not get anyone to care for them. Some of Chou's colleagues had said, well, why don't they just lock up the house and bring the whole family? But Chou had said that this wasn't practical.

Finally, Dudman succeeded in shifting the subject to political issues, asking the Premier if he had any new advice for Kissinger on how to end the war in Indochina. Chou said he would start out by quoting to Kissinger a remark made by Dudman to the effect that it wasn't North Vietnam that was carrying on an invasion, but the United States. Actually, as it developed, the Premier had been misinformed—the remark had been made not by Dudman but by the Swedish Foreign Minister. Chou apologized to Dudman, and then asked my opinion of the war. I said it had been a mistake from the start and that it could be ended any time the United States wished to end it. I said I thought my opinion was shared by many Americans.

Chou was now well engaged on the subject of Vietnam. It was clear that this was what he had wanted to talk about, and I had the feeling that he was running over in his mind the points he was going to put to Kissinger. I did not think Kissinger was going to have a very easy time of it.

Chou's thoughts turned back to the Korean War. He recalled that a number of American generals came to the conclusion that that was the wrong war, at the wrong time, in the wrong place. Eisenhower had pledged himself to end it and, in fact, went to Korea and did bring the conflict to an end "in a very straightforward manner." But Chou had not seen any similar phenomenon with regard to Vietnam.

Jerry Cohen said he thought that if Senator McGovern was elected, he would end the war.

"So it seems that you are campaigning for Senator McGovern," Chou laughed. "Do you think he will really end the war?"

Cohen recalled that a year earlier, the scientist, Arthur Galston, had been discussing the American presidential race with Chou and failed to mention McGovern's name. Chou then asked Galston some questions about McGovern. This, observed Cohen, showed that Chou understood American politics better than we did.

Chou bristled a bit. He said he didn't think he had a better understanding of American politics. I noticed that he bristled every time a question was asked that seemed to imply flattery of China or himself. I had previously noted the same sharp response by Chou in the stenographic accounts of some of his other talks with Americans. He had been almost angry with a group of the Association of Concerned Asian Scholars who sought to praise China for achievements that Chou felt had not actually been accomplished.

And I thought he showed a bit of skepticism where McGovern was concerned. Chou wanted to know whether McGovern would back a national coalition government in Saigon without Thieu. I pointed out that McGovern had made an unqualified statement that he would go to Hanoi, if elected, and end the war and bring back the prisoners.

That pleased Chou, but what he really wanted to know was whether the American generals, as opposed to the presidential candidates, were making known their opinions as they had in the Korean War. Fairbank said they had been far less frank, possibly because they lacked combat experience.

"But," added Fairbank, "we have no MacArthur, thank God!"

"Yet," interjected Chou, "before he died MacArthur said that the United States should not fight another war on the Asian continent. So perhaps before his death he realized the truth."

The role of the American generals continued to trouble Chou. He asked what had happened to Maxwell Taylor. Since there was so much anti-war sentiment among the rank and file, it should find reflection among the officers. He believed that, whereas the air force, perhaps, favored the war, the army had a different sentiment.

There was some talk among the Americans concerning defense appropriations, and Chou noted that President Nixon's bombing offensive in Vietnam had shot costs up by $3 billion, and possibly by $5 billion before the year was out.

Jeremy Stone pointed out that McGovern's defense budget would cut spending by one-third. Again the Premier's skepticism came to the fore. "Do you think he can do that?" he asked.

I said that the prestige of the military was deeply involved in Vietnam. If our enormous war machine could not defeat a poor, backward country, how could we defeat other countries, in other parts of the world? This, I thought, was a very important factor in prolonging the war.

Chou agreed, but returned again to his basic question—why had not American generals come forward against the war in Vietnam as they had in Korea? He retraced the history of the Vietnam conflict—first the introduction of U.S. advisory groups, then the overthrow of the Bao Dai government, the Diem regime, the elimination of Diem, the intensification of the war, the invasion of Cambodia, the battle on Route Nine and the gradual involvement of all of Indochina. What the people of Indochina want, he said, is simply independence.

"That is where the root of the trouble lies," he added. Indochina had never been conquered—not by the French in 100 years, not by the feudal Chinese in hundreds of years. Mendès-France had finally ended the French involvement after Dienbienphu. He had shown courage. But then came the Geneva Conference of 1954, and the Chinese were taken in. He personally was taken in. According to the agreement, there was to be only a provisional partition at the 17th parallel. It was not a state boundary, and wasn't intended to be one. It was not the same situation as the two Germanys, nor even like North and South Korea. The 17th parallel was supposed to be a temporary line, and there was to be a year of consultation between North and South, then elections within two years under international supervision.

"They were intended to be held then," he said, "and almost all foreign friends understood there could be no doubt that President Ho would win."

He turned to me, recalling that I had been in Hanoi, and asked if I agreed that Ho would have been the victor. I did, and added that even John Foster Dulles had admitted as much. Dudman pointed out that President Eisenhower had said the same thing in his memoirs.

This information delighted Chou. He had heard from Premier Pham Van Dong of North Vietnam that Anthony Eden had also said something like that in his memoirs. Dulles, Chou said, was already planning to violate the Geneva agreements before they were concluded. That was why the United States took the precaution of not signing.

I said that this had been brought out quite clearly in the "Pentagon papers." That was right, Chou agreed.

"So," he said, sadly, "you must not say that we know how to handle foreign affairs well. We were greatly taken in at that time. That was my first experience in an international conference. We were taken in. I have also said as much to Premier Pham Van Dong. I have said that we were both taken in."

As he talked, Chou En-lai became more and more caught up with his feelings. He talked of the pain it gave Ho Chi Minh to order his supporters to leave the South after the demarcation line was fixed, and of the division of families between North and South, which had now continued for almost 20 years. How could one not have sympathy for the Vietnamese people after what they had gone through? He mentioned the American pilots, the POW's shot down after coming from great distances to drop bombs on North Vietnam. It was said that one should have sympathy for these men, but what of the people of Vietnam, the victims of the bombing? He had sympathy for them and also sympathy for the American people who opposed the war so strongly. He had even heard of officers throwing down their medals on the steps of the capitol and of anti-war activity in the army—something not seen in the Korean War. So the Chinese had not only sympathy for the people of Vietnam, but respect for the people of the United States, and that was why Chairman Mao had said he had great hope for the people of the United States.

But what was most deeply on his conscience was his own role in the Geneva Conference—the very negotiation that had left him in such high spirits when I first saw him in Moscow in 1954.

"I was the representative who put my signature to the agreement," he said, "and if we are to be forgiven, it is only because we lacked experience."

Now, he said, China had more experience. Her representatives would not make the same mistake in the United Nations. At this point, Chou pulled himself up short. He was visibly shaken, and his voice trembled with feeling. We must stop this discussion, he said, getting a grip on himself, or it will become too emotional. Someone suggested that if he went on he would be giving a lecture. "No," Chou said wryly, "I will be making a speech."

We rose, and Chou, taking Mrs. Fairbank's arm, led the way to the Anhwei room, where we were to dine. He had not actually answered Dudman's question in a good hour of talking, but he had given a clear picture of his thinking on Vietnam.

Conversation at the dinner table was relaxed. Possibly that was because of the meal—a triumph of Chinese cuisine. First, there were hors d'oeuvres of chicken bits, tomatoes, shrimp, ancient eggs, hard-boiled eggs, cucumber slices and fish bits. This was followed by water-green soup, the greens coming from the Imperial West Lake in Hang-chow and found only there. Then, crisp rice with three delicacies—chicken, sea slugs and a third that I neglected to note. We then were served crisp fried chicken and duck; French beans with fresh mushrooms; baked shad (very much like Hudson River shad), found only in the Yangtze; a purée of bean soup with crushed almonds; sticky rice cakes; meat patties; bread and butter; plain rice in a bowl; and a watermelon. There were three liquors—wine, brandy and *mao t'ai*, the special 150-proof rice liquor discovered by the Communists in Kweichow Province during their Long March.

We were served by silent and efficient waiters and waitresses at a round table, the center of which was decorated with feathery greens. Behind Chou En-lai was a mural of an Anhwei mountain scene.

The Premier began talking about the United Nations. China hadn't expected to get in in 1971. They had expected it would take another year. But he had overlooked one thing. He recalled back to the 1930's, when Chiang Kai-shek had gotten into secret contact with the Communists. Chiang told his generals to fight the Communists while he was negotiating with them. It wasn't exactly a parallel situation, but it was a good deal like that involving the United Nations. The U.N. delegates knew Dr. Kissinger had been to China in July, that he had gone back in October, and so they began to say—well, since you Americans can have contacts with China we, too, can have contacts.

Chou said he hadn't seen the possibility of getting into the U.N. in 1971, but some of the younger people had. Just after he had bid goodbye to Kissinger, and while Kissinger's plane was leaving the ground, word came in that China had been admitted. The younger people were very happy because they had predicted the outcome, while "we of the older generation were put in a rather passive position."

He said China's admission had an accidental appearance, but all events had an inevitable cause. They only seemed to be accidental. Fairbank recalled hearing that the American ping-pong team was standing waiting for a taxi. While they were waiting, the Chinese came up and said, "Come to Peking."

That was just a matter of timing, Chou said. The decision to invite the American team had been made by Chairman Mao. There had been many applications from various teams—the Algerians, the English and others. These were official applications. The Americans had asked only unofficially. While they were deciding what to do, Chairman Mao asked, "Why shouldn't the American team be permitted to come?" So the Americans had been asked. But he and his comrades had not been able to conceive of such a thing, nor had they been able to predict its results. So they had to be thankful that there were direct communications with Japan, so that, with one telephone call, the

Americans were invited, and many people—including the State Department and the Chinese Foreign Office—were taken by surprise.

Cohen recalled that he and Fairbank and some of their colleagues had sent a recommendation to President Nixon and Kissinger in late November, recommending they send someone to China to explore the possibility of improving relations. They had been convinced, Fairbank added, that the vast majority of Americans wanted to end the stalemate on China.

Chou said that Fairbank and Cohen obviously could feel the pulse of the American people, but that for the U.S. government to put this policy into effect required them to travel a tortuous path because of hostility on both sides. It wasn't only U.S. hostility to China. China had taken a hostile attitude to the United States because of U.S. support of Taiwan.

He proposed a toast to the friendship of the Chinese and American peoples, and for the exchange of some scientists, educators, and cultural groups. He paused, and after a significant glance at Dudman and myself, added journalists to the roster. He walked around the table with his cat-like pace, raising his glass with everyone present, and then said: "Let's take off our coats. It's getting warm in here. Let us be liberated."

Fairbank thanked the Premier for the remarkable opportunity he and his wife had been given to see Chinese life and to renew contacts with their old friends. Stone thanked the Premier for permitting his scientific organization to come, the first American science group to visit China in a quarter-century. The talk then swung to the question of exchanges—particularly scholarly and scientific exchanges. Fairbank was eager to get the Premier's approval for exchanges of language students and teachers, pointing to the great need on both sides. The Premier was a bit reserved, fearing, he said, that if Chinese students went to Harvard, they might have confrontations with Chinese Nationalist students. He seemed to be bothered not only by the possibility of incidents, but by the implication that Taiwan and Peking might be placed on an equal plane. Stone suggested that the problem could be solved if a special institution were set up to handle Chinese studying English in the United States. The Chinese might go to colleges where there were no Taiwan students, so the problem would not arise. Chou didn't seem to think that was such a good idea either. It sounded to him like "looking at flowers from the back of a horse." Moreover, he said, he was not objecting to Taiwan students studying in the United States. After all, frequently they wound up coming to the mainland. Stone explained that he hadn't meant that the Chinese would have to travel from one school to another, he was just suggesting that there were many ways to skin a cat. This figure of speech brought the banquet to a dead halt for about five minutes as Nancy Tang, all of the English-speaking Chinese and Chinese-speaking Americans tried to work skin-a-cat out in good Mandarin.

I switched the subject by offering a toast to exchanges of journalists, and a tribute to the role played by Edgar Snow in U.S.-Chinese understanding. Chou responded positively. The press exchanges had gone very well. He asked Dudman about the *St. Louis Post-Dispatch*, which he had heard was a midwestern paper. Dudman said his paper was a liberal one, published on the banks of the Mississippi, in the heart of the United States. He added that in 1954, at the time of Dienbienphu, the *Post-Dispatch* had published a cartoon showing a great swamp marked "Indochina," and a U.S. soldier marching in. The caption said: "A war to stay out of."

Chou was enchanted. "That's really something!" he said. "Thank you for giving me that knowledge." It had taken real foresight, he said, to publish that cartoon. Dulles was then in full swing. His policy of brinksmanship had really begun in Korea, but it was already bankrupt. Chou mused. It was not possible to foresee things. Sihanouk, for instance. Who could have foreseen two years ago that he would be in Peking? "I couldn't have foreseen it," he said. He asked Dudman and me what was behind the coup in Cambodia. Was it the CIA or was it something else. I am afraid we didn't cast much light on the situation. Then he asked if we had read Neville Maxwell's *India's China War*. It was a remarkable book. Maxwell had used only Indian documentation. He had no Chinese sources, and he had shown that India, not China, was the *provocateur* in the conflict.

I picked up his point about forecasts—had he been able to foresee the split between China and the Soviet Union? Yes, he said, they had envisaged that difficulty, but they could not envisage the circumstances under which the rift would occur. He said he understood I had been in Mongolia. I told him of the 1959 reception, when the Chinese and Russians stood on either side of the room, and the Russian general wanted me to stand together with "us" against "them."

That amused Chou. He laughed and observed: "Yes, you are quite an honest friend." He added that one reason they had not invited me to be the first *New York Times* correspondent in China was that it would have involved inviting "the leading anti-Soviet champion." They hadn't wanted to cause more complications with the Russians over such a minor question, so instead, they had invited the "son-in-law of our old friend, Chester Ronning." Ronning was the former Canadian Ambassador to China, born in China of a missionary family. Seymour Topping, his son-in-law, is my colleague on *The Times*, an Assistant Managing Editor.

There was a brief pause. Chou looked at his watch. "I like a roving discussion like this," he said. "This is the way it used to be. Once you become official then everything becomes very tense." We had been talking about four hours. The evening had come to an end. There were a few more remarks. Cohen expressed hope that the Vietnam War would soon end. Chou pounded the table. "This is the western way of showing approval," he said. Cohen said that he hoped diplomatic relations would be established, and that soon the Premier and all the others at the table would be in the United States.

A note of sadness crept into Chou's voice. He could not applaud Cohen's last point. He believed all the others in the room would go to the United States, but at his advanced age, he did not have this hope. After a few more words, Chou looked again at his watch, said again it had been a good evening of talk and that now perhaps it was time to break it up. He rose, took a cat-like stretch and, looking a bit tired, gracefully started around the table, shaking hands. He shook hands with Dudman and told him he would use the story of the *Post-Dispatch* cartoon on Kissinger.

"But you never did answer my question," said Dudman. Chou smiled slyly and offered his hand to me, again apologizing for not inviting me to China sooner, and also for having to mix up his American guests. He wished that he could see us separately, but there wasn't time. But there would be occasions in the future. We walked down the hall, everyone taking pictures of each other, and everyone somehow very loath now to call the evening over. We stood in the reception hall for a time. The Premier bid farewell warmly to the Fairbanks. They were the only American guests whom he really knew. "See you next year," he said. Then, we went out into the night. It was cooler now, after the very hot day. The wind had sprung up on the great north China plain and it was beginning to whip into Peking, bringing with it the dust. We got into the car with Ma Yu-chen and were back at the Chien Men Hotel at 10:30. It had been not quite four hours.

What would the Premier do now, I wondered, as we walked up the wide steps of the hotel. Surely his day was not yet over. Surely he would go back to his office and pick up once again the endless task of running one of the greatest of countries. There were those who wondered how the Premier was able to devote evening after evening to this kind of conversation. But I thought I knew. It was a relaxation. He could, for a few hours, talk very much as he wished. And it was not idle conversation. He had known precisely who each of the individuals was who made up the dinner party. He knew what they had done and what subjects they were informed on. He had matched that knowledge against his own interests. He had spurred all of us to talk about American politics, the presidential campaign and the war. He had drawn out Dudman and me in our special fields of expertise. He had garnered some nuggets of information and anecdote for use with Kissinger. He had run through his own thoughts on Vietnam and put them once again into order. It had not been, as he said, a tense evening. It was a relaxed occasion. He had been a skilled and suave host. He had made each guest feel that he was present because he had a particular role and a particular contribution. He had shown his grace and charm with the ladies, and his wit and realism with the men.

With it all, there had been an undeniable note of nostalgia—nostalgia for the old days, the days of Yenan and Chungking, when evening after evening had been spent in conversation like this, or even more lively, interspersed with the songs the Fairbanks remembered but he had almost forgotten. There was in all this a special fondness for Americans and things American. That had been marked throughout Chou En-lai's life. True, he had been educated in France, not the United States, but his interest in and preference for Americans had been demonstrated decades before the Communists came to power. It had not been displayed for a long time—not during the 20 years of deep antagonism between official Washington and official Peking. But, even then, the Premier had always shown a special fondness for the handful of Americans who moved behind the barriers and into China.

I did not really credit his renunciation of all hope of coming to the United States. Surely, it could not be a question of his years. He was as full of vitality today as he had been 20 years earlier. In fact, I felt certain that he would, indeed, come to the United States when the time was ripe—probably not until after the establishment of diplomatic relations. One thing and only one, I believed, might prevent it. That was the enormous responsibility and burden that he carried in China—a responsibility and burden which, inevitably, would be increased even more on that day when Chairman Mao passed from the scene.

21

Thermidor in Peking

The Yangtze River at Wuhan is a mile wide, and chocolate-hued from the heavy burden of silt it gathers in a long course through western and central China. The current is swift, and near the center of the tri-cities, the River Han meets the Yangtze and adds its flux to all the rest.

In the heart of Wuhan, on the Hankow side, just below the old British Customs House where the chimes that once played *God Save the King* now resound to the *Internationale* is the ferry station. Here we boarded a trim harbor cutter for a sight-seeing trip on the Yangtze. The trip was Charlotte's idea. At first, the Wuhan officials seemed startled by the notion, but then they enthusiastically arranged the excursion, not a long cruise, just a few miles up the river and across to a landing below the new Yangtze bridge, a sail, as we quickly learned, on an historic course, none other than that followed by Chairman Mao on his famous Yangtze swim.

Twice the Chairman had swum the river, entering at a point above the bridge on the Wuhan side, and emerging nearly eight miles downstream on the Hankow side, at the ferry slip where our cutter took off. The current is swift at Wuhan, and pulls the swimmer downstream quite rapidly. (The Chairman's swim required only a bit more than an hour.) But to strike a diagonal course across the river as the Chairman did is not so easy. The Chairman swam the Yangtze at Wuhan first on July 16, 1964, and then again on July 16, 1966. The second swim was the most notable, for it was portrayed to the country in newsreels and photos, and warned the Chairman's political opponents that, at the age of 73, his vigor was unimpaired. He made the swim just two days before returning to Peking for the first time in more than eight months. Once there, he took command of the Cultural Revolution, then beginning to gather overwhelming momentum.

The picture of the Chairman swimming the Yangtze, his head massive above its choppy surface, appeared in every newspaper in China on July 24. On each subsequent July 16, thousands of Chinese have joined in a massive swim, following the Chairman's route down the Yangtze. They swim in phalanxes of 100 each, sometimes as many as 10,000 or 20,000 swimmers, filling the river almost shore-to-shore.

I did not meet Mao Tse-tung, nor even see him at a distance, but wherever I went in China, I found his presence pervasive. I do not mean in the form of little red books. I actually saw only two persons with little red books in hand during my visit to China. One was a thoughtful man, studying the texts as one might a prayer missal on an airplane. The other was a five-year-old girl who waved the book to attract my attention and get her picture taken. Mao's picture was generally displayed but not excessively. In fact, I often saw tell-tale patches on hotel and office walls that showed where a picture had been taken down, obviously Mao's. To be sure there were many statues of Mao, usually of plaster, and usually within buildings rather than in public squares. But these were being removed. In fact, adjacent to the Sian railroad station, I saw the scaffolding around a statue that was about to come down. In the huts of peasants and flats of workers, I usually saw a Mao portrait, often a badly tinted oleograph, and medallions and portraits were on sale in the stores.

Bookstores seemed largely devoted to Mao's works, sometimes to the extent of 90 percent of the display. But the once universal habit of wearing Mao buttons was in sharp decline. Many higher officials and academics no longer wore the button, although it was common among girl elevator operators, chauffeurs and waiters. On the streets, passersby might or might not wear it. Higher officials were more apt to wear a small enamel emblem saying "Serve the People." Sometimes these carried a cameo of Mao, sometimes not. It was obvious that Mao's words to Edgar Snow in his talk on December 10, 1970, were being carried into action. Mao said then that his cult of personality had been necessary to achieve the purposes of the Cultural Revolution but that it had been overdone and was going to be dismantled. The flamboyant titles that had been associated with his name: Great Leader, Great Teacher, Great Helmsman—all these would be done away with. Only the single word "teacher" would remain.

I had forgotten this remark of Mao's when we went to Changsha.

Changsha was the metropolis of Mao's youth. It was there he went from his little village of Shao Shan in 1911, walking the 40 miles, to enter the Changsha middle school. Then and now, Changsha was an intellectual center, a center of schools, of study and, inevitably, of revolutionary agitation. Here was one of Dr. Sun Yat-sen's strongholds and, in time, Changsha became one of Mao Tse-tung's strongholds. It was not surprising, given this background, that some of the bitterest battles of the Cultural Revolution raged here.

Changsha, for the first time, gave me a feeling of Mao's character. It is always difficult to separate myth from man, but here at Changsha No. 1 Normal School, where Mao studied and to which he returned as principal of the primary school in July, 1920, I thought I was getting close to the essential man.

The No. 1 Normal School is not a museum. It is still a busy teacher's school, with 1,500 students in primary, middle and normal classes. The rooms associated with Mao—his principal's office and his study—are preserved more or less as he used them. But the rest of the building buzzes with activity, just as it did when he first came there more than half a century before.

When Mao attended school, he went in for physical culture—ice-cold baths, setting-up exercises. He and his comrades walked in the rain to harden their bodies, and sunbathed in summer. In winter, he went for long walks in blizzards and bitter winds. He was developing his body as well as his mind. And, like most of the students of his day, Mao was caught up in nationalist and revolutionary agitation, but it was not until he became a schoolmaster at Changsha, a married man of 27, in 1920, that he began to move actively toward Communism.

I saw two quotations from Mao at the Changsha No. 1 Normal School. One said: "Always respect the fact and never be subjective." The other said: "To become a teacher of pupils, you must first be a pupil of the people."

It was then that I jotted down in my notebook the heading: "Mao as a teacher." For this, it seemed to me, was his natural role. This was how he envisaged himself. Later on, when I reread Snow's interview, I found my intuition supported.

From the start, Mao was strongly drawn toward using educational methods to move his countrymen. He set up a New Citizens' Society in 1918, which was designed to help people help themselves. And in 1921, he organized what he called the Hunan Self-Help University, a kind of night school in which students with little or no money could enroll.

It was only gradually that Mao moved toward the Communist Party and the doctrines of Karl Marx. He had not, for example, read *The Communist Manifesto* until 1919.* That was during his brief stay at Peking University, where he worked in the library as an assistant and fell under the influence of Li Ta-chao, a brilliant young man who single-handedly introduced China's intellectuals to Lenin and the ideology of the Russian Bolshevik Revolution.

What was the greatest influence on Mao's life? My guess is that it was life in the village of Shao Shan, where he was born and lived until adolescence. It is hard to recapture the feeling of that life today. Shao Shan has become a shrine. It is visited by 1.6 million persons a year. They come from the ends of China, on excursions arranged by communes, factories and schools, riding trucks for dusty hundreds of miles, sleeping in the hard cars of the railroad trains, or walking for weeks on foot.

As a shrine, Shao Shan has lost its character as a village. There are three good-sized hotels to house the many foreign delegations—4,000 foreigners from 60 countries came to Shao Shan in 1971. A railroad line has been built to the village, and an imposing railroad station, with Mao's statue beside it, stands where there were once rice paddies. There is a huge museum, but it, like so many other museums in China, was closed when I was there, the exhibits being rearranged to reflect the latest political realities—that is, the fall of Liu Shao-chi and Lin Piao.

But I could still envisage much of the Shao Shan where Mao grew up. Shao Shan lay 120 *li* from Changsha, and that was a distance great enough to isolate it from the main currents of Chinese life. Mao was a fortunate child. His father was a poor peasant who made himself well-to-do through grain trading and carting. The house in which the Mao family lived seems even today almost luxurious in contrast with the usual peasant hut. The family gods still stand on a shelf in the entranceway. There is a reception room; two kitchens (summer and winter); a dairy room; a dining room; a bedroom for Mao's father and mother; one for Mao (decorated with pictures of his mother and his younger brothers—but not his father, whom Mao hated); a room for storing

---

* *The Communist Manifesto* was not translated into Chinese until that year.

farm implements; a room for rice milling and storage; a woodshed; a pigpen; a room for Mao's younger brother, Mao Tse-tan, who was killed in battle with the Nationalists in 1935; a room for his middle brother, Mao Tse-min, who was killed in 1943 in Urumchi; and finally, a fine hard-clay threshing floor.

Not many boys in Shao Shan came from so large or luxurious a home. Yet Mao's childhood differed little from his comrades'. He tended the water buffalo, helped transplant rice, harrowed the fields, gathered straw and firewood, cleaned the pigsty and did all the other chores a peasant boy does. Almost everyone in Shao Shan was named Mao (and most of them still are). There are dozens of third, fourth, fifth and sixth cousins of Mao's still living there.

Life in the village was simple and hard. Cholera was common, and so were most other epidemic diseases. Drought brought famine, and famine brought starvation, and starvation brought death. There was a high birth rate in Shao Shan, but the population did not increase. Disease and starvation controlled the population. Mao's first intimation of revolution came one day when he and his fellow primary-school students noticed that many of the Shao Shan bean merchants were coming back to town. They reported rebellion had broken out in Changsha because of the famine.

In these villages, the saying was: "Three days of rain and we have a flood; three days without rain and we have a drought."

That was the life Mao grew up knowing; this was the life that at some point he became determined to change—first by pedagogical methods, and then by revolutionary tactics. But I do not think that he ever gave up his concept of himself as a teacher. Not that his ideas of teaching were entirely conventional.

Many of Mao's sayings, at least those attributed to him during the Cultural Revolution, seemed to me to place enormous reliance on young people and students as a catalytic influence in society, possibly tracing back to his own youth and the time when almost all of China's youth was fulfilling that role in the heyday of Sun Yat-sen's national independence movement. Mao relied very, very strongly on practical experience, pragmatic wisdom, and what used to be called vocational training. Mao proclaimed the superiority of peasant wisdom and the virtue of learning-by-doing. He was strongly antagonistic (almost to the point of anti-intellectualism) toward book learning, rote library study, closet theory, ivory-tower concepts and, of course, bureaucracy. At least, so he sounded in his *ad hoc* pronouncements, although he himself had always been a passionate student of Chinese classical literature—to the point that his Russian critics, for instance, accused him of having failed to read or study many of the Marxist classics.

Mao was quite willing, as he demonstrated in the Cultural Revolution, to put up with an enormous amount of confusion, of *luan*, of disorder, of struggle and contention, of turbulence and even anarchy, because he felt that in the end this would clear the air, refresh the spirit and move China back onto that course that it had followed, in his opinion, in the simpler and purer days of the Long March and Yenan. This was in the spirit of the earthy words he was said to have spoken to his comrades in 1959, summing up the Great Leap Forward: "Comrades, you should analyze your responsibility, and your stomachs will feel much more comfortable if you move your bowels and break wind."

In fact, it seemed to me that one of the characteristics of the Chinese Revolution had been periodic, highly emotional upheavals, breaking of wind on a national scale. Contrary to the image that many westerners had of China as a nation of "blue ants," highly disciplined, governed by rigid and inflexible rules, the reality seemed to me to have been one of violent national outbreaks. There had been the period of Let One Hundred Flowers Bloom in 1956, when everyone in China was encouraged to speak out his thoughts about the Revolution, which produced a national cacophony so violent and critical that the Flowers were suppressed within a matter of weeks, and the frankest and most outspoken critics of the Revolution found themselves behind bars. That had been followed by the Great Leap Forward, Mao's effort to lift China up by her bootstraps, building small iron furnaces in the courtyards of collective farms, and engaging in a welter of do-it-yourself activities all over the country. This was abandoned in a new hurricane of controversy and debate that had hardly ended when the country was wracked by the quarrel with the Soviet Union, which had simmered and bubbled for a decade. In the midst of it all arose the climacteric Cultural Revolution, in which the whole country, as it were, went into the streets.

Whatever else might be said about Mao's pedagogy, you could not call it placid.

Without question, the Cultural Revolution was *sui generis*. Even Mao had not expected such *luan* and, as he told a Central Committee Work Conference in October, 1966, "It was beyond my expectation that the publication of the Big Character poster at Peking University would stir up the whole country . . . I myself caused this big trouble, and I cannot blame you if you have complaints against me."

He had thought, he admitted, that the Cultural Revolution would be completed within a few months. When it continued, as it did, for the better part of two years, and provoked, as it did, extraordinary divisions and deep splits within the country, massive confrontations, battles in which hundreds were killed, and when the life of the country was brought almost to a standstill, he obviously felt that matters had gone too far.

But what was it that Mao was striving for in the Cultural Revolution? Was it simply to eliminate Liu Shao-chi and the men of Liu's groups whose influence he thought was pernicious, moving the country away from idealistic, revolutionary goals and back onto the path of materialist subjectivism?

Certainly, that was a major factor. It could be no accident, in view of Mao's deep commitment to the pedagogic tradition, that one of the strongest charges he brought against Liu Shao-chi was Liu's failure to support the Socialist Education Movement, which Mao envisaged as carrying back into the countryside the basic precepts of the Chinese Revolution.

And Mao's belief that the country had to be re-educated was underscored in the letter he wrote to Lin Piao on May 7, 1966, which laid the theoretical foundations for the May Seventh schools. Mao's theme in this letter was that the Chinese armed forces "should be a great school." And he felt the same approach should apply to all other sectors of Chinese society, and particularly to the cadres and the leaders.

Mao's efforts to derail China from the bureaucratic, materialistic course onto which he felt Liu Shao-chi was directing her were not without significant precedent. Almost the same thing had happened after the Bolshevik Revolution in Russia. During the last year of his active political career, before successive strokes by March, 1923, removed him completely from public affairs, Vladimir Lenin was struggling with the same problem. It had become apparent to him that, despite the Revolution, despite the noble ideals and lofty objectives of the revolutionaries, Russia was falling back into her old rut. The bureaucrats were moving into control; the government apparatus more and more resembled that of the czars; the commissars were behaving like the czar's ministers; the party was becoming a clique. That was the motivation behind Lenin's Last Testament, in which he inveighed against Stalin and his tendencies, urging the party to remove him from the secretaryship and find another leader more suitable. It was conveyed in a whole series of minutes, speeches, and position papers as Lenin struggled with the Minotaur he saw emerging from the Romanov wreckage. Lenin did not have the vigor nor the years of life to carry his battle to victory (if indeed such a thing was possible), and with his death in 1924, the struggle in Russia was lost. Mao, with his energy and years of experience, was better able to confront the dragon, but whether he had slain it, or whether it, like the dragons of legend, would spring to life again and again remained to be seen.

All of this puts to one side the more personal political aspects of the Cultural Revolution, that is, Mao's determination to drive out of office Liu Shao-chi and the bureaucrats and political figures associated with Liu. This task had been essentially completed by the time I visited China. Liu was on the scrap heap, along with all his close associates. Whether Liu was physically among the living I could not say. For a long time, obviously, Liu had been kept under guard in his home, while a great investigation went forward. During that period, there was much talk about Mao's doctrine of rehabilitation. Mao did not, it was said, believe in execution. He believed, instead, in changing a man's conscience, in transforming him, so that he would be capable of performing a useful function in society. An important Chinese official mentioned this belief to me during a discussion of Stalin and his purges. He felt they were wrong. "One must be very careful whom one kills in a revolution," he said.

But whether the doctrine of rehabilitation still applied to Liu and his 60 closest and oldest supporters I did not know. It seemed to me that the path of redemption might have been closed, because I now heard open denunciation of Liu and his group as traitors, and treason was a crime normally punished by execution. The intimation seemed to be that Liu had passed across the line. I did not think he was likely ever to come to the surface again.

There was another question that I had difficulty in evaluating. That was the extent to which the Sino-Soviet quarrel underlay the conflict between Liu and Mao. It was said that Liu had been an advocate of reconciliation with Russia, that he had favored the Russian "revisionist" line inside China, that he had backed programs for heavy industrialization over building up agriculture, that he supported Soviet educational methods and Soviet attitudes on culture (whatever that meant). He was, in a word, smeared as pro-Russian. It seemed to me that there was at least a nub of truth in the denunciation, but this did not leave the point entirely clear. Perhaps the situation was not black and white. In totalitarian politics, it seldom is.

But this left dangling the biggest question of all—the question of Lin Piao, Minister of Defense. Throughout my stay in China I kept getting hints that the denouement of the Lin Piao affair was at hand. In fact, I had good reason to believe that so far as the Chinese party members were concerned, the explanations had already been given. That was implied by several persons. To them, the principal unresolved question was the fate of several thousand persons who were still being held while their cases were examined.

In almost every institution, there were one or two persons, or sometimes more, who were still in custody while their records were examined. It seemed to be believed that almost all of these would ultimately be released, but not until the complexities of the so-called "May 16th" group and its relationship to Lin had been clarified.

This was one of the thorny puzzles of the Cultural Revolution. A group of ultra-radicals seized control of the Chinese Foreign Ministry during the late summer of 1966. Their principal target, apparently, was Chou En-lai. Demonstrations against him were conducted around his residence in the Imperial City, and Big Character posters denouncing him were put up. His long-time associate, Marshal Chen Yi, Minister of Foreign Affairs, was heavily attacked and virtually driven from office. Some reports said Chen was refused medical aid, and that this contributed to his death in early 1972. Mao himself attended Chen's funeral in a demonstration that left no doubt of his attitude toward Chen's persecutors. This group was charged, as well, with a variety of acts that embarrassed Chinese foreign policy—the attack on the British Embassy in Peking, riots in Macao and Hong Kong, rude and insulting behavior to many foreign diplomats and to many foreign friends of China (including Edgar Snow and Han Suyin), and an effort to halt Chinese relations with all countries except those that were revolutionary supporters of China. These men, it was said, virtually ran the Foreign Office during 1967 and part of 1968. Several names were mentioned as participants. Yao Teng-shan, former attaché in Indonesia, was said to be a leader. He and another attaché, Hsu Yen, had resisted bravely an attack on the Chinese Embassy in Jakarta, and on returning to Peking, had been received by Chairman Mao. For a period of several months, apparently beginning in the summer of

1967, Yao Teng-shan was in *de facto* charge of the Foreign Office and virtually acted as Foreign Minister. Many, many other individuals of prominence were said to be affiliated with this group, including Sydney Rittenberg, an American long resident in Peking. For a time, Rittenberg apparently took control of Radio Peking.

Were these people and their violent tactics connected with Lin Piao in any way? It was whispered that they were. Not that Lin Piao instigated them, but that he had made use of them. Exactly how he did so was not specified, but the implication was that, in some way, by embarrassing China in her foreign relations, Lin was able to further his own game.

What was that game?

There was no easy answer, and there is not likely to be for many years. Lin Piao's association with Mao had been long and close, but until recent years, Lin had been known primarily as a brilliant military man, a general who had faithfully and skillfully applied Mao's tactics, a man who had won many key battles in guerrilla days and in the civil war against Chiang Kai-shek, but not a charismatic leader, not a figure warmly admired by the Chinese public, and, moreover, a man whose health was notoriously feeble, so uncertain that on occasions he was compelled to withdraw from active political life for two, three or even five years at a time.

Never a man in the spotlight, Lin Piao had been pushed toward center stage after 1959, when Peng Teh-huai was dismissed as Defense Minister, because, among other things, Mao felt that Peng had grown too friendly with the Soviet Union. Lin was selected to replace Peng.

No record of any significant deviation between Lin and Mao up to 1959 had been brought to light, nor did any emerge in the following years. It was Lin who, on September 2, 1965, published the elaborate gloss on Mao's long-held theory of guerrilla war, which Lin called "Long Live the Victory of the People's War." In this declaration, Lin set forth the thesis that the peoples of the backward nations of the world, led by China, ultimately would overwhelm the advanced nations—the European countries, Russia and the United States.

When the Cultural Revolution finally got under way with the attack on *Hai Jui Dismissed from Office* (it is worth recalling that Mao equated Hai Jui with Peng Teh-huai and saw the play as a criticism of Peng's dismissal), it was Lin Piao, as Minister of Defense, who stood steadfast beside Mao, again and again mustering the authority of the People's Liberation Army to advance Mao's offensive against Liu

Shao-chi and to bring under control the unruly and turbulent great cities when anarchy spread under the *luan* of the Red Guards. On December 31, 1967, the *People's Daily* published a picture of Mao, Lin and Chou. Lin was in center place—a clearly symbolic suggestion that both Mao and Chou depended on him. Peking now said that, under cover of the confusion of the Cultural Revolution, Lin had begun to advance his own fortune; begun to isolate Chairman Mao with a rampant cult of personality; to divorce him from the people and other associates and plot to become his successor. At first Lin advanced his cause through maneuver, thus succeeding in having himself designated by the first plenary session of the Ninth Party Congress that met in March, 1969, as Mao's political successor, his official heir-apparent. Lin had reached the pinnacle. On Mao's death, he would automatically take the helm of the greatest nation on earth. It could not but have been a heady moment.

The designation of Lin was incorporated in the new Chinese Communist Party Constitution in these words:

"Comrade Lin Piao has consistently held high the great banner of Mao Tse-tung Thought and has most loyally and resolutely carried out and defended Comrade Mao Tse-tung's proletarian revolutionary line. Comrade Lin Piao is Comrade Mao Tse-tung's close comrade-in-arms and successor."

On September 12, 1971, a British Trident jetliner, owned by the Chinese National Airways, crashed in eastern Mongolia, and all those on board perished. Rumors spread almost instantly that one of the passengers was Lin Piao. This rumor was officially confirmed in July, 1972—first, in statements made by Chairman Mao himself to Madame Bandaranaike of Ceylon and French Foreign Minister Maurice Schumann, and then, within a day or two, in an official statement issued by the Chinese Embassy in Algiers and in a statement to correspondents in Peking by Wang Hai-jung, a Chinese Foreign Office aide and interpreter, who is a protegée and niece, by blood or courtesy, of Chairman Mao.

These versions declared that Lin was killed while escaping from China with a number of close associates, after plotting a *coup d'état* to assassinate Chairman Mao and seize power in China. No specific details of the plot, the *coup d'état* or the crash were presented.

Many varying accounts of the Lin Piao affair had long been in circulation, and I heard some of them in Peking. According to one version, Lin had plotted to kill Chairman Mao while Mao was en route from Shanghai to Peking, but the plan was exposed to the Chairman by Lin's daughter, Lin Dodo, a member of the staff of the *Liberation Daily*. Lin, his wife, his son and several military associates then boarded the Trident and sought to flee to the Soviet Union.

There were several versions of what happened to the plane. One was that it was shot down over Mongolia by Chinese fighter planes. Another was that a gunfight broke out inside the plane, possibly between the plane's crew, loyal to Mao, and the escaping party. One version said a grenade had been exploded inside the cabin; another that most of the bodies had gunshot wounds.

Speaking to a group of American editors in October, 1972, Premier Chou En-lai said that China's leadership had no advance knowledge of any plot by Lin. The first clue that something was afoot came when Lin's son secretly ordered a Trident civil aviation plane sent to Peipaiho, a seashore resort east of Peking where Lin Piao was staying. The secrecy of the order and the fact that it was given by Lin's son, an air force commander, aroused suspicions and Lin's wife was asked about the matter. She denied any order had been given. This produced further suspicion and Peking ordered all civil airplanes grounded while an investigation took place. At that point, according to Chou, Lin took fright and hurriedly boarded the plane with the intention of flying to the Soviet Union. However, in his haste he only had a few air charts and radio call signals, no navigator and no radio operator. The plane ran out of gas and crashed while attempting to land near Ulan Bator, Mongolia.

The plane skidded in landing, a wing hit the ground, caught fire and the nine persons aboard were burned to death. The Mongol government notified the Chinese on the second day after the crash and Chinese officials visited the site, took pictures and established the identity of the victims. Only later, said Chou, did the Russians learn about the accident. They then exhumed the bodies in an effort to identify them.

After Lin took off in the Trident, a military helicopter carrying some of his confederates attempted to flee the country.* The helicopter was forced down by the Chinese Air Force. From documents confiscated on the helicopter, Chou said, authorities for the first time learned that Lin Piao had been plotting against Chairman Mao. Chou did not

---

* It may be significant, particularly with respect to Tsinghua University's role in the Cultural Revolution and Lin Piao's relation to the "May 16th" group that the helicopter took off from the grounds of Tsinghua University.

name any of those who died with Lin but others identified two victims as Lin's wife and his Air Force son. Lin's wife had been known as a very strong-minded supporter of her husband. She won a reputation for ferocity during the Cultural Revolution. His son held a high post in the Air Force.

Chou said that Lin and a small group of supporters backed the idea of naming Lin Piao officially as Chairman Mao's successor at the Ninth Party Congress. Chou implied that there had been opposition to this course for, as he said, "China is such a big country, how is it possible to have only one successor?" He also said that the report which Lin Piao presented to the Ninth Congress did not represent Lin's own ideas. These had been stated in an earlier version which Lin persuaded Chairman Mao's secretary, Chen Po-ta to draft. This version was rejected by the Central Committee and, presumably, Mao. Then another version was substituted which Lin read even though he did not agree with its contents.

Chou said that a report on the circumstances of Lin's death and conspiracy had been distributed to all party members so that everyone in China had been informed of the situation. Chou bridled when some American editors indicated skepticism about his account and suggested that not all the details of the "jigsaw puzzle" had been fitted together.

"What puzzle?" Chou inquired. "There's no puzzle about it. I have told you every thing. It's much clearer than your Warren Report on the assassination of Kennedy."

I heard several conflicting stories about the Trident from Soviet sources. The first version was that careful examination of the bodies revealed that Lin could not have been aboard the aircraft because no body of the appropriate age (Lin was 64) was recovered. Another story was that the bodies had been consumed by fire, and could not be identified. A third version, which I heard much later and from a source much more likely to have access to the facts, was that Soviet authorities had identified Lin through dental work done in the Soviet Union. They had made no statement, however, because they felt that would play into the Chinese propagandists' hands: Peking would contend that Soviet identification of Lin meant the Russians had prior knowledge of his flight, and that, in fact, Lin was plotting with the Russians for the overthrow of Mao.

When the Chinese finally announced Lin's death in July, 1972, the Russians affected a low profile. They did not immediately pick up the story and use it as propaganda against the Chinese.

Beyond the question of specifics—what actually happened on the airplane, who shot whom, where the plane was flying and the rest—lay a question that was much larger; if Lin actually did move against Mao, why did he do so?

This question seemed infinitely more important to me and infinitely more difficult to resolve. Some facts were obvious. As the Cultural Revolution gathered momentum, it carried everything before it like an Alpine glacier. The whole country became engulfed in chaos, such chaos that there were times when it clearly threatened the viability of the Chinese state, as well as Mao's leadership.

In this situation, Mao had two pillars of strength—Lin and Premier Chou En-lai. Again and again, one or the other or both moved into a complex and dangerous situation and worked out a solution. Only rarely during the Cultural Revolution, so far as I was able to ascertain, was Lin ever challenged or criticized. Never did the Red Guards turn against him. The only Big Character poster put up against him of which I heard was one written by his oldest daughter, a PLA member in Harbin.

This was not true of Premier Chou En-lai. He was the target of attack, a very serious attack. The initial target was his closest government associate, the big, bluff Marshal Chen Yi who was Foreign Minister. But it was clear from the beginning that those who criticized Chen Yi had bigger game in mind, and, shortly after mid-summer, 1967, their slogans directly assaulted Premier Chou En-lai. As Chou himself told Edgar Snow, that campaign came to a climax in August, 1967, when Chou was besieged for 48 hours by tens or even hundreds of thousands of demonstrators in the Great Hall of the People on Tien-an Men Square. The action came at a moment when neither Mao nor Lin were in Peking. It was a dangerous situation, but in two days of almost continuous talk with the Red Guards, Chou succeeded in convincing them that he should be released.

That incident is attributed in Peking today to the "May 16th" group. The name is significant. It derives from the date of May 16, 1966, when a new Cultural Revolution Committee was set up at Mao's order. After the violence against Chou, four members of the Cultural Revolution Committee—Wang Li, Kuan Feng, Lin Chieh and Mu Hsin—were dismissed from their posts and taken into custody. All were said to be members of the conspiratorial May 16th group. Since that time Chen Po-ta and Kang Sheng, both members of the Cultural Revolution Committee, have also dropped from sight, both charged with links to the May 16th group.

Thus, in effect, virtually all of the officials who were charged with carrying on the Cultural Revolution in May, 1966, have in the aftermath been removed on charges of conspiratorial action aimed at disrupting the state. They were said to have tried to drive Chou En-lai from office, and also, a bit later, to have made efforts to disrupt the army. Very little was known of the May 16th activity in the army, but there were hints that it had been even more serious than in the Foreign Office.

Was this group allied with Lin Piao? That is the implication many Chinese have conveyed to me. That was the insinuation conveyed by Chu Yung chia in Shanghai. That was the major charge against Kuai Ta-fu, the Tsinghua University leader of The Regiment, and mainspring of so much fatal violence there.

These violent demonstrations and their leaders were said to have a "link to heaven"—that is, a connection with the very highest circles. In other words, Lin Piao.

The implication was that Lin, by encouraging and protecting the most radical elements in the Cultural Revolution, hoped to emerge on top. And the suggestion was that he found Premier Chou En-lai a formidable obstacle to his progress and, hence, encouraged the attacks on Chen Yi and finally on Chou himself.

This may be true. But, if so, it required a remarkably Machiavellian character, because the suggestion is that, on the one hand, Lin Piao was secretly inspiring, suggesting and protecting the instigators of *luan* while, on the other hand, he was employing his disciplined PLA military forces to put down *luan*.

From what I know of what went on during the Cultural Revolution, almost anything seems possible. But I confess I find it hard to believe that Lin Piao played such a bizarre game.

That Lin and Chou should have emerged as rivals for authority and influence seems much more probable. It also seems probable that the rivalry or antagonism had its roots not in personalities but in policy.

As the Cultural Revolution raged, China's foreign policy fell into disarray, and this could clearly be traced to the anarchical conduct of affairs in the semi-revolutionized Foreign Office. Relations between the Soviet Union and China took a sharp downward course.

In November, 1968, a significant event occurred. For two years the Chinese had refused to meet with the Americans in the ambassadorial conferences that had been in progress in Warsaw since 1956. Now, a few days after Richard Nixon's election, Peking advised Washington that it was prepared to resume talks. Coming after the election of a new American President, the Chinese action was obviously significant. Mr. Nixon immediately let it be known that he favored new contacts. The State Department advised China of its willingness to meet. A date was fixed for the first meeting in early February—after the Nixon administration had taken office—further indication that the Chinese move was linked to the U.S. election and to the possibility of positive negotiation.

Professionals in the State Department had long favored these talks and moves toward a détente with China. They prepared for the meeting with excitement, making ready a small package of concessions which they proposed to present to the Chinese as evidence of their good faith and willingness to engage in meaningful discussion. The U.S. delegates were en route, and China had dispatched a top interpreter from London to Warsaw, when the Chinese suddenly cancelled the meeting on the flimsy grounds that a minor Chinese diplomat in The Hague had defected to the west through the urgings of the CIA.

This curious sequence of events delayed the opening of U.S.-China private talks for more than a year. It was never explained. But if a disagreement in principle was building up between Lin and Chou over China's course in foreign policy, this incident may have been a skirmish in what later became a battle.

Lin is now described as having favored a *rapprochement* with the U.S.S.R. Chou favored an approach to the U.S.A. The aborted U.S.–Chinese meeting would have been held on the eve of the Ninth Party Congress, which named Lin as Mao's successor. In retrospect, it seems plausible that Lin opposed the meeting with the U.S.A. and was powerful enough not only to block Chou's plans but to have himself named Mao's successor a month later.

But China and Russia came to the brink of nuclear war in September, 1969, and were pulled back only by Chou's skillful diplomacy. By the turn of the year, contacts with the United States had been renewed. Chou's policy of restoring links with the nations of the world had begun to gather momentum, and in September, 1970, a second plenary session of the Chinese Central Committee was held at which the basic question (I was told) was put: Which way should China turn—back toward the Soviet Union, or toward the United States?

The question was not finally resolved, but Chou's supporters were gathering strength.

By this time, I think, other issues were in conflict—the question of renewing and reviving the party apparatus shattered by the Cultural Revolution (which Chou favored) and another issue of very great importance—the return to their positions in the party, the government, the state apparatus and state institutions of thousands of persons who had been "set aside" for investigation during the Cultural Revolution. Chairman Mao had said that this should be done. Chou favored it. Lin Piao, it is now said, opposed the rehabilitation, and opposed rebuilding the party, perhaps because without the party his control of the army gave him internal control of the country. So matters stood until December, 1970. On December 10, 1970, Chairman Mao received Edgar Snow and told him that President Nixon would be welcome to come to China. The die was cast. Already, of course, the maneuvering for direct high-level U.S.–China talks had been going on. Now, Chairman Mao had clearly opted for the move toward the United States, the move favored by Chou, against that favored by Lin Piao (or said to be favored by him).

The developments of 1971 tumbled one after the other—the visit of the U.S. ping-pong team (at the instruction of the Chairman), the entry of U.S. foreign correspondents, the Kissinger visits, and the announcement of July 15 that President Nixon would be coming to China.

Could it be that Lin Piao felt time was running out? He had seen one after another of his colleagues fall when they had been on the wrong side of a question. The decisions on policy were going against him. Chou's diplomatic offensive had taken on remarkable proportions. What went on in the inner councils? We do not know. Lin continued to hold office. Articles, perhaps inspired by him, that could be read as critical of China's American initiative appeared in the press—even during the Kissinger visit. Yet Premier Chou still spoke of Lin to a group of Americans in normal conventional terms as late as July 19.

But it must have been apparent to Lin by now that any hope of succeeding Mao was slithering away. Did he then, in early September, seek to force a showdown—either by military or by political means? We simply do not know. We know that the Trident crashed on the night of September 12–13, and that for several days the Chinese grounded all of their civil aircraft (and possibly military as well).

Then flights resumed, and surface normality prevailed. Except for one thing. The name of Lin Piao, "comrade-at-arms and successor" of Chairman Mao, had vanished.

Whatever the tangled history of Lin Piao might have been, he no longer would play a role in China. One more of the small band who had started the Long March with Chairman Mao had vanished. One more revolutionary had been devoured by the Revolution he created. One day in late summer 1972, the Peking press carried a long article on the French Revolution. It centered attention on the fate of Robespierre, the great tactician of the French Revolution. As the article noted:

"Robespierre was after all a bourgeois revolutionary. No sooner was the revolution won than he started to ignore the interest of the masses and, even worse, he suppressed them. The result was he lost their support and became powerless in withstanding the forces of reaction that struck back. He himself was finally sent to the guillotine. . . ."

Thus, on July 28, 1794, Robespierre, together with Saint-Just and Couthon, perished on the same guillotine to which they had sent Louis XVI and the aristocrats. On that day in France, the tenth day of Thermidor, the French Revolution had come full circle. Perhaps on September 12-13, 1971, the Chinese Revolution had its Thermidor. But of that, only time would tell.

22

The Present and the Future

"Palace lights!"

I do not know how to convey the nuance that Mme. Soong Ching-ling put into those simple words—irony, contempt, worldly sophistication, a sense of being a victim of protocol. Not that she looked or seemed a victim. The lights she was speaking of were tall, eight-sided Chinese lanterns, fitted with electric bulbs, and they hung in the dining room of the palace she occupied on the shore of one of the Imperial lakes in Peking. The palace was rather large but not very beautiful, and it had been built for a Manchu prince. It was, in fact, the palace in which Henry Pu-yi, the last of the Manchus, the puppet Emperor of Manchukuo under the Japanese, was born and lived as a boy. Now it was occupied by Mme. Soong in her role as Vice-Chairman of the People's Republic of China, that is, Vice President.

Mme. Soong was not fond of Peking. For many many years she had lived in Shanghai. That was where she considered her home. She was not fond of the old Manchu palace, despite its beautiful gardens and roses. To her taste it was too ostentatious. She felt the palace lights were symbolic of that ostentation, without taste or comfort, that was the hallmark of the Manchu for whom the building was originally built.

But, as an officer of the People's Republic, in fact, not infrequently its presiding officer in the absence or illness of the President, she was compelled to spend a good deal of her time in Peking, and when there, she lived in the old Manchu Palace behind a high brick wall and an enormous red-painted gate, at least 30 feet high and seeming even higher, guarded by a detachment of young PLA soldiers in their slouchy uniforms and caps.

Mme. Soong was one of the great ladies of the world, the widow of Dr. Sun Yat-sen, whom she married on October 25, 1914, at the age of 20, when Dr. Sun was 48. The marriage was, in its time, a great scandal. Dr. Sun had been married for years and had three children by his first wife, and, while it certainly was not unusual in China for a man to take a second wife, Dr. Sun's action stirred both Chinese society and the American missionary colony. But Mme. Soong knew what she wanted, and knew what she was doing. She and Dr. Sun were madly in love, and she dedicated her life to him, and with his death in 1925, she continued to place herself at the service of her country. She cast her fate with the Communist cause, while her sister, Mei-ling, married Generalissimo Chiang Kai-shek and cast her lot with the Nationalists. There were three Soong sisters—Ai-ling (Friendly Life) who married H. H. Kung, the banking tycoon of the Nationalists after earlier serving as Dr. Sun's secretary; Ching-ling (Glorious Life) who married Dr. Sun; and Mei-ling (Beautiful Life) who married Chiang. Their brother, T. V. Soong, was for many years Chiang's Foreign Minister.

Perhaps there have been three women more beautiful, more gifted, more important in China's history, but I doubt it, and of the three, I had long been fascinated by Mme. Soong and her role in the Chinese Revolution. In recent years I had struck up a correspondence with her, and, on learning I was in China, she had invited Charlotte and me to dinner.

A Foreign Office car picked us up at the Peking hotel where we had been watching a movie, at about 6:15 P.M., and we drove north past the Forbidden City, finally coming out on the Imperial lakes where we arrived at the palace occupied by Mme. Soong. There were six PLA men at the gate, which swung wide for us, and we drove into a large park with a fine English lawn. Two or three cars stood at the portico, including a handsome old Mercedes touring car. We walked down several long corridors into a reception room, where Mme. Soong awaited us. There was no mistaking her. She was as handsome as I had imagined, with long, fiercely black hair, pulled back in a bun, a strong, broad face and a family resemblance to her sisters. She was shorter than I had imagined, and looked very chic in a silk tunic, which was gray with thin pinstripes, and gray trousers. She was sitting on a comfortable settee with two other guests—very old friends of hers, we learned—Liao Cheng-chin, a former member of the Party Central Committee and long head of the Overseas Chinese Administration, and his wife, Ching Pu-chun, both English-speaking.* A bit later, a very good friend of mine (and of Mme. Soong's) Paul Lin, a

* Liao Cheng-chin was born in Japan in 1908. When Japan's Premier Tanaka came to Peking in September, 1972, Liao participated in the diplomatic discussions with Premier Chou En-lai, and Chairman Mao suggested that he be sent to Tokyo as Communist China's first ambassador.

McGill University professor, and his wife, Aileen, walked in. On the wall behind Mme. Soong was a picture of Dr. Sun Yat-sen, and on the other wall was a large but rather informal photograph of Chairman Mao, very relaxed, and standing, I think, beside a lake.

Some months before, I had sent Mme. Soong a volume of reminiscences of Mme. Borodina, widow of Mikhail Borodin, the famous Soviet agent whom Lenin had sent to Dr. Sun. I knew that Mme. Soong and Mme. Borodina had been close friends, and when I thanked her for receiving us she thanked me for the book.

I was interested in her for more reasons than simple curiosity. She was one of the leaders of the People's Republic, a leadership that was unique in many ways, and particularly from the standpoint of age. No country in the world had a leadership group so old, and this had been commented upon several times by Premier Chou En-lai to American visitors, most recently in the course of the visit of President Nixon. The Chinese had been struck by the comparative youthfulness of the Americans, and the Americans had been equally impressed by the relative age of the Chinese.

Indeed, the statistics were impressive. Chairman Mao would celebrate his 80th birthday in 1973. Premier Chou was 74. The Acting President, Tung Pi-wu, was 87. Marshal Yeh Chien-ying, who assumed the senior military role after Lin Piao vanished, was 74. The top economics-and-finance man, Vice-Premier Li Hsien-nien, was 68 or 69. Chu Teh, the former head of the PLA and head of the standing committee of the National People's Congress, was 87. This was the group that was running China, and in the galaxy, Mme. Soong was a leading star. I did not know her age, but I presumed that it must be in the upper 70's. I later found that reference books give her age variously, but apparently she was born in 1894, which meant that she, too, was on the verge of her 80's.

I was fortunate enough to spend evenings with two of this remarkable company, Premier Chou En-lai and Mme. Soong, and I concluded that if all of China's leadership was as vigorous, as sparkling and sharp-witted, China was not ill-served by relying on age rather than youth.

I knew no contemporary statesman for whom Chou would not be a formidable opponent. And the same was true of Mme. Soong. She had not been in the United States, as she said, "for half a century," but she began speaking of it as though she had left China only yesterday to study at the little Wesleyan college in Macon, Georgia. Actually, she entered Wesleyan in 1908 and graduated in 1913. This had been a happy experience, and it had marked her whole life. She studied there before World War I, but she had not forgotten Americans, nor lost her competent command of English. The Americans of her memory were so open, so kind, so generous, that her face came alight at their memory.

How had it happened, I asked her, that she had gone all the way from China to an obscure college in the south of the United States?

"My father made me," she said, her eyes sparkling. There was no doubt whatever that her father had decided what he wanted his girls to do, and they had done it. Papa's word was law, and when Mme. Soong spoke of him, she seemed, in a way, again a young girl being sent off on a long mission by a fond and determined parent.

Her father, she said, had simply fallen in love with America. He had been born on Hainan Island and he had an uncle who had gone to America and started a grocery store. She couldn't remember where —New York or Boston (it was, as a matter of fact, Boston). Her uncle raved about the United States in the letters he sent back home. When her father was eight, he made friends with the captain of an American sailing ship and got the captain to take him to America. He ran off without telling his family a word, and it was only months later, after the youngster had gotten to America and sought out his uncle, that the family knew what had happened. Charlie Soong went to work in his uncle's store. The uncle wanted him to take over the business, but Charlie wanted an education. He was befriended by James Duke of the tobacco family, who sent him to Trinity College (later to become Duke, when Duke family money was poured into Trinity's endowment) and then, a bit later, he went to Vanderbilt University.

Finally, Charlie Soong came back to China, to Hainan Island, to the pepper and spice business, to one enterprise after another, all successful, all very successful. But he never lost his love for Americans—particularly southerners, who he thought were more like Chinese than anyone else in the world, with their open hospitality, their warm friendship, their quick humor. When his daughters grew old enough for education, there was no doubt in Charlie Soong's mind as to where they were to be educated—in the United States, and in a Methodist school (for he himself had been a Methodist).

There had not been many Chinese in the United States, Mme. Soong said, in the days when she was going to school there—only a few in New York City and some in San Francisco. She had never gone back to the United States, but she remembered it all as though it were yesterday. I said that she must come to America, but she shook her head. She didn't know what she would do with the television crews if she were to come. Paul Lin said they were very hard to escape, and I agreed that she would have a difficult time not to fall into their hands. We left it at that, but I was convinced that—like Chou En-lai—Mme. Soong would love to visit the United States, and I hoped that it might be possible. It seemed to me that she was vigorous enough to stand the rigors of the trip, and, with that in mind, I mentioned that I had heard she had been ill but was delighted to find her looking so well, which, to be sure, she did—her face hardly lined, her hair black as ink, her handclasp strong. True, she liked to have someone's arm as she walked but, all in all, I thought she was in remarkably fine health.

She had been suffering, she said, from an allergy that had resulted from terramycin that her doctor had given her a year ago, which had not yet cleared up. She was sorry to have to admit that it had been given her by a woman doctor, who had failed to test her for sensitivity before administering the drug. As it happened, three doctors were coming to see her on the morrow, including a specialist from Shanghai and a doctor from abroad. And so, since they would be giving her a thorough examination, she couldn't eat, because she had to be in good shape for them. I thought her disease sounded something like shingles, but, on the other hand, I was reminded of her sister, Mme. Chiang Kai-shek, who also had a skin sensitivity, so severe that when she visited the White House during World War II she brought her own silk sheets, much to Eleanor Roosevelt's amazement. Later on I was told that in fact all the Soongs suffered from the affliction.

After a little more conversation, we walked into the dining room —a rather long walk down a palace corridor—to a big room in which there was a large round table, decorated with flowers. Several waiters in neat jackets stood by. The room was lighted by the big Chinese lanterns to which Mme. Soong applied the derisive term of "palace lights."

The meal began with a clear broth with a pigeon's egg in it— very rich and nourishing. Paul Lin said it was very rejuvenating and good for reviving the sexual powers. Mme. Soong laughed and said that this was the soup that President Nixon had called "quail-egg soup." It wasn't. She happened to keep some pigeons, and it was pigeon-egg soup.

As each course was served, Mme. Soong rose in her chair, although it was not too easy (her figure is short and she had a tuffet under her feet) and insisted on serving me, as is the Chinese custom. She had said, with a little snort, as we sat down: "We'll just have to serve ourselves. These waiters don't know how to do a thing." Her old servants had been packed off to May Seventh schools, and the new ones hadn't had any training. Actually, I had seldom seen more skillful service at any dinner table.

Soon we were eating enormous prawns, and then a Peking fish—mandarin fish, I believe—with sweet and sour sauce. Mme. Soong kept urging me to use knife and fork rather than chopsticks (with which I was rather proud of my ability), insisting that if I didn't "you will starve."

The dinner went on and on, from one delight to another. There was Peking duck, some kind of potato salad, several other vegetable dishes, small green pickles, green beans served almost raw but extremely tender, almond milk (made of crushed almonds and cream), eight-treasures pudding, which Mme. Soong said Americans call "poor man's pudding"—no one at the dinner could remember all the eight treasures that went into it—and finally Canton oranges, Tientsin apples and delicious pears.

It was impossible to eat all the food, and I told her about the American custom of doggy bags. I said I thought the contents often went to feed the masters, rather than the dogs. She laughed and said that when she was a girl in Canton, a servant accompanied you to big banquets and carried home all the food you couldn't consume.

We talked a bit about Chinese food and how good it was. That was one art, I said, that had not been lost in Peking. Not so, she replied. The old cooks were all dying off, and none of the young people wanted to take up cooking. They thought it was too menial.

I said that was the trouble with youngsters—they don't know that cooking is an art. She agreed, and said that the young do not understand. I thought that later on they would. But she seemed dubious.

What about art in general? I asked. What is the state of art and culture in China? Well, she responded, *All Men Are Brothers* and *The Dream of the Red Chamber* were being published again. She seemed a bit surprised at this, adding that the Red Guards had thrown them all out. They just didn't know what was good and what was bad. But now things were getting better.

There was more than a little bite in her remarks about the Red Guards. Natural enough, I thought, since I had heard that in September, 1966, Red Guards had burst into her Shanghai home, demanding to see her, and insisting that they would cut her hair, to which she was said to have responded: "I'll cut *their* hair!"

What, I asked, should I see in China—how would she advise me? "Of course," she responded, "you must see the factories and communes. That is the most important. But also, you must see our art. You must see our ballet, particularly *Red Detachment of Women*, which the Nixons saw." It was set on Hainan island in 1936, and that was where she had been born and had lived until she was four years old.

Mme. Soong smoked an occasional cigarette—Panda brand. They were very, very mild, she said—all Virginia tobacco, with no chemicals or harmful additives. The conversation turned to pandas and the ones the Chinese had sent to Washington. Paul Lin said so many people had gone to the zoo to see the pandas that the authorities had had to limit the crowds, because the mass of humanity was raising the temperature of the air around them too much.

What about the musk oxen we had sent? I asked. How was their health?

"Humph!" Mme. Soong exclaimed, "That was a bad deal. It was typical of Nixon." But the musk oxen were getting better. They had been treated and their health was improving. They hadn't been put on exhibition yet but soon would be. (I saw them a few days later—they seemed a bit mangy but otherwise looked as well as their cousins at the University of Alaska at Fairbanks that I'd seen a year earlier.)

We got to talking about America again, and she asked about hippies and drugs. She had heard that teenage children took drugs in the United States. This was a terrible problem. It had been resolved in China by the Revolution. Education and care for the addicts and an end of the supply by pushers and retailers had eliminated it. It was no longer a problem. I said I wished I could say the same of the United States. Times had changed, she mused. When she was in school in Georgia it was a very moral place. The girls couldn't even go to the store without a chaperone.

I asked about her father and his origins. That reminded her of an argument she had once had with Ed Snow. It was about her father. She was very fond of Ed, but he had made a mistake. He wrote in one of his books that her father was a coolie. That was not true, and she had told Ed that. Not that there was anything wrong with being a coolie. To work was honorable. But her father had not been a coolie, and she had never told Ed that he was. So Ed had corrected the error in the second edition of his book, *The Other Side of the River*.

When I praised the Peking duck, it reminded her of a story about Nikita Khrushchev. When he had come to China, he admired Chinese food very much, particularly Peking duck, and asked if they wouldn't send some Chinese cooks to Moscow to show the Russians how to cook Chinese dishes. So the cooks were sent, but when they got there, they found there was no way they could cook Peking duck, because the Russians did not force-feed their fowl and the Russian ducks were too thin for the traditional Peking cooking.

That was right, I said. There was no Chinese food to be had in Moscow. I told her about the Peking restaurant the Russians had opened in the '50's, and how I had visited it a year after it opened. The menu was very long and listed one delicious Chinese dish after another. But when I tried to order them, they were all "off." The only thing I could get was *shashlyk* and *borshch*. "Not even Chinese *borshch*," she laughed.

But in the United States I said, Chinese food was very popular. "Yes," she observed drily, "chop suey."

It was not a late evening. Mme. Soong had a strenuous day ahead with her doctors, and we didn't want to tire her. But before we left she insisted on piling oranges and apples and pears into the bags of Charlotte and Aileen. "For your doggy bags" she said.

I left Mme. Soong with the feeling of having been in a presence. I don't know how else to say it. She was, I knew, a wise woman, a worldly woman, a woman who had given her life to China and would go on giving it to the end. She didn't like Peking very much, nor the big draughty palace, very cool downstairs, but, she said, several degrees warmer on the upper floors. She missed her own house and gardens in Shanghai where she had lived for so long and where the headquarters of her China Welfare Association were located. But now, as a member of the government, she had to spend at least two-thirds of her time in Peking, carrying on official duties.

I left Mme. Soong with the same feeling I had on leaving Premier Chou En-lai—so long as these remarkably energetic and sophisticated persons were at the head of China's affairs, the country would sail a smooth, and, I felt certain, successful course. They had been at the top a long time. They knew China and they knew the world. They were dedicated and intelligent. Whatever whirlpools China had been through, she had now emerged into sunnier, calmer waters.

But what of the future? The laws of probability could not be defied forever. Sooner or later this older generation, so remarkable in its survival and its ability, would be moving off the stage. What next? That is a question on which Chou En-lai had mused with several Americans in past months. He recognized its reality. But he had not offered any specifics, nor had any appointments been made in 1972 that tended to bring new men, new faces, new blood into the higher echelons of government.

Again and again, rumors went about that something was going to be done. But, in fact, when vacancies had to be filled, they were filled temporarily or on an acting basis by men of the senior generation—men over 70.

When one looked down the list of active members of the Politburo, there were only two younger names: Chang Chun-chiao and Yao Wen-yuan, the two Shanghai men who came to the aid of Chairman Mao in the autumn of 1965, when he could find nowhere else to turn in his effort to launch the Cultural Revolution.

So far as I knew, only these two men had emerged from the turbulence of the Cultural Revolution, their reputations unscathed, their role and their eminence enhanced. To put it in dialectical terms, they had emerged from the thesis of Liu Shao-chi and the antithesis of Lin Piao safely into the synthesis of Chou En-lai. Yao was about 42, I was told. Chang was 60. They were younger by one to three decades than the others in China's leadership. Not that youth would insure survival. In fact, just the contrary had been the rule in recent years. One group of younger leaders after another had been swept away in the currents and cross currents of the most turbulent politics of our age.

Nonetheless, Chang and Yao seemed tested. They had been at Mao's side during the critical times of the Cultural Revolution. They had gone up to Peking with him from Shanghai, when the Chairman transferred his base to Peking in August, 1966. They had moved into crisis after crisis. When the 30,000 workers were sent out to Tsinghua University in July, 1968, to bring the fratricidal war of the students to an end, Chang and Yao went with them and were in the thick of the efforts to bring peace to the campus. They played the leading roles in the Shanghai "storm" in January, 1967, and they had been present again when the climax of the situation came at the diesel plant in August, 1967.

Both men were members of the Politburo and had been since 1969. Chang was a member of the Shanghai Party Committee in 1965, when Chairman Mao moved his base there. With the success of the Cultural Revolution, Chang became head of the party organization in Shanghai, a post he still held, although he spent most of his time in Peking. He served on the Cultural Revolutionary Committee with the now purged Chen Po-ta and with Chairman Mao's wife, Chiang Ching, and, with her, was one of the few survivors of that group.

Yao Wen-yuan was junior to Chang and almost invariably associated closely with him. He wrote the article attacking *Hai Jui Dismissed from Office* that kicked off the Cultural Revolution in November, 1965, and many other important political and dialectical contributions during the Cultural Revolution. He had not held any important post before the Cultural Revolution but was the son of a well-known left-wing critic and writer. He served on the Cultural Revolution Committee with Chang and Chiang Ching and, like them, survived the experience. He was Chang's number-one deputy in Shanghai, and divided his time between Shanghai and Peking.

Neither Chang nor Yao made many public appearances with foreigners. But when Premier Chou En-lai met, in the summer of 1971, with a group from the Concerned Asian Scholars, both participated in the discussion, largely dealing with U.S.–China relations and with China's internal policies. Their presence at this meeting only a few weeks before Lin Piao's fateful disappearance could not have been accidental. Possibly it was designed to symbolize their important role in the emerging government in which Premier Chou En-lai was to play so vital a part. When President Nixon came to China, Yao participated in the Peking discussions, and Chang was host at the farewell banquet for the President in Shanghai. When Premier Tanaka came to China, the two men played an equally prominent role. And when the American newspaper editors visited China in October, 1972, Premier Chou En-lai singled out Yao as an example of the many able, younger men in the party from whom the future leadership would be drawn.

However, I would hardly speculate that the baton of Chinese leadership might ultimately come to rest in the hands of Chang or Yao. Such predictions have a way of turning inward upon their author. I could not but be reminded of the situation in the Soviet Union in the last years of Stalin, when I was a correspondent in Moscow. In those days, a favorite diplomatic sport was trying to deduce what might happen when Stalin died—who would succeed him. The odds-on favorite was Georgi M. Malenkov. His chances were enhanced when Stalin personally named him his "closest comrade-at-arms" (a designation remarkably similar to that with which Lin Piao was endowed in March, 1969). When Malenkov delivered the main report at the 19th Communist Party Congress in Moscow in October, 1952, he seemed a dead-on shot. And when Stalin died in March, 1953, and Malenkov became Premier, it looked as though history was following a preordained course. But nothing could have been more deceptive. Under the cover of Malenkov's promotion, Nikita S. Khrushchev, a name hardly known in the west, was skillfully greasing the skids down which Malenkov would slide from his pinnacle within two years into an oblivion so complete that hardly a Russian even remembers his name today.

Possibly Lin Piao was the Malenkov of China (I mean not in policy but in the inevitability of his slide into oblivion). But that did not necessarily enhance the prospects that Chang and Yao had donned the mantle of heirs prospective. There probably was no more dangerous position that could be held by any man in a dictatorship than that of heir presumptive. It was a position without power, and a position that miraculously united the remainder of the court against the chosen favorite.

The best, therefore, that could probably be said in late 1972 was that there were no candidates other than Chang and Yao for the ultimate succession on the horizon at that time. But much could change. Should Mao Tse-tung die within the fairly near future, his post would certainly fall into the capable hands of Premier Chou En-lai, who was already functioning as the active director of the Chinese government and the architect in detail of its foreign policy. What was at issue, actually, was what might happen when, as, and if Chou En-lai were to die. Any prudent man would be bound to assume that Chou himself might have some specific ideas in that regard, and until or unless Chou's ideas had been made manifest, speculation seemed simply ignorant.

Undoubtedly China had many men in the middle brackets who possessed remarkable leadership qualities. The fact that they did not seem as yet to be playing a central role was not necessarily important, since, in honesty, westerners knew so little of the behind-the-scenes relationships that in China are probably vital.

The name of the man who might succeed Chou was not the key question. He could be Wei or Yao or Chang or Wang. What was important was the policy he would follow. Would China's leadership of the future be consistent with that of the present? Would the new centrist line that foreigners identified with Premier Chou survive his stewardship? This was the central question, and the answer to it, I thought, lay not in personalities so much as in basic policy orientation. What, in a word, was the direction in which China was moving? And would she continue on this course regardless of the disappearance of one set of personalities and the rise of new and unknown men?

23

The Continents Shake

I walked back across the bridge at Shumchun, my heels hitting the wooden planks with a hollow echo, leaving the red flag of China, with its five golden stars, fluttering behind, and coming up toward the Union Jack. It was hot, and I was tired and a bit depressed at leaving China. As I reached the British side, I saw that the train from Hong Kong had just come in and passengers were streaming off, bound for China, excited, interested and apprehensive. A woman in the station was selling Coca-Cola and cigarettes and candy and chewing gum and half a dozen different newspapers. As I bought a copy of each paper, a teenage youngster panted up. He had papers, too, but he was too late. I was back in the land of free enterprise. I tucked the papers under my arm and we boarded the train for "Sin City," as the Canton papers called Hong Kong, seeking to stem the trickle of escapees, mostly young boys who each night tried the perilous swim past the guards with their Tommy guns, over the dangerous coral reefs and into the other world—several hundred a month, sometimes more. Why did they go? In part, at least, because of the propaganda articles describing the awful things that happened in "Sin City."

I settled back in the Hong Kong train. It was as clean and comfortable as the Canton train. But there were no antimacassars, no oil paintings of the Yangtze bridge or the Taching oilfields. Instead, a white-jacketed steward served beer, scotch and soda or gin and tonic. I looked out the window at the sloppy land, the fields not cultivated. the hills not terraced, the rubbish and refuse, the tin can heaps and dirty paper blowing in the wind, the shacks built of oil cans, the hundreds of cars—yellow, orange, blue, tan, white—every color in the world, more cars than I had seen in all of China, the bulldozers clearing land for highrise apartments, the places where walls had caved in and landslides had cut the railroad in last month's monsoon and, in some perverse sense, I was happy to see the jumble and clutter and turbulent energy of Hong Kong spewing out almost to the fringe of China. Was it all so bad? Of course, the slums, the beggars, the child prostitutes, the sweated labor, the lack of education, the violent contrast between rich and poor were shameful.

But there was more to it. Hong Kong, with all its squalor and filth and wretchedness, had a standard of living higher than China's—the housing, on average, was better; there were more consumer conveniences; clothing was better; the automobile was within reach of a remarkable number; the population was well fed; sanitation was not bad; neither was public health. No New Men or Women here—yet, of the thousands of Hong Kong visitors to China every year, few stayed. Of course Hong Kong belonged to China; would revert to it under treaty in the last year of the century. And, of course, China could take over Hong Kong and Macao at any time she wished. But that did not seem likely. Or so I had been told by a Chinese who had some reason to know. So long as Hong Kong's standard of living remained higher than that of the mainland, he said, there would be no change. I thought that meant no change for a good long time.

I stared out the window as the train made its slow progress across the Leased Territories. It was a suburban train now, halting at frequent stations. There were throngs of youngsters on the platforms, boys neat in dark blue jackets, girls in white, school children going to or from their classes. It was, I thought, a moment for summing up, for taking stock of the great experience. Where was China going? Where had she arrived? What about China's New Man?

I thought of a story that Yao Wei had told me about Edgar Snow's last meeting with Mao Tse-tung in December, 1970. As Snow was about to leave, Mao remarked that he was only a lone monk walking the world with a leaky umbrella. Snow quoted the phrase to give a feeling of Mao's sense of isolation and humbleness.

"But," said Yao Wei with a laugh, "this was not what the Chairman had meant at all." In fact, it illustrated the subtlety of the Chinese language and the perils of trying to interpret China to the West.

The Chairman had been speaking to Snow about the fact that China was not a member of the United Nations, and he then added a phrase about China being like a monk walking with a leaky umbrella. This was a complicated and rather amusing Chinese pun that revolved around the word for umbrella, which is made up of two characters, *fa* which means hair (or law) and *tien,* which means sky (or heaven). A Chinese monk shaves his head, so he has no hair, but if he holds an umbrella he has, in a punning sense, hair, and he has thus defied human law. At the same time, the umbrella cuts off the sky, and thus there is no sky, or as Chinese usage has it, there is no heaven. So the monk with the umbrella is defying the law, both human and divine. And that was what Mao was suggesting that China was doing as a non-member of the United Nations—she was walking the world in defiance of the law, human and divine.

The story stuck in my mind as a lesson against drawing hasty conclusions about China. China was so much more complex than it seemed, and at the moment you thought that you began to understand, probably you were only penetrating the first layer of meaning. Understanding China was like peeling an onion.

For instance, what was the real state of the quarrel with Russia? Tensions seemed to have lessened, yet the more I studied the problem the more I became convinced that it was one of those blood enmities that rule great-power relationships and would continue to rule China and Russia for a long, long time. I had dug deeper and deeper into the secret history of the Russian and Chinese Communists, particularly Mao's relations with a long succession of Russians. The deeper I dug, the more wonderment I felt—not that Moscow and Peking had quarrelled, but that they had for a long time been able to present a smooth and unbroken façade to the world.

The Russians, in their polemics against Mao, had opened up their archives going back to the early 1920's to quote characterizations of Mao made by Mikhail Borodin from 1923 to 1927.

Borodin fled China in 1927, when Chiang Kai-shek turned on the Communists and slaughtered them by the hundreds of thousands. He was removed from any connection with Chinese affairs from that time on by Stalin, ultimately to be arrested in January, 1949. He died in a Stalinist concentration camp in 1952.

The Soviet polemicists, however, had been given access to Borodin's unpublished and unknown archives and extracted from them comments concerning Mao's views on the peasantry.

Mao, Borodin was quoted as saying, possesses "an inner confidence in the superiority of the peasantry to other classes and to the superior revolutionary possibilities of the peasants and simultaneously underevaluates the leading role of the proletariat.

"Mao Tse-tung clearly undervalued the role of the proletariat as an initiator and leader of the Chinese Revolution and as a leader of the Chinese peasants. This is characteristic of the speeches of Mao Tse-tung in the 1920's and I often heard him state these views during the time I was in China."

The Russians thus raised the very point that lay at the core of the mistaken indictment brought by Senator Joseph McCarthy against the State Department China specialists. The Russians, Borodin among them, raised the question of whether, in fact, Mao, with his emphasis on the primacy of the peasant, actually was a Communist, a genuine Marxist. They answered the questions in the negative. McCarthy had contended that the American diplomatists regarded Mao as an "agrarian reformer" and not a Communist. This, as it happened, was not exactly the view of the American China specialists. Among the Americans who met Mao in Yenan in 1944–45, only the violently anti-Communist General Patrick Hurley ever took the view that Mao was not a real Communist, and he had picked up the idea from Stalin himself. Now, the Russian polemical documents revealed that Soviet representatives who met Mao in Yenan in 1941–43 also concluded that he was not actually a Communist. (Part of their evidence was that Mao had no books on his library shelves in foreign languages; no translations of foreign literary works; only a few foreign Marxist works translated into Chinese. What probably bothered them most was the absence of Russian works.)

Most striking in the Russian case against Mao was the charge that he was pro-American, had been pro-American from the earliest times, and continued to be right down through 1949, when he came to power. They cited repeated instances in which, they alleged, Mao had refused to support Soviet policy, particularly after Hitler's attack on Russia in June, 1941. The Chinese, according to the Russians, had not believed that Russia's 24-year-old Socialist state would be able to defeat Germany's eight-year-old Fascist state. Mao was said to have recommended that the Russians abandon Moscow, Leningrad and Stalingrad, retiring to the east beyond the Urals, leaving it to the Americans and English to cope with Hitler.

In contrast to this, said the Russians, Mao welcomed Americans to Yenan, maintained close military and political liaison with them, hoped to collaborate with them in operations against Japan and in the post-war period.

In fact, Moscow charged, on the eve of coming to power in 1949

Mao proposed, at the second plenary session of the Seventh Party Congress, that China abstain for at least two years from establishing diplomatic relations not only with the United States and England but also with the Soviet Union. Mao's intention, said the Russians, was to sever his connections with Russia and make China a neutral nation, with no alliances to the Communist world whatever.

Whatever else must be said about the Moscow thesis, a mass of American evidence supporting the view that Mao hoped to follow a pro-U.S. position has been recently uncovered. Much of it actually was long known to a small circle of specialists but lay unassayed and uncollected in the wreckage that remained of U.S. China policy after the McCarthy days. In the extended conversations that American military and diplomatic personnel conducted with Mao and Chou En-lai in Yenan in 1944–45, the desire of the Chinese Communists for close, fruitful and friendly links with the United States was repeatedly emphasized. Further evidence was turned up by the historian Barbara Tuchman in 1972, in the form of a proposal by Mao and Chou that they come to Washington in January, 1945, to confer with President Roosevelt. The proposal never reached the President, having been intercepted by Ambassador Hurley in Chungking. Until Mrs. Tuchman published its text, the existence of the message had never been known.

There had been parallel illuminations as to the real relationship of China and Russia from the Chinese side. Mao, for example, told the 19th plenary of the Eighth Party Congress in September, 1962, that Stalin had attempted to stop the Chinese Communists in 1945 from carrying out the Revolution. Stalin insisted that the Communists collaborate with Chiang Kai-shek in a coalition government. The Chinese ignored the Russian advice, defeated Chiang Kai-shek and took over the country. In the same speech, Mao said that Stalin had not wanted to sign the Sino-Soviet alliance after Mao went to negotiate with him in December, 1949. That was why the talks lasted two months. (The late Nikita Khrushchev had previously revealed that these negotiations had been very difficult and marked by a grandiose attitude on the part of Stalin who, Khrushchev said, treated Mao like a "colonial flunky.") Mao said Stalin remained hostile toward the Chinese Communists until after the Chinese intervention in the Korean War. By 1956, relations had turned sour again. As early as November 15, 1956, Mao made a speech raising the question before his party colleagues as to whether the Soviet Union had not abandoned Communism, the principles of the Bolshevik Revolution, the teachings of Lenin and Stalin.

It seemed to me that the depth and breadth of the Sino-Soviet conflict and the tenacity with which it had persisted over the decades made certain that it would continue indefinitely into the future as a fixed pole of Chinese conduct.

This did not mean that the quarrel might not be, and could not be, ameliorated. Frontier tensions might be eased. The enormous garrisons on either side of the Siberian-Mongolian line could be cut back. But I did not think close Sino-Soviet collaboration was likely in the foreseeable future. At best it would be prickly, arms-length, stiff and suspicious. And that would be true even when Mao vanished from Peking and Brezhnev and Kosygin were replaced by another duo, trio or quartet of equally gray mediocrity in Moscow.

In fact, whoever came into power in Moscow would always keep before him the possibility that "a quick little war" with China might serve the national interest—that is, strengthen his personal regime, revive flagging Russian patriotism and eliminate sources of unrest and discomfort by rallying the nation against the "yellow devils" beyond the Amur and Ussuri. It was an old line. It had enticed Nicholas II into war with Japan, defeat and ultimate downfall. But I doubted that this lesson was likely to be absorbed by the current generation of Communist bureaucrats.

I did not, however, really share the radical vision of the provocative Soviet historian, Andrei Amalrik, who postulated a colossal war between Russia and China sometime before 1984, and very likely, between 1975 and 1980. Amalrik (who had been sent to concentration camps for his views) saw this as arising from the intensification of internal contradictions within Russia, inevitably causing the regime to seek salvation through a foreign adventure.

I did, however, accept Amalrik's contention that the Soviet state would not survive war with China should it come about, and I suspected that it was concern over the internal consequences of a China adventure that had caused Kosygin and Brezhnev to restrain their more impetuous military associates from launching a blitz in September, 1969.

From China's standpoint, the Russian danger was bound to be paramount in foreign policy. It had led Chairman Mao to give approval to Chou's "opening to the west," the ping-pong exercise, the Kissinger conversations and the Nixon visit. China would hew to this course, although she could not achieve full normalization of relations with the United States until the Vietnam War had been brought to at least a tentative end. Only with this would the United States be able to carry out the Shanghai communiqué pledge to withdraw its forces from Taiwan.

But China had no intention of waiting idly for this day to come. She had embarked full-scale on the strengthening of her international position in every part of the world. I had been struck in Peking by the low-pitched tenor of Chinese comment on Japan—indeed, Japan had hardly been mentioned by Chinese officials unless I had brought up the subject. This contrasted with the sensitivity on Japan displayed a year earlier in the talks between Chou En-lai and Scotty Reston. I had found a different tone—a de-emphasis of the specter of an aggressive militaristic Japan and a stress on the possibilities of peaceful collaboration. I did not know, on that July day when I left China, that within a few weeks, the new Premier, Tanaka, would be visiting Peking, that diplomatic relations between Japan and China would be restored, diplomatic ties between Tokyo and Taiwan severed and the foundation of enduring Sino-Japanese cooperation established.

This clearly was a powerful second string to Chou's bow. Now China's foreign policy could march forward even more positively. For this meant that China had created the basis for a partnership with Japan that could change the face of Asia.

The union of China's masses and Japan's technology; of a billion Chinese and the world's greatest GNP; of the largest land power in the world and the contemporary equivalent of early 19th-century England—the potential was without horizon. If Japan and China could work together; if Japan's technical know-how and productive capacity could be harnessed to China's enormous pool of human talent and energy, was there any goal the partnership could not achieve?

The visit of Nixon to Peking had been a brilliant coup. But in a sense, Tanaka's was even more brilliant. It meant that the long, vigorous and imaginative Soviet effort to draw Japan into Russia's train, to tempt Japanese industrialists with sugar-plum dreams of developing Siberia, of billion-dollar deals and new-built industrial empires, must fade. The Tanaka mission was a knock-out blow to Moscow's attempt to interdict just such a Sino-Japanese union. I feared greatly that my old friend, Oleg Troyanovsky, the personable and persuasive Soviet Ambassador in Tokyo, would never now return from Moscow, where, it was said, he was undergoing medical treatment. I could well believe that treatment was necessary. To Moscow the Tanaka-Chou arrangement was a disaster.

Nor was it a necessary plus for the Nixon-Kissinger team. By working together, Japan and China could win a remarkable measure of independence from U.S. influence—whether or not they wished to take advantage of it. The weight of both Japan and China had spectacularly increased on the international scales. If they spoke in a single voice, no one in Asia could fail to listen, indeed, in tandem, they easily matched either the U.S.A. or the U.S.S.R. as a political and economic entity. To be sure, there was some distance from an agreement to renew diplomatic relations to the formation of a working partnership, but each side clearly perceived the potential.

This, then, seemed to me the immediate goal of Premier Chou's foreign policy—the establishment of a triangular relationship of China, the United States and Japan that would clearly overbalance any combination the Russians might forge against it.

In China, it was taken as an axiom that the Soviet Union and India had concluded a working partnership hostile to, and directed against, China. A Sino-Japanese relationship should prove stronger than the Russo-Indian.

Would the United States tip the balance toward China? Or toward Russia? More likely toward neither, so long as U.S. policy was dominated by the Metternich inheritance of Dr. Kissinger. Balance-of-power theory inevitably viewed with favor an equation in which India-Russia was weighted against China-Japan. The United States, then, could use its power and influence to maintain equilibrium.

It was a tempting analysis—almost a textbook case. What bothered me was its textbook classicism. World events did not conform to such tidy patterns. And too much of the world had been left out of the sketch—the uneasy Third World, the tumultuous nations of Asia, Africa, the Middle East and Latin America—where social, economic and political factors constantly contributed to disequilibrium; Europe, where assiduous Soviet policy worked to shift a subtle balance in Russia's direction; and the Communist countries of eastern Europe, tied to Moscow but always restive, often emotional, in Russia's iron grip.

Yet, when all had been said, the outline of the emerging China policy and its architect, Chou En-lai, took on pyramidal dimensions. China's diplomatic potential had by no means been exhausted. It was not impossible that Taiwan might react to the tidal wave of world diplomacy set off by Chou and agree to negotiate a complex settlement of its quarrel with Peking. This should not be ruled out. I had good reason to believe that there had been quiet, peripheral soundings between the two sides. An arrangement on Chinese terms and in Chinese style might not be as difficult as the world supposed—perhaps an agreement that Chiang Kai-shek would remain in power and his son after him—provided only that Peking's sovereignty was acknowledged. Or an agreement for Peking's sovereignty to be acknowledged after Chiang's death with his son, Chiang Ching-kuo, recognized as provincial governor. Or as Chou En-lai had lately suggested Peking might pick up Taiwan's tax tab and guarantee to buy out Taiwan's industry in return for acknowledgement of sovereignty. Oh, there are many subtle permutations that the Chinese might work out. Chinese ingenuity could resolve almost any problem—if the desire was there.

A sudden Peking-Taipei arrangement did not seem beyond calculation. After all, China had demonstrated remarkable diplomatic skill in liquidating impacted problems, not only those of the United States and Japan, but in lesser instances. Korea, for example, or Burma, where the intense hostility that had led Burma and China almost to the brink of war in 1965–67, had been overcome. Premier Ne Win of Burma had come to Peking and the two countries had resumed normal diplomatic and trade relations (even though it seemed certain that clandestine Chinese aid to the hill-country rebels against Ne Win had far from ceased). And even the Thais, staunchest of U.S. allies in the Vietnam War, had cautiously begun to feel out possibilities for regularizing their China relationships.

Around the world, the Chinese had shown that few could match them in diplomatic skill. The era of surprises had not ended. Even in Europe, Chinese diplomacy was reaching out in a low-key way to establish, if not a presence, at least a voice in the Balkans, right at Russia's doorstep. China had excellent relations with Rumania. She had turned hostility to friendship in Yugoslavia. She numbered Albania as her lone ally, and now she had entered into diplomatic relations with Greece. In an unassuming way, China was trying to encourage the creation of an "island of friendship" at the base of the Balkan peninsula.

The striking fact about all of this diplomacy was that it was old-fashioned, great-power, classic diplomacy. It had not a whit to do with revolution or Marxism. China was not making ideology or leftist sympathy a factor in her campaign. Kings, emperors, dictators, right-wing colonels—you name them—all were welcome into China's diplomatic family. It was *Realpolitik* conducted by one of the world's greatest masters of *Realpolitik*.

These fireworks on the international front could not mask the fact that China was industrially and economically still, in the words of Chou En-lai, a backward nation. True, she had been producing hydrogen weapons since June, 1967. She had sent up satellites in 1970 and 1971. She had her long-range rocket weapons. But militarily, she was a conventional Asian land power—the strongest in Asia, but her strength was based on a remarkably well-trained and disciplined force of about 120 divisions comprising 2.8 million men, not highly mechanized. The PLA was backed by 30 million militia. She could handle limited threats, but against Russia's nuclear power, Russia's armor, Russia's jets, Russia's missiles, China must rely on distance, space, population, guerrilla war—and her network of anti-nuclear shelters. Her air force was largely obsolete, and the 200 submarines in her navy were a threat to no one. Steel production had been only 27 million tons in 1971—more than double the 13 million of the Great Leap Forward in 1959—but only a quarter of that of the Soviet Union. Oil reached 20 million tons in 1970. Fertilizer touched 14 million tons, in the same year—not even half of China's requirements. The total GNP for 1970, Premier Chou told Edgar Snow, was $90 billion, exclusive of agriculture and services. Agriculture added about $30 billion to that total.

These were respectable totals for a nation that was emerging from feudalism, but they clearly revealed China's industrial weakness, just as the agricultural figures revealed her strength. By 1970, she had become the world's largest cotton producer, and she harvested a wheat crop of 240 million tons. Her wheat reserves totaled 40 million tons in that year. The 1971 crop was another bumper one, 246 million tons. In fact, there had been nine bumber crops in the past ten years, each year's production exceeding that of the previous year. In 1972, drought hit hard in many areas in which I had traveled—the northern plains around Peking, the northwest and parts of central China. Crop totals were held down, but the overall yield was still high—almost 250 million tons by Chou En-lai's estimate. China was not yet an industrialized state. Chou En-lai was correct in that. The pace in the factories was almost leisurely, and the rush to build plants did not equal the pace, for example, of the Soviet Union in the early five-year plans. But perhaps China was building more slowly and more solidly. Such, at least, was my feeling.

These were some of the thoughts that ran through my mind as our train gradually made its way closer and closer to Kowloon, entering the areas of great population density, the sprawling outskirts of one of the world's busiest collections of human beings.

China, it seemed to me, had won a substantial measure of security in the past three years—much of it the by-product of Chou En-lai's brilliant diplomacy, and much of it the result of what the Chinese called the tempering of the Cultural Revolution.

Her foreign policy was dynamic but not revolutionary; pragmatic rather than propagandistic. The ultra-leftist slogans of the Cultural Revolution had vanished without trace. No more was heard the rhetoric of Lin Piao's September, 1965, call: "Long live the victory of the people's war." The emissaries being received by Chou and Mao were not Black Panthers and violent Asian revolutionaries, or, if revolutionaries were being received, they were not getting the spotlight attention of the conventional diplomats, premiers, scholars and businessmen. China was buying Boeings from the United States and Concordes from Europe, rather than exporting revolution to San Francisco or Rome.

At home and abroad, China was treading a centrist line. But the men and women on whom China relied were not centrist—at least I did not think so. They did possess a new spirit, one that was in black-and-white contradiction to the spirit of the old China. A price had been paid for this. Perhaps you now did not often hear the sound of a solitary flute player in a Peking courtyard, sending a sad sweet message to his lover. Perhaps, at dusk, you no longer heard the symphony of the pigeons, as the flocks, whistles attached, whirled through the air above the monochrome roofs. Perhaps the cries of *dowzha* no longer resounded through the towns of north China as peddlers hawked their steaming wares. Nor did many Chinese women still fashion their men's clothes of homespun.

In a word, China had lost some of its color, some of its street life, some of its diversity, some of its craftsmanship for the sake of an egalitarian life, for the sake of a life in which no one was very rich, no one was very poor, no one lived luxuriously, no one lived in want. The thrill and excitement of the Hong Kong streets could not be matched in Shanghai.

But there was a new China, there was a new life. Part of it had come into being with the Revolution in 1949. That laid the foundation. Then, in some manner, the Cultural Revolution, with its turbulence, its fighting, its conflict, its passion, its argument, its *luan,* had completed the process. There *is*—at least for a time—a New Chinese

Man and a New Chinese Woman. They had stood up. They had self-respect and dignity. They were admirable in their fellowship, kindness and sense of self-sacrifice. I admired them but I did not think they were for export, or that their spirit could simply be imitated in the United States, or anywhere else. It was as specifically Chinese as Chairman Mao's poetry.

Before I left China, I talked about this with a rather high official. We had been speaking of the Soviet Union. He—like every Chinese—was fascinated at my observations of Russia. I had said that it seemed to me that Russia had lost the spark of its Revolution. That it had been overtaken by materialism. The young people chased western fads like butterflies—the latest song, the latest dance, the latest style. Hippy clothing. Hippy haircuts. Drugs. They were trying to ape the western drug culture. It was hard to see what remnants of the Revolution were left. Soviet foreign policy differed hardly an iota from czarist foreign policy. I could not but feel that when the Chinese called the Soviet rulers the "new czars" they had touched a very elemental truth.

But in China, there was something new. I agreed with those who said that the greatest change in China was in the spirit of the people.

The Chinese official smiled. They had made only a start. The task that China now faced was to turn her spiritual force into a material force. It was a great task, and China was only at its beginning. China was still very backward. He was sorry that I had not known the old China so that I could measure it by my own yardstick.

"I'm sorry, too," I said. "But nonetheless I think it is the miracle of the modern world."

"Perhaps," he said gently, "you are going a bit too far."

"No," I replied, "I don't think I'm going too far. I think that it is a great achievement to put a man on the moon. But to put a man on the earth—that is even more."

The official smiled. He did not deny my statement. But he added a word of caution. "If we lag in our efforts," he said, "we will slip back. We must move ahead. The time is still very short."

He turned to the United States. "Whatever your opinion of Nixon, or our opinion," he said, "he has done one thing right—China. Now it is up to the people—the people in both China and America. There is so much to be done. But no matter how long it will take, we think it can be achieved. The people will do it. The people of China and the people of America. They cannot be resisted."

I agree with that. The peoples of America and of China—if they joined their strength—would be irresistible. I wished that I could feel more confident that they actually would come together in a human torrent that would sweep the world toward a better life. But I had reservations. I had come to certain conclusions in China. I had convinced myself that there was in China a new spirit among men, a contagious spirit, one on which China could build. But could America match it? This was the question. I did not believe China's New Man and New Woman could be replicated outside of China. Such spirit must rise, as it had in China, from the roots of national consciousness, out of the turmoil and agony of ages.

I thought of one of Chairman Mao's poems that I had read in Peking, one from which President Nixon had quoted a couplet. It had been written to the venerable Kuo Mo-jo, China's leading literary scholar, in 1963, at a moment when the Sino-Soviet conflict was much in Mao's mind.

He wrote:

> So many deeds cry out to be done,
> And always urgently;
> The world rolls on,
> Time presses.
> Ten thousand years are too long,
> Seize the day, seize the hour!
> The Four Seas boil, clouds and waters rage,
> The Five Continents rock in the wind and roaring thunder.
> Away with all pests;
> Our force is irresistible.

That, I thought, was China today. That was the strength of its spirit after the *luan* of the Cultural Revolution. But where was that of America? When would the New American Man and the New American Woman walk the earth, proud and confident, making the oceans boil and the continents shake?

INDEX

HARRISON E. SALISBURY is the only western correspondent to visit all of the Communist nations in Asia — the vast reaches of Soviet Siberia and the Arctic North, the hidden lands of Central Asia, Mongolia, North Korea, China and two states closely aligned: Cambodia and Laos — and the first to set foot on North Korean soil since the end of the Japanese regime in 1945.

Presently the Associate Editor of The New York Times and editor of its Op-Ed page, Mr. Salisbury's reporting from Russia won the Pulitzer Prize, the George Polk Memorial Award and the Sigma Delta Chi Award. His stories from Vietnam and the Chinese periphery have won the George Polk Memorial Award and the Asia Award.